914.92
L23

W9-ADQ-158

THE UNITED NATIONS SERIES

ROBERT J. KERNER, GENERAL EDITOR

SATHER PROFESSOR OF HISTORY IN THE
UNIVERSITY OF CALIFORNIA

❖

CZECHOSLOVAKIA: TWENTY YEARS OF INDEPENDENCE

EDITED BY ROBERT J. KERNER

THE NETHERLANDS

EDITED BY BARTHOLOMEW LANDHEER

❖

Other volumes in preparation

THE NETHERLANDS

WILHELMINA
QUEEN OF THE NETHERLANDS

DJ
L3
10

The Netherlands

Chapters by Johan Willem Albarda, Adriaan Jacob Barnouw,
Hendrik Nicolaas Boon, Jan O. M. Broek, Paul Bromberg,
Henri Emile Enthoven, David Friedman, Jan Greshoff,
J. Anton de Haas, Philip Hanson Hiss, James H. Huizinga,
Raymond Kennedy, Bartholomew Landheer, Marinus Michiel
Lourens, Raden Moehammad Moesa Soerianatadjoemena,
Joep Nicolas, Hendrik Riemens, Peter H. W. Sitsen, Samuel
van Valkenburg, Amry J. Vandenbosch, Bernard H. M. Vlekke

JE MAINTIENDRAI

EDITED BY BARTHOLOMEW LANDHEER

UNIVERSITY OF CALIFORNIA PRESS
BERKELEY AND LOS ANGELES · 1944

UNIVERSITY OF CALIFORNIA PRESS
BERKELEY AND LOS ANGELES
CALIFORNIA

❖

CAMBRIDGE UNIVERSITY PRESS
LONDON, ENGLAND

COPYRIGHT, 1943, BY
THE REGENTS OF THE UNIVERSITY OF CALIFORNIA

Second printing

PRINTED IN THE UNITED STATES OF AMERICA
BY THE UNIVERSITY OF CALIFORNIA PRESS

TO HER MAJESTY
QUEEN WILHELMINA OF THE NETHERLANDS

May 45

35141

The United Nations Series

THE UNITED NATIONS SERIES *is dedicated to the task of mutual understanding among the Allies and to the achievement of successful coöperation in this war and in the coming peace. In the measure that the United Nations understand one another they will march triumphantly through total victory to lasting peace.*

The University of California offers this series as a part of its contribution to the war effort of this state and nation and of the nations united in the greatest conflict known to history, and it heartily thanks the editors of the respective volumes and their collaborators for their devoted service in this cause and for their effort to present an honest, sincere, and objective appraisal of the United Nations.

ROBERT J. KERNER
General Editor

Editor's Preface

WE CANNOT EXPECT *a better world after this war if the United Nations do not have a broader understanding of one another—a knowledge based upon unbiased and objective information. It has become evident that in our literature there is a dearth of books which give this information about the various countries. We, therefore, owe a considerable debt of gratitude to Professor Robert J. Kerner and to the University of California Press for having realized this need and taken such energetic action to remedy it.*

As the editor of this volume in The United Nations Series, I wish to express my sincere appreciation to the contributors who produced their chapters, with great devotion, in record time. In many instances we would have welcomed additional space in which to present information which had to remain untold or be only briefly mentioned. But a too-bulky volume might not have fulfilled the function which The United Nations Series hopes to fulfill, namely, to offer in a readable book as much concise information as possible about the various aspects of a nation—in this instance, the Netherlands. It has been our purpose to achieve an interpretative treatment and not to offer a mere summary of facts which could be found elsewhere; therefore, considerable weight has been given to matters on which the literature is meager or entirely lacking.

A nation is a living and growing entity. The contributors would feel themselves well rewarded if they had succeeded, at least partially, in giving an impression of what conditions in the Netherlands really are. The love of one's country should not alter the capacity to judge matters objectively, as objectivity merely means the realization of life as a continued process which does not tolerate perfection at a

[ix]

*given moment. Belief in the future can never be based upon com-
placency and self-satisfaction. Our world will need the combined
effort of all the United Nations in order to avoid the errors of the past.*

*In ending this preface, I should like to express again my apprecia-
tion of the very pleasant collaboration with Professor Kerner. Thanks
are due also to Miss Marian B. Harris of the University of California
Press, to Mrs. Lenore Sorsby for editorial assistance on a number of
the chapters, to Dr. George C. O. Haas for an excellent translation
of the chapter on literature, to Miss Jenny Broekman for her assistance on the chapter on architecture, and to Mrs. Loretta Korch and
Miss Marion Turner Sheehan for aiding on various details in the
preparation of the manuscript.*

*The University of California Press deserves to be complimented
on the very attractive format, and on the efficient and prompt manner
in which the volume was brought out.*

BARTHOLOMEW LANDHEER

Contents

PART THREE:
POLITICAL AND CONSTITUTIONAL DEVELOPMENT

xiv

CONTENTS

PART FOUR: ECONOMIC AND SOCIAL DEVELOPMENT

PART FIVE: CULTURAL ASPECTS

Dutch artist; awarded Grand Prix, Paris Exposition of Decorative Arts (1925) for his first stained glass window; produced stained glass windows for important commemorative occasions and won mural government competition in Holland; engaged on a series of thirty-six stained glass windows in the Fairmount Presbyterian Church, Cleveland, Ohio; author of articles on painting.

Netherlands Information Bureau, New York; interior decorator, Netherlands Pavilion, 1939 World's Fair, New York; manager, The Fireplace (*De Schouw*), and Consulting Bureau of Interior Decorating, 1914–17; with Metz and Company, 1919–25; later with H. Pander and Sons; author of *Het Hollandsche Interieur* (1928); *De praktische kleine Woning* (1930); and *Praktische Huis Inrichting* (1933).

Poet and essayist; with Radio Department of the Netherlands Information Bureau; journalist and correspondent for Dutch and Netherlands Indies newspapers at Brussels; author of many works of poetry and prose, includ-

CONTENTS

List of Illustrations

THE DUTCH NATIONAL ANTHEM

WILLIAM OF NASSAU

(WILHELMUS VAN NASSOUWEN)

By MARNIX VAN ST. ALDEGONDE

William of Nassau, scion of a Dutch and ancient line,
I dedicate undying Faith to this land of mine.
A Prince I am, undaunted, of Orange, ever free.
To the King of Spain I've granted a lifelong loyalty.

I've ever tried to live in the fear of God's command.
And therefore I've been driven from people, home, and land.
But God, I trust, will rate me his willing instrument
And one day reinstate me into my government.

Let no despair betray you, my subjects true and good.
The Lord will surely stay you though now you are pursued.
He who would live devoutly must pray God day and night
To throw His power about me as champion of your right.

My God, I pray Thee, save me from all who do pursue,
And threaten to enslave me, Thy trusted servant true.
O Father, do not sanction their wicked, foul design.
Don't let them wash their hands in this guiltless blood of mine.

Alas! my flock. To sever is hard on us. Farewell.
Your shepherd wakes, wherever dispersed you may dwell.
Pray God that He may ease you. His gospel be your cure.
Walk in the steps of Jesu. This life will not endure.

The first five stanzas translated by
ADRIAAN JACOB BARNOUW

Part One

The Scene

CHAPTER I

Land and People

BY SAMUEL VAN VALKENBURG

AS IT STOOD before the fateful invasion of May 10, 1940, the Netherlands, known also as Holland, may be used to illustrate the qualities of one of the best types of civilization to be found in Europe. In many ways no finer example could be chosen. A successful combination of agriculture, industry, and trade had given to Holland a position superior to its size and population. Even a casual visitor to the Netherlands would have been impressed by the prevalent atmosphere of contentment, prosperity, and culture. Although Holland, like other countries, occasionally faced difficult times, it did not seem to suffer greatly.

Besides its enjoyment of the general geographical advantages of western Europe, of which climate is the most important, three factors had special weight in giving Holland its outstanding rank among the smaller nations. First and foremost was physical background, and the consequent battle between man and water. The Dutch, like the Swiss, are products of an originally unproductive physical environment; and, like the Swiss, they have not only conquered their land and wrested a livelihood therefrom, but have also molded themselves into a nation of strong individualists.

The second factor which contributed to Holland's outstanding position was the lure of the sea. The Dutch, by the very nature of their country, are a seafaring people. Although the period of their world supremacy in maritime affairs had ended at the close of the Napoleonic Wars, with the cession of strategic bases to Great Britain, their ocean trade in later years was to be of the utmost importance. Moreover, seafaring had been the basic factor involved in the establishment of Holland's great overseas empire, which once included areas in all parts of the world. Although the empire was restricted to only two parts before the Second World War, even then it contained a population of more than 70,000,000. One part, Surinam, or Dutch Guiana, together with certain of the neighboring Antilles, more recently had exercised only a minor influence; but the other part, the Netherlands East Indies, with their wealth of tropical products, was a tremendous factor in the life of Holland. They supplied an outlet for Dutch energy and a source of national wealth in the form of raw products which in good years provided a sizable part of the national income. Almost every family in Holland had friends and relatives who spent a great part of their lives in "tropical Holland."

The third factor which contributed to Holland's outstanding position was its location not only at the outlet of the Rhine, the most important river in Europe, but especially in the center of Europe's greatest industrial region. Its location on the Rhine made Rotterdam one of the most important harbors in Europe. The traffic on this river, however, consisted chiefly of goods in transit between Germany or Switzerland and regions across the water and, hence, did not greatly affect Holland. Its situation in relation to the large industrial centers, on the contrary, was chiefly responsible for the way in which Holland developed into a country of intensive agriculture during the nineteenth century. For scores of miles the region immediately to the south and southeast of Holland in Belgium and in Germany resembled a great city, where fruits, vegetables, and dairy products, all of which Holland can produce, were used in vast quantities. In later years strong nationalistic tendencies hampered the logical exchange of food for manufactured products, and the Dutch farmers were forced to grow crops for the subsistence of Holland alone, rather than for sales abroad.

Physical background.—During the Ice Age the thick ice sheet covered northern Holland, and extended across the present North Sea into England. In its retreat it left sandy glaciofluvial deposits, with many glacial ridges, which now cover eastern Holland north of the Rhine. At the same time, the swift-flowing Rhine and Meuse (Maas) rivers laid down the sands which now form the uplands in the provinces of Brabant and Limburg south of the Rhine. These provinces may be called uplands only in contrast to the lower western part of the country. Their loose, dry soil made them an ideal site for the homes of the first men who followed the retreat of the ice. In the shallow depressions which now form the North Sea, the rivers at first flowed northward, probably uniting with other rivers from England and from southern Scandinavia to form a single great stream.

In time, however, because of the melting of the ice and the sinking of the land, the rising ocean permitted the sea to encroach inland more and more. The process of inundating the land culminated only after the sea had broken the land connection between England and France. As a result the sandy uplands became the coastline of the Continent. Along the shore, however, from the protruding Nose of Calais (Nez de Calais) northeastward the winds and currents formed a sandy bar, with a broad closed lagoon behind. This extended as far as the low morainic upland of Denmark. The bar in time became a narrow zone of sand dunes, broken in many places to give outlet to the deltaic branches of the Scheldt, Meuse, and Rhine rivers.

The next stage was the gradual filling of large portions of the lagoon, partly with clay brought by ocean currents and by rivers, and partly with peat, the by-product of lagoon vegetation. In this way the lagoon was transformed into a swamp below sea level. At later times stormy seas attacked the sandbar and broke through at many places, flooding the swamps beyond and forming inland basins of salt water. The present map of Holland still shows evidence of this process in the disconnected formation of the dune islands of the northern, or Frisian, coast, as well as the central basin of the Zuiderzee, and the ragged coastline of Zeeland in the far southwest.

Historical development.—On the dry dune strip the Romans fortified the outlet of the Rhine, west of the present city of Leyden (Leiden); here the modern residence of the Sovereign and the Government had its origin as the garden of a count, indicated by the Dutch term, 's Gravenhage (now known as The Hague).

The swamp itself, with its many lakes and peatlands, was less attractive. In some places small groups of people ventured to migrate from the uplands to the lowlands, and to build artificial mounds in order that their dwellings might stand high above the tides and the storm waves. Groups of fishermen also settled along the shores of the inland basins and used the protected waters as fishing grounds. Such settlements grew in importance. Seafaring as well as fishing became an important occupation. In the Middle Ages many of the towns thus started became members of the Hanseatic League and traded along the coasts of the North Sea and the Baltic.

But man cannot subsist on the products of the sea alone, and the need of land on which to produce other kinds of food confronted the inhabitants of the fishing settlements. This need led to the discovery that the swamps, and even the floors of the shallower parts of the many lakes and of the inland marine basin, contained fertile soils which, if protected by dikes and drained, could be used for grazing and for the growing of crops. In this way the Dutch polders (areas of drained land) originated. The Dutch lowland is still an intricate system of reclaimed lake and marine floors, surrounded by dikes and drainage canals, into which the surplus water may be pumped. It was expected that this system would work to great advantage during an emergency because, in event of an invasion, the water which had been controlled with such difficulty could be used to reflood the land.

The area reclaimed from the water was at one time an unimportant part of the Holy Roman Empire and later a possession of Spain. For a long time its position was overshadowed by the high type of culture in Flanders near by on the south. But the small groups of individualists who had founded their country and had fought for its freedom gradually gained power until for a time they saw it become the dominant nation of Europe. A decline soon followed, however, because Holland was too small to maintain leadership in world politics. Nevertheless, much of the old spirit remained a part of the Dutch character and is responsible, in large part, for Holland's high cultural standing before the Second World War.

Draining the land.—As the fertile fields and grasslands were formerly the bottom of the lagoons, it is therefore understandable why a great part of Holland is now below sea level. Exceptionally low tides make possible, at fairly frequent intervals, the draining of much of this low area by means of canals; at high tide, closed locks keep the ocean out. The isles of Zeeland in the southwest were reclaimed by means of dikes, as were also the provinces called North Holland and South Holland, which lie along the coast from Rotterdam northward. After the First World War the last and greatest task of reclamation, that of drying up the Zuiderzee, was attempted. A large dike across the northern part of the Zuiderzee changed the sea body into a fresh-water lake (Lake IJssel). The plan included the reclaiming of large parts of what was formerly the sea bottom. The polder south of Wieringen was constructed first, and added fifty thousand acres of excellent land to Netherlands territory. During the Second World War the second unit (the northeastern part) was completed, and the first harvest was brought in. Altogether this was a gigantic undertaking, proving that Dutch energy and efficiency were still up to the highest level.

On the northern coast, east of the Zuiderzee, most of Friesland and the northern part of Groningen belong to the same original type of swampy, half-drained or half-flooded country. Numerous lakes in this region remained undrained because their peaty bottoms were unfit for agriculture. In summer these Frisian lakes were much used for the sport of sailing. When they froze during the severe winters they were used so continuously for skating that industry was almost crippled for the short time that the ice remained solid. Leeuwarden, the capital of Friesland, now in the center of the province, grew up as a seaport on the shore of a former inland basin which no longer exists.

This historical treatment of the physical background of the Netherlands is necessary in order to explain the present geography. It lays a basis for the discussion of the three natural divisions: the dunes, the lowland, and the upland.

The dunes.—Except where the sea has broken through, the dunes form an almost continuous band. Because the sand is usually fixed by vegetation, the dunes are a bulwark against the fury of waves and winds. On the outer side is a beach, wide at low tide and protected by

THE NETHERLANDS

many stone piers, used for bathing in summer. Before the present war, many summer resorts lined the coast, the best known of these having been Scheveningen, the beach of The Hague ('s Gravenhage). Besides the waterways of the Scheldt and the Rhine, two artificial shipping canals were cut across the dunes—the New Waterway leading seaward from Rotterdam on one of the Rhine branches, and the North Sea Canal giving an outlet to Amsterdam. The Rhine outlet itself was of minor economic importance, but the Scheldt opened the way first to the Dutch harbor of Flushing (Vlissingen), the continental terminus of one of the main crossings to England on the route between London and Berlin, and then farther inland to Antwerp.

The straight Dutch coast does not favor fishing. Nevertheless, fishing was still important before the Second World War. Steam trawlers had replaced the old flat-bottomed boats, and fishing was concentrated in a few important harbors, notably IJmuiden on the North Sea Canal, where herring was the main catch.

On the inner side of the dunes a zone of sand forms a transition to the polder region. Here the soil is very favorable for the growing of fruits, vegetables, flowers, and nursery stock in the form of young trees and bushes. Near Haarlem were the famous bulb fields, which supplied a somewhat unusual item in the exports of Holland. The many hothouses in which grapes and tomatoes of high quality were grown for export formed a truly unique feature; they illustrate how effectively Dutch energy mastered such geographical disadvantages as summers too cool for the development of many of the finer fruits. This transition zone is the site of many towns and villages which flourished before the Second World War. The firm soil on which these towns were built made possible the beautiful parks and gardens which could not have been grown on the polders. The Hague (500,000 inhabitants), the residence of the Queen and of Parliament, although Amsterdam is the actual capital, is the largest city in the transitional zone. Before the war it was comparable with Washington in its dignity, and in its large proportion of official residences; it, too, was a center of wealth and a retreat for pensioned officials and retired business people.

The lowland.—The Dutch lowland (polderland), most of which is below sea level, represents Holland in its most typical form. Seen from the air or on a large-scale map, it appears as an intricate pattern of polders with innumerable ditches separating the fields and providing drainage toward steam pumping stations. These stations ordinarily pump the excess water into the wide drainage canals, but in dry seasons they are used to pump water from the canals back upon the land, thus making Holland doubly secure against crop failures. Windmills, which many people regard as the most characteristic feature of Dutch scenery, have lost a great deal of their importance. Extensive bodies of water represent parts of the former swamps where the underlying soil of peat or sand was not worth reclaiming; others occur where peat was once dug out for fuel and the depressions were not refilled. Dikes, higher and broader than those of the canals, protect the lowland from the waters of the inland marine basin of Lake IJssel, as the Zuiderzee is now called, and from the two branches of the Rhine River which flow across this polderland. Most interesting is the new polder south of the island of Wieringen. This dotted area was once a part of the Zuiderzee; now it is a flat, treeless plain on which the shell-like soil and the remnants of shipwrecks lying on the meadows among grazing cattle combine with the new and gaily colored brick houses to betray how recently the polder had been reclaimed.

In the polder region as a whole, grass is the dominant vegetation, both on the peat and on part of the clay. Green meadows studded with large farmsteads are surrounded by borders of trees. Roads, canals, tramways, and railroads provide transportation facilities to bring milk, butter, and cheese from the dairies to the towns.

On the higher clay soils, grain flourished; it was the dominant product in Zeeland at the southwest corner of Holland and also in Groningen at the northeast corner. Besides wheat, the major crops were sugar beets, fodder, and seed. The type of garden agriculture prevailing on the inner edge of the dune zone with its sandy soils extended into the polder region, where local areas were well known for their nurseries of vegetables, fruits, and trees. Moreover, especially between Rotterdam and The Hague, the hothouse type of agriculture invaded the lowland.

Cities of the polderland.—Two cities dominate the polder region: Amsterdam, the capital, and Rotterdam, Holland's greatest seaport. Amsterdam, originally a fishing settlement beside the IJ, a gulf of the Zuiderzee at the mouth of the little Amstel River, became one of Europe's principal cities in the seventeenth century. Its colonial connections were one factor of its growth, and profits made in Far Eastern trade were the basis of its prosperity before the Second World War. With the decline of the Dutch Republic, Amsterdam's glory for a time was also eclipsed, and its rise during the nineteenth century was restricted by harbors unsuitable for modern trade. The Zuiderzee was too shallow for large seagoing vessels; a canal extending northward was too long to be satisfactory; and it was not until the straight, short North Sea Canal was built that the problem was solved. At the seaward end of the canal, at IJmuiden, the great locks, the largest in the world, have a depth of forty feet, while the IJ, now closed off from the former Zuiderzee, has become an excellent harbor.

Before the Nazi invasion, trade was still chiefly with the Indies. Amsterdam imported such products as tobacco, copra, coffee, tea, rubber, quinine, kapok, tin, spices, cocoa, and teak. For some of these imports, especially tobacco, quinine, kapok, and pepper, Amsterdam was the chief European market. A very special local industry was that of diamond cutting and polishing. Amsterdam and Antwerp supplied the world market in this field. The canal connecting Amsterdam with the Rhine gave to it a share of the Rhenish trade, although this was of small importance compared with similar trade passing through Rotterdam. The Amsterdam Stock Exchange, the largest in Holland, made of this city a financial center. With its 800,000 inhabitants, its strong hold on the Dutch colonial trade, and its prestige as the capital, Amsterdam formed a busy center of Dutch economic life. Unlike most cities, it is surrounded by a broad expanse of grassland, and only beyond this soft, damp area does one find the garden suburbs such as Hilversum on the sandy upland to the east and Haarlem on the dunes to the west. In the country surrounding Amsterdam, especially along the IJ, the North Sea Canal, and the little Zaan Canal, important manufacturing developed under the combined advantages of ocean transportation and a comparatively large neighboring market.

The position of Rotterdam (600,000 inhabitants) at the mouth of the Rhine, with its vast economic hinterland, made it an international transit harbor rather than a Dutch terminus. The canal known as the New Waterway provides easy access from the sea to the city, and along both the canal and the Rhine from the Hook of Holland to

Rotterdam stretched busy communities which shared the city's trade and industries. Grain, ore, timber, oil seeds, cotton, and petroleum were imported and reshipped on long barges which were towed in strings up the Rhine. They returned to Rotterdam bearing the greater part of Dutch imports, even more imports than were carried to Amsterdam. As at Amsterdam, various types of manufacturing plants bordered the New Waterway and the neighboring waterways, making Rotterdam a local, but nevertheless important, industrial center. So many ships frequented this port that it was one of the chief harbors of the world. In contrast to Amsterdam, which had regular steamship services to India and to South America, the trade of Rotterdam was largely borne in tramp ships, although there were also well-known lines to the Dutch East Indies and to the United States.

Among the other cities are Delft, Leyden, Utrecht, and Groningen. Each was not only an important market town but also the seat of a well-known university. All four cities are near the border of the lowland, Delft and Leyden near the dunes, Utrecht and Groningen near the eastern sandy uplands, and their garden suburbs extend into the drier sandy region.

The eastern upland.—Quite different is the picture in the east, where sand and high moors replace the lowland peat and clay. The elevation is still low, although above sea level, but in many places glacial ridges of sand give a rolling aspect to the country, contrasting strongly with the broad river valleys of flat clays. In some places there is still much wasteland, but even there the scenery is beautiful in summer when the purple heather stands out against the dark green patches of forest with their stately pines and majestic oaks and beeches. The present value of this wasteland, in addition to its timber, is its recreation resources for the adjacent, densely populated cities.

Before the present war a great shift took place in the use of the sandy uplands. Once they were the most backward section of Holland, a region of meager fields of rye, buckwheat, and potatoes, and a place for wandering herds of sheep; but the need of arable land and the possibility of growing highly productive crops were instrumental in changing the aspect of land utilization much as occurred in the peninsula of Florida in the United States. Heavy fertilization was necessary to make the soil productive, but prosperous villages showed the successful result of man's effort to challenge nature.

Wheat, oats, and sugar beets were gaining in importance, and governmental aid helped to double the acreage of wheat in recent years. Nevertheless, the main emphasis was placed on dairying, which was based on grassland as well as fodder crops. Orchards and vegetable gardens, as well as field crops, did well on the river clays, and the raising of swine and chickens was a profitable local industry. The increase of population had been very rapid, brought about by the development of manufacturing.

Aside from the general industrial development, two regions gained prominence: one, in the eastern part of the province of Overijssel (Twente) east of the Zuiderzee, specialized in textiles and machinery; the other, in North Brabant, which forms the southern part of Holland, manufactured more diverse goods such as textiles, shoes, tobacco goods, machinery, and electrical supplies. No really large cities grew up in this eastern sandy area, although a number of flourishing cities reflected its increasing importance.

Limburg, Holland's southeastern province, extends far south along the Meuse River, touching a part of the fertile loess uplands so typical of adjacent Belgium. The landscape is very different from that of the rest of Holland. Here, elevations up to 1,000 feet are reached, whereas the glacial ridge of the eastern upland scarcely passes 300 feet; here are real valleys and hilly divides; here are quarries of stone unknown elsewhere in Holland except in the form of glacial boulders. The main value of this southern offshoot of Holland is not so much the rich cropland as the coal mines, which are a part of the coal field extending from northern France to the Rhine. Before the war, the production almost equaled the consumption in Holland as a whole, but the location of the mines made it profitable to sell the coal to the neighboring manufacturing regions of Belgium and Germany, whereas the coal for most of Holland was brought from Germany by way of the Rhine.

General picture.—In spite of its diversity, Holland has a somewhat uniform quality. Before the war its 9,000,000 population gave it a density of 600 inhabitants per square mile and made it vie with Belgium as the most densely populated country of Europe. In eastern Europe a much lower density led to overpopulation, but this was by no means true in Holland, where an intensive use of the land and a high development of manufacturing and commerce were achieved. Although certain factors such as the central location of the country have influenced this progress, much was attributable to the energy of the population. This energy is partly maintained by a climate which approaches the human optimum, and partly by a constant and successful struggle against nature.

However, apart from factual geographical material, another aspect of the Netherlands should be mentioned as important in the geographical picture. That is the beauty of the Dutch landscape before the present war. There were the green meadows in which cattle grazed, the numerous canals and lakes which reflected the ever-changing interplay of the clouds, the large red-roofed farmhouses hidden by dark green foliage, and finally, the villages and small towns, with bright red-brick houses which always looked as though they had been carefully scrubbed. At the edges of the dignified cities were the suburbs with gardens of colorful flowers, and with stately country houses which, set in beautiful parks, reflected the wealth of an overseas empire. There were the eastern uplands with dark pines and low, yellow sandy ridges and the straw-thatched farmhouses which rose from fields of waving wheat and rye. An unforgettable memory is the contrasting beauty of the bulbfields in April and the grandeur of the winter landscape when the water is frozen and Holland is ice-mad. All this is the Holland which the great painters have immortalized. All this is dear to Dutchmen who have only one hope, one desire—to see their land freed from the invader and returned to those who created and loved it.

Part Two

Historical Background

CHAPTER II

The Dutch Before 1581

BY BERNARD H. M. VLEKKE

LATE IN THE PALEOLITHIC PERIOD the primitive hunters who visited the eastern districts of the Netherlands, along the banks of the Meuse and the IJssel, left scattered traces of their temporary settlements; later these were unearthed by the earnest archaeologist and the casual farmer. Marshlands separated these sandy eastern plains, now the provinces of Brabant, Limburg, Gelderland, Overijssel, and Drenthe, from the fringe of dunes which formed the uninhabitable western section of the country—its sole bulwark against the angry floods of the North Sea. Although the marshlands then were not so low as they are now and actually must have lain well above sea level, the enormous volume of the Rhine, the Meuse, and the Scheldt, seeking outlet through the Dutch lowlands, turned them into impenetrable swamps. In time, because of the gradual sinking of the soil, the danger of floods continually increased; there was also pressure on the land from the sea. Under the incessant pounding of wind and waves, even the dunes themselves receded slowly inland; but as long as their protecting front line was unbroken, the land within remained relatively safe.

The people who inhabited the more solid parts of the countryside, the Paleolithic Netherlanders, seem to have been the direct ancestors of their Mesolithic successors and lived in a period which saw the birth of new races and new forms of civilization. The *Hunebedden,* or Giants' Graves, which still lie within the inner range of low hills skirting the Groningen Marshes in the far north, are Neolithic monuments, huge Megalithic, or rock memorials to the dead, supposedly constructed around 2000 B.C. In the central part of Holland, the sandy plains of the Veluwe contain other burial places which are of a different character but are approximately of the same period.

Little is known of the racial characteristics of the early Netherlanders, since their derivation is historically as obscure as that of people in the other parts of Europe. The difference in type between the dark-haired, broad-faced people of Walcheren, in Zeeland, the southwest corner of the Netherlands, and the fair-haired Nordics of Friesland is attributable to the Alpine tribes who lived in southern Holland before the Nordics invaded their domain from the northeast. Even around Limburg in the southeast corner the Alpine type seems to prevail, although the mixture of bloods is more equal.

Anthropology and archaeology do not agree in their analysis of the antecedents of present-day Hollanders. An example is the traditional classification by Roman historians and geographers of the ancient inhabitants as tribes of Celtic and Germanic descent, which classification does not seem sound. For instance, it is known that the settlements along the coast on the narrow strip of solid land behind the dunes are not so old as those on the eastern plains. And certainly the cattle-breeding tribes of the interior lived only in the marshy districts between the dunes and the sandy plains. The marshes, which supplied good pasture for the herds, were also flooded periodically. In order to provide refuge for their cattle in flood time, the tribesmen erected mounds of earth called *terpen,* which gradually were enlarged and raised to provide shelter for the people as well.

When the Romans entered Holland in the first years of the present era, they could make little use of either the marshes or the sandy plains of the north. They built well-fortified naval stations on the banks of the Rhine and the IJssel and manned them with small garrisons. From these strongholds they made war, under Drusus and Germanicus, with the Germanic tribes along the Weser and the Elbe bringing troops and supplies up the rivers to whatever points had been selected for attack. But the dreary, damp land north of the rivers seemed wholly unsuitable for settlements even to the hardened veterans of the Roman legions. In fact, the only district the Romans were interested in was the hilly countryside east of the Meuse, between the villages of Maastricht (*Trajectum*), and Aachen (*Aquae Grani*). Here, along the highway connecting Cologne with the Channel ports, numerous Roman country houses were built and some measure of Roman civilization prospered.

Had it not been for the Romanized warrior Civilis and his Batavi who have become interwoven with Dutch historical tradition, the northern tribes then living on Netherlands soil would have been completely forgotten. The tale of their brief but violent uprising against Rome in 69 A.D. fascinated Tacitus, the Roman historian. As he has told the story, the Batavi, a small tribe living between Waal and the Rhine, had served Rome and had even formed part of the bodyguard of the emperors of the Julian Dynasty. When that dynasty fell, their special privileges ended and the uprising which followed was suppressed with some difficulty. In the long and turbulent history of the Roman Empire, this insurrection in northern Netherlands was of minor importance; but through the writings of Tacitus, Civilis and his Batavi have attained immortality. The Batavian warrior was acclaimed, long after his death, as the first of Holland's many fighters for freedom. Indeed, the Netherlands was called Batavia by the Latins, and eventually the name was even given to the capital of an Asiatic empire.

The decline of Roman authority in the Low Countries began in the third century, with the first invasions by Germanic tribes from across the Rhine. The Romans promptly gave up control of the northern half of the territory, but to the sea, not to the human invaders. Storms from the southwest had finally broken down the front line of the guardian dunes and the marshlands behind had sunk so low they were open to inundation by the swollen sea. The northern section of the coast split into numerous islands. Behind them the Zuiderzee took form and continued to grow and extend for the next ten centuries. The Batavi disappeared from history, to be revived a thousand years later in the legends of the country.

By the end of the fourth century the Romans were maintaining their hold only in the southeast corner, and the southern part of the

Netherlands was overrun by the Franks. In the fortified and desolate southeastern village of Maastricht, a Roman priest, Servatius, organized the first Christian community in the Low Countries.

From the south of the Netherlands, the Frankish war lord, Clovis, led some of his people on expeditions into central Gaul. After he had founded a large and rich kingdom between the Somme and the Loire, he returned to the land of his people firmly determined to establish his power over his unruly compatriots and their barbaric neighbors. He found that to the north the scattered inhabitants of the islands and marshes had united under the King of the Frisians. It was a difficult and tedious task to subdue these men, who rejected both the political domination of the Franks and their Christian religion, although that faith was preached to them by their kindred Anglo-Saxons. In 695 A.D. Pope Sergius appointed the Anglo-Saxon, Willibrord, Bishop of Utrecht, but Christendom did not conquer Germanic paganism until the Frankish kings had established their political supremacy on the battlefields. The murder of St. Boniface, the German apostle, in 754 A.D. near Dokkum in Friesland, marked the last violent outbreak of pagan resentment against the newly organized Christian Church. Eventually, under Charlemagne's rule, a certain degree of political and religious unity came to the Netherlands.

These changes, however, did not greatly affect the social institutions of the people. The Low Countries remained, as they had been in the old Germanic period, a territory of small estates and free landowners. Such bondage and serfdom as still existed gave way rapidly to more liberal social forms. The *latifundia,* or enormous estates, such as the French possessed, were unknown and the Church did not achieve extensive landholdership. Of the few monasteries, Egmond, on the northwestern coast was the most important. A part of the Church property was early appropriated by the Frankish kings for the benefit of their personal followers, or vassals. Certain of these vassals were made counts and were assigned to rule over various local Netherlands districts.

During, and immediately following Charlemagne's reign there was a short period of internal peace which offered some scope for trading and industry. Frisian weavers fabricated the impressive gift of cloth presented by the Emperor to the Caliph of Bagdad, Harun-al-Rashid. The skippers and fishermen of the Rhine villages traveled between Cologne and England. But in the ninth century this brief interval of prosperity was rudely disturbed by invasions of the North-men (Scandinavians), during which time no part of the Low Coun-tries escaped destruction by fire or by sword. And what the Northmen left, the floods ruined, floods more extensive and more devastating than any seen before. The Netherlands was in a desperate plight both economically and politically. Politically, conditions were bad because the Frankish Monarchy had split into the kingdoms of France and Germany and the counts of the Netherlands were uncertain to whom they should transfer their allegiance. Finally the rulers of Lorraine, which included present-day Belgium, reluctantly accepted the over-lordship of Henry I of Germany, as did also the rulers of the northern Netherlands.

The tenth century brought some relief to the country. For one thing, the Scandinavian invasions ceased. At about 1000 A.D. the first of the Dutch dikes was built to protect the continually sinking land against the floods. In the course of succeeding centuries, part of the inundated land was recovered, but the northwestern section, behind the present islands of Tessel, Vlieland, and Terschelling was lost forever.

Henry I's successors, the German kings of the Saxon Dynasty, tried to reorganize the Netherlands politically. But the half-barbaric counts of the western marshes proved to be indomitable rebels. Two counties had been formed in the north and northwest, that of Holland, soon to be united with Zeeland, and that of Friesland. The German kings deputized the bishops of Utrecht to be guardians of the peace in the Low Countries and gave them large grants of land. And the bishops, sometimes supported by the ducal troops of Lorraine, attempted to subdue the unruly borderlands from 975 until 1150. Once Holland was conquered, but immediately was restored to independence by the Count of Flanders, a vassal of the King of France who was as rebellious against his overlord as were the northern counts against the

Holy Roman Emperor. In 1075 the power of the counts was broken in Friesland; the inhabitants not only proved to be completely intractable, they succeeded in keeping free of all supervising authority for five centuries. Until 1523, Friesland was actually an anarchic republic where no authority was recognized except that of the village chiefs and the abbots of the monasteries.

In the eleventh century the bishops of Utrecht freed themselves from the German kings but lost, at the same time, their own power which had been derived from them. Promptly the counts of Holland occupied the entire western coast. The northeastern district of Drenthe, nominally subject to the bishops, formed a republic of almost free peasants, presided over by the local lords of the fortified hamlet of Coevorden. East of Utrecht, the counts of Gelderland united numerous scattered domains into one strong princedom. South of the rivers, the counts of Louvain extended their authority north to the Meuse and changed their modest title for the more ambitious one of dukes of Brabant and Lorraine (1106).

Politically, the country was in chaos. It continually suffered from overpopulation which could be relieved only by emigration either to England or to the empty spaces east of the Elbe. Colonists from Holland and Flanders had settled a large part of Brandenburg. The country had remained economically backward until the beginning of the twelfth century. Culture scarcely existed at this period. And yet, somehow, a Netherlands nation rose from this amorphous, unpromising beginning.

To the south a clear-cut linguistic boundary separated the Dutch from the French-speaking populations, but it differed from the political demarcation between Flanders and the other Dutch-speaking territories. Besides its political separation from the rest of the Low Countries, Flanders had a different economic system. On the contrary, no definite dividing line, either linguistic or economic, separated the Netherlands from the Low German districts. Sufficient proof exists to show that the Netherlands dialects were not understood in central or upper Germany, yet the transition from *Dietsch,* or Old Dutch, to Middle German took place gradually. The increasing differentiation between the western and the eastern Low German territories resulted from the tendency of the Netherlands to turn toward the west and south rather than toward the east, a tendency manifested during the Crusades.

Dutch nobles usually joined the French or the German kings in their overland expeditions. The common people, however, preferred the sea route around Spain. At least three times as many Netherlanders as other nationalities, sometimes united with people from Cologne and from other cities on the Rhine, joined the British in a common naval pilgrimage to the Holy Land. On one of these expeditions, in 1147, the British and the Dutch conquered Lisbon for the King of Portugal, and thus gave that new kingdom its capital. At least two of the naval crusades were remarkable for their democratic organization, with all authority delegated to the elected spokesmen of the free soldiers of the expedition. This was the first expression of the seafaring Dutch character, founded in the social institutions of Holland where, more successfully than in most neighboring territories, a free peasantry maintained itself.

Political events outside Holland intensified the Dutch trend toward the south and the west, and hastened separation from Germany. After the death of Frederick Barbarossa, the last emperor of the Holy Roman Empire to have any great influence in the Netherlands, not only was the power of the German kings broken by internal strife, but the English and French kings opened the series of wars which kept western Europe divided for two hundred years. The counts of Flanders were perforce embroiled in these conflicts because of political connections with France and economic ties with England.

The English kings sought an alliance with the princes of Holland, Brabant, and Gelderland in order to secure a continental bulwark against France. As such an alignment was highly profitable, the counts of Holland ceased to look much farther east than Utrecht and concentrated, instead, on the struggle in the south. Once the dukes of Brabant had secured possession of Limburg and Valkenburg—thus establishing a bridgehead east of Maastricht, which was still under the sovereignty of the Netherlands—they, too, felt sufficiently safe to turn their attention to the west. Gradually Holland, Zeeland, Brabant, and northern Flanders developed a new unity of political interests and shortly afterwards of economic and cultural life, in which they were closely connected with France and England. The oldest works of Dutch literature were of Flemish origin. And most of the epic and lyric poems were either translated from the French or displayed strong French influence, although some of the great contributions, such as the epic of *Reynard the Fox,* held no trace of foreign thought.

Although Bruges, an important center of commerce as early as the eleventh century, maintained close relations with the North German towns from the beginning of the Hanseatic League and most of the cities of the Netherlands east of Utrecht also became members, the towns of Holland, Brabant, and Flanders kept aloof. In language, too, the three provinces remained individual. In the thirteenth century, Jacob van Maerland, one of the first Dutch poets about whom much biographical data are known, clearly distinguished between the common Dutch language, or *Dietsch,* and the Flemish, Holland, and Brabant dialects. By the fifteenth century the common tongue was called *Nederlandsch;* however, the northeastern dialects, those of Gelderland, Overijssel, and Utrecht, were not considered a part of it, but were grouped under "Eastern," or even "Low Saxon," *Nedersassisch* dialects. Hollanders counted the Frisians among the easterners, but the Frisians during the Middle Ages considered themselves a separate national group.

But the conviction of belonging to an independent linguistic branch does not necessarily imply a common national sentiment. Netherlanders of the Middle Ages recognized no political allegiance except to their city or, at most, to their native province. This sectional feeling was intensified during the thirteenth century, when the founding of townships actually began. The only two towns in the Netherlands which could trace their histories to the Romans were Nijmegen and Maastricht. Both of these towns owed their survival to accidental factors; at Maastricht was the church of St. Servatius, which was revered by all the people of Lorraine; at Nijmegen was the imperial residence, near to its ancient walls. All the other Netherlands cities came into being wherever a good harbor or a crossroad of waterways offered commercial opportunities to tradespeople and fishermen. Almost all Dutch rulers promoted these thriving communities by granting city rights to small hamlets and even to entire country districts. By doing so they not only encouraged economic prosperity, but practically eliminated the differences in legal status between township and countryside.

Not only the rapidly flourishing commercial communities, but also the reclamation of the marshlands changed the economically stagnant western part of the Netherlands into one of the most prosperous areas of northern Europe. This change marked a sharp contrast between the southern and the northern sections of the Low Countries, especially between Flanders and Holland.

Flanders prospered because her close relations with England permitted her to procure the raw materials needed by the Flemish weavers; thus she was free to exchange merchandise not only between Bruges and the Hansa but also with the Italian cities. Early in the Middle Ages the Flemish gave up shipping in order to mediate between the northern and southern traders. Holland, however, competed energetically with the shipping of the Hansa merchants and indirectly, therefore, with Flanders. By the middle of the fourteenth century, the trade with Prussia and Poland which was to be the "mother trade of all Dutch commerce," was in full swing. In the fifteenth century the competition became sharp enough to provoke bloody conflicts.

Now that the Netherlands had grown important commercially and politically, the dynasties disputing the Crown of Germany felt it vitally necessary to gain a foothold where the German, French, and English currents of influence met. Since, in that day, intermarriage was the normal method of acquiring political power, the Luxemburger married into the ducal family of Brabant, and the Bavarians into that of the counts of Holland, but in both instances the German princes, once settled in the Netherlands, became instead fully involved in western European affairs.

The English kings fared no better. For a while they retained their alliance with the counts of Holland, but they failed to obtain the succession to Flanders. And the interests of Flanders, Brabant, and Holland had become so interwoven that if a powerful dynasty could secure possession of one, it could not but exercise great influence in the other two. Political unity of the Low Countries was finally achieved by the French royal house of Valois, represented by its younger branch, that of Burgundy.

Between 1385 and 1433, the provinces of Flanders, Brabant, Holland, Zeeland, and Limburg, together with the Walloon provinces of Hainaut and Namur, one after another fell to Philip, Duke of Burgundy, and his successors. Although the French language was widely used in official circles and French modes of chivalry are reflected in the official historiography of the Burgundian period, which was modeled on French lines, by the time the Burgundians came to power the peak of French influence had already passed. A center of Dutch civilization had flourished in the triangle of northern Flanders, Brabant, and Holland long before. And, whereas with a few exceptions, all literature of the thirteenth and fourteenth centuries had been imitations of French and Latin models, by the second half of the fourteenth century and more markedly in the fifteenth, all this had changed. A vigorous reaction against the use of the French language had forced several provincial governments to give equal rank and sometimes precedence to the Dutch tongue. After the founding of the first German universities, Dutch students began to attend at Cologne and Heidelberg as well as at Paris, Orleans, and Montpellier. In recognition of the new trend, Philip II established the University of Louvain in 1423 as an independent center of learning for the Low Countries.

In this and in other ways, the Burgundians contributed a great deal to the political and cultural life of the Netherlands. But, despite frequent assumption to the contrary, they were not solely responsible either for creating the unity of the Netherlands or for determining its cultural course. In as much as the northeastern section of the country was never so close to the western powers as were Brabant, Flanders, and Holland and clung instead, to ties with the counties of the lower Rhine and Westphalia, the Burgundians there met with much less response to their arguments for unity and coöperation than they did among the people along the seaboard. The antagonism between the the east and the west inspired the Low Saxons of Gelderland, Friesland, and Overijssel to resist successfully for more than a century all Burgundian attempts to conquer them.

During the twelfth and early thirteenth centuries architecture, which had followed the Rhineland school of Romanesque art, turned to the Gothic style which had been directly imported from France. But the French Gothic was only the foundation on which the Netherlands determined by its nature and its building materials rapidly developed its own characteristic Gothic style. As with architecture, literature became more original, although the Chambers of Rhetoric—associations of townspeople exercising the art of letters as a pastime—did not raise the level very high.

The most significant and original contribution to civilization by the Dutch was the Flemish school of painting, born in the fifteenth century. This school of art shows no trace of French influence. Flanders was the most prosperous and best known of all Netherlands provinces, but only half the painters of the Flemish school were Flemings, whereas the remainder included men from all Dutch provinces. The Flemish painters and musicians certainly profited from the patronage of the dukes of Burgundy, but their principal supporters were the wealthy burghers of Flanders and Antwerp. On the whole, the true importance of the Burgundian period consists of the permanent fixing, under the ducal policy, of the final boundary between the Netherlands and Germany.

As in all medieval states, the legal authority of the Dutch rulers was strictly limited. Whenever the expenses of government outstripped the normal resources of the princes, additional funds could be obtained only by voluntary concessions from the free men of the county. This was the origin of the assemblies of landowners and townships, known in western European countries as estates (*Estats, Stände*). In Holland these assemblies were called "States." The assembly called together all the members of the council, including the more important noblemen and ecclesiastics. And once the towns had become sources of revenue, their representatives had also to be included.

But the ancient meetings, attended by all the free men of the county, were not immediately dropped from the practice of government, especially in Holland, Friesland, and the northeastern territories. There seems to be little doubt that at least in the beginning, and in certain districts, contributions were granted or refused by the free men as well as by the gentry and the townships. In the later assemblies of the estates composed along traditional lines, the gentry represented the countryside. But until the fifteenth century, the free peasants had some influence and occasionally took matters into their own hands. Twice in 1426–1427 the peasants of Holland rose against their prince and the states (Provincial Assembly of Estates), because of taxes levied upon them to which they had not consented. The free men of Friesland defended their independence successfully until 1523, and the peasants of Drenthe, protected by the poverty of their district, did not relinquish their own customs.

Because the Church was never allowed to become an important landholder in the Netherlands, the lay element remained strongly predominant, except in the province of Utrecht, a part of the episcopal state of the same name, where the clergy had considerable influence in the representative body. In other provinces, for instance in Holland, the clergy was not represented at all. The degree of clerical strength in the various assemblies gives a fair idea of the proportion of land held by the Church, much of which was entrusted to lay wardens. The counts of Holland even obtained the guardianship of the province of Utrecht from its bishops several times.

Inside city walls, the town councils forbade by law the transfer of real estate to the Church. By other laws they limited ecclesiastical jurisdiction over people not directly connected with the Church. These activities attested to an anticlerical sentiment which was incongruous with the Dutch tendency toward dogmatic concept of religion, and theological discussions, both of which factors have strongly influenced the entire history of the Netherlands.

Education in the Netherlands was colored less by the formal Church than by the Brethren of the Common Life, a religious organization, developed in 1382 at Deventer, Overijssel, by Floriszoon Radewijnsz who was a follower of the famous preacher, Geert Groote. Through Groote the group was affiliated with the Netherlands mystics, the greatest of whom was Jan van Ruysbroeck. During the fifteenth century the new fraternity gained supporters in the Netherlands, and the adjoining districts of Germany, and gave excellent instruction, by modern methods, graduating many famous scholars and producing one of the most widely read books of all time, the *Imitatio Christi*. The Brethren and their Latin schools undoubtedly helped to shape the cultural development of the country and to lay the foundations whereby later generations might make the Netherlands a prominent center of humanist learning.

In most provinces the states obtained and held predominance in the government, at least after the beginning of the fifteenth century. This was in part because the local princes incessantly had to ask for financial assistance from them. It was also the result of the dynastic changes in almost all the provinces. It had become the custom not to recognize a new prince until the charters and privileges, not only of individual cities but of the entire province, had been sworn to and the prince had been duly inaugurated. Although only the great Charter of Brabant, the *Joyeuse Entrée*, or *Blijde Inkomste*, specified it to be a right of the subjects to revolt if the prince exceeded his legal power, the same rule was considered binding in most other provinces. Thus, in 1418, the states of Gelderland solemnly covenanted not to recognize a successor to the ruling Duke Reynold without unanimous agreement on the choice of candidate. They further pledged themselves to the common defense of all the privileges and liberties of the province.

The most striking example, however, of the sovereign power of the states is the decision of the states of Brabant over succession to their ducal throne between the imperial German family of Luxemburg and the French Burgundian dynasty. The reigning Duchess Johanna had bequeathed her possessions and lands to her nephew, Duke Philip of Burgundy. The German Emperor, also a candidate, in his capacity of emperor, and thus overlord of Brabant, opposed the succession of Duke Philip.

The states disregarded both the testament of their Duchess and the pretensions of the Emperor and forced both contestants to plead their causes before their assembly. They finally recognized Philip as heir to the throne, but only under condition that he would transfer his rights to a younger son and renounce his scheme to incorporate Brabant into the Burgundian State.

In Holland the majority of the states, especially the town delegates, unhesitatingly supported Duke Philip II of Burgundy against the lawful heir of the country, the romantic princess, Jacqueline of Bavaria, because they considered the Burgundian to be more capable of protecting their commercial interests and of assuring general peace in the Netherlands. With their help the Burgundian duke easily secured the county for himself and his line, and when, by 1433, Duke Philip II became master of the western and central part of the Low Countries, he did so through the support of the people.[1]

Although still greatly divided politically, the Netherlanders evidently felt a further unification of the provinces to be not only unavoidable but also highly advantageous, and tending toward a lasting peace. The sharing of this opinion by most of the inhabitants, especially by the townspeople, however, did not create a common national sentiment any more than did the consciousness of belonging to a separate language group bring it to the Frisians.

The situation in the Netherlands after 1433 was not unlike that of the British colonies along the Atlantic seaboard around 1700, in that although they were united under a common ruler, the provinces felt no obligation to help one another in minor wars or in commerce

---

[1] In order to avoid confusion, reference should be made to the list of princes of the Netherlands of the Burgundian-Habsburg dynasty:

    Philip I (Philippe le Hardi), 1385–1404
    John (Jean sans Peur), 1404–1419
    Philip II (Philippe le Bon), 1419–1467
    Charles the Bold, 1467–1477
    Mary of Burgundy and Maximilian of Habsburg, 1477–1482
    Philip III (Philippe le Beau), King of Castile, 1482–1555
    Charles I (V as Emperor of Germany), 1506–1555
    Philip IV (II as King of Spain), 1555–1581

and industry. In commerce, especially, the rivalry was intense. Competition became so fierce in the fifteenth century between the merchants of the Hansa, whose products cleared through Flemish ports and those of Holland and Zeeland, that the Hanseatic League prohibited direct communication between Holland and the Baltic area. The contest was as much one between two systems and trading routes as between trading communities.

The Hollanders sailed around Denmark, the path nearest to Hamburg and Lübeck. In coöperation with the King of Denmark, and later the King of Sweden, implacable enemies of the economic hegemony of the League, they prospered on mass transportation of cheaper cloth and foodstuffs. Lübeck and the League were supported by Bruges and Flanders, but the Hollanders also had allies within the hostile camp, Danzig, and the Prussian ports. In 1426 Lübeck closed the Sound against all Dutch shipping. The Hollanders retaliated with a war of privateers. Four years later a fleet equipped by the cities of Holland appeared in the Sound and intervened in the Scandinavian wars of succession. But not until the third quarter of the sixteenth century did Dutch trade and shipping triumph over that of northern Germany.

The beginning of a centralized form of government came through the Burgundian dukes and resulted naturally enough from the unification of Netherlands territory. But they had to fight hard for the reform against the stubborn resistance of the provincial states. Gradually, fostered by joint meetings of the states in the States-General (or Parliament), a feeling of national unity developed among the people. After fifty years of Burgundian rule the Netherlanders could appreciate so clearly the advantages of political unity that when they rebelled against the autocratic regime which followed the death of Charles the Bold in 1447, it was not each province separately, but all the provinces together that revolted against the central government, in joint action expressing an outspoken desire to remain united.

The northeastern provinces were finally added to the Burgundian patrimony by Charles V of Habsburg, the last of the Burgundians, Emperor of Germany and King of Spain, known, also, as Prince

Charles I of the Netherlands. Except for the fact that only the first steps toward reducing the status of the Low Countries were taken during Charles' reign, union with so many other states might have led to the complete subordination of the Netherlands under one of the more powerful components of the Habsburg Empire.

But the final conquest of the northeastern provinces was a long and tedious job, chiefly because the western provinces refused to support what they considered purely a scheme to expand the dynasty. The whole undertaking might easily have failed had it not been for the peculiar character of Emperor Charles' chief opponent, Charles of Egmond, Duke of Gelderland (1492–1538). This singular, rough and indomitable potentate knew only one passion, to annoy his imperial enemy by thwarting his plans for the unification of the Low Countries. He was eager for the help of the French King and of the Low German princes, but not eager enough to take the one step which would have assured him prompt assistance from a powerful German League—to become a Lutheran and introduce the Reformation in his realm. On the contrary, in his persecution of the Lutherans, Duke Charles emulated the very emperor against whom he fought so bitterly on the battlefield. At his death, Charles of Egmond tried in vain to transfer his lands to the King of France. Instead, his subjects recognized the Duke of Cleves and Jülich. The circle of frustration completed itself when the new Duke, who sympathized with the Reformation, was immediately attacked by the Emperor with an overwhelming force and had to cede sovereignty of the territory to him (1543).

The Emperor devised two measures by which to weld the loosely connected provinces into a perfect whole. The first, approved by the Diet of the Empire at Augsburg in 1548 under strong pressure, organized the Netherlands provinces into a separate district (*Kreits, Kreis*), of the Empire, which was to be forever withdrawn from the jurisdiction of the Imperial Chamber (Reichskammergericht). In this way relations between the Netherlands and the Empire were at once regulated and reduced to a minimum. In 1549 the States-General of all provinces approved another decree which made the rules of succession identical in all parts of the Netherlands. Thus the state of the "Seventeen Provinces of the United Netherlands"[2] came into existence.

Emperor Charles V, as Prince Charles I of the Netherlands, installed a central government for his new state with its capital at Brussels. Under a governor (or *landvoogd*), a Council of State embraced the members of the high nobility, a few personal advisers of the prince, ecclesiastics, and legal experts. Separate councils for legal and financial affairs, and a supreme court, held at Malines, completed the central government. The sovereign was represented in each province by a stadholder (*stadhouder*), or lieutenant, who commanded the troops in his area and administered his province with a provincial council.

One characteristic aspect of the Burgundian-Habsburg period was the creation of a new nobility, personal companions of the sovereign and superior in rank and wealth to the gentry who had formerly been the followers of provincial rulers. In the reign of Prince Charles I (Charles V of the Empire), they took part in all the campaigns from Algiers and Tunis to the Elbe and the Baltic, acted as stadholders, belonged to the Council of State, and were admitted to the Order of the Golden Fleece which had been founded by Philip II of Burgundy. The rolls of this nobility contain such names as the Nassaus of Breda who later inherited the principality of Orange, the Lalaings, the counts of Bergen and lords of Montigny, the Egmonds, the Chièvres, the dukes of Aarschot, etc.

When Charles came to the throne, the most crucial problem confronting him was the Reformation. Since the Netherlands, of which he was ruler, had close ties with Germany, of which he was emperor, Lutheranism had rapidly permeated the Netherlands. But Charles had no intention of allying himself with the revolt against the Church. The first decree against heresy, on March 20, 1521, was followed a few months later by an extremely severe one entrusting the persecution of the adherents of the Reformation to secular authorities. This marked the beginning of a state inquisition, in addition to and superimposed

---

[2] Historians have tried to identify the "seventeen provinces," but Professor Huizinga has proved that "seventeen" here is a figurative number used for a "large number," in the same way that the term "Seven Seas" is used.

over that of the bishops. At that time the Pope was a Netherlander, Adriaan Floriszoon of Utrecht, Charles' former teacher and the only Dutchman ever to attain the highest post in the Roman Catholic Church.

At the instigation of Charles, the Pope gave full power to the State Inquisitor who had been appointed by his pupil. A storm of protests from the local and provincial authorities was directed against this innovation in jurisdiction. The inquisition proceeded, nevertheless. From 1525 to 1526 the first victims of the persecution died at the stake in Holland and in Utrecht.

Probably more than two thousand persons in the Netherlands died for their religious beliefs, but that number includes the very large percentage of Anabaptists who were killed not only because they rebelled against the Church, but also because they were revolutionaries against the established social and political order. After the Anabaptists began to gather strength in 1530, and consequently to receive increased persecution by civil and inquisitorial authorities, part of them fled to Westphalia, where under Jan Mathijszoon of Haarlem and Jan Beukelszoon of Leyden, they founded the Realm of Sion, in the city of Münster. There new adherents gathered around the two leaders. Simultaneous revolutionary upheavals occurred in Amsterdam and in other cities near the Zuiderzee and resulted in the intervention of armed forces. When, after the fall of Münster, the sect changed into a pacifist group under Menno Simonszoon, former pastor of Witmarsum in Friesland, they were still persecuted by a distrustful State.

The doctrine of John Calvin first made an impression on Dutch minds around 1540, beginning in the southern Netherlands, in the industrial center of the Walloon country, and then sweeping through all the larger cities, particularly in the south. Whereas before 1560 there were very few Calvinists in northern Netherlands, the revolt against Spain concentrated its forces on Holland and Zeeland and eventually wiped out the movement in the southern provinces.

When Charles V abdicated in favor of his son, Philip, in 1555, the last ties with Germany and Austria proper virtually fell away. But the

Netherlands was reduced to little more than a province of the Spanish Kingdom. The Dutch feeling against the new king, (Philip II of Spain, Philip IV, as Prince of the Netherlands), stirred and troubled the country. Philip was by education a Spaniard and refused to learn Dutch, or even to speak French, which would have brought him into more direct contact with his new subjects. Without an understanding of Dutch ways, good and bad, he loathed their rather boisterous, often even uncouth manner of rejoicing, their intemperance, their luxury at table, quite as much as he resented their stubborn insistence on local independence. He was blind to their shrewdness in commerce and to their progressive economic system. Philip was an authoritarian and the Dutch legalistic attitude, inspiring prompt argument on every far-reaching scheme for political and clerical reorganization which would necessarily change local customs and limit sworn privileges, was intensely irritating to him. His loyalty to the Church demanded unconditional obedience to his appointed ecclesiastics, when the frankly anticlerical Netherlanders resisted any undue influence from the priesthood.

It seemed reasonable that the Netherlands geographically should become the pivot of Philip's foreign policy and military enterprises. But the logical Dutch failed to understand why they should have to pay for political adventures often contrary to their own interests. Even the new nobility had no direct contact with their sovereign and resented his giving to a few chosen favorites the power which had been theirs. The only remedy which appeals to a dictatorial mind is discipline. Philip tried to enforce his authority by gradually removing all real power from the country's institutions of local self-government, reducing them to mere figurative corporations. The meetings of the Council of State, for instance, became an empty formality.

Philip's next move was to subordinate the Church by reorganizing the dioceses and making all bishops appointees of the Crown. By a "readjustment" of ecclesiastical property the new bishops were to be provided with an income and a certain amount of power in the assemblies of the states. In this way even these representative bodies which had guarded the national liberties were endangered. Philip failed to accomplish his next aim, which was to regulate the tax system and remove it from the jurisdiction of the states which voted the taxes and controlled the use of the money thus appropriated. The high nobility, the gentry, and the merchant class revolted one after another and were joined by the adherents of the Reformation who soon became leaders of the rebellion. Philip's repressive measures had precipitated the Eighty-Years' War for freedom (1568–1648).

Historians have thoroughly described the military and political aspects of that war but still do not agree on either its motives or character. For those who lived during it and fought in it, the Eighty-Years' War was decidedly a struggle for freedom. When the hard-pressed city of Leyden minted new money, the town council had the coins inscribed, *Haec libertatis ergo* (*This for Freedom*). But what did the merchants and townsfolk of Holland mean by "freedom"? Surely not what was understood by John L. Motley, who identified it with a democratic, individualistic way of living. Under the "liberties of the nation," sixteenth-century Netherlanders meant the privileges, the charters and what they contained—the right of local self-government and independence of social groups. So it has been said that the love of freedom of the old Netherlanders was merely conservatism, a desire to maintain their antiquated institutions which, in a well-organized state, were bound to give way to the more efficient system of a centralized government. But to call the Eighty-Years' War a "conservative revolution," as is frequently done, is inaccurate because it touches on only one aspect of that war.

The determination of the sixteenth-century Netherlanders to retain their charters and privileges was buttressed by a belief in certain principles of government perhaps more modern than the Spanish tendency toward centralization which actually sought to replace all lawful barriers against tyranny with the arbitrary power of the king. One of the maxims of the revolutionary leaders was that law and not arbitrary power should rule, and there is no reason not to accept these words in their normal meaning. This was the same principle which made the Dutch resist extension of the Church prerogatives, unavoidable if Church and State were to combine in order to suppress heresy.

WILLIAM THE SILENT, PRINCE OF ORANGE

Although probably at that time the Netherlanders cared little for tolerance as a principle, and they did not question the theoretical right of the authorities to suppress heresy by force, public opinion protested the extermination of dissenters without regard to the effect of this policy on the public welfare. However, a few Netherlanders did uphold tolerance as the ideal, and insisted that persecution anywhere and against anyone was a crime. Dirk Volkertszoon Coornhert, secretary of the city of Haarlem (1522–1590), not only fearlessly expressed this opinion in his writings but also verbally in his public life. As a consequence, he was in constant danger of his life or banishment by the Spaniards, the revolutionary Calvinists, and his own town council. But the common opinion among most Netherlanders was that enforced unity in religion led to hypocrisy, and that religious persecution disorganized social life. Also their innate sense of moderation prompted their leaders, Catholic as well as Calvinist, to protest repeatedly against the religious extremists in their midst.

Even though the liberties of the nation were believed to have been embodied in the charters and sworn privileges, the people always maintained that laws and regulations should be interpreted with moderation. From the privileges themselves it followed that the sovereign was not entitled to absolute power and that his power ceased to be legal whenever he encroached upon the rights guaranteed to the local communities by the privileges. This principle was formulated by Prince William of Orange in a proclamation when he took the field against the Spaniards in 1568: "The privileges are not free grants of the sovereign to his subjects, but form contracts binding both prince and people."

These words constitute what was known as the contract theory which had already been propounded in France. The theory found vigorous support among the Netherlanders because, unlike the French, they could prove its soundness by historic arguments of the fourteenth and fifteenth centuries. Indeed, recognition of the first Burgundians by their Netherlands provinces was often in the nature of a bilateral agreement and at least in Brabant the privileges stipulated the right of the people to deny obedience to a prince who failed to keep his word.

The contractual basis was further developed by Joannes-Junius (Jan de Jonge), Governor of the town of Veere, who advanced the thesis that the "natural rights" of the people could be ceded temporarily to the prince, but could never be completely surrendered. In 1581 the States-General employed the full meaning of these theories when they deposed King Philip because, they said, a prince is ordained for the well-being of his people and not the people for the well-being of the prince. When a prince, instead of protecting his people oppresses them, the people have a right to defend their *innate liberty,* and in doing so, according to natural law, must be willing to sacrifice everything they have. Thus the States-General held that all people are born free, and not only have the right but also the duty to protect their freedom against tyranny.

This, then, was the broad principle on which the Republic of the United Netherlands was founded. The further development of the platform under the strictly aristocratic government of the Republic in the seventeenth century belongs to another chapter in this book.

Of the seventeen provinces, however, only seven (really eight) could join the new republic, since the unity of the "seventeen" was broken by war and by internal strife. In those districts where the revolution had gained momentum, the Calvinists quickly seized control of public life. The reaction of the Catholics, especially in the Walloon provinces, was to make a separate union at Arras and to conclude a treaty of peace with Alexander Farnese, Duke of Parma, Commander in Chief of the Spanish army. The northern provinces counteracted this move, which had long been under way, by forming the Union of Utrecht, January 23, 1579, promising to help each other in war against the pretensions of the King of Spain and to remain forever united against all foreign aggression.

The military situation, however, was grave. At the time when King Philip was deposed (June 22, 1581), the Duke of Parma had reason to hope that he could crush the rebellion completely. Ten years of anxiety for the Netherlanders were to pass before the tide began to turn.

CHAPTER III

The Seventeenth Century: The Golden Age

BY ADRIAAN JACOB BARNOUW

THE LAST QUARTER of the sixteenth century was a crucial period for the Low Countries. In the late 'seventies most of the southern provinces, more concerned for the maintenance of the Roman Catholic religion than for their freedom from tyranny, showed a willingness to make peace with the Spanish King, Philip II, and bow again under his rule. The northerners, on the contrary, determined to continue the struggle until freedom was won, banded together in the Union of Utrecht. Two years later they asserted their will to freedom by a solemn renunciation of allegiance to their hereditary sovereign. Philip II was declared to have forfeited the right to rule his Dutch people because, as a faithless shepherd, he had maltreated and forsaken his flock. In 1584 the Prince of Orange, the great leader of the revolt, was assassinated. The Earl of Leicester, sent to the aid of the Dutch by Queen Elizabeth, proved to be an ambitious schemer, more eager to make himself Lord of the Netherlands than to see the Netherlands free. French support proved equally unreliable. Self-help, the Dutch realized, was the surest way to freedom. They found a great military leader in Maurice of Nassau, a son of the murdered prince. In a lightning campaign Maurice recaptured city after city from the Spaniard until, by 1595, the territory of the Republic was cleared of Spanish soldiers.

The seventeenth century opened auspiciously. In 1609 the war-weary Spaniards agreed to a cessation of hostilities, and concluded with the Dutch rebels a twelve-year truce. The young republic, secure in its newly won independence, entered upon an era of peace, prosperity, and glory, which the Dutch have called the Golden Age.

Its gold was not of that pristine purity that marked the age of innocence of which the poets have fabled. It was an age rich in material gold and in the cultural treasures that art and science, with the aid of generous wealth, could produce. The golden age of the poets lay in the unrecoverable past. It did not know the value of gold and did not exert itself in digging for gold, because man was innocent of greed and private property did not exist. When man became covetous he fell from grace, and his moral state turned from bad to worse with each new generation. "The age of our parents, which was worse than that of our grandparents, has produced us more wicked still, who will soon bring forth an even worse offspring." Thus spoke Horace in the Augustan age of Rome, and the Dutch poets of the seventeenth century pretended at times to share his fanciful pessimism. But when they dismissed Horace as a prompter and wrote spontaneously, there was a purer ring in the music of their verse, though it sang not of innocence but of enterprise born of greed, and praised, next to God, the donor of all blessings, the Dutch nation for possessing these blessings in abundance.

God had blessed Holland with prosperity in reward for the sacrifice it had made for the sake of its conscience. The Dutch of the seventeenth century honestly believed that their wealth was a material token of God's approval. They were allowed to enjoy the fruits of their parents' and grandparents' heroic resistance to Spanish tyranny. The fight for freedom had given them more than freedom, it had given them peace and prosperity in which to enjoy freedom. The unbridled amassing of wealth, which was a striking feature of that capitalistic era, was therefore not felt to be an evil. The love of commercial enterprise was a God-given urge, the financial success that crowned it a God-given reward. "Help thyself, and God will help thee," began a song of the Sea Beggars. The Dutch had helped themselves to freedom, and God had come to the aid of those brave fighters by giving them prosperity and peace.

The Dutch themselves marveled at the sudden upswing of trade and commerce, and at the rising flow of products from all lands into the ports and storehouses of Holland. Only divine aid could account for it. Foreigners were equally impressed by the phenomenal expansion of the Dutch in all fields of human endeavor. Visitors from abroad came to the Dutch Republic to study the causes of its welfare and the functioning of its social and political institutions.

It is clear from all accounts that one of these causes was the industry of the Dutch people. Labor to them was not a curse. Every man was busy at his trade or craft and worked at it with the skill that had come from pride in family training. The child assisted his father in the workshop, and acquired from him both knowledge and skill in the trade. The industries and handicrafts that produced such a variety of exquisite manufactures did not spring up over night like mushroom growths. They were the full flowering of skills that had occupied the hands and brains of Dutchmen in past generations and owed the high quality of their output to the accumulated experience of centuries. The medieval towns of the Low Countries had hummed with the industry of the weavers, the clothmakers, the dyers, the goldsmiths, the carpenters, the painters, the carvers, the sculptors, the shipbuilders, the ropemakers. The craftsmen of that age were better than mere workers at their trade; they were artists, with pride in their skill and love of the product of their art. One need only look at the paintings of the Dutch primitives of the fifteenth century to realize that the homes of the Dutch people were rich in objects of beauty. Each piece of furniture bore the stamp of its maker's individual talent. The simplest jug of earthenware revealed the potter's love of the beautiful article he had made on his wheel. The carpenter was a woodcarver, the blacksmith could fashion decorative designs in wrought iron, the sign painter was an artist and the artist thought it not beneath him to paint signs, the linen weaver wove decorative patterns into his batistes, the goldsmith was an artist in his own right.

The medieval institution of the itinerant journeyman increased the number of skilled workers in the Low Countries. For the fame of the Netherlands as an industrial center spread far and wide and attracted from all parts of Europe wanderers who had skill to offer and energy to sell. Albrecht Dürer's father, a native of Hungary, had worked in the Netherlands as a goldsmith's apprentice before he went to Nürnberg. Many workers did not return to their homeland, but settled in a Dutch town where wages were good and life offered amenities that could not be found elsewhere. And this influx of foreign labor and fresh ingenuity furthered the development of new techniques. The art of tinglazed faience, among others, was brought to Holland from Italy in the early sixteenth century, but it became distinctly a Dutch industry whose precious products spread the fame of Delft over the entire Continent.

The ravages of the long war with Spain did not destroy this industrial activity. Fortunes declined, industries were sacked or abandoned, flourishing enterprises went bankrupt, and markets were lost; but the native skill and energy survived the havoc of war and resumed their labors with redoubled vigor when peace and order were restored to the Netherlands. The supply of foreign labor in the early seventeenth century far surpassed that in any previous period. The Dutch Republic, because of its determined struggle for independence, became a haven of refuge for all who sought freedom of worship, or safety from coercion. The Flemings and Walloons from the southern Netherlands who refused to bow their necks under the Spanish yoke, the Separatists from the Church of England, the Jews from Spain and Portugal, the German Protestants who found life unbearable under a Catholic prince, all flocked to the Dutch Republic, where they found freedom of conscience, employment, and economic security.

There was, then, nothing miraculous about the flowering of Dutch life into the radiant magnificence that won for that era the name of the Golden Age of the Netherlands. Holland's soil had been fertilized for that phenomenal harvest by the industry of previous generations. The people's triumphant emergence from a perilous war against the superior power of the Spanish Empire had given them a self-confidence that hesitated at no enterprise which promised abundant reward for their daring. When King Philip closed the ports of Spain and Portugal to them, the traders from Holland decided to sail to the

Indies themselves, and buy direct the precious spices the Portuguese obtained from the Moluccas. The first squadron of Dutch ships reached Java in 1596. But in the hope of finding a sea route to the Indies that was not infested by Spanish men-of-war the Dutch undertook to force the northeast passage across the arctic ice. The first attempt ended in disaster. The small band of sailors who survived returned to Holland with a stirring story of their wintering on the desolate island of Novaia Zemlia. That was in 1596. Ten years later, Henry Hudson headed an expedition that had been ordered to steer the same course. But finding the ice pack impenetrable, he steered his ship in the opposite direction, and tried to find the northwest passage. That voyage led to the rediscovery of the river which bears his name and to the founding of New Amsterdam, which the British, half a century later, rechristened New York.

Holland's navigators have marked the map of the world with many a Dutch name that still bears testimony to Dutch enterprise and lust for adventure. William Schouten made his native city of Hoorn the godmother of the southernmost cape of South America; Barents (Barentsz) gave to the mountainous island he discovered in the arctic seas the name of Spitzbergen; Abel Tasman's memory is preserved in the name Tasmania; New Zealand and Van Diemensland, Staten Island, and the names of numerous kills and creeks along the eastern seaboard of the United States still testify to the ubiquity of the seafaring Dutch in the past.

Such voyages widened the sphere of Holland's overseas commerce. Until the 'nineties of the sixteenth century the Dutch merchants had traded with the ports along the Baltic Sea, with the harbors of Scotland and England, and the coasts of France and Portugal. But in that last decade a mighty impulse filled their sails to seek profit and adventure in ever-farther regions, in the Mediterranean, in the Western Hemisphere, in the East Indies, in China, in Japan, in South Africa, on the island of Ceylon and along the coasts of Coromandel and Malabar. Competition between rival shipowners was eliminated by their merging into chartered companies. The United East India Company, founded in 1602, was given the monopoly of the trade with Java and the Moluccas; the West India Company of 1621 received sole control of the trade with the Americas; the Greenland Company pooled the interests of all shipowners who sent their crews on whaling expeditions in the arctic seas.

After the initial period of exploration and investment was past, the dividends began to flow. Especially the East India trade reaped golden harvests. And yet, none of these enterprises could vie in importance with the herring trade which remained, as of old, the chief and perennial source of Holland's wealth. Holland knew a secret process of curing herring which had been practiced as early as the fourteenth century and had since been improved and refined. The herring catch was the gold mine of Holland. The fish were salted, barreled, and stored, or shipped to foreign parts for sale or barter. An English pamphleteer who called himself Tobias Gentleman complained in the early seventeenth century that the British fishermen "have not yet the right use of making barreled fish wherewith they might serve France as do the Hollanders."

The Dutch historian, Emanuel van Meteren, who wrote in the early seventeenth century, appraised the number of ships employed in 1610 in the herring trade at 1,600. Subsidiary industries and handicrafts shared in the vicissitudes of the fisheries. The salt imported from France was refined in Holland, and the surplus not required for the curing of the fish and for home consumption was exported to the Baltic ports. So large a fleet, continually in need of repairs, gave employment to thousands of ships' carpenters, ropemakers, and knitters of nets. "By reason of their industrious fisher trade," wrote Tobias Gentleman, "it is said of the Hollanders that not one of their people are idle, nor none seem to be amongst them, except they be some of our own English nation."

In addition to their fishing fleet the Dutch employed a large merchant navy for the carrying trade. The Dutch industries that worked for foreign markets supplied these ships with an abundance of cargo. On their return voyages from the Baltic ports they brought back timber for their shipyards, iron ore, copper, grain, and raw materials for various Dutch manufactures. The grain imports were of special significance to the prosperity of Amsterdam which, in those days, was the granary of Europe. Almost every country in western Europe was dependent on Holland for its import of wheat. And these grain ships, on their return to Holland, carried freight from the foreign ports where they had unloaded to other ports at home or abroad. Thus the Dutch merchantmen became the freight-carriers of all Europe. They even carried French commodities from one French harbor to another. So dependent was Spain on the imports of wheat from Amsterdam that the Government, in spite of the King's ban on the admission of Dutch ships to Spanish harbors, had to connive at this illicit trade, because without it Spanish subjects would have starved.

Through all these channels, the fisheries, the carrying trade, the Amsterdam grain staple, the East and the West India companies, the whaling industry, and the export and import of innumerable products of national and foreign manufacture, an unprecedented wealth poured into the land. Amsterdam was the chief beneficiary of this plentiful harvest, but every town in the Republic, large and small, participated in the general prosperity. The poet Constantijn Huygens makes Amsterdam address the foreigner in these words:

> My marvels do deserve a more than common awe.
> The stranger ought to faint who came to see and saw
> And, having seen, should say, "How broughtst thou all the powers
> Of all that's powerful within thy moats and towers?
> O golden swamp with heaven's plentitude replete,
> Storehouse of east and west, all water and all street,
> Twice-Venice, whither reach the ramparts that embrace thee?"
> But, stranger, speak not thus. Better in silence face me.
> Praise Rome, praise Paris, praise Cairo's pageantry.
> Who stands in dumbstruck awe has spoken best of me.

The urge for exploration and adventure which impelled merchants and navigators to sail for distant regions of the globe possessed the minds of stay-at-home scholars in no less degree. The seventeenth century in Holland brought forth a group of original thinkers who opened uncharted fields of knowledge.

One such thinker was Hugo Grotius (1583–1645), who formulated entirely new ideas about international law and interstate relations. His ideas were revolutionary in scope in so far as Grotius rejected the then universally accepted theory of unrestricted sovereignty. He denied the right of a sovereign prince to wage war on his neighbors for no better reason than to aggrandize his own realm. Such a war was iniquitous, and the wager of such a war was a criminal under international law who deserved to be punished by international coöperation. Nations and states should be subject to the same moral laws as were individuals. If it was a crime for an individual to attack, rob, or murder his neighbor, it was a crime for a state to attack and plunder a neighboring state, and the comity of nations should consider it a duty to restrain and punish the criminal. A punitive war of this character, therefore, was the only just war in Grotius' judgment. Aggressive wars were criminal and could not be justified by the aggressor's appeal to his unrestricted right of sovereignty to do as he pleased. Universal recognition of that right would lead to anarchy, Grotius argued. Hence, for a state to waive its supposed right to declare an aggressive war was not a question of noble virtue or Christian self-denial, but a matter of self-interest.

That was indeed a revolutionary doctrine. For the practice of the seventeenth century was the very opposite of Grotius' teaching. He considered a state's right to its own territory no more assailable than, within its frontiers, a citizen's right to his own property; the age of Richelieu, on the other hand, dealt with border states as if they were designed for no other purpose than to change hands continually. Unjust is a war, maintained Grotius, which is waged for the maintenance of the balance of power. But the only wars which the seventeenth century considered righteous were of that very nature. Offensive and defensive alliances were condemned by Grotius as unavoidably entailing injustice and crime; the practice of his age made them the base of international relations. His wisdom was far in advance of his time; it is even ahead of ours. When the world shall have emerged from the anarchy into which stubborn disregard of his teaching has plunged it, mankind may awaken to a recognition of his wisdom.

Order, clarity, precision were characteristic of his thinking, and he wished that the same restraining elements would canalize the turbulent stream of human life. He had seen the chaos war had made. He loved liberty, but wanted it circumscribed by precise and unassailable rules that were based on reason and justice.

That same love of precision and order pervades the work of another original thinker—the mathematician, Simon Stevin. One does him an injustice, it is true, in labeling him the exponent of one particular science. He lived in that happy age when scholars could be universalists. Stevin played with many sciences, but he conducted each game with such ingenuity and originality that he left the experts of his day far behind, and impressed those of later days as a pioneer who deserved wider fame than his small native country could give him. He was a pioneer in many fields. He was the founder of the modern sciences of statics and hydrostatics. He proved, for example—anticipating Galileo—that the rapidity of an object's fall is independent of its mass. As an astronomer he wrote an ingenious defense of the Copernican system. For his seafaring countrymen he wrote a handbook on the method of determining position at sea. He made algebra a manageable tool by devising a system of notation that embodied most of the ingenious methods of later mathematicians such as Descartes and Newton. He wrote a manual of Italian bookkeeping, which was used as a guide by Sully, superintendent of finances under King Henry IV of France, in straightening out the badly entangled finances of the kingdom. He was the instructor and counselor of Prince Maurice and director of works on fortifications. He was the author of a theory of music, of books on civics, on the use of the Dutch language; in short, there was scarcely a field of human interest and endeavor on which his versatile mind did not formulate opinions.

The motive power behind Stevin's multifarious activity was his love of law and order. He wanted also to find law and order in nature, and to prove to his countrymen that what happened in the cosmos was the effect of traceable causes and not an accident or a miracle. In that age of superstition, in which the Dutch Reformed Church upheld the belief in the devil, when it even unfrocked one of its ministers for denying that comets were harbingers of divine wrath, Stevin's bold rationalism served to disinfect the popular mind of unwholesome and dangerous poisons.

He did not care for science that stopped at formulating theories. Mere speculation was like building a solid foundation fit to support a heavy structure without any intention of erecting an edifice. He was eager to see the new knowledge he had found applied to the needs of his countrymen. It was for that reason that he wrote all his books in Dutch. His style bears the stamp of that clarity and order for which he strove in every phase of endeavor. By rejecting the use of Latin he renounced international fame in order to benefit the average Dutch layman. Stevin died in 1620; but not until the present time has he received recognition from the learned world at large.

Nine years after Stevin's death, Christiaen Huygens was born. He belongs to the intellectual giants of that age. Any encyclopedia will give the reader an account of his achievements. He was the son of a distinguished father, the diplomat and poet, Constantijn Huygens, who supervised the boy's education, intellectually aware of his originality. When Christiaen was in his early thirties he was a European celebrity, conducting a busy correspondence with the learned in all parts of the continent. Scientific journals did not yet exist; the exchange of letters between scholars was their method of publishing the articles in which they gave account of their discoveries and speculations. In 1666, when he was thirty-seven years of age, Christiaen Huygens received from King Louis XIV a royal pension of six thousand francs, a spacious apartment in the royal library, and the commission to draft the work program for the newly erected Academy of Sciences, of which he was the first president. When six years later his native country was invaded by the armies of the King of France, he remained the latter's guest in the royal library and continued to direct the proceedings of the Academy. "The world is my country, to promote science my religion," he said. During a serious illness he entertained himself, to the dismay of a younger, more conventional brother, "with deliberating, while face to face with immortality, the pros and cons of our faith in the life hereafter, as if that were a problem subject to doubt." His rationalism made him a solitary figure. He told his brother Constantijn, who reported it in his diary, "The people will tear me to shreds when they hear of my opinions and sentiments about religion." Doubt and skepticism had made him the insatiable explorer of nature's secrets. Probability, he said, was the nearest that man could attain to truth, and in his austere devotion to reason and experiment as sole guides along the way to that inaccessible goal he would go no farther than not to exclude the deity from the probable that he knew to be within his reach. But reason and experiment did not find God there, and without Him he died a melancholy hermit.

Huygens shared Stevin's aversion to speculation for speculation's sake. He was anxious to see his discoveries in mathematics, astronomy, and mechanics utilized for practical purposes. He had the good fortune to see one of these turned into an indubitable blessing. His perfection of the pendulum clock gave to the measurement of time that exactitude which his age espoused, and his invention of the balance spring enabled every owner of a pocket watch to have a reliable time measure at his beck and call at all hours. He rang the death knell of Dutch placidity and composure. Having taught his countrymen to count the minutes, he made of them niggardly consumers of time.

It is no accident that the greatest Jew of the seventeenth century was born a Dutch citizen. The Jewish people, by giving Spinoza to Holland, paid a debt of gratitude to a people that alone among the civilized nations of Europe allowed them to live as free burghers according to their own customs and traditions. They were not forced to live within the walls of a ghetto, nor to wear a badge that marked them as members of a despised race. No poll tax was exacted from them, and their admission to the city of Amsterdam was not limited to a fixed number. They were, indeed, excluded from the guilds and from holding office in the state and city, but they shared the latter handicap with all non-Jewish citizens who did not belong to the Calvinist State church, and inasmuch as the majority of them were engaged in commerce and foreign trade, their exclusion from the guilds worked no hardship on them.

The Jews were allowed to have their own Thora school, where the only subjects taught were Hebrew and Hebrew literature in connection with the Jewish religion and sacred rites. In "The Tree of Life," as this school was called, young Baruch de Spinoza received his education. The rabbis who taught there were learned men, but their dogmatism made them intolerant of independent reasoning. When the brilliant Spinoza, after graduation, struck out on a course of thought that led him away from Jewish orthodoxy and into the path of Cartesian philosophy, they threw up their hands in horror and demanded from him, under threat of excommunication, a confession of guilt and an open disavowal of his heresies.

But Spinoza could not be frightened into a confession of beliefs that his reason had taught him to reject and he was expelled from the synagogue with the major excommunication. He left Amsterdam, lived for a number of years in rural retirement at Rijnsburg, not far from Leyden, and spent the last fourteen years of his short life at The Hague.

Spinoza had many friends in Holland who realized the nobility of his thought. But they formed a small group in respect to the mass of the people who, without having read a word of his writings, believed him to be a dangerous, immoral atheist. The ministers of the Dutch Reformed Church were among his bitterest enemies. He incurred their wrath with the *Theological-Political Treatise* in which he treated the Bible as a historical document embodying institutions ordained only for a particular people, the ancient Jews. The storm of indignation aroused by this thesis was a warning signal to him to delay the publication of his *Ethics*. It did not see the light until after his death.

Ernest Renan said of the Spinoza house at Rijnsburg that from it, perhaps, God had been seen at closest range. That was a truer estimate of Spinoza than his contemporaries were able to form of him. He was a mystic in search of oneness with God, but he sought it not through epileptic trances and emotional exaltation, as did so many mystics of the later Middle Ages, but through the austere process of severely logical reasoning. He saw the universe as an organic whole, denying that matter and mind were separate. Material objects were "modes" of God, and God was partially expressed in them. To see oneself as a whole and that whole in its relation to God is the way for man to become free from servitude to the passions, and ultimately to attain his highest goal, the intellectual love of God.

Spinoza earned a modest livelihood with the grinding of lenses. His glasses gave better eyesight to his contemporaries, his books have given clearer vision to succeeding generations. His wisdom has become part of modern thinking. Even the thought of those who have never read his philosophy does not escape his influence. Modern man is his pupil, whether he knows it or not. He looks at the world through the glasses Spinoza left him.

Another genius of the age who gave man a new conception of life was the biologist Jan Swammerdam. He was the first to study insect life in its circular course from egg to egg, and to devise a classification of insects on the basis of their various metamorphoses which retains its value to this day. It was generally assumed in his time that insects came to life by spontaneous generation from mud, manure, and putrid matter. He proved such theory to be a superstition and taught that "just as all vegetation evolves from a perceptible and fertile seed, even so all other creatures and animals spring from a seed or egg."

He wrote about snails, which he discovered to be hermaphrodites, about bees, describing their anatomy and the distribution of labor in the hive, about ink fish and other creatures that had never been studied scientifically. He was a deeply religious man. Behind the natural phenomena that he studied he looked for the divine power which alone could explain them. In 1675 he published a little book on the May fly. "Among the various traits that we have observed in the story of the May fly," he wrote, "nothing seems to me more remarkable than that it does not try to postpone the time of its metamorphosis. It casts off as soon as it can the shape of a creeping and swimming worm to assume the figure of a flying creature. This teaches man that he should quickly and readily leave the wet and cold waters of this muddy vale and raise himself on the wings of hope and love, which are the two arms of faith, into the air of divine affections." His transformation took place on February 17, 1680, in his forty-third year. Boerhave, who brought out an edition of Swammerdam's biological works, gave it a title which did justice to the scholar who had served science to the glory of God. He called the book, *Biblia Naturae.*

While Swammerdam revealed to his contemporaries the fundamental oneness of animal and insect life, Anthonie van Leeuwenhoek was opening up a world of living creatures of whose existence the lay people had no suspicion. He was the discoverer of the microbes, the "little beasties" as he called them in his quaintly phrased reports on the progress of his research. He made his startling discoveries with microscopes that he constructed with his own hands. In his hunt for the "little beasties" he made side expeditions into the field of biology. It was he who, in 1674, gave the first accurate description of the red corpuscles which he found to be circular in man, but oval in frogs and fishes. He demonstrated the accuracy of Swammerdam's account of the circular course of insect life by tracing the entire history of the flea, "that minute and despised creature," from its first emergence from the egg through its subsequent metamorphoses. He even noted the fact that the pupa of the flea is sometimes attacked and fed upon by a certain mite, a discovery that suggested to Jonathan Swift the often quoted lines:

> Nat'ralists observe a flea
> Hath smaller fleas that on him prey,
> And these have smaller still to bite 'em,
> And so proceed ad infinitum.

Van Leeuwenhoek, indeed, explored infinity in the invisibly small. He was akin to the great navigators of that age who discovered new lands in distant seas and gave to man a more accurate knowledge of his earth. Stevin, Huygens, Swammerdam, and Van Leeuwenhoek were greater than these navigators, however. They brought proof of a cosmic order that pervades all manifestations of existence, not only the stars but also the infinitesimally small particles of the earth, and leaves no scope for accident or miracle.

None of the five pioneers of science was a member of a university faculty. Stevin, it is true, lectured for a time at Leyden, but this academic connection was only a minor incident in his varied career. Grotius and Huygens were men of patrician birth to whom a professor's chair was not a seat of honor and a professor's salary no temptation. Swammerdam was financially independent and loved too much his freedom from routine duties to covet a professorship. And Van Leeuwenhoek was a humble burgher, untrained in the knowledge of Latin and Greek which was then considered an essential mark of learning. He was the burgomasters' usher at the town hall of Delft, and his scientific discoveries were made in his private study at home.

In a modern estimate, these men were gifted amateurs. It has become so customary to connect the advancement of learning with university and laboratory study that people marvel at one who accomplishes something great in science without academic support and patronage. But the physical equipment that universities in the seventeenth century supplied to the research worker was not much better than that which the independent worker could make himself, or could buy at a sacrifice which, in his passion for knowledge, he considered but slight. Van Leeuwenhoek ground his own lenses and constructed his microscopes himself. There was nothing amateurish in either him or Swammerdam. They were experts in every detail of their science, down to the manufacture of the tools they employed.

They probably would not have found in themselves this passion for truth if the schools they attended in their youth had not given them a solid foundation of general knowledge and encouraged in them the inquisitive urge. The Dutch had always taken good care of their schools. "In Holland," says the English historian G. N. Clark in his great book, *The Seventeenth Century,* "the general level of education was probably higher than in most parts of France and the British isles." Especially the Latin schools of the Republic were staffed with masters who earnestly tried to follow in the footsteps of Erasmus, and each Dutch town was ambitious to see its Latin school excel those in other cities. This type of rivalry, stimulated by local pride, kept education up to a high mark.

There was a similar rivalry among the Seven Provinces in the field

of higher education. After Holland had founded a university at Leyden, the other provinces followed. Each had to have a university of
its own. Leyden, however, maintained by the wealthiest citizens in
the Seven Provinces, remained first in importance among the universities. As Latin was the vehicle of instruction, there was no linguistic
bar to the admission of foreigners. They came from all parts of Europe,
and Holland spared no funds in attracting to its university the leading scholars of the Continent who were most likely to attract, in turn,
the greatest number of students from abroad.

The University of Leyden was originally intended as a training
school for theologians who had to provide learned ministers for the
Dutch Reformed Church. But its curriculum soon included Latin
and Greek, Hebrew and Arabic, medicine and natural history. Leyden's Arabists were famous throughout Europe. Erpenius published
a grammar of Arabic; his successor Golius supplied a dictionary;
Warner brought together the manuscripts that formed the nucleus
of Leyden's Oriental collection; and Albert Schultens, benefiting by
the work of these three pioneers, became the founder of the comparative study of Semitic languages.

The Dutch Reformed had fully earned their right to a learned
seminary for their ministry. For it was the fervor of the orthodox
Calvinists that had fired the courage and steeled the endurance of
the people during the crucial years of the Spanish war. The ministers
often rebuked the civil magistrates for telling the people that the
war had been fought for freedom's sake. The Dutch had fought for
religion's sake, they claimed, for the Calvinist religion, to the exclusion of other creeds. Having triumphed over the intolerance of Spanish Catholicism, the Calvinist ministers proved themselves equally
intolerant toward dissenters in their own midst. They ousted from
their pulpits the followers of Arminius who had rejected the doctrine
of predestination; they prevailed upon the secular rulers of the Republic to keep all dissenters out of office; and they often fulminated
against the municipal magistrates for their tolerant admission of Jews
and other foreign refugees. But though they were a domineering body
of men, they never became dominant in the Republic; their intol-

erance was stubbornly and successfully resisted by a native love of independence so characteristic of most Netherlanders.

It must be admitted, however, that the ministry of the Church was made up of learned men who labored hard to edify their flocks with solid and well-documented sermons. But learning is not equivalent to culture. The early reformers, in their iconoclastic zeal against everything popish, had removed the organs from the medieval churches the Reformed had taken over; and the choral music for which the Netherlands had been famous in the early sixteenth century had been silenced by them forever. Organ music, it is true, was reintroduced in the course of the seventeenth century. Jan Pieterszoon Sweelinck, the last in the long procession of Dutch composers, was organist of the Nieuwekerk at Amsterdam until his death in 1621. After his passing, however, Dutch music declined until the twentieth century. Under the rule of the Calvinist Church, hostile to all forms of art as allurements of the devil, the Dutch people were musically starved.

The theater also suffered from Calvinist antagonism. In pre-Reformation days almost every town of any importance had its theater guild, known by the term, Chamber of Rhetorics. Annual competitions between rival chambers were held with great pomp and circumstance. The competing guilds, in colorful procession, would enter the town that acted as host; the streets through which they passed would be decorated in festive style by the local artists, costly prizes would be awarded and a banquet would close the Country Jewel (*Landjuweel*), as these gatherings were called. But the Reformed Church frowned on these frivolities. Only in Amsterdam, under the powerful protection of the burgomasters, did a Dutch theater flourish in Holland's Golden Age. The noblest drama, that of Vondel, the greatest of Dutch poets, did not escape the ministers' censure. It was a transformation of the medieval mystery play into a classical drama in Senecan style, enlivened by *tableaux vivants* and the musical accompaniment of the chorus. Romantic drama was more popular with the groundlings because of its realism and unrestrained production of horrors. The pious were told to shun these shows and to look upon actors as social outcasts. The theatrical profession was, in consequence, held in low esteem. In the late eighteenth century players were still disqualified as witnesses in court on the ground that they belonged to a disreputable calling.

Vondel saw in tragic drama the highest form of poetry, and he looked upon himself as, first and foremost, a dramatic poet. But posterity honors him rather as a lyricist. His voluminous poetic works bear the stamp of his time. He was not, as were the great navigators and scientists of seventeenth-century Holland, an explorer and discoverer. He was satisfied with being a follower. The creative genius of Holland does not tend toward the literary. Even the most gifted of Dutch writers had a self-conscious feeling of inferiority, which made them hesitate to strike out upon untrodden paths. Vondel felt safest when following in the footsteps of the ancients, especially of Virgil. He had a magnificent mastery of language and attained a poetic diction that has the quality of organ music. But for the modern reader much of the nobility of his poetry is marred by the fact that he tended to present the life he knew in Holland as a modern counterpart of life in ancient Rome. In his poetry the burgomasters of Amsterdam were consuls, the councilmen senators, Neptune wielded his trident above the waters of the IJ and Amstel, and in his epithalamiums the gods of Mount Olympus often were guests at Amsterdam wedding parties. Admirers of baroque art may be able to enjoy the beauty of his verse, which had, indeed, no equal in his time. He was the Rubens of Dutch literature, and his art equals the painter's in vastness of range and grandeur of execution.

Vondel's taste was the conventional taste of the upper class of his day. He did not write for the masses. Their poet was Jacob Cats, a pedestrian didacticist, who put his homely wisdom into prolix and monotonous verse. His collected works, in two folio volumes, were, next to the Bible, the best read books in every Dutch household.

Hooft, son of an Amsterdam burgomaster, brought the Italian pastoral to Holland. He wrote sonnets and exquisite lyrics, turned a comedy by Plautus into a farce of Amsterdam life, and crowned his literary labors with a magnificent history of the first twenty years of the war with Spain, written in a terse and eloquent prose that is modeled on the diction of Tacitus.

Constantijn Huygens wrote a great deal of autobiographic verse that mirrors the life of his time and people. His diction is the very opposite of that of Cats. He strove for distinction through brevity, often at the risk of obscuring his meaning. He admired the startling felicities of Donne and skillfully translated nineteen of Donne's poems into Dutch. The epigram was a form of expression that suited Huygens' peculiar talent for succinctness. Thousands of short poems in his collected works testify to his wit and ingenuity in selecting the terse and telling phrase.

The poet who was most thoroughly Dutch because he dared seek beauty in every aspect of life at home was Gerbrand Adriaenszoon Bredero. He died young, at an age at which Vondel was writing poetry far inferior to his. Bredero left a volume of lyrical verse and a collection of comedies and farces that form the best literary counterpart of the work of the Dutch genre painters.

The discovery of beauty at home, which made Bredero kin of the great explorers of his age, was the outstanding achievement of the painters. In art the Dutch dared to be themselves; they showed foreigners the way to unsuspected sources of artistic inspiration. They discovered and proved that the beauty of a work of art is not in its subject but in the artist's interpretation. They dared paint subjects that had never been considered artistic, a landscape for its own sake and not as background for a scene of human activity, a simple indoor scene of domestic life, a breakfast table, a still life of books, or of flowers, or fish, or poultry. The production of pictures was a highly specialized craft in those days. Few were the artists like Rembrandt whose scope was as wide and varied as life itself. The majority of his brother craftsmen, even the most talented among them, narrowed the range of their pictorial interest. There were artists who painted exclusively winter scenes, others who excelled in the portrayal of woodlands, others in river views, in church interiors, in architectural pictures of city streets and canals, in pastures with cattle, in poultry yards, in still-life paintings of flowers, fish, books, venison, fruit. This narrow specialization enabled even the artist of modest talent to achieve high excellence within his limited field, and made the Dutch school of painting of the seventeenth century rich and prolific in variety of output. The population of Holland in those days was less than a million, yet the number of skilled artists was so great that all the galleries of Europe and of the United States are hung with their works. Dutch art is the chief glory of the Golden Age of the Netherlands.

The great masters all belong to the first three-quarters of the seventeenth century. Rembrandt died in 1669, Frans Hals in 1666, Vermeer in 1675, Jacob van Ruysdael in 1682, Jan Steen in 1679. The third quarter was a period of naval war with England. Three times in succession peace was broken and the fleets of both nations met in combat. The Republic, although attacked in the third of these wars by England from the sea and by the King of France and the Bishops of Münster and Cologne on land, came out victorious but not unscathed. After 1680 the decline set in.

At that perilous juncture in its history, Holland was fortunate in having a man of genius at the head of her navy. As commander in chief of the Admiralty of Amsterdam, Michiel Adriaenszoon de Ruyter stood first among his contemporaries. Backed by the authority of Jan de Witt, the Great Pensionary of Holland and, as such, also the leader of her foreign policy, De Ruyter built up a navy that no longer needed to rely on armed merchantmen for reinforcement. He saw to it that all the new men-of-war were built of one type so that replacements and repairs could be obtained without delay from the stores and arsenals on land; he supplied the shortage of trained officers by the formation of a professional cadre, and had the fleet accompanied by supply ships on its extended expeditions. In former days the captains were responsible for the victualing of their own ships, and the grafters among them enriched themselves at the expense of their crews, charging the Admiralty for more and better food than they actually bought. De Ruyter insisted on the establishment of an efficient supply and rationing system. Thus the makeshift conglomeration of privateering merchantmen with which Holland had fought her naval wars in the past was superseded by a disciplined and firmly organized battle fleet, whose striking power was demonstrated in the second war with England.

Young French noblemen who served on his ships as volunteers, in order to learn the art of naval warfare, were amazed to see De Ruyter, at the victorious close of the greatest battle he had ever fought, seize a broom and sweep the floor of his cabin, then visit the hencoop to feed his chickens. De Ruyter possessed an inborn dignity that could not suffer from participation in such menial tasks. His mariners called him *"Bestevaar,"* an affectionate equivalent to "granddad." He had risen from their midst, but had remained one of them, an unassuming hero without pretensions, never humble nor obsequious with his superiors, and always genial with the men who obeyed his commands. That was the secret of his popularity. Believing liberty to be the highest good, he respected love of freedom in others. His mariners willingly obeyed him because they knew him to be prompted not by pride of authority, but by zeal for the common good.

After the peace with England had been signed, the States-General, in their shortsightedness, were disinclined to appropriate funds for the maintenance of the navy's wartime efficiency. They needed De Ruyter again, however, in 1676, to rush to the assistance of Spain against France in the Mediterranean. He objected to sailing with a fleet so inadequately equipped. One of the pompous merchant rulers had the impudence to ask him if he had lost his courage in his old age. "Where the States-General are willing to risk their flag, I am willing to risk my life," was his dignified reply. His dead body was brought back from that expedition and was buried on March 18, 1677, in the Nieuwekerk at Amsterdam. With the passing of De Ruyter, there passed, also, an era of great achievements in war and of greater ones in the efforts for peace. His death marked the end of the Golden Age of the Netherlands.

CHAPTER IV

Decline and Reawakening

BY HENDRIK NICOLAAS BOON

THE ULTIMATE REASONS for the rise and fall of nations or civilizations will always challenge even the most searching analysis. The symptoms which betrayed the cultural and political decline of the eighteenth-century Republic of the United Netherlands have been ably diagnosed. Many reasons have been advanced for the disappearance of daring and initiative abundantly manifest in the Golden Age, but none has explained it.

One argument is that the unprecedented rise of the Republic—its attainment of cultural and political leadership—was possible only because the political situation in the surrounding countries favored its development. A succession of extremely capable leaders enabled the country to assume this role of a Great Power even though its organization actually lacked the qualifications. Once the other Great Powers came into their own, however, the Republic of the United Netherlands could no longer hold the balance of power.

It is almost a truism that cultural decline comes gradually. Only by comparing the cultural attainments of the Golden Age with those at the time of the French Revolution can the progress of decay be measured. Lack of a well-directed foreign policy had involved the country in wars which ruined its trade; the colonial companies were nearly bankrupt; initiative and constructive genius slept; the period of greatness had saddled the state with debts which could be met only by reducing the strength of the army and the navy below a safe minimum. In international relations, the Republic was still treated as a Great Power but it was exhausted, unable to carry its burdens.

The weakness at the core of the Republic was its internal organization as a state; this weakness was exposed when there was no effective leadership to compensate for governmental defects. The constitutional frame of the Republic had been drawn up at a time when the leaders found it vitally necessary to unite the provinces against Spain. Although the inherent weaknesses of the union were overcome when capable leaders governed with a firm hand, the last princes of Orange, who had even greater power than their predecessors, were unable to put through the necessary reforms. Partisanship so completely divided the country that in 1787 the authority of Prince William V had to be reëstablished through the intervention of a foreign power.

The story was ever the same: in peacetime the people were reluctant to change the historic articles of union; during emergencies, other matters required more immediate attention. Governmental efficiency was handicapped by the independence of the provinces, since decisions had to be reached by unanimous vote. When even one province dissented, a decision could be achieved only by persuasion. And once a decision was reached, there was still no guarantee that it would be carried out. Government consists equally as much in accomplishing certain objectives as in avoiding others. In the Republic the easiest method was to leave problems unsolved. As a consequence, among the other powers the Netherlands Government became famous for its incredible slowness.

Time and again attempts were made to improve conditions. The last in the line of dynamic political leaders of the country, Van de Spiegel, changed the antiquated division of contributions among the individual provinces. But he did not succeed in replacing with a central authority for naval affairs the five admiralties which were unable to put a modest fleet to sea. And his plan to create a council of ministers to advise the Prince of Orange did not even reach a state of discussion. The need for reforms was quite generally recognized, but no more than patchwork was achieved. Instead of devoting their energies to reconstructing the State, the groups in power wasted themselves in persecuting their opponents, the Patriots, of whom many emigrated to France.

Despairing of carrying out the essential reforms in a constitutional way, the more radical elements among these Patriots in exile were inspired by the French Revolution to start a movement for the violent overthrow of the Republic of the United Netherlands, and the authority of the House of Orange. They remained in active correspondence with their sympathizers in Holland, organized clubs and debating societies in France through which to study the writings of the French revolutionary philosophers and to draft plans for a Dutch revolution. But despite their feverish verbal activity, none of these groups was able to start a serious revolutionary movement. They could only wait impatiently for the victorious French armies which would soon be fighting in Belgium.

The fortunes of war postponed the arrival of the Patriots for some time, but in December, 1794, French troops in need of supplies entered Holland. Aided by a severe frost, the invaders swept across the wide rivers in the southern part of the country.

No one, not even the leaders of the country, believed that the Republic could survive. The resistance put up by the ill-armed defending soldiers was necessarily halfhearted, since their equipment was in such a deplorable state that even the most confident troops would have been almost ineffective. While the tottering State thus swayed under the first blow, there was an insurrection in Amsterdam which, however, proved abortive.

This development itself was typical of the whole situation prevailing in the Netherlands. Although the old patricians and the Prince of Orange both realized that their days in power were numbered, they abdicated only after the presence of the French army had left them no choice. On the contrary, the revolutionaries were impotent to start a spontaneous movement and would have been ineffective except for the protection of the French troops.

Van de Spiegel and others tried in vain to induce Prince William to lead his people against the invader as his forefathers had done. Instead, William agreed to postpone his departure for a few days but, on January 18, 1795, refusing to wait any longer, he left with his family in a fishing boat for England. Such an ignominious leave-taking of the ruling prince marked the inglorious end of the Dutch Republic, the same Republic which his ancestors had established with such great effort.

In the wake of the French armies the Dutch counterpart of the French Revolution finally took place. But it completely lacked the spontaneity and the power of the movement which had shaken France to its foundations. Plans had been made to avoid bloodshed or "incidents." The patricians ceded their places willingly to the "provisional representatives of the people," who took over the government until a new constitution could be approved. Indeed, many patricians were glad to relinquish responsibility in the trying and uncertain period which was foreseen. But even so, some patricians, in certain parts of Holland where French pressure was less strong, succeeded in retaining much of their influence under the guise of the new order.

A central revolutionary committee in Amsterdam directed the entire movement, maintaining close contact with local committees in each of the important towns. After the change in the local and provincial governments had been completed, logically the next step would have been to establish a national assembly for the Batavian Republic (1795–1805) on the French model. But at this point the revolution lost its impetus and more than a year elapsed before the first truly democratic national assembly met in The Hague. However, during that interval many reforms had been carried out and these completely changed the aspect of the country. The privileged status of the nobility was abolished and the existing remnants of medieval and feudal servitudes were done away with. The five admiralties were reorganized and consolidated into one committee for naval affairs; the famous United East India Company was taken over by the State. In fact, a general simplification of the complicated government organism was brought about.

Because the French army had been instrumental in effecting these changes it was not long until France presented a bill for her assistance. Important cessions of territory and the maintenance of 25,000 French soldiers stationed in Holland were the price demanded for a defensive and offensive alliance. And this was only the first installment of the large payments which France exacted from Holland, in later years, in exchange for a status of semi-independence which became more and more a fiction until, finally, Napoleon incorporated the Low Countries into his gigantic empire.

For the time being, however, French ideas exercised a beneficial influence. From them stemmed the reforms which converted the rambling organization of the Seven Provinces into a modern centralized state. The French "big stick" was actually indispensable, especially so when the National Assembly failed to formulate a constitution acceptable to the people. Because the revolution in the Netherlands lacked the rejuvenating force of the French Revolution, the old struggle between the unitary and the federalist elements persisted unabated in the new assemblies. The infirmities of old age corrupted the strength of the new Republic. It was clear that the deadlock of endless and sterile discussions could be overcome only by force. With the coöperation of the French Minister in The Hague, a coup d'état gave the country a tailor-made constitution modeled on the French pattern. A slavish imitation of the French model was all that the harassed Dutch nation of the time could achieve.

With this change in constitution came, at last, definite sanction of the reforms of previous years. The constitution in time was to be replaced by others, but many of its innovations were permanent. It has been said of this constitution that the country threw away the bottle but drank the medicine. Under it provincial debts were amalgamated; the budgets were unified; inequality in the treatment of Jews and Catholics disappeared; a strict separation between Church and State was accomplished; the old provinces were replaced by departments with different boundaries; judicial procedure was unified and simplified; and the numberless varieties of taxes were systematized to a certain extent. This constitution was the first really democratic framework the Netherlands had ever had, but it did not work.

For one thing, the lower middle class, which was now called upon to fill important posts in the Government, was insufficiently educated. The Jacobin party which governed, although it was the only party with a positive program, was a minority in the country. Corruption and ineptitude prevailed. Because they were a minority, the Jacobins, while theoretically pledged to the democratic process, could rule only by the use of force. Even after the coup d'état brought moderate elements into control, the new organization was incapable of constructive legislation. Although the old order had collapsed and was gone forever, the new government showed no greater enterprise nor energy. It seemed as though the nation was beyond regeneration.

Napoleon in the meantime had achieved absolute power in France and he soon extended his control to the Batavian Republic. At his direction General Augereau on September 14, 1801, sponsored a last coup d'état which strengthened executive authority in the Netherlands and, in fact, ended the period of democracy in the Government. Men from all parties were now invited to participate in the administration and they readily agreed. Naturally the leadership reverted to those who had had previous experience. Improvement of general conditions, however, was hampered by the increasing demands from Napoleon for men and money for his campaigns. The Dutch authorities could not oppose him, so they incurred his disfavor by their deliberate slowness and inefficiency.

Napoleon planned a reorganization of Europe in which there would be no place for even a semi-independent Dutch Republic. In this system, under his direct control, Napoleon's brothers were to be kings of the different vassal states. As a beginning, and in order to accustom the Hollanders to a monarchical form of government, Napoleon appointed Rutger Jan Schimmelpenninck as head of the State under the time-honored title of Grand Pensionary. That rule lasted only one year, but during it Schimmelpenninck accomplished several lasting reforms. He selected his ministers regardless of party or social class, and some of them were among the most efficient the Netherlands had ever known. A fair system of taxes replaced the hundreds of uneconomical and unjust forms of taxation. The Government was empowered by law for the first time to supervise education. Thus, the country was conditioned to a strong central government without provincial or local autonomy.

Although Schimmelpenninck did very well for Holland, Napoleon did not intend to let him remain. He was replaced on the flimsiest of pretexts by the Emperor's brother, Louis Napoleon, who was King of Holland for four years (1806–1810). Louis sincerely tried to serve his adopted country, but he was powerless against his omnipotent brother who was interested only in getting a firmer personal grasp on the country.

Holland was in a desperate plight. Napoleon's wars had ruined the trade which had been the main source of Dutch prosperity. England's command of the seas had severed Holland's communication with her colonies. Confined to her own small territory on the Continent, Holland was unable to breathe. Only agriculture prospered, and that but moderately. Poverty increased at an appalling rate. In once powerful Amsterdam, more than one-fourth of the population lived on charity. Grass grew between the stones on the quays at which thousands of ships formerly had moored every year.

It was vitally important to Holland's interest to come to an early peace with England, but that was an achievement Napoleon wanted least of all. He not only nullified all of Louis' efforts in behalf of his adopted country, but finally became so irritated that he dismissed him with scant formality and, by the decree of July 9, 1810, declared Holland to be a part of France.

Although this annexation was the logical conclusion of previous political developments, the final and formal loss of independence came as a shock to many Netherlanders. They realized at last to what depth the country had fallen. Impoverished by the loss of its colonies, with its trade ruined, its finances so disordered that interest had to be cut to one-third, its youth conscripted for Napoleon's innumerable wars, and its territory governed by Frenchmen, Holland seemed beaten too low ever to rise again.

Increasing misery and oppression, however, made a fertile field for the seeds of revolt. Gysbert Karel van Hogendorp, who had consistently refused favors from revolution and empire alike, had been unceasingly at work for years to give form to a national restoration. In the dark and dismal year of 1812 he completed an outline for a constitution and started discussing with others a general plan for the liberation of the country. He was moved by the knowledge that when the hour struck, Holland should be prepared to liberate itself.

The Allies decisively defeated Napoleon at Leipzig in October, 1813, after his retreat from Russia. French troops in Holland began to withdraw to the south of the country. The moment for action approached. On November 15th an insurrection inspired by Van Hogendorp broke out in Amsterdam among the shipyard workers who had always been sympathetic to the House of Orange. The prosperous members of the citizenry were reluctant to commit themselves too far, but they were carried along by the people. Two days later, Count van Limburg Stirum, one of Van Hogendorp's closest friends, appeared on the streets of The Hague wearing an Orange decoration; in this way was started a widespread popular movement. An eloquent proclamation beginning "Long live Orange, Holland is free!" called upon the Hollanders to liberate themselves.

Once the movement had got well under way, Van Hogendorp called on all the patricians of the period before 1795 to take over governmental authority until the arrival of the new Prince of Orange, son of William V, from England. Unlike the people as a whole, the venerable assembly was reluctant to declare itself openly in as much as the French were still very near and might possibly return to mete out a terrible vengeance.

At this critical moment, when the inertia of the aristocracy threatened to defeat the spontaneous nature of the revolution and to force the country to wait passively for freedom by the Allied armies, Van Hogendorp, Van Limburg Stirum, and Van der Duyn van Maasdam courageously took control themselves. In a bold proclamation they accepted the responsibility of maintaining the functions of administration until the Prince of Orange should come. "God helps those who help themselves," was their watchword. In the days of feverish activity which followed, these three men undertook virtually singlehanded the gigantic task of creating ministries, of running the government, and of forming a national army. Because of Van Hogendorp, Holland did not have to accept her independence from the hands of her Allies. She freed herself.

The national tension was relieved by the landing of Prince William on November 30th at Scheveningen, the same town from which his father had left the country eighteen years before. William's arrival immediately raised several questions of great importance to the future of the new state. And all those questions were implicit in the one crucial question: Would the new ruler restore the old order in its entirety, or would some of the reforms of the revolution be retained? Because of the insight and vision of both Van Hogendorp and the Prince, the newly formed Dutch State was a blend of the old and the new, while in almost all other European countries the old order was restored as completely as possible.

The principal issue concerned the political nature of the Prince's domain. Was he to return as stadholder of a federation of provinces, or as sovereign of a unitary state? The decision, which had to be made immediately would affect the entire course of the nation's life. The proclamation which welcomed the Prince was formulated by Van Hogendorp, Van Limburg Stirum, and Van Maasdam and indicated a complete break with the past in these words: "It is not William the Sixth, of whom the country does not know what to expect, but William the First who, as Sovereign-Prince, is being welcomed by the people." Thus the sovereignty which had been jealously retained by the States-General for centuries was finally transferred to the House of Orange. In his answer, William accepted the rule of the country, but only under the guarantee of a constitution.

Here at last was a bold and courageous decision, ending forever the century-old struggle between a federal and a unitary state. The hard lessons of the years of frustration and misery had not been wasted. As a unified state, Holland resumed her place among the nations of Europe.

In the further elaboration of the Constitution, on the basis of Van Hogendorp's outline, by a committee of fourteen members, practically no questions of principle were raised. Political thought was inarticulate after years of oppression. Among the assembly of notables which accepted the Constitution, the great majority considered it more a necessary form than a living principle for the new state. This resulted in the powers of the king being rather too extensive: he was commander of the army and the navy, he had supreme authority over foreign policy, he decided on war and peace. The new States-General was a combination of its namesake in the Republic and the legislative assemblies of the French period. Decisions could now be made by a majority vote of individual members, elected by the provinces proportionately to the number of their inhabitants, but the elective system was still far from democratic.

The recreated Netherlands State was regarded favorably by the Great Powers, who returned to it nearly all the overseas possessions. The Kingdom of the Netherlands also received increased responsibilities in reorganized Europe by the union with the Belgian provinces. But the new order was still in the process of formation when it was challenged by the return of Napoleon from exile. In the brief but perilous campaign which defeated Napoleon, the Netherlands troops under the Prince of Orange made an honorable showing.

Thus the basis was laid for the new national life of the Kingdom. The union with Belgium did not last, but otherwise the year 1813 marked the rebirth of a nation under the leadership of the House of Orange. No longer was the Netherlands a first-class power on the decline, as it had been in the eighteenth century; it now took its place in the foreground as one of the more important secondary powers, destined by geography, history, and cultural achievements to occupy the position with honor.

Within the country, the new order was received enthusiastically. Everyone expected a renewal of better times, now that the House of Orange was restored to power and the country was free. But, in the main, reaction against French oppression was negative, and, although tempered by the moderation of the Dutch character, it remained negative. Positive concepts of the task of the Netherlands in a reconstructed Europe were advanced only by Van Hogendorp, and he was soon sidetracked.

Now the dry rot of the French period became evident. Because the innovations of the French Revolution had been imposed on Holland, they were never completely accepted by the people as part of the national heritage. Since the nation had grown accustomed to accepting leadership and had forgotten how to think for itself, the Netherlanders had not been capable of effecting the necessary reforms themselves. And whereas the French occupation lasted long enough to stamp out the early divisions of partisanship, it lasted too short a time to bring to the fore a new generation with fresh, progressive ideas. For a time the return to freedom was applauded, but once the miseries of the occupation were over, a large part of the population was quite happy to return to their pipes and their cups of coffee and to leave the affairs of state to the King. And still there was an enormous task ahead. Much of the commerce and industry of the country had to be developed anew; ships had to be built and the nation's ties with its colonies reëstablished and strengthened.

However, although there was little energy in the country, King William was eager to give it the kind of dynamic government for which he had prepared himself in his long and bitter years of exile. It was a stroke of good fortune for the country that its first king was a man with a strong hand who was willing to provide able leadership. Because of the firm foundations he laid in the many years of hard and patient work, a younger generation finally succeeded in rejuvenating thought and in bringing to new bloom, under the banner of liberalism, the arts, sciences, and the political life of the nation.

CHAPTER V

Modern Development

BY BARTHOLOMEW LANDHEER

IN HOLLAND, AFTER THE RESTORATION, much of the French system was retained. French laws on taxation, the system of military conscription with a voluntary homeguard, the entire civil-law system, and numerous other innovations were continued, in contrast to most other countries where strong reactionary measures continued to prevail.

King William I immediately appointed a commission to prepare a constitution on the basis of Van Hogendorp's draft. A few months later the draft of the commission was submitted to an assembly of six hundred notables who could vote only "for" or "against" without discussion. The meeting was held in the Nieuwekerk in Amsterdam on March 29, 1814. Of the 474 present in the assembly, 448 voted in favor of the new constitution.

The Constitution of 1814 contained the provisions that the sovereign should share the legislative power with the States-General and exercise the executive power alone. All sovereign power, formerly possessed by provinces, districts, or towns, was to be transferred to the king. The king was to appoint and dismiss ministers, declare war and make peace, have control of finance, and govern the overseas possessions. He was to be assisted by a Council of State of twelve members. The States-General was to consist of fifty-five members, elected by the provinces on the basis of population. The members, of whom one-fourth should belong to the nobility, were to be elected for three years. The sovereign was to be a member of the Reformed Church but equal protection was given to all religious beliefs.

The Constitution was fundamentally absolutistic and rested on an oligarchic-aristocratic foundation. The influence of the people was negligible; only in the towns did a small number of those who made the largest contribution in taxes become electors for the Provincial Estates. It should not be forgotten, however, that the country was in a serious condition and that centralization of power was necessary in order to reëstablish more normal conditions. The following measures were taken by the King entirely independently: the reorganization of the Dutch Reformed Church, the creation of the Netherlands Bank, and the regulation of higher education. Only the very serious problem of the national debt was dealt with in collaboration with the States-General.

The entire matter of the territory of the Netherlands was handled in the true manner of the period, namely, by endless bickering between the various Great Powers. Holland had received assurances from the British that it would be strengthened to form a barrier against French aggression. The conversations between the British plenipotentiary and the Sovereign-Prince resulted in a proposal to unite with Holland the Belgian provinces as far as the Meuse and, in addition, to include the region between the Meuse and the Rhine. Prussia objected, however, to the cession of cis-Rhenan territory, and this plan was abandoned. In the preliminary Treaty of Paris of 1814, matters were left vague. It was stated only that the frontiers on the right bank of the Meuse would be regulated in accordance with the military requirements of Prussia.

In the meantime William, with the assistance of his minister, Van Nagell, had drawn up the fundamental conditions for the creation of the new state. These proposals were adopted by the Allied sovereigns in London on June 21, 1814.

After the intermezzo of Napoleon's return, the work of reconstruction was continued. King William summoned a commission of Dutch and Belgian notables to draft a new constitution. The States-General was now to consist of two chambers, of which the first was to be appointed. The second chamber, of 110 members, was to be equally divided between north and south on the basis of a very restricted franchise. The proposal was approved by the Dutch States-General by a unanimous vote, but it was promptly rejected by the Belgians. The grievances were mostly of a religious and financial character, as the Catholic south dreaded domination by the Protestant north and also was reluctant to share the heavy debts of Holland. Nevertheless, by counting the absentees as having voted favorably, the proposal was considered acceptable. This maneuver undoubtedly did not add to the popularity of the new union. The Congress of Vienna gave its official sanction and added the Duchy of Luxemburg to the enlarged Netherlands.

In economic matters the King proved to be a capable and energetic leader. He did his best to promote Belgian industries, as well as to encourage the carrying trade of the north. He considered limited protection the best way in which to achieve these ends and did not favor Van Hogendorp's ideas of free trade. Numerous new waterways were built to improve the system of communications and the Netherlands Trading Company (*Nederlandsche Handelsmaatschappij*) was founded in order to promote trade relations with the Indies. Cultural matters also had the attention of the King who continued to be too autocratic only in politics.

His chief mistake was to aggravate the Belgians, particularly in religious matters. His demand that all candidates for the priesthood first attend the Collegium Philosophicum in Louvain, which he himself had founded in 1825, met with strenuous opposition. Supported by the Pope, the Belgian Catholics scored a victory over King William who had to relinquish his attempt to regulate the education of Belgian priests. The Belgians also felt that they were taxed too heavily for their insignificant share in the official positions of the Netherlands. The language problem created additional difficulties, and laws favoring Dutch as the official language were resented by the Belgians.

Conditions finally became so acute that they led to a revolt which, at the beginning, was scarcely more than a riot. Large sections of the Belgian population had grievances, but the King personally was popular and it was fully realized that Belgian industry had profited from his care. Rather unexpectedly a performance in one of the cities of

La Muette de Portici, with its revolutionary songs, led to rioting which gradually spread to other cities. When the Dutch failed to take energetic measures, a Provisional Government was formed and the Belgians declared their independence.

King William appealed to the Great Powers which met in London on November 4, 1830. Contrary to the expectations of the King, it was immediately made clear that the intervention of the Great Powers would be based on the principle of separation. In the meantime the Belgian National Congress in Brussels, with overwhelming majority, declared Belgium an independent state in which the House of Orange-Nassau should forever be excluded from the throne.

The London conference decided that Holland was to retain her old boundaries of 1790, but Belgium was eager to incorporate Maastricht, Limburg, and the Dutch part of Flanders. When Leopold of Saxe-Coburg was elected King of Belgium, William I protested sharply and decided on a military expedition against the new country. A Dutch army of 30,000 men invaded Belgium, defeated a numerically superior army, and had Brussels at its mercy.

But the Dutch army did not advance beyond Louvain because it had accomplished its task. The Ten Days' Campaign improved matters considerably for Holland. In 1832 the Great Powers sent an army to Belgium and began a blockade of Dutch ports to force a final settlement. However, it took until 1842 to reach a final arrangement, because William I refused to move on a number of points. Holland was now given a part of Belgian Limburg and the debt ratio was also altered in favor of the Netherlands.

Since 1840 the Netherlands has been one of the smaller European powers, a fact which was accepted with resignation since memories of the glorious past remained vivid. There was a certain satisfaction among the population, however, that matters had been clarified and that Holland could concentrate on its own affairs. Culturally, the new period brought a process of intensification called the *Réveil,* which meant a break with rationalism and a return to Calvinism under the leadership of Bilderdijk, Da Costa, and Capadose. A tendency, perhaps stimulated by the *Réveil,* was the Liberal revolt against the orthodoxy of the Dordrecht Synod (1619) of the Calvinist Church. This group, under the leadership of Professor Hofstede de Groot and of the preachers De Cocq and Scholte, resolved to secede from the Reformed Church. These Separatists (*De Afgescheidenen*) suffered severe persecution in the beginning since the Government refused to recognize their church. Because of these unfavorable conditions a number of the Separatists, led by the preacher Van Raalte, migrated to the State of Michigan in the United States where they became the nucleus of what is now a flourishing colony of Michigan Dutch.

Politically, the last years of the reign of William I were not happy. He had lost contact with the people who more and more had come to resent his absolutistic policies. The country was on the verge of bankruptcy, and the poor financial conditions were in part attributed to the long drawn-out conflict with Belgium. The clamor for a more liberal constitution became so loud that the King had to relent. The Reform of 1840 brought only insignificant reforms: the province of Holland was divided into two parts, the civil list was reduced, the number of deputies in the Second Chamber was decreased in accordance with the separation of Belgium, the States-General was to be informed of the colonial budget, the distinction between ordinary and extraordinary budget was to be abolished.

The principle of ministerial responsibility was introduced, but against the will of the King, who abdicated in 1840 in favor of his son, William Frederick, Prince of Orange. King William II was more liberal than his predecessor, although he lacked the energy which William I had shown in his early reign.

The new king began his reign by openly presenting the financial difficulties of the nation to the public. The interest, in guilders, due on the national debt, amounted to the staggering sum of 25,500,000, with an additional 10,000,000 for the Indies. On January 1, 1841, there was a deficit of 34,000,000. Relations with Belgium were considerably improved when the Belgian share in the national debt was reduced. A more tolerant arrangement was made for the Separatists, although they received no claim on property or income of any of the recognized churches.

Although financial difficulties were much improved by the energetic measures of Van Hall, conditions in general remained stagnant and uneasy. It was obvious that the time was ripe for more general reforms which were advocated by the liberal faction under the leadership of Thorbecke in the Second Chamber. It was the revolutionary wave which swept over Europe in 1848 that really brought about the necessary changes. Because Holland was still chiefly rural, the movement for social and economic improvement remained moderate.

The pressure of the Liberal movements in Germany and France prompted the King to hasten the revision of the Constitution. He invited the Second Chamber to submit proposals, without consulting the ministers who promptly offered their resignations. The King formed a commission of Liberals (Thorbecke, Donker-Curtius, Kempenaer, Luzac, and Storm) to draft a constitution which would consider the wishes of the Second Chamber. In the meantime the King formed for the first time a cabinet which was made up according to the wishes, and at the initiative of the prime minister.

After a few changes, the proposals of the committee were accepted and Holland had a really liberal and democratic constitution. As the father of this Constitution, Thorbecke said: "The Constitution excluded the strength of the people; now it will flow through all the veins of the State." Holland had become a political democracy and it had taken the first step on the road toward complete democracy, of which the economic and social aspects were still a part of the future.

The monarchical power remained extensive, but the new constitution brought full ministerial responsibility. The franchise was extended considerably and included all citizens of full age who paid at least from 20 to 160 guilders (depending upon local conditions) in direct taxes. These same voters now also elected the provincial estates and the municipal councils.

The power of the States-General was extended through the right to make changes in the proposals of the king, for example, right of amendments, and right of inquiry. The budget became annual and was under the complete control of the States-General, while this institution also received a voice in the government of the colonies.

The new constitution also guaranteed freedom of the press on a broader scale, the right of petition, the right of assembly, and freedom of religion. On the whole, the Constitution of 1848 meant that the power of the oligarchy which had ruled Holland too long had been broken and that the group of active citizens had been enlarged to include the more progressive elements. The changes of 1848 enabled Holland to regain, in part, the position it had held in the seventeenth century when it was the champion of freedom in the civilized world. In many aspects the Thorbeckian Liberals were a continuation of the Patriots of the period before 1795. As in the period of the Republic, Holland again had two parties—the Liberals and the Anti-Liberals, or Conservatives.

It is possible to observe various trends in the Conservative party under the combined leadership of F. A. van Hall and G. Groen van Prinsterer. The latter was the creator of a Christian Historical or Anti-Revolutionary trend of social thinking which condemned the principles of Liberals as an outflow of the French Revolution. He also condemned the separation of Church and State, which act he considered anti-Christian. In the beginning he secured only small support because Holland was still far from having the organized party-life that it had in later periods. It was the middle class which found admission to political life and became more active. Also, under the Liberal principles, Catholicism gradually began to grope toward a stronger position in the life of the nation.

King William II did not live long to see the fruits of his work. He died in 1849, only a month after the new States-General had met for the first time. He was succeeded by the Crown Prince who was inaugurated as King William III on May 12, 1849. One of William III's first deeds, although after long hesitation, was to make Johan Rudolf Thorbecke the leader of the new cabinet. Thorbecke had been the driving force of liberalism, but had been ignored in the formation of earlier ministries. He immediately showed his mettle with the election laws, the provincial statute, and the basic municipal law. These organic laws long remained the basis of Dutch administration. Provinces and municipalities became autonomous bodies while their relation with the central government was maintained by provincial commissioners and by the mayors of the cities. Under the ministry of Thorbecke, Holland also entered upon a period of economic liberalism which, more than protectionism, undoubtedly was in accordance with its economic position as a commercial center.

In 1853 Thorbecke fell as a victim of the conflict between Protestantism and conservatism on one side and liberalism and Catholicism on the other. A proposed Papal treaty led to a flare-up of Protestant activity which focused its hostility on Thorbecke as the leader of liberalism. The King, apparently eager to use this opportunity to rid himself of the powerful Thorbecke, appointed Van Hall as the leader of the new cabinet. Nevertheless, the proposed organization of Holland into an archbishopric with four bishoprics passed without too great opposition.

Thorbecke's personal leadership was very strongly missed, however, and there was a noticeable decrease of public interest in political matters. The electorate remained largely liberal, but it became increasingly evident that the King was more conservative and, as a result, the political machinery began to function less rapidly and less smoothly. Cabinets came and passed in quick succession without achieving much of significance. Only in the matter of railroads, in which Holland had lagged behind its neighbors, was greater activity shown, particularly after 1860. In economic matters, the trend remained liberal, and a steady upward movement may be observed from the middle of the nineteenth century.

The Netherlands Trading Company, the modern continuation of the East India Company, was deprived of its monopolistic position, various customs and local tariffs were gradually abolished, and the harbors of Rotterdam and Amsterdam were improved by modern connections with the sea. Thorbecke, following his return to the Cabinet in 1862, was instrumental in creating an efficient system of secondary education. This meant another step forward in preparing a larger group of the population to take an active part in economic progress. Of great significance was the agitation against the Culture System (*cultuurstelsel*) in the Indies which had gradually developed

many abuses although it had functioned well enough in the beginning. Eduard Douwes Dekker (Multatuli, 1820–1887) who wrote
the book, *Max Havelaar,* which dealt with conditions in the Indies,
created a great impression, although its presentation was one-sided
and exaggerated. It brought about in Holland an increased interest
in the Indies which eventually led to many improvements in that
territory. Control over the budget of the Indies was granted to the
States-General while, at the same time, the state monopoly in spices
was abolished.

In 1865 foreign problems again began to occupy most of Holland's
interest. After the defeat of Austria by Prussia, Napoleon III was
also eager to enlarge his territory and attempted to purchase Luxemburg from the Netherlands. Although the King had already given
his consent, the arrangement was cancelled at the eleventh hour
because of the furious protests of Prussia. France was not prepared
to risk war on this issue and accepted an arrangement whereby Luxemburg became independent. The increasing power of Prussian Germany began to cast its shadow over Holland, and sympathies in the
Franco-Prussian War were with France, which country had had such
a great influence on Dutch civilization. It must be admitted, however,
that the economic unification and growth of Germany stimulated
Dutch commerce; particularly did Rotterdam profit from the prosperous hinterland. After 1870 the influence of German culture increased enormously, particularly in the fields of philosophy, medicine,
and the exact sciences.

Catholicism began to move away from liberalism, and in the school
problem the tendency against the public and nonreligious schools
began to grow more pronounced under the leadership of Schaepman
who followed the principles of the encyclical letter, *Syllabus Errorum,*
of Pope Pius IX. Liberalism, on the other hand, made a move toward
increased democracy by advocating more and more the interests of
the rising middle class. This trend found a very eminent exponent
in Samuel van Houten who based his policies on the idea of the sovereignty of the people. Extension of the franchise, protection of the
economically weak, and extension of governmental control over eco-

nomic activities were points in the program of the Liberals. This tendency toward greater democracy also became evident among the Anti-Revolutionaries who, under Abraham Kuyper, began to devote themselves to the interests of the common people (*kleine luyden*). This led to a closer collaboration with the Catholics who held the same attitude toward secular schools.

In the 'seventies Dutch political life included the following parties: Progressive and Conservative Liberals, Anti-Revolutionaries, and the increasingly conservative Catholics. There was still no labor party, although industry had developed considerably. In 1866 the first labor union was formed. It continued in existence until 1871 when the General Netherlands Workers Union (*Algemeen Nederlandsch Werkliedenverbond*) was organized. In 1878, under German influence, the first Social Democratic association was started while Domela Nieuwenhuis was leader of the Union of Socialists.

Then came the recent period which in Holland, as in other countries, was dominated by class conflict. At times serious disturbances developed, but they were not of more than passing importance. It was not until 1874, however, that social legislation began to develop although this was relatively early compared with other states. Van Houten's law against child labor was passed as the first measure of its kind.

In many other instances progressive legislation was blocked by the resistance of the Conservatives, of the religious groups, and the Thorbeckian Liberals. On the whole, the attitude of *laissez faire, laissez aller* continued to dominate practical politics. The matter of extension of the franchise and the improvement of education remained the object of much bickering until Heemskerk brought about a partial solution with the Constitutional Revision of 1887. The immediate reason for this change was a rapid succession of deaths in the royal family which made it necessary to reconsider the succession laws. The main innovation of the revision was an extension of the franchise since the financial status of the citizen was no longer the essential qualification. This liberal point was granted by the Conservatives, because they, in turn, received some consideration in the school question whereby subsidies to be granted to the religious schools were regarded as permissible.

After 1890 Holland entered upon a period of rapid progress in commerce and industry, as well as in the arts and sciences. It began to regain, at least partially, the position it had held in the seventeenth century in these matters, although that century remained, as it has been so justly called, the Golden Age of Holland.

A few figures may illustrate the changes which had taken place in Holland within a relatively short period. In 1916 Holland had a population of about 6,500,000 (now it is over 9,000,000); in 1850 the population figure was about 3,000,000. The population of Amsterdam rose from 200,000 inhabitants in 1820 to more than 600,000 in 1916; that of Rotterdam from 200,000 in 1849 to more than 500,000 in 1916; The Hague from a small provincial town of 40,000 in 1813 to a large city of 325,000 in 1916. The urbanization of the country was rapid, not only in the provinces of north and south Holland, but also in the industrial districts of Twente where factory towns had quickly sprung up. The national income mounted sharply as the income, in guilders, from direct taxes increased from 169,000,000 in 1897 to 227,000,000 in 1913. Wages increased considerably. In Twente, for instance, wages rose from 100 to 150 per cent in a period of thirty years.

Also, in the south, industrial life had become more and more important. Around Tilburg and Eindhoven some of the most important factory districts developed. Shipbuilding, and the manufacture of shoes, leather, and paper were all rapidly growing industries. Mention might also be made of the metal industry, as well as of a number of consumers' goods industries which all showed an amazing development. Since 1890 Holland had had more than its share in the economic expansion of the world. Its shipping tonnage had risen in accordance with this expansion. In 1867 Amsterdam had 306 sailing vessels and 18 steamships, Rotterdam respectively 162 and 20. In 1910 Holland had 686 ships, of which 283 were steamships. Holland attained eighth place at that time in world tonnage. In all fields Holland was regaining the place to which it was entitled.

This renaissance was also evident in cultural matters. In literature there was the school of 1880 which broke with bourgeois tradition; in painting there was The Hague School of Israels and Maris, not on the same level as the seventeenth century but, nevertheless, of respectable achievement. In science the names of Lorentz, Bosscha, Kamalingh Onnes, and Hugo de Vries made Holland known throughout the world. The large cities developed into international centers, no longer peaceful, sleepy provincial towns. It has truly been said that Holland was beginning to be great in those things in which a small nation can show greatness. However, an impression must not be given that this progress was brought about easily.

From 1880, Holland's foreign policy had been one of neutrality but there was a growing interest in international law and international organization. Van Houten dreamed of a world federation while Van Vollenhoven pointed to the desirability of a world police force. In the creation of a system of international private law the eminent jurist, T. M. C. Asser, took a significant role. The peace conferences of 1899 and 1907 were held in The Hague, and Holland was associated in the public opinion of the world with international law, a fact further emphasized by the knowledge that The Hague was the site of the Permanent Court of Arbitration and the Peace Palace.

In internal politics it has been rightly said that Thorbecke made the merchant a member of the political community, while Schaepman and Kuyper did the same for the small middle class and the farmer, and Domela Nieuwenhuis and Troelstra for the worker. Since 1890 the workers have gained tremendously in political importance, especially after the creation of the Social-Democratic Labor party (*Social-Democratische Arbeiters Partij—S.D.A.P.*) in 1894. At first quite revolutionary in tendency, this party soon developed into a progressive labor party which was instrumental in bringing about the wage increases and the extensive social legislation of which Holland may be justly proud.

Another amazing phenomenon was the rapid growth of Prime Minister Kuyper's Anti-Revolutionary party, even though in 1895 a conservative group under Lohman separated from it, followed in

1897 by the Christian Historical group. These two united again later. In the Catholic party greater unity was preserved, and it gradually grew into a most powerful organization. Among the Liberals various factions became independent, namely the Liberal Union and the Liberal Democratic parties.

The extension of the franchise in 1887 led to the winning of a majority by the religious parties. They immediately legislated an improvement in the condition of the religious schools which now became eligible for state subsidies.

In the cabinets which followed, there was a continual shift from Liberals to Conservatives. On the whole, this may have benefited the country, as each was likely to show its good intentions in order to remain in power. Social legislation progressed rapidly and economic progress was aided by innovations in tax legislation. The franchise was again extended in 1896 and remained unchanged until 1917 when the franchise became universal. The parliamentary struggles of the intermediary period centered around the universal franchise which was ardently advocated by the parties on the Left. But in the beginning of the twentieth century Holland came under the Conservative leader, Kuyper who, for a considerable length of time succeeded in maintaining a reactionary government.

He kept radical tendencies, which led to the railroad strike of 1903, within reasonable boundaries. After the strike, laws were proposed which threatened severe penalties on those who attacked the right to work, and strikes by persons in the public services were made punishable as misdemeanors. Labor threatened a general strike, but the laws were passed after minor modifications. The general strike was called, but failed in part because labor was too greatly divided and in part because the Government took a very determined attitude. The Christian unions declined to join the strike, and this made it possible to continue the running of trains on a limited scale.

The Socialists under Troelstra had not been strong enough to defy the power of "Abraham the Terrible," as Dr. Kuyper was called in Holland. Dr. Kuyper came to a severe clash with the Liberals on the matter of higher education. He wanted to give the private universities, especially the Free (Calvinist) University of Amsterdam, the same rights as those held by the state universities. Very cleverly, Dr. Kuyper took the stand that liberalism itself, in its purpose to respect the rights of the various social and political groups, should welcome such a measure. The Liberals vehemently attacked the bill; they saw in it a grave threat to the established principles of the separation of Church and State. The Bill was passed in the Second Chamber by fifty-six against forty-one votes, evidence of the division of power at that time. The First Chamber, however, which still had a Liberal majority, rejected the measure but was promptly dissolved by Dr. Kuyper. A new chamber passed the law. Liberalism had been forced back to the more formal ideology which it was to show in later years.

Gradually resistance against the willful attitude of Dr. Kuyper, as well as against his efforts to monopolize Christianity for one political party, began to grow. In 1905 his coalition was defeated, although the new majority was divided among Liberals and Socialists.

The new Prime Minister de Meester concentrated on improvement of the army, which suffered from the antiquated system of substituted service by which induction could be avoided through finding a paid substitute. This undemocratic condition was abolished, and this meant another step forward in abolishing discrimination between the rich and the poor. The matter of building additional fortifications along the Dutch coastline created quite a furor in Europe as it was felt—unjustly—that this was done at the instigation of Berlin. After the Boer War, tension in Europe was high, and the British protested strongly against the possibility of aiding Germany's defenses. After a number of arguments on both sides, the Ministry weathered the criticisms from abroad and the plan went through, although with several restrictions.

The controversy over military matters had led, however, to the downfall of De Meester who was succeeded by Heemskerk. The latter brought the Anti-Revolutionaries back to power. Although Dr. Kuyper did not approve of the new coalition cabinet which he described as "born in imprudence," it nevertheless had a long and relatively successful life. On the whole, progressive legislation continued, particularly in the social field, while a sterner moral attitude was displayed than by the Liberals. Laws against betting and indecent literature among others were passed, although none of these vices was of great significance in the Netherlands. Insurance against sickness and disability, old-age pensions, and other social security measures were introduced, thus greatly assisting Holland in becoming, on the whole, the harmonious country into which it developed under the wise and democratic leadership of Queen Wilhelmina, who has ruled with great impartiality and justice since 1898.

The second decade of the twentieth century shows a marked increase in the power of the Social Democrats. The general elections of 1913 gave 225,800 votes to the Liberals, 308,260 to the Christian coalition, and 145,332 to the Social Democratic Labor party. According to the principles of the International Socialist Congress of 1904, the socialists refused to participate directly in the Government but were willing to support the Liberals in order to get the franchise laws accepted. This move led to a split in the party as the more radical members under Wijnkoop were reluctant to join a reformist party which did not hold to Marxian principles.

As the Liberals were not strong enough to form a cabinet, for the first time an extraparliamentary cabinet under the leadership of Cort van der Linden was set up.

While Holland was thus trying to solve its own problems, and recording in 1913 a century of progress, the First World War broke out. Holland found itself unprepared and startled. It had developed a firm belief in international agreements and had not regarded the European tension too seriously. Nevertheless, necessary measures were taken to protect its borders; the 200,000 men whom the country could bring under arms, because of the precautions of Minister of War Hendrik Colijn, were immediately mobilized and supplemented by the Landstorm, until about 450,000 men were in the field under Lieutenant General C. I. Snijders.

For four years the armed forces stood guard over the country which was threatened several times by invasion, a danger which fortunately never materialized. Holland suffered severe privations in the war, and its losses from the unrestricted submarine warfare of the Germans were considerable. This cruel warfare destroyed the last vestiges of sympathy which Holland may have had for Germany, although its feelings had been predominantly pro-Allied from the very beginning of the war. Dutch neutrality continued to be respected by both warring powers, because England was not eager to have Germany on the Dutch coastline and Germany, in turn, did not see any advantage in lengthening its front. But the path of neutrality was a tortuous and difficult one which demanded real diplomacy on the part of the Dutch.

Although international relations and economic shortages absorbed most of the energy of the country, political progress was slow but nevertheless present. Even the Constitutional Revision of 1917 which introduced universal male suffrage and proportional representation did not cause much excitement. There was some agitation for women to vote in the elections, but it remained a minor conflict in a period which was dominated by war and disaster.

The most positive feature of the war period was the scheme for reclamation of the Zuiderzee which was expected to add almost 500,000 acres of fertile soil to the Netherlands. The plan, to cost 80,000,000 guilders, was of old date but the economic duress of the war made its execution more feasible than it had been before. As a public work it was of great significance in easing unemployment which had developed alarmingly during the war.

The First World War brought to the Dutch a taste of the world to come—government control over economic activities, large-scale unemployment, and increasing political differentiation. When in relief the Dutch welcomed the return of peace, they little suspected that later on they would have to solve again many of the same problems which the war period had brought to them.

In 1918 the first elections were held on the basis of proportional representation. They resulted in a very feeble majority of the Coalition over the parties of the Right. This made the formation of a cabinet very difficult, and it took two months to find a premier in Ruys de Beerenbrouck of the Roman Catholic party. But the Government found unsuspected support from all sides when the Socialists made an abortive move toward revolution under Troelstra, who thought that the German example could be followed in Holland. As the bid for power of the Social Democratic party could expect support only from its own members—about 22 per cent of the population—it was an ill-advised attempt which led to some rioting in the large cities but to no consequences of any importance. The Socialists themselves made a hasty retreat from the statements of their leader, and the country saw great demonstrations of loyalty to the Queen and to the Government.

It would be incorrect, however, to say that the war did not leave its mark on Holland. The entire postwar period was characterized by the same phenomena which menaced other European countries, a growing restlessness, a bitter jealousy among the different classes, a predominant materialistic attitude, and an increasing number of political beliefs and trends which, because they presented philosophies instead of practical political programs, showed a gross lack of restraint in aim. Democracy became too much a formalistic concept instead of a doctrine which gave to people a definite outlook on life.

On the whole, however, the problems of Holland did not reach such proportions as did the problems in neighboring countries. The extremist parties like the Communists and, later on, the National Socialists (Nazis) failed to win much support. The most serious problem in Holland, as in other countries, was unemployment, for which a satisfactory solution was never found. Perhaps the leader of Holland in the prewar days, Dr. Colijn, was right in his attempt to solve this problem by returning to a simpler type of living. But the times were against him, as liberal economic beliefs were still uppermost in Holland. Perhaps the coming postwar period will bring a solution of the problems which seemed insurmountable before the Second World War.

Part Three

Political and Constitutional Development

CHAPTER VI

Constitutional and Political Aspects

BY JOHAN WILLEM ALBARDA

THE NETHERLANDS was a republic until 1806, and until 1795 a prince of Orange had often been the stadholder. In 1806 the Netherlands became a vassal state under Napoleon who made his brother, Louis, the king. After having been absorbed into the French Empire in 1810, the Netherlands again obtained its independence in 1813, when it became a monarchy. The son of the last stadholder was elevated to the position of sovereign prince. The hereditary prince of Orange and those who had held the leadership as representatives of the Dutch people during the recovery of independence were in agreement that a constitution which would guarantee the people's rights should be established at once.

The Constitution of 1814, in which the head of the State was known only as "prince," had to be replaced by a new one the following year. In that year, as a result of a decision reached by the Great Powers, the Netherlands and Belgium were united to form a kingdom of which the sovereign prince of the Netherlands was the crowned head. The Netherlands remained a kingdom even when, after many difficulties, it was separated from Belgium. The separation was ratified by the Great Powers in 1839.

The Kingdom of the Netherlands was at first a limited monarchy, in which the power of the king exceeded that of the representatives in very important respects. This limited monarchy has developed gradually into a parliamentary democracy. The principal milestones in its development were the constitutional revisions of 1848, 1887, 1917 1922, and 1938, and the Parliamentary Decision of 1868.

In the brief scope of this chapter it will be possible to sketch only the principal lines of the governmental organization of the Netherlands, giving here and there a résumé of the process by which it took its present form.

The democratic character of the Netherlands State is first of all shown in the constitutional guarantees of freedom and justice for citizens. Among the fundamental rights assured in the first section of the Constitution are equal rights to protection of person and property for all who live within the territory of the Kingdom; all Netherlanders equally eligible for all government services; freedom of the press, without any preventive censure; the right of petition before qualified authorities; the right of meeting and assembly. In the section of the Constitution which deals with religion, the freedom of all faiths is expressly established. All confessions are also guaranteed equal protection. It is further stated that the members of the various churches shall all enjoy the same civic rights, and have equal claim to be vested with honors, offices, and administrative posts. Finally, the Constitution declares that all public religious services are permitted in buildings and enclosed places.

Mention must also be made of the fundamental rights which are guaranteed to Netherlanders in the section on justice. There exists no other judiciary besides that which the law has indicated. No one can be kept against his will from the justice entitled to him by law. Expropriation for the general good can only take place after a legal declaration that the general good requires it, and then only on payment of a previously determined indemnity. Except in special cases fixed by law, no one may be taken into custody without an order from the judge. The order must state the reasons for the detention. Also, no residence may be entered against the will of the owner, except when authorized by law, and by order of the legally appointed authority. The privacy of letters sent by post or by other public means of communication may not be violated, except on order of the judge in legally specified cases. The verdict, with certain exceptions, is pub-

ROYAL PALACE, AMSTERDAM

THE BINNENHOF, AT THE HAGUE

lic. The sentence must always be given publicly. Judges are named for life, and are thus independent of the government. This, then, though not a complete sketch, is a clear enough presentation of the constitutional rights of the Netherlands people.

It is impossible to become adequately acquainted with the division of powers, authorities, and responsibilities in the Netherlands State by studying the Constitution and other laws of the Kingdom. Although the Constitution contains the fundamental principles, a constitutional practice has grown up on this foundation which only after many years made a place for itself. This was accompanied by a shifting of the division of power. Thus in the Netherlands, also, there exists beside the written law of the land an unwritten one: a collection of conventions considered as belonging to the living law.

The king governs with the ministers. All royal decrees, appointments and regulations are also signed by one or more of the ministers. The king is assisted by a Council of State, the members of which are named by him. The Constitution stipulates that the king shall previously take the advice of the Council of State on all proposals made by him to the States-General and on all general governing measures to be established by him. The States-General consists of two chambers. The Second Chamber has a membership of one hundred representatives directly elected by the electorate. The First Chamber consists of fifty members elected by the states of the eleven provinces, each province electing a certain number.

The members of the Second Chamber are elected for four years. Their terms of office expire at the same time. In the First Chamber the members are elected for six years, the terms of one-half the members expiring every three years. Members of both chambers may be reëlected forthwith.

The king shares the legislative authority with the States-General. The proposed legislation is presented by the king to the Second Chamber, which has the right to make changes in it. After the Second Chamber has decided to accept the proposed legislation, changed or unchanged, it is then sent to the First Chamber. If it is accepted by the First Chamber it still must have the royal sanction. Immediately on receiving the royal sanction it is published in the Government Record (*Staatsblad*), and becomes law.

Among legislative measures dealt with in the States-General are those concerning the approval of the budget of government expenses. In dealing with the budget and its parts, the chambers are given an opportunity to discuss critically the conduct of the Government as a whole and that of each of the ministers. Budgets may be proposed only by the Government. The right of initiative in this matter does not extend to the Second Chamber. In legislative matters the Second Chamber has one more right which the First Chamber does not have. The Second Chamber may initiate legislative proposals. If these proposals are accepted by the First Chamber, royal sanction is required before they become law.

There is, perhaps, no provision in the Constitution which is more important for legal relations in the Netherlands than that in the article which states: "The King is inviolable, the Ministers are responsible." Their responsibility is to the States-General, and they are held accountable for the management of the Government. There was much contention before this principle of responsibility was included in the Constitution of 1848, and there was a great struggle before it acquired the full significance which it has had since 1868.

The king is inviolable. For none of his acts of government can he be called to account or be held responsible by the representatives of the people. In each act of government those ministers alone are responsible who have given their indispensable coöperation to the transaction. If an act of government displeases the people or their representatives, the criticism is directed not against the king, but against the responsible ministers. The king remains above and outside the political scene. He takes no part in the struggle. He is the head of the State, standing above the stir and bustle of parties and oppositions, and therefore is the symbol of national unity.

Nothing has contributed so much to the firmness of the monarchy in the Netherlands as this principle of placing responsibility. Even among the Netherlands people who are attached by strong historical bonds to the House of Orange, a sporadic interest in a republican form of government flared up now and then during the nineteenth century, but it never became a movement of any importance. Because the principle of ministerial responsibility with all its consequences has been honored, not only for legislative acts but for administrative ones as well, there has not been a single move against the monarchy. This is doubtlessly because of the great conscientiousness with which Queen Wilhelmina during the course of her long reign has observed the Constitution and the unwritten laws.

The ministers are responsible. In consequence no cabinet can maintain itself, if its conduct is not approved by the States-General, or if it does not have the confidence of the majority of the representatives of the people. If a cabinet or a minister should remain in control, in spite of important differences in principle and objectives from the representatives of the people, then the representatives have a means of forcing a resignation. They can declare lack of confidence in the cabinet or in the minister. They can reject proposals made by the cabinet or by the minister. In extreme instances, although this is seldom done, they can reject the budget of the minister, and thus, by withholding the money, make the progress of the Government impossible.

The Constitution stipulates that the king shall appoint and dismiss ministers at his pleasure; however, his actions are covered by ministerial responsibility. The minister-president, or the organizer of the cabinet who signs the royal decree appointing or dismissing one or more ministers, by this signature, has become responsible for the appointment or dimissal.

It has become the custom for the cabinet to offer its resignation after the election of a new Second Chamber. Other circumstances may also lead to the resignation of the cabinet, first of all, a conflict with the States-General. The custom, faithfully followed by Queen Wilhelmina, has been to take counsel of the foremost political leaders in the Second Chamber.

Naturally the Queen always takes into consideration the result of the most recent election. After this she proceeds to choose a cabinet-organizer who then presents to her, as Queen, the persons considered

by him to be qualified for ministers. The cabinet-organizer is responsible for the composition of the cabinet. It is obvious that he therefore
tries to form a group which may be expected to coöperate successfully
with the representatives of the people.

In event of serious conflict the Government does not always have
to bow before the decisions of the States-General. If the Government
feels that the attitude of the States-General is not in accord with the
feeling of the majority of the voters, then it can appeal to the people.
The ruler has the constitutional power to dismiss one or both chambers. If the Government uses this power, then another election takes
place immediately. If the result of this election is unfavorable to the
Government, then the cabinet must resign. This has been the rule
in the Netherlands since 1868.

The rights of the two chambers are not limited to collaboration in
lawmaking and in judging the Government's leadership. Both chambers also have the right of interpellation. The ministers are obliged
to give any information requested, as long as the giving of the information is not in conflict with the interests of the State. Both chambers
also have the right to institute investigations. The way in which this
is done is regulated by law.

The sessions of the chambers are not dependent on the judgment
or will of the Government. The Constitution states that each year on
the third Tuesday in September the ordinary sitting of the States-
General shall be opened, and that the session shall last for at least
twenty days. In practice, the session is closed approximately four days
before the opening of the following one. This may also be considered
as an unwritten law. During the session each chamber arranges its
own schedule. The chairmen call the meetings whenever and as often
as they find it necessary. In this matter the Government can make
its wishes known to the chairmen, but it cannot give orders. Nor can
it prescribe to either chamber what business should be taken up.

The ministers may attend the meetings of the chambers, but
they are members of neither one. A member of the chambers, if he
is appointed minister, therefore ceases to be a member.

Here it may also be stated that the members of the chambers, on entering office, take two oaths: an oath of allegiance to the Constitution, and a so-called oath of integrity. In the latter oath the member declares that he has neither given nor promised gifts in order to obtain his election, and that in the course of his duties he will receive no gifts or promises either directly or indirectly.

The integrity of the members of the chambers has always been highly regarded in the Netherlands. Only by the rarest exception has there been an instance where suspicion was cast on a member's integrity. In an exceptionally evident case the member is at once forced to resign by his own political friends.

In the matter of abuse of power, both the members of the chambers and the ministers would be tried before the Supreme Court, the highest court of justice. The Attorney-General of the Supreme Court who would institute the prosecution is appointed for life, and thus cannot be dismissed by the Government. However, it has never been necessary to prosecute in a case of this kind.

The Constitution declares that the laws are inviolable. This means that the judge is not permitted to disagree with the soundness of the established law.

The Constitution which guarantees the rights of the people is protected against inconsiderate and hasty changes. A measure for changing the Constitution must be considered twice by each chamber. The first time it has to receive only an ordinary majority of votes. If it is accepted, then both chambers are dissolved and at once new elections are held for the membership of the new chambers. In each of the new chambers the constitutional amendment then requires a two-thirds majority before it can be accepted. Thus the final decision in each revision of the Constitution lies in the hands of the voters.

But, however justly the liberties of citizens may be assured, and however fairly the balance of authority may be arranged, the result does not always form a democratic state. A state is fully democratic only when in ascribing the political rights of voting and of being a political candidate no distinction is made between citizens.

In this respect the Netherlands has grown in the course of a century into a democratic state. In the first half of the nineteenth century the Second Chamber was not even directly elected. A powerful movement among the Liberals, under the leadership of the great Thorbecke, and greatly influenced by the foreign situation in the year of revolution, 1848, was necessary in order to insert into the Constitution of that year the principle of direct vote. But the electorate was still very limited. Voters were limited to men with property who paid a certain amount of taxes.

Only in 1887 was the Constitution changed to state that the right to vote should be given to those who were fit and who stood well in the community; through this change the electoral law could apply to others as well as to taxpayers. Just before this amendment to the Constitution, the number of voters was only about 100,000, whereas the total population was approximately 5,000,000. After 1887, in accordance with the reform of that year, the electoral law was repeatedly expanded. The Constitution barred the way to the adoption of universal suffrage. The action in favor of this movement, largely but not entirely supported by the Social Democratic Workers party, which was developing powerfully, succeeded in the Constitutional Revision of 1917. The principle of universal suffrage was then included in the Constitution. Another movement also succeeded in 1917—abolishment of the limitation to men only of the right to vote. As a result of this accomplishment universal suffrage for women was recognized in 1919. The partisans of votes for women were thoroughly satisfied only when the electoral rights of women were included next to that of men in the revised Constitution of 1922.

Before the Second World War the number of voters included almost one-half the population. With a census figure of approximately 9,000,000 persons, the number of voters before the German invasion was approximately 4,500,000.

A similar democratization also took place in the election of the First Chamber. Called into being in 1815, at the insistence of the Belgians, the First Chamber was originally composed of aristocrats. The members were not elected but were selected for life by the King. They were chosen from those who by birth or by wealth, or by services rendered to the State, belonged to the most distinguished families in the country. The Chamber did not meet publicly. This was the group which was called, in ridicule, "the King's ménagerie."

An important change was made in this situation by the Constitutional Revision of 1848. The members of the First Chamber were to be elected from then on by the provincial states. However, the candidates were chosen only from among those who belonged to the limited group of the highest taxpayers. The First Chamber thus became plutocratic instead of aristocratic. Then in the Constitutional Revision of 1887 persons who had distinguished themselves in some manner also were included.

This limitation was first given up in the Constitutional Revision of 1917. The requirements for candidates for the First Chamber were made the same as those for the Second Chamber. Before the war, every man and woman of the required age, in practice, was eligible for the First, as well as the Second Chamber. Proportional representation was instituted at the same time as universal suffrage. It was applicable to both chambers, to the provincial states, and to the city councils.

In order to explain completely the advantages and disadvantages of proportional representation, too great detail would be needed. Two advantages which time has proved may be mentioned. One is that proportional representation has caused the election contest to become far more than formerly a contest of principles, directions, and objectives, and far less than formerly a contest for and in behalf of the personality of the candidate. The other is that proportional representation has brought a certain stability into the political balance of power. At least local and more or less accidental circumstances no longer play a decisive role in election results. The difference in a few election districts can no longer cause an important political party to lose its rightful representation in the States-General. Each party obtains a number of seats dependent on the proportional representation of its followers in the entire country. The changes in political balance among the people are clearly reflected in an altered proportion of the composition of the States-General. In general, the majority in the chamber reflects the majority in the population. It is no longer possible for a minority to rule.

Among the disadvantages attached to the system of proportional representation in the Netherlands, one especially has been definitely uncovered. In the Netherlands may be found a greater number of important political parties than in most other countries. This is a result of the place which religion formerly occupied in political life. Not only are there a Catholic party and two Protestant Christian political parties, but also a Christian Democratic party, and a Reformed party. Furthermore, there is the Social Democratic party, the Liberal party and the Progressive Liberal party, the Communist party, and in the past few years the National Socialist party.

With the institution of the plan for proportional representation there has been a sincere effort to offer equal rights to all minorities. Indeed, the recognition of the rights of minorities is one of the fundamentals of democracy. Therefore an effort is made to achieve the most exact possible proportional representation. This has had an unexpected and unwanted result. A number of interest groups (pressure groups) saw a clear opportunity to obtain a representative in the States-General. Thus there arose a number of unimportant parties who offered candidates. This created a confused and scattered image which made voting very difficult for many electors. Fortunately, this evil was at once lessened by a technical revision of the election law, and it can be completely eliminated by further technical measures. But during its temporary existence it has been detrimental to the political life of the Netherlands. The last elections for the Second Chamber, held in 1937, gave the following results:

Political Parties	Percentage of the total number of votes	Number of seats in the Second Chamber
Catholic party	28.8%	31
Social Democratic party	22.0%	23
Anti-Revolutionary party (Calvinist)	16.4%	17
Christian Historical party	7.5%	8
Democratic Liberals	5.9%	6
National Socialists	4.2%	4
Liberal party	3.9%	4
Communist party	3.4%	3
Christian Democratic party	2.1%	2
Reformed party	1.9%	2
Other parties and groups	3.9%	—
	100%	100

It should be remarked that the National Socialists, who obtained 4.2 per cent of the votes in 1937, were on the decline. Two years previously they had almost doubled this number of votes in the elections for the Provincial States. Had it not been for the war they would certainly have been pushed back even farther in the following election. At present, the people of the Netherlands are awaiting the day of liberation, when national socialism will receive its final blow.

As the figures above show, no single party in the Netherlands is strong enough to obtain by itself a parliamentary majority and to support a government with it. This has been the situation for a score of years. Thus the government can be based only on a coalition of two or more parties. And such a coalition government can maintain itself only as long as it has a majority among the representatives of the people. This has often been difficult to accomplish and more than once has led to cabinet crises when there was opposition between the collaborating parties, often on questions of social policy. Such a crisis in 1939, considering the circumstances of that year, led to a very fortunate solution. In the face of the approaching war a government was then formed in which Social Democrats took part for the first time. This particular government was given the support of more than 75 per cent of the members of the chambers, while the majority of the remaining members were favorable to it. No government during more than half a century had been built on such a broad basis. In this strong position, more fully united than ever, the Dutch people prepared to meet the approaching war. This has certainly contributed much to the single-mindedness with which the Dutch have regarded the war, withstood the difficult test of the German invasion, and maintained a strong national unity during the German occupation.

Some mention has been made of the provinces and municipalities, the territorial units which are the divisions of the Kingdom. They have self-elected governments and a great degree of self-government, guaranteed them by a favorable interpretation of the principle of decentralization.

During the last twenty-five years a need has been increasingly felt for another sort of decentralization. This is the result of the great expansion which the Government has undergone, and the resulting increase in the extent and the difficulties of its duties and those of the representatives of the people.

Formerly the lawgiver acted in a strictly limited field. He followed the interpretation which corresponded to the requirements of community life in former times; law remained remote from interference in economic and social questions. With the changes which took place so rapidly in economic affairs during the second half of the nineteenth century, new requirements and new conceptions developed. This went together with important changes in the political balance of power. Thus both the Government and the representatives of the people were obliged to enter the field of social laws and that of preoccupation with economic conditions, and to go even further into it. Just as in many other lands, the representatives of the people did not appear to be equal to the difficulties and extent of their ever-growing task. This led in many instances to a real feeling of dissatisfaction, and in some even to a doubt of the merits of the parliamentary system.

In the Netherlands the way was already opened in 1917, at the time of the revision of the Constitution, along which grievances could be adjusted. At that time a provision was written into the Constitution which made it possible to create public groups, in addition to the existing chambers, whose collaboration could be called upon in certain branches of governmental duties. Through the activities of these bodies, the States-General was able to free itself from much detail work. Here is the introduction of a new principle of decentralization, not according to territories, but according to divisions of governmental duties.

In the Constitutional Revision of 1938 this new principle was further developed. The Constitution now specifies that the lawmakers may call into being groups which can act upon the regulation of certain trades and industries, or certain groups of trades and industries. Regulating authority may be given to these bodies. Naturally their work must be subject to the control of the Government. The Government, therefore, is empowered to suspend or to annul their decisions whenever it feels that these are in conflict with the general good. Besides bodies for certain professions and industries, a central group for professional and industrial life may also be formed, and given regulatory powers.

Here new perspectives have been opened up for democracy. In these new organs contractors, workers, consumers, specialists, and representatives of general interests are brought together in order jointly to handle and solve questions of industrial life. This means democracy in industry, and as a result it brings competent and experienced citizens far more than formerly into coöperation in pursuit of the general good. These new organs may also be called to collaborate on the preparation and execution of social laws and thus transfer the task largely from bureaucratic hands to those of the groups concerned.

Such new organs appear not only in the field of industry. They may also, states the Constitution, be created in other provinces of governmental activity. Thus a body with authority to regulate the teaching profession, one for workmen's housing, another for public health, and still others may be organized. Here is perceived again the perspective of a large measure of sharing by citizens in the task of government, for the furtherance of the general good.

This functional decentralization, as it is often called, means the possibility of strengthening and improving the democratic organization.

In concluding this limited survey the relation of the Netherlands to the overseas territories must not be omitted. The Netherlands Constitution, in general, is only in effect in the European part of the Kingdom, although it also contains the principles which control the relations with the overseas territories.

This relationship has very radically altered in the course of a century. Although in the first half of the nineteenth century, the territories were considered principally as conquered countries from which even income for the Netherlands treasury was obtained, and although they were governed only by the Netherlands authorities without the coöperation of their native population, in the second half of the nineteenth century a new orientation took place. An end was made quickly to the practice of taking income from them for the State. The idea became more and more general that the Netherlands should not consider the overseas territories as countries from which benefits were to be derived, but should also see them and treat them as lands whose welfare should be considered and whose populations should be more and more occupied with exercising governmental functions, and thus be prepared for self-government within the bounds of the Kingdom.

The Netherlands' altered relationship to its territories was strikingly expressed in the Constitutional Revision of 1922. Whereas the Constitution formerly spoke of "colonies and possessions in other parts of the world" this entire terminology disappeared in 1922. After that year the Constitution spoke of the "Netherlands Indies, Surinam, and Curaçao," naming these lands as parts of the Kingdom equal in importance to the Netherlands. It does not detract from the value of the new constitutional interpretation that the minister in charge of the affairs of these territories was still called the "Minister of Colonies," even after 1922. This is to be explained principally because of human inertia, and because of a preference for short titles.

In the Netherlands Indies, Surinam, and Curaçao representative bodies have long assisted the governors in their administrative responsibilities. In 1916 the Netherlands Indies received a People's Council through which it became possible for the population in an organized way to be heard on questions of administration. In 1925 the obsolete regulation of the government was replaced by a law on the governmental organization of the Netherlands Indies in which the authority of the People's Council was not inconsiderably extended.

At present the Constitution contains the following description of the governmental division of authority: the king has the supreme direction of the Netherlands Indies, Surinam, and Curaçao. In his name the general direction of the Netherlands Indies is exercised by the governor-general, and of Curaçao and Surinam by the governors. The king annually makes a report to the States-General on the government and the condition of the territories. The governmental policies are regulated by the Netherlands legislature, but not before the representative body of the territory concerned has been heard.

The conduct of internal affairs is left to the established organs in each of the territories. However, the regulations decided upon by these organs can be legally annulled in instances where they clash with the Constitution or with the general interest.

Although the Constitution still offers opportunity for a further development of the self-government of overseas territories, it is generally felt in the Netherlands, as well as in the Netherlands Indies, Surinam, and Curaçao, that a more radical revision is necessary. This conviction was already shared by many people before the Second World War. It has become even more seriously considered on all sides during the war, partially as a result of the sincere attachment which the populations of these territories have shown to the Netherlands and to the Queen. The war has now delayed the conversion of these convictions into deeds of reform. As long as the Netherlands and the Indies are not freed from the enemy, neither the Netherlands nor the Netherlands Indies can consult with the people and their lawful representatives on projects of reform, nor can decisions be made. However, the question of the new arrangement of the whole Kingdom belongs to the problems which will be solved by mutual deliberation between the parts of the Kingdom immediately after the liberation.

Shortly after the Netherlands was drawn into the Second World War, the Government disclosed its decision to take up the deliberations between the parts of the Kingdom for a revision of their relation to each other and to their internal governments. The extension of the war into the Far East has not altered this decision.

Queen Wilhelmina has repeatedly explained the decision of the Government in her radio addresses. No statement has made a greater impression than that of December 6, 1942, in which the Queen said:

"In previous addresses I announced that it is my intention after the liberation to create the occasion for a joint consultation about the structure of the Kingdom and its parts in order to adapt it to the changed circumstances. The conference of the entire Kingdom which will be convoked for this purpose has been further outlined in a Government Declaration of January 27th, 1942. The preparation of this Conference, in which prominent representatives of the three overseas parts of the Kingdom will be united with those of the Netherlands at a round table, had already been begun in the Netherlands

Indies, Surinam, and Curaçao, the parts of the Kingdom which then still enjoyed their freedom.

"Although it is beyond doubt that a political reconstruction of the Kingdom as a whole, and of the Netherlands and the Overseas Territories as its parts, is a natural evolution, it would be neither right nor possible to define its precise form at this moment.

"I realize that much which is great and good is growing in the Netherlands, despite the pressure of the occupation. I know that this is the case in the Indies, where our unity is fortified by common suffering. These developing ideas can only be shaped in free consultation in which both parts of the Kingdom will want to take cognizance of each others' opinions."

The Queen has made it clear that it would be trespassing on the rights of the people if important decisions should be made during the occupation, without the people's coöperation. She continued:

"I am convinced, and history, as well as reports from the occupied territories confirm me in this, that after the war it will be possible to reconstruct the Kingdom on the solid foundation of complete partnership, which will mean the consummation of all that has been developed in the past. I know that no political unity nor national cohesion can continue to exist which are not supported by the voluntary acceptance and the faith of the great majority of the citizenry.

"It is my opinion that such a combination of independence and collaboration can give the Kingdom and its parts the strength to carry fully their responsibility, both internally and externally.

"This would leave no room for discrimination according to race or nationality. Only the ability of the individual citizens and the needs of the various groups of the population will determine the policy of the Government. A political unity which rests on this foundation moves far toward a realization of the purpose for which the United Nations are fighting, as it has been embodied, for instance, in the Atlantic Charter and with which we could instantly agree because it contains our own conception of freedom and justice for which we have sacrificed blood and possessions in the course of our history."

CHAPTER VII

Political Parties

BY DAVID FRIEDMAN

THE SOCIAL SYSTEM of the Netherlands is democratic; the Netherlands State has been a constitutional monarchy theoretically since 1848, and in practice since the last quarter of the nineteenth century. It is shaped on the pattern of a parliamentary democracy into which not only its political institutions, but also its other institutions somehow are integrated.

The principle of democracy is not and cannot be limited to its political form and expression. In its ideal form it is hardly a system; rather, it is a view of life which accounts for a more or less harmonious collaboration between various social groups with conflicting interests which entail a certain self-control in their aims and ends. At the same time democracy is an arrangement of social relations dependent upon the culture, the mentality, and the nature or character of the people as well as upon the present situation of that people. Democracy affords to both individuals and groups an opportunity to express themselves freely on their opinions concerning such matters as political affairs, economic views, or even the promotion of their private interests. Although such opinions usually are at variance, democracy should nevertheless rest on a generally accepted rational as well as moral homogeneous public opinion which has, as its essential basis and condition, mutual respect of individual natural rights, whatever these may be, and the public interest of the people. In a way, this public opinion should also be considered as the greatest common denominator of the various individual and group opinions which makes coöperation possible. Democracy as a political system has at the same time an educational value. Because it calls upon the population as a whole to coöperate in the formation and establishment of its own government, it educates the people to judge and act independently or, at least, it provides an opportunity to do so. As such—and conscious of human and humanitarian values—democracy stresses the development of the personality and individuality of all the citizens, a factor which, according to circumstances, may turn out to be an asset or—if overdone, as is frequently true in the Netherlands—a liability in political and social relations. In order to make the principles of democracy practical in their application, and to arrive at a proper working policy it is necessary that a sufficient number of individuals, groups, or parties combine as a coalition to form a working parliamentary majority even if this should involve the risk that the principles or rather the interests of the minority will not always appear to their full advantage. At all times opportunity must be left to the oppositional minority groups to assert themselves fully and to exert their influence on the decisions of the majority. Accordingly, parliament as a political expression of these democratic principles should be, by its composition, an immediate reflex of the political ideas, wishes, and intentions which the masses, groups, or aggregate of the population hold.

There is no doubt that to a great extent, the Dutch social system is ideally and theoretically patterned on the principles outlined here. By its historical development as well as by the general character of the people it might be stated that democracy, however interpreted, is ingrained in its life. Nonetheless, the actual situation does not always correspond to the ideal pattern, which certainly is true for the political situation in Holland during recent decades.

The Dutch Parliament, or States-General, since the constitutional revisions of 1917 and 1922, has been constituted by a system of proportional representation on a basis of universal, though compulsory, active as well as passive suffrage, comprising both men and women. Under this system there were, in April 1933, at the elections for the Second Chamber, the Dutch House of Representatives, 54 political parties, factions and groups which entered candidates to be elected as

TOWN HALL, HILVERSUM

BLAST-FURNACE WORKS, IJMUIDEN

representatives in the States-General. This number showed a marked increase compared with previous years when there were already an extraordinary high number of political groups: 32 in 1918, 48 in 1922, 33 in 1925, and 37 in 1929. Because of a change in the electoral law certain limits were set to this anomalous situation, with the result that in 1937 there were only 20 parties left—still a high number—which were able to enter candidates at the polls. From 1918 to 1937 there were at the six quadrennial elections respectively 17, 10, 12, 10, 14, and 10 parties which succeeded in gaining seats in the States-General. As the system of proportional representation is meant to convey a faithful and almost mathematically exact picture of the political thoughts of the people, although determined by the party formations, it is interesting by way of example to examine the list of parties in 1933, the result of the first parliamentary election after the great economic depression of 1929, particularly since the major parties invariably top all the preceding and subsequent election-lists. In order to fill the 100 seats of the Second Chamber, candidates of 14 political groups were elected:

	Seats
The Roman Catholic State party	28
The Social Democratic Labor party	22
The Anti-Revolutionary party	14
The Christian Historical Union	10
The Liberal State party, the "League of Freedom"	7
The Liberal Democratic party	6
The Communist party	4
The (Conservative Calvinist) Political Reformed party	3
The Revolutionary Socialist party	1
The National Farmer Horticulturist and Middle-Class party	1
The Roman Catholic People's party	1
The Christian Democratic Union	1
The Reformed State party	1
The (semi-Fascist) League of National Rehabilitation	1

As the electoral law provides that parties which do not poll at least 75 per cent of the electoral quotient are ignored in the distribution of parliamentary seats, forty small groups and factions failed to obtain representation in the legislature. Besides seven varying Socialist or Labor groups, three Roman Catholic Democratic or Labor parties, and six Fascist or National Socialist factions, these forty included groups of market-vendors, taxpayers, independent merchants, tenants, the trading middle class, brain-and-manual workers, parties in favor of "Justice and Liberty," of "National Prosperity" and of "Reconstruction and Fraternity," as well as a "Zuiderzee" party, an "Anti-Depression" party and a certain number of individual groups without any specification for a comprehensive political program but with a plan for the promotion of private middle-class interests.

These smaller groups—although responsible for a waste of votes and, as such, impairing the system of proportional representation—did not really influence the political situation dominated by the major parties. They served rather as an additional indicator of the various forms of dissatisfaction prevailing among the electorate, as well as of a certain political disintegration reflected to a much wider degree by the grouping and differentiation of the great parties in the States-General. There are several reasons for this multiplicity. Apart from the traditionally individualistic disposition of the average Dutchman, the primary cause perhaps is that in no other country have political and religious issues or, for that matter, political and religious conflicts been so closely and consistently connected as in Holland. By the very way in which religious situations are integrated into the life of the people, religious divisions cut horizontally across the vertical political groupings along economic and social lines elsewhere in vogue. This multiplicity, however, can be reduced to four predominant ideological categories which intrinsically bring out the socio- and religio-political structure of the Dutch people.

Although these categories—apart from the Catholics—do not form homogeneous units, their political organizations are nonetheless the crystallization and actual projection of the chief trends of nineteenth- and twentieth-century political thinking. According to their number of seats in the States-General they comprised respectively: the Roman Catholics, the Socialists, the Protestants, and the Liberals, each of which had its own independent Right and Left Wing formations. Before the invasion there existed scarcely a sphere of Dutch social life in which this differentiation did not manifest itself, be it the labor unions, the farmer-coöperative movements, the organization of the radio societies, cultural institutions, the youth movement, the educational system, or the press. Consequently, the relation between party system and social stratification became very complex. The five main vertical strata of Dutch society, labor, trading middle class (retailers and small farmers, etc.), big farmers, new middle class (small employers, public functionaries, intellectuals, etc.) and big employers were all organized within their own various organizations, but always horizontally divided according to one or more of the four great ideologies. This made nearly all the major political parties more general than class organizations, especially those of the Roman Catholics and the Neo-Calvinist Anti-Revolutionaries, both of which united in their organizations the conflicting interests of the "capitalist" upper class and lower middle and laboring classes. It is obvious that this situation led to ever-recurring dissensions and controversies within the ranks of these confessional parties, as much as it prevented a truly constructive and fruitful collaboration or coalition with the secular groups even where matters of general importance or questions purely social and economic were concerned. It also accounts for the many extraparliamentary, intermezzo- or business-cabinets of the last decades which almost without interruption made their appearance on the political scene. In order to give an analysis of the Dutch political system, it will therefore be necessary to survey the main party-groupings.

Liberals.—The Liberal Prime Minister, Kappeyne van de Coppello (1877–1879), once said: "It may be true that the sun of liberalism is frequently obscured by clouds. It does not always shine in full splendor and luster. Nonetheless all light and consequently all power is derived from that sun." It would be impossible to deny that the Dutch people are extremely indebted to liberalism and the Liberals. There is perhaps no other political group, or rather, trend of thought in the modern history of the Netherlands which exerted such a great influence on all spheres of Dutch life or definitely marked it with its stamp. This remains true in spite of the fact that in 1937, at the last elections for the Second Chamber prior to the German invasion, the party dwindled into a small political semiconservative group, represented by only four members.

The rise and development of liberalism in the nineteenth century, its decline in the twentieth, and its loss of *raison d'être* in later years must be considered within the sphere of contemporaneous European and world history which produced it. It was inspired in Holland by an age-old tradition of liberty and tolerance which formed one of the basic elements of Dutch cultural and political life. To its spiritual heritage belong such comparatively heterogeneous trends of thought as were developed by the great humanists and philosophers of the sixteenth and seventeenth centuries (Erasmus, William of Orange, Coornhert, Grotius, etc.), as well as by the "moderates" in the Reformed Church and many of the numerous dissident Protestant groups outside that church. The spiritually libertinistic "regents" of the seventeenth century, as well as the "enlightened" adversaries of the fossilized, oligarchic, nepotistic "regent" class of the late eighteenth century—the bourgeois Patriots active before and during the French revolution—must also be ranged among the spiritual ancestors of modern liberalism.[1]

It is difficult to give an exact definition of this political trend as it gradually developed throughout the nineteenth century. Previous to 1848 it was by no means a well-defined homogeneous political system based on a well-elaborated political program. At that time a Liberal party did not exist. After a long "incubation" period it continued to gain in political power. Its comparatively progressive ideas were chiefly carried by enlightened, rationalistic, and anticlerical intellectuals and members of the wealthy bourgeoisie, who, because of the antiquated aristocratic-autocratic constitutions of 1814 and 1815, were deprived of any real influence on the conduct of the state. Another factor was the Belgian *status quo* policy of King William I, with its ruinous effects on the financial position and the trade of the country. Liberalism, however, did not appeal to the larger masses of the population who were neither politically minded nor politically educated and were more concerned with religious and economic than with political issues. Nonetheless, the general dissatisfaction prevailing among all classes of the population after the final separation between

---

[1] See the chapters on "Philosophy and Religious Trends," and "Social Structure of the Netherlands."

Holland and Belgium in 1839 was great. This dissatisfaction was by no means removed by the Constitutional Revision of 1840, in spite of the fact that it introduced partial ministerial responsibility. The King and Conservatives alike were of the opinion that a financial stabilization should precede a constitutional reform. This stabilization was accomplished in 1844 by the Conservative Liberal Minister, F. A. van Hall, through a voluntary loan and through other measures which established an equilibrium in the budget between receipts and expenditures.

A great factor in this financial reorganization was the large annual payments derived from the Indian Culture System. It was in these years that liberalism was molded into an effective political system which subsequently effected the sweeping and radical political and social reforms which essentially changed the structure of Dutch life. The soul, inspirer, and leader of the Liberals was the Netherlands' greatest statesman of the nineteenth century, Johan Rudolf Thorbecke (1798–1872), at that time a professor of jurisprudence at Leyden and in later years three times prime minister (1849–1853, 1862–1866, 1870–1872). In an earlier period of his life, Thorbecke was strongly influenced by some of the leading philosophers of the German romantic movement, particularly by the ideas of the historical school of jurisprudence of K. F. Eichhorn and F. C. von Savigny. In a long series of outstanding articles and books, Thorbecke laid down the essential principles and theoretical bases of a liberal, constitutional parliamentary conduct of state and society. He had many followers; and the cause he championed had the support of every Progressive in the country, as well as of such brilliant politicians, writers, and publicists as Donker-Curtius, Luzac, Potgieter, Bakhuizen van den Brink and others. He exerted such an immense influence that for a long time liberalism was identified with Thorbeckianism, and politicians divided themselves into Pro- and Anti-Thorbeckians. Under his leadership a body of nine members of the Second Chamber drew up a definite proposal for a moderate liberal democratic revision of the Constitution in 1844 which, however, failed to obtain the approval of King William II. In 1848 a Liberal state was finally established.

Alarmed by the revolutionary events which stirred Europe in 1848, notably by the sudden overthrow of the monarchy of Louis Philippe and the proclamation of a republic at Paris, the King consented to the ardently desired revision, to a large extent Thorbecke's outstanding achievement.

The revision of 1848, together with its attendant organic laws, ushered in an era of social reform of which the following were the most striking features: parliamentary democracy; full political emancipation of all religious denominations; freedom of press, assembly, and speech; improved jurisprudence; and the stimulation of economic prosperity and industrial life, patterned on a basis of free enterprise and free trade, and accomplished by the abolition or alleviation of tariffs, customs, duties, and taxes. Liberalism was responsible for improvement in the means of communication, including highways, waterways, and the railway system. Freedom and independence in all spheres of life, rather than equality, constituted its basic principle.

The dogma of economic freedom was based on the principle of "spontaneous economic harmony," accompanied by a strong optimistic faith in the future and in progress. Consequently, with the rise of big industry in the Netherlands from 1870 on, more attention was given to production, less to distribution. However, the liberal doctrine that economic prosperity of the industrial and commercial leaders—of the upper middle class—would equally and spontaneously extend itself to the lower strata of society turned out to be only partially true. It cannot be denied, however, that the new period of industrialization in many ways improved the conditions of labor. The opening of new world markets, which made free competition possible, the intensified trade with the Dutch East Indies, and the very great increase in population which stimulated internal trade, all contributed to an improvement in labor conditions.

In the second half of the nineteenth century there arose a new industrial and agricultural proletariat. This group, which lived on the verge of pauperism and worked under very bad conditions, owed its existence chiefly to the fact that the period of transition from small industry and handicraft to large industry was too brief, and adjustment to the new situation too incomplete. A peculiar point in this development was the attitude of the old Liberals themselves. More and more their freedom proved to be the freedom of the wealthy bourgeoisie, not that of the lower classes of society. Their attitude was marked by social indifference. Moreover, the principle of freedom entailed a strict noninterference by the State in economic life, which principle prevented the realization of consistent social legislation. This, however, provoked a strong opposition within the ranks of the Liberals themselves who, indeed, since 1848 had been divided on such major issues as the broadening of the franchise, the colonial policy, tax-reform, and the military service. It was this disunity which time and again gave their political opponents, the Conservatives and Anti-Revolutionaries, opportunities to take office even when in the minority. Time and again Conservative cabinets realized essentially Liberal programs. One of the causes of this situation was the increasing tendency of many Liberals toward conservatism, whereas the Conservatives adopted the Liberal conceptions for their own political-constitutional views. Already, in 1862 the leader of the Anti-Revolutionaries, Groen van Prinsterer, exclaimed that the Conservatives came into office with the support of the Anti-Revolutionaries, but governed with the Liberals.[2] Subsequently, the Conservatives finally submerged in the Anti-Revolutionary and Liberal parties (c. 1885). Among the Liberals, however, arose a younger progressive school of thought, focused on social legislation and a broadening of the franchise. They opposed the traditional school which adhered to the principles of 1848. Prominent leaders of this progressive school were Fransen van der Putte, Kappeyne van de Coppello, and Samuel van Houten. In subsequent years these dissensions led to the formation of various Conservative and Left (or radical) Liberal groups. The fundamental difference between these groups has been strikingly expressed by the Liberal Minister, P. W. A. Cort van den Linden:

"The essential mistake of the old economy and old liberal policy is contained in its conception of men as individuals, who, uniting as self-sufficient independent beings, form society.

---

[2] K. E. van der Mandele, *Het Liberalisme in Nederland,* p. 199.

"The new doctrine, on the contrary, requires that individual interest be subordinated to common interest. 'Be a man,' the individualists say. 'But above all, be a human being,' is the answer."

In 1885 the Liberal Progressive Union was founded. Its members were more united by their common anticlerical sentiments than by a commonly accepted political program. The union originally comprised all shades of Liberals who disagreed upon essential points. A radical group (Treub and others), in 1888 in Amsterdam, formed a separate electoral society which, in 1894, became the Radical League with members throughout the country. Dissatisfied with the insufficient Constitutional Revision of 1887, they favored universal suffrage, compulsory education, and a consistent social legislation. A Right Wing group, the Old Independent Liberals, in 1894 broke away from the Liberal Union.

From 1885 to 1917 extension of the franchise remained the principal issue. The Constitutional Revision of 1887 created an electorate of male persons of not less than twenty-five years of age who possessed residential qualification and "signs of fitness and social well-being." In 1894 the Progressive Liberal Minister, Tak van Poortvliet tried to interpret these words in the sense of "all who could write and did not receive doles from charity." This proposal, which would practically have introduced universal male suffrage, met with such fierce opposition that not only the Liberals but also the Anti-Revolutionaries and Catholics broke up into hostile groups—Takkians and Anti-Takkians. The electoral law of 1896 (Van Houten), though practically doubling the number of voters, also failed to pacify the varying shades of Progressives. This led in 1901 to a new split in the Liberal Union which had not been able to attain the support of a majority of its members for its plans of constitutional revision to provide universal suffrage. The Progressives subsequently formed the Liberal Democratic League which incorporated the older Radical League.

In 1921 a fusion was effected between the Liberal Union, the old Independent Liberals, and five other groups, under the name of "League for Freedom" to which in later years the title "Liberal State Party" was added. Stressing individual freedom in all spheres of life and the value of the human personality, it adhered essentially to Thorbecke's principles, though adjusted to the new exigencies of the time. Recognizing the Christian character of the Dutch nation and wishing to maintain this character, it rejected, as of old, any theological or dogmatical basis for the political conduct of the State. The Liberal State party strongly favored coöperation with the League of Nations. But it also stood for a policy of well-planned armament. It advocated democratic administration, while opposing socialization of industry and restriction of free competition. It adhered to the maintenance of nondenominational public schools, as well as to complete equality of rights for men and women. It was chiefly its traditional policy of nonstate interference in the social and economic life of the people which estranged it from the larger masses in the period preceding the Second World War.

The "radicals" and Liberal Democrats, of the Liberal Democratic League, chiefly progressive intellectuals, have greatly contributed to the social betterment of the labor class. Like the Liberals, the Liberal Democrats stood for economic prosperity, free trade, and the public nondenominational school. In addition to the principle of liberty, they emphasized equality. They favored political as well as economic democracy and advocated state interference, social legislation, state pensions, and graded income taxes. Opposing monopolistic private concessions, which made life unnecessarily expensive, they stimulated government management of these public services of a monopolistic character, but were, like the Liberals, opposed to socialization in general. By their opponents they were frequently called "academic socialists," although they were far removed from the basic socialistic principles. Because of this policy they gained considerably in power and influence after the First World War. From 1933 to 1937 they were represented in Colijn's Cabinet of National Unity. Conforming to articles 8 and 16 of the Covenant of the League of Nations, from 1924 to 1936 they strongly advocated a policy of progressive disarmament.

The Protestant Parties.—The great opponents of the Liberals in both the political and the spiritual field were the Anti-Revolutionaries, or Christian Historicals. Their history, though less complicated is certainly not less interesting than that of the Liberals. As a political body they owed their existence largely to the conflict over the schools. Spiritually they were the exponents of the renaissance of Calvinism which, together with the rise of liberalism, dominated the cultural and political life of the nineteenth century.

The three principal leaders of the Anti-Revolutionaries were successively Guillaume Groen van Prinsterer (1801–1876), Abraham Kuyper (1837–1920) and Hendrik Colijn (1869–). The first was the philosophic creator of the basic ideas and principles, the second the dynamic and versatile founder of the Anti-Revolutionary party, the third is the efficient and practical statesman devoted to the realization of these principles in political life.

Although the antirevolutionary starting point in life was entirely different from that of the Liberals, the Anti-Revolutionaries nevertheless stood for their own (Calvinist) interpretation of liberty and freedom of conscience. They drew their inspiration from the great Calvinist principles of the Reformation which had guided the Dutch in their long struggle for freedom and independence against the Spaniards. Groen van Prinsterer enunciated the motto "Against the revolution, the Gospels." Yet, he explicitly stated that the antirevolutionary trend of thought was not "counter" revolutionary or reactionary, but "anti" the humanistic-rationalistic spirit which actuated the French Revolution. In their opinion this revolution started with the declaration of human rights; it could only end, however, with the declaration of the rights of God. Above the sovereignty of man they placed the sovereignty and omnipotence of God.

After many preliminary discussions a new general organization of the Netherlands Reformed Church, arbitrarily instituted by Royal Decree, became effective in 1816. Although since the constitutions of 1798, 1814, and 1815 a full political separation between State and Church had been established, with freedom of religion and equal protection to all the existing denominations guaranteed, this new arrangement gave strong ecclesiastic-legislative power and influence to King, Government, and Synod. This, however, did not give the

State *"jus in sacra,"* but only the supervisory power of *"jus circa sacra,"* which found its expression in the establishment of a ministerial department for the Reformed, and for other forms of public worship. The new arrangement met with fierce opposition, as many considered it to threaten the independence and internal freedom of the Church. Essentially, the old antithesis between the strict Calvinists (Precisionists) and Liberal Calvinists (Libertines) of the early seventeenth century made itself once more manifest with the Liberals or "moderns" preëminently in charge. The new organization of the State, in the opinion of its orthodox opponents based more on the "enlightened" rationalistic conceptions of "natural law" than on the theocratic ideas of the Calvinists—and primarily benefiting the Liberal Conservative higher bourgeoisie—created great discontent in certain aristocratic circles, as well as in the lower classes of society. A reaction against this situation set in. Inspired by kindred movements in Scotland and Switzerland a *Réveil,* a new religious awakening, made itself manifest. It centered around such distinguished and aristocratic men as William Bilderdijk and his disciples, Isaac da Costa, who published his startling *Objections Against the Spirit of the Age* and who said, "Our freedom be the Evangelical, not the philosophical," William and Dirk van Hogendorp, William de Clercq, Elout van Soeterwoude, A. Capadose, Groen van Prinsterer, and many others. The *Réveil,* among other points emphasizing personal, living piety, faith, the divine authority of the Holy Bible, the divinity of Christ, and original sin, formed a mighty factor in the spiritual development of the early nineteenth century, the more so because it stressed evangelistic and philanthropic work.[3] It was, however, a typically aristocratic movement and politically antirevolutionary. Most of its adherents opposed the French Revolution in its principles as well as in its consequences, whereas some Anti-Revolutionaries, such as Groen van Prinsterer, agreed with many of the political-social reforms directly or indirectly caused by that revolution.

A more popular movement was represented by the many small oppositional congregations—seceding from the Netherlands Re-

---

[3] H. Bavink, *A General View of the Netherlands,* Number XVII, p. 14.

formed Church—which after a period of much persecution united in 1869 in the officially recognized Christian Reformed Church, with many followers among the smaller middle and farmer classes. These groups outside the Church, together with the orthodox groups within the Church backed the rising antirevolutionary movement. Groen van Prinsterer entered the States-General in 1840, as a "general without an army," and in subsequent years, time and again, came into conflict with his parliamentary "friends," who were more counterrevolutionary, antiliberal and conservative than antirevolutionary or Christian Historical. He terminated his coöperation with the Conservatives in 1871, when the party realized its full independence. Groen van Prinsterer's basic conception was the divine right, implying that the source of governmental authority transcends the human will. In his *Irreligiosity and Revolution* (*Ongeloof en Revolutie*) he wrote: "The Bible is the book of books, especially in the antirevolutionary bookery. The new wisdom of our age, even if not flatly rejecting 'Revelation,' entails that higher judgment (divine authority) is not to be applied to the sphere of constitutional law (*staatsrecht*). We, however, maintain that the Holy Scriptures indicate the fundamental bases of justice and morality, of authority and freedom for nations and governments. The Bible is the infallible touchstone. Unconditional submission to God's Word has always been a guarantee not only for dutiful obedience, but also for dutiful resistance. No doctrine of proud self-perfection or of gross licentiousness can be in harmony with the pronouncements of the 'Revelation.' *It is written!*' That is the axe which cuts off every root of the revolutionary crop." As a second "pillar," Van Prinsterer took the motto: "*It happened*," intimating that the antirevolutionary or Christian Historical trend had its roots and support in "Revelation" and in history.

It was only in 1878 that the Anti-Revolutionaries organized into a political party in the strict sense of the word. This was mainly the outstanding achievement of Dr. A. Kuyper, successor *jure suo* to Groen van Prinsterer, and Prime Minister from 1901 to 1905. Kuyper's versatile genius accounts for the many activities in which he indulged. He acquired fame as a minister of the Reformed Church, as chief editor, parliamentary representative, author of many theological works, and as professor at the "Free University on Reformed Principles," which was his creation. He was the "democrat" in the party, spreading his ideas and ideals among the smaller middle classes and the farmers. Aiming at the restoration of the church government of the Synod of Dordt, he was in 1885 and 1886 chiefly responsible for a new secession in the Reformed Church. The seceding groups assumed the name of Suffering Church (*Doleerende Kerk*). In 1892 they united with the aforementioned Christian Reformed Church, under the new name of "Reformed Churches of the Netherlands," which became closely affiliated with the Anti-Revolutionary party.

Like the Liberals, the Anti-Revolutionaries were not able to maintain integral unity within their own ranks. Dr. Kuyper's democratic policy, favoring a system of broader suffrage, his predominant position as party leader, his efforts to mold the party into a centrally organized political mass-organization, which made the parliamentary representatives too dependent upon the party government, as well as his attitude in ecclesiastic and academic affairs (Free-University, *Doleantie*), induced the more aristocratic conservatives among the Anti-Revolutionaries in 1897–1898 to break away and to form an independent organization under the name of Free Anti-Revolutionaries.

Previously, in 1893, the Second Chamber faction had split into two independent groups on the issue of the progressive electoral law of Tak van Poortvliet. The leader of the Free Anti-Revolutionaries was Jhr. A. F. de Savornin Lohman. Their primary aim was full adherence to Van Prinsterer's principles from which they felt Kuyper had strayed. They were less concerned with obtaining a majority among the electorate than with establishing authority, i.e., the authority of "God's Word"; not the (democratic) success of the party, but rather the power of the principle counted with them. Another important factor was Kuyper's Right Wing "coalition" policy with the Roman Catholics, when he claimed that the Christian parties "sprang from the same root of faith." This coalition was essentially the consequence of Kappeyne van de Coppello's "illiberal" Education Act of 1878 which denied state support to the private confessional schools and was bitterly resented by Anti-Revolutionaries and Roman Catholics alike. The rising political power and influence of the Catholics, however, stirred large groups of Protestants, who feared that the nation was losing its reformed character. This gave rise to the creation of various independent Protestant electoral societies, the most prominent of which became the Christian Historical Electoral League (1898) and the Frisian Christian Historical party. In the years 1903 and 1908 these parties respectively joined the Free Anti-Revolutionaries and were henceforth known as the Christian Historical Union. To a certain extent this Protestant political differentiation reflects the theological disunity of the various Reformed churches. The Christian Historical Union mainly recruited its members from the adherents of the Netherlands Reformed Church. In spite of its latent or professed anti-Roman Catholic tendencies the C. H. U. formed part of the "coalition" till 1925, when it seconded a parliamentary motion— handed in by the Ultra-Calvinist Political Reformed party (*Staatkundig Gereformeerde partij*)—to discontinue the Netherlands Legation at the Vatican. This terminated the long-standing coalition between the Roman Catholic State party and the great Protestant parties which, on the whole, also disagreed on social and economic issues. Space does not permit exhaustive treatment of the various small Right and Left Wing Protestant political groups which originated in opposition to the policies pursued by the major parties.

The Anti-Revolutionaries gained considerably in political strength in the years just preceding the Second World War. This was because of the outstanding personality of their eminent leader, Hendrik Colijn, rather than because of an agreement with the Anti-Revolutionary principles. There is no doubt that a growing *rapprochement* between Liberals and Anti-Revolutionaries became effective, especially in the economic field. It was chiefly dissatisfied Liberals and Christian Historicals who joined the Anti-Revolutionaries at the election of 1937. In 1933 Colijn formed his Cabinet of National Unity in which Protestants, Catholics, Liberals, and Liberal Democrats coöperated. The masses of the population were originally strongly in favor of this Cabinet, which, however, in 1937 was not continued, principally because the major groups represented could not reach agreement on certain highly essential economic issues.

The Catholics.—Since the introduction of proportional representation the Catholics have formed the strongest united group in the States-General. From the role of a "stepchild" in Dutch political life the group developed, in the course of one century, into a most powerful political and cultural force.

Even in the heyday of the Reformation the Roman Catholics were not totally eclipsed. In the middle of the seventeenth century they were able to organize themselves anew under the leadership of Sasbout Vosmeer, Apostolic Vicar of Cologne. They lived for the greater part in the so-called "Lands of the Generality," the conquered territory in Brabant, Flanders, and Limburg. As small farmers or as workers in the textile industry they were kept backward politically, economically, and culturally by heavy taxes, as well as by other restrictive measures. Just as the Jews and adherents of numerous dissident Protestant sects were deprived of the full rights of citizenship, so were the Roman Catholics. They were not officially permitted to hold public religious services but were, on the other hand, entitled to their personal beliefs and to freedom of conscience. In the days preceding the French Revolution many joined the more liberal Patriots. The Constitution of 1798 introduced, for the first time, their political emancipation. At that time, however, they had only a few strong and capable personalities at their disposal. Throughout the nineteenth century the Catholics gradually and steadily rose in influence, although as a political and cultural body they remained largely in an isolated position. In his encyclical, *Mirare Vos* (1832), Pope Gregory XVI repudiated in principle the liberal ideals. The fact, however, that the prevailing liberal policy greatly benefited the religious and political emancipation of the Catholics, induced them to support Thorbecke and the Liberals in their political aspirations. The Constitutional Revision of 1848 brought complete freedom of worship and of organization to every form of religious belief. Before 1848 the Catholics had already obtained an indemnification for their Church, emancipation of monasteries, and the right to form associations and to hold public meetings. Among the Catholics a growing desire to restore the episcopal hierarchy made itself manifest. By a papal decree of March 4, 1853, a Catholic episcopate was established. It was particularly the phrasing of this decree with its denunciation of the great principles of the Reformation, as well as of Holland's long war against the Spaniards, which awakened among the Protestants throughout the country a storm of fierce indignation. The intensity of the subsequent "April Movement" even caused Thorbecke to proffer his resignation soon thereafter.

It was primarily the school policy which brought about gradual estrangement between Catholics and Liberals. In the papal encyclical *Quanta Cura* of 1844 and the accompanying *Syllabus Errorum* the fundamental principles of liberalism and liberal culture were once more rejected. This was followed in 1868 by a pastoral letter of the Dutch bishops in which they emphasized the insufficiency and danger of public secular education for Catholic children. It was Van de Coppello's Education Act of 1878 which sealed the cleavage between Catholics and Liberals. Henceforth they held a "center" position in politics and sided more and more with the Anti-Revolutionaries, their allies in the school conflict.

Although from 1853 on, Catholic electoral societies were founded throughout the country, many years elapsed before the Catholics were able to organize themselves into one political party. The stimulating force in this development was Monseigneur Dr. Hermanus J. A. M. Schaepman (1844–1903), Catholic priest, poet, writer, professor, and statesman, who, like Dr. A. Kuyper, advocated democratic ideals. He entered the States-General in 1880 favoring extension of the franchise and social legislation. In 1883 he published a pamphlet, *Approach to a Program,* in which he emphatically stated that a Catholic party did not of necessity imply disruption of religious peace or Catholic supremacy. Not as Catholics versus Protestants, but as Catholic citizens versus Liberals and Conservatives they should pursue their own political ideals, which were based, however, on the great principles and traditions as professed and outlined by the Roman Catholic Church. Their program, too, should be "antirevolutionary," though revealing its own origin, color, and character. Accordingly, Schaepman set about to overcome the partiality of his fellow-believers for the Liberals, and their prejudice against the Protestants. In collaboration with Dr. Kuyper and Jhr. de Savornin Lohman, he brought about the coalition of the Right Wing parties, denounced by political opponents as a "Monster Union" between Rome and Dordrecht.

From 1888 on this coalition resulted in various Right Wing cabinets in which the Catholics were strongly represented. Like the Protestants and Liberals, the Catholics were originally hopelessly divided on such issues as military service and the franchise. Prior to the elections of 1897, however, a definite general program accepted by the various electoral societies was drawn up, which showed a certain affinity to the antirevolutionary program. Its most important items were principally based on Schaepman's *Approach,* on the papal encyclicals *Quanta Cura* (1864), and *Immortale Dei* (1885), and in agreement with the *Syllabus Errorum.* The program covered social questions, education, the army, law, taxes, agriculture, and industry as well as the problems of the overseas territories. It was mainly the heterogeneous structure of Netherlands Catholic Society with its great internal contrasts in social stratification and economic interests which prevented a truly effective unified organization of the Catholics, even after this program had become effective. This called for a reorganization. In 1905 the Roman Catholic State party acquired its definite form. Although the 1896 program was maintained, it was modified in accordance with the papal encyclicals, *Rerum Novarum* and *Quadragesimo Anno,* and in 1936 totally adjusted to the new exigencies of the time. This firm organization henceforth guaranteed the Catholics the largest number of seats in the States-General, as well as a predominant position in the government of the country.

The postwar events, the rising influence of the Socialist movement to stimulate the Catholic workers in their demands for social improvement, the interests of the Catholic industrial employers, better served by protection than by unlimited free trade, as well as the dissatisfaction among progressive Catholics, causing, time and again, the creation of Left Wing, independent, popular democratic Catholic parties, induced the Roman Catholic State party to advocate social legislation, economic planning, the establishment of a corporative structure of society, as well as state interference in economic life. Most particularly, after the termination of the coalition in 1925, did a slight tendency to coöperate with the Social Democrats make itself manifest. Monseigneur William H. Nolens, its prominent leader, however, explicitly stated that such coöperation could only be realized "in case of utmost urgency." The predominant position of the Right Wing group, the opposing stand taken by Catholics and Social Democrats towards the Spanish Civil War, their entirely antagonistic world philosophies, as well as their conflicting interests in the labor movement made the realization of this coöperation totally impossible. Though essentially divided on social and economic issues the Catholics continued also after 1925 to coöperate with the great Protestant parties, but always on the basis of special extraparliamentary programs. The Roman Catholic State party was not ecclesiastic in function and emphasized its national aspect. It safeguarded the "positive Christian" bases of Dutch society, especially the integral maintenance of religion, family, and property. It strongly advocated social justice.

The Socialists.—Notwithstanding the backward and impoverished living conditions of the laboring classes during the nineteenth century, socialism asserted itself very late in the Netherlands, as compared with the surrounding countries. Before 1870 this was principally because big industry had not yet been developed and the concentration of industrial workers and the creation of an industrial proletariat had not occurred. The new industrialization of the last quarter of the nineteenth century brought about an essential change in this situation.

The introduction of socialism in the Netherlands is primarily the achievement of progressive intellectuals. It arose in opposition to the rigid liberal and Christian bourgeois structure of Dutch society and cut across the old Liberal Christian antithesis. Socialism was stimulated by such movements as the atheistic The Dawn (*Dageraad*), a society which had as its objective the furtherance of free thought, and by the sharp, ironical writings of Eduard Douwes Dekker, the great fighter against hypocrisy and backwardness. In 1869 short-lived sections of the London International Labor Association (The First Internationale) were organized at Amsterdam and elsewhere; in 1871—as a reaction—it was followed by the antisocialistic General Netherlands Workers' Union. A Christian social organization, *Patrimonium,* was founded in 1877. Its purpose was the promotion and improvement of the Christian (Protestant) labor class but was, at the same time, strongly in favor of the House of Orange.

The antisocialistic attitude of the General Netherlanders Workers' Union, led to the establishment of several independent Social Democratic groups which, in 1881, united to form the Social Democratic League. This League gained marked influence through its campaign for universal suffrage. The prominent leader was Frederik Domela Nieuwenhuis (1846–1919), a former Lutheran pastor, who through his publication *Justice for All* (*Recht voor Allen*) greatly furthered the socialist cause.

The same conflict which kept Socialists (Karl Marx) and Anarchists (Bakunin) divided throughout the world caused also a split in the ranks of the Dutch Social Democrats who broke up into parliamentary and antiparliamentary anarchistic Free Socialist groups. In 1894, under the leadership of the so-called twelve Apostles (P. J. Troelstra, W. H. Vliegen, F. van der Goes, J. H. Schaper, Henri Polak, J. W. Gerhard, and others), the Social Democratic Labor Party (S.D.A.P.) was founded. In subsequent years this party became the second strongest political group in parliament and in the country. At first the new organization met with fierce resistance on the part of the Anarchists, organized under Domela Nieuwenhuis in the group of Free Socialists. From 1897, however, the young party proved at every recurrent election to have gained in votes. It is therefore no overstatement to say that the history of socialism in the Netherlands is the history of the S.D.A.P. notwithstanding the fact that Left Wing groups broke away several times, to continue as independent socialist-radical organizations, the strongest of which, in the years following the First World War, became the extremist Communist party (D.

Wijnkoop, L. L. H. de Visser, and others). Communism, however, was never able to gain a strong foothold in the Netherlands. Its representation in the States-General was never over four seats, an event which happened in 1933 after four years of economic depression.

The S.D.A.P. was originally a semirevolutionary, anti-ecclesiastical, oppositional, though parliamentary, labor group with a strong class consciousness, advocating class warfare, and greatly influenced by German Marxist doctrines. In the course of forty years it developed into a progressive, semibourgeois, reformistic, humanistic, pacifist socialist-oppositional folk party, with a religious tendency among many of its followers (Woodbrokers, Religious Socialist Union). In its political program the S.D.A.P. emphasized that its struggle for social justice was essentially based on respect for the dignity of the human personality. Accordingly it considered socialism and democracy as indissoluble, and socialism and dictatorship, including the dictatorship of the proletariat, as incompatible entities. It therefore aimed at the acquisition of political power through democratic methods. In order to realize its political and cultural ideals it created many subsidiary organizations which covered the interests of youth, women, radio, sports, and other forms of social life. Its leader was until 1924 the dynamic, romantic poet and Frisian politician, P. J. Troelstra who was succeeded by J. W. Albarda. Whereas the S.D.A.P. until 1939 consistently refrained from taking part in the government of the country, it became prominent in the administrations and municipal councils of both the large and the small cities. Because of its constant activity a program of social legislation was carried through, chiefly by the Right Wing parties which made Holland one of the most progressive of countries in the social conditions of organized laboring classes, although the position of the many unemployed—in spite of relief and official support—remained bad. Before the occupation of the Nazis, the new, excellent and cheap housing projects for workmen in all the big industrial cities were the most striking manifestation of this social improvement.

The goal of the S.D.A.P. was radical labor legislation, reduction of unemployment by industrialization and public works, and gradual nationalization of industries and land. It advocated more self-government for the colonies, local option, and state pensions. Until 1937 the Social Democrats were strongly opposed to all military expenditures. The precarious European situation, however, caused them to change this attitude. A few years earlier they had virtually dropped their republicanism and had taken a view more closely approaching that of the English Labor party. The new constructive policy of the S.D.A.P. found its expression in various reports in which its opinions concerning the gradual socialization of big, private industry and enterprise were outlined. In 1933 the S.D.A.P. published, in collaboration with the Social Democratic Labor Union, a project of economic planning, the so-called "Labor Plan." The huge costs, however, made the realization of this plan impossible. In subsequent years it served no other purpose than to become a means of propaganda for the Social Democratic movement. From 1939 on, the party was represented in the Cabinet.

National Socialists.—It is against the background of the almost impenetrable normal party system with its stable and practically unshakable parliamentary traditions that national socialism made its appearance during the period preceding the German invasion. It was a movement which did not meet with sympathy on the part of the Dutch population as a whole. National socialism took concrete shape in 1931–1932 when Anton Mussert—a civil engineer in the employ of the Netherlands Government and known through his firm opposition to the treaty with Belgium—founded his National Socialist Movement (*Nationaal Socialistische Beweging* N.S.B.). Previous to this, several smaller fascist organizations, frequently in conflict with one another, had sprung up, but were hardly noticed by the majority of the people. The N.S.B. was a typical phenomenon of the economic depression because it was able to exploit the discontent prevalent among the lower middle class, the farmers, and among youth generally. At the electoral polls the N.S.B. had its vicissitudes. In 1935, at the elections for the Provincial Estates it obtained 7.9 per cent of all the votes cast. In 1937 it acquired four seats in the Second Chamber. In reality, however, the N.S.B. suffered a crushing defeat, because its number of votes was reduced to 4.2 per cent. In 1939 it won only 3.7 per cent of the votes for the Provincial Estates.

The N.S.B. was strongly opposed to the parliamentary system. It advocated the abolition of the political parties, favored authoritarianism and dictatorial leadership and denounced the internationalism of the Socialists and the Catholics. These principles, diametrically opposed to all the old established Dutch institutions and traditions of tolerance and democracy, together with the aggressive events in Germany, rallied the people of all classes and parties to the House of Orange. The N.S.B. stood for the "Great Netherlands idea" based on the "Dietsch" race. It supported Flemish extremism against Belgian unity, and attacked British imperialism in South Africa.

Contrary to the situation in Germany, where the national socialist ideology had a longer tradition, national socialism in the Netherlands was never recognized as a typical Dutch movement. It was felt to be "outlandish" in spite of the fact that, in complying with Dutch tradition, it originally did not incorporate virulent anti-Semitism in its political program. Both before and after the invasion, however, it fully adopted the German pattern, despite fierce opposition on the part of the population. Post-invasion events show clearly how greatly the National Socialists misunderstood the real spiritual and political disposition of the Netherlanders. It is a noteworthy fact that the N.S.B., in order to justify itself as a typical Dutch movement and to substantiate its propagandistic appeal asserted that it considered such great leaders as the Anti-Revolutionary statesman, Abraham Kuyper or the Social Democratic leader, P. J. Troelstra as its precursors, whose respective political ideals it wanted to realize. At the same time it emphasized its adherence to the Queen and the House of Orange. This sham patriotic attitude, however, did not blind the average Dutchman to the national socialist danger threatening national independence. Farsighted men knew that the pretense of patriotism was a mere camouflage for pro-German treachery. The ignominious and insolent attitude of the N.S.B. before, during, and after the invasion proved only too well that this political organization was merely a secret outpost of the German national socialist movement.

On July 5, 1941, all the great political parties were dissolved by decree of the German Reichskommissar Seyss-Inquart. This terminated temporarily an episode of Dutch cultural and political history which strikingly revealed the abundant diversity of Dutch life, as well as the richly variegated aspects of the Netherlands national character. The splendid attitude of the people, however, maintained against the brutal and terrible odds of the German occupation, has clearly demonstrated that the predominant trait of the national character is not "diversity" but, above all, "unity in diversity."

CHAPTER VIII

Netherlands Foreign Policy

BY AMRY J. VANDENBOSCH

IN THE YEARS when the Republic was in its glory the Netherlands played an active part in world politics. Intermittently for eighty years it fought against the mighty power of Spain until its independence was finally acknowledged. During this same period it frequently engaged in active warfare on the Seven Seas against the great maritime powers of the day, and established colonies and trading posts on four continents. In the century after it won its independence, the Dutch Republic was alternately the ally of England in waging war against ambitious France or the enemy of England in a gigantic struggle for commercial supremacy. Whenever France renewed its periodic drive toward the Rhine, the British and the Dutch, recognizing their common peril, united against her, but as soon as the danger was over they resumed their old struggle until finally Britain had so far outstripped Holland that Dutch commercial rivalry was no longer a source of fear.

With large commercial interests and a vast colonial empire, it is not surprising that the Netherlands played so important a part in world politics. After the Treaty of Utrecht (1713) the oligarchies which controlled the United Provinces became so engrossed in commerce and gain that the Republic lost its vitality. Its foreign policy was one of nonintervention and peace at any price. The prestige and power of the country declined steadily throughout the century and ended in a long period of French domination (1795–1813).

The new kingdom as a buffer state, 1814–1839.—The end of the Napoleonic Wars saw the creation of a new Netherlands. Bel-

gium, or southern Netherlands, was then united to Holland, or
northern Netherlands, to form the Kingdom of the Netherlands,
with a member of the House of Orange as sovereign-prince. The recreation and enlargement of the Netherlands, and the determination
of its position in the European state system of the time was the work
of the Great Powers and especially of Great Britain. The British desire
to see the Low Countries united to form a buffer state represented no
radical departure in British foreign policy. It was based on two and
a half centuries of British experience and was a natural development
of this time-honored policy.

The independence of the Low Countries had been a principle of
British foreign policy since the beginning of the national states in the
sixteenth century. Because of its insular position across a narrow
channel from Europe, Great Britain could not permit the European
coast opposite the Thames estuary, and particularly the Rhine-Meuse-
Scheldt delta to come under the control of a hostile or potentially hostile power. As a corollary of this principle, Britain was interested in
the maintenance of the balance of power in Europe, in order that the
independence of the Low Countries might not be endangered by a
strong continental power or coalition of powers. This had been the
policy of Britain in the past and was to continue to be its policy in
the future, but in a situation greatly more complicated by the unification of Germany in 1870.

This British policy accorded well with the interests of the Netherlands. Traditional French policy threatened the security of both countries. Because of her colonies, shipping and trade, Dutch interests
were chiefly on the seas or overseas and, hence, largely dependent on
British good will for their protection. On the contrary, because Great
Britain was not a great military power, it was not in its interest to
acquire any territory on the Continent. Thus, in friendly relations
with Great Britain, the Netherlands found the best guarantee of protection not only of its great overseas interests but also the territory of
its European kingdom. It was chiefly because the British wished a
friendly Netherlands capable of serving as a strong barrier against
France that Great Britain returned nearly all of the Dutch colonies

which she had occupied at the time when the Netherlands fell under the control of France.

The role of the Netherlands as a strong second-class power was not of long duration, nor did the Dutch-Belgian state play a significant role in European politics during the brief period of its existence. The French occupation had left the Low Countries in a very weakened condition. Moreover, in spite of King William I's best efforts, Holland and Belgium failed to develop the close unity of which he had dreamed and for which he had labored so diligently. Much of the difficulty lay with the King himself, as he was often arbitrary and obstinate, but it may be doubted whether the union ever did have any chance of success. The two peoples had grown apart during the two centuries of separate national existence. Indeed, the Belgians constituted two peoples instead of one. The Flemish—the northern Belgian provinces—were closely related to the Dutch in race, language, and culture, but they did not play a leading role in the political, economic, and cultural life of the Belgians. The Walloons, the French-speaking Belgians, dominated the life of the Belgian provinces. The Dutch and the Belgians showed little sympathy for each other and differed in economic interests as well as in religious outlook. King William's government did everything in its power to improve the welfare of the southern provinces but paid little or no attention to just grievances in the political and administrative field. The Belgians greatly outnumbered the Dutch, yet they had no more representatives in parliament than the Dutch and the number of Belgians in administrative posts was small. However, strict equality would have given control to the politically inexperienced Belgians. It was too much to expect that the Dutch, who had a long tradition of cultural and political independence, and who saw little advantage in the union, would accept Belgian predominance.

The discontent of the Belgians flared up in open revolt with the outbreak of the insurrection in France in 1830. King William I appealed to the four powers of the Congress of Vienna by whose aid and approval the Kingdom of the Netherlands had been created, but the powers did not come to his aid. Austria and Prussia feared a general war and were preoccupied with uprisings in Poland and revolutionary movements in Italy. Nicholas I of Russia showed some inclination to go to the aid of William, but he was too distant to be of any possible assistance. France naturally had no desire to see the barrier on her northern border continued, and threatened invasion if there was military intervention by any of the four powers. The Belgian revolution was a blow to British interests, but there was little Great Britain could do about it. The Belgians threatened to throw themselves into the arms of France rather than submit to any form of intervention. Short of the annexation of southern Netherlands to France, the British Government was prepared to yield almost anything in order to preserve the peace. A conference of Great Powers was speedily called to meet in London, which conference in effect intervened diplomatically on behalf of the Belgians. Long negotiations, however, were required to bring a settlement agreeable to all participants concerned. Pressure had to be exerted on Belgium and coercion against Holland at various stages of the negotiations. The outcome of it all was that the Netherlands was again reduced to very nearly its old boundaries. William I continued as Grand Duke of Luxemburg, which was somewhat reduced in size by cession of territories to Belgium.

Neutrality, 1839–1919.—The Netherlands as a strong buffer state was gone. As a substitute there was devised the "perpetual neutralization" of Belgium, guaranteed by the five Great Powers. For Dutch foreign policy of the future the neutralization of Belgium had great significance. The Netherlands could not have maintained its independence if Belgium had fallen under French control or influence, nor could the Dutch have followed the policy of making no commitments. After the separation the Netherlands steadily and more positively settled into the policy of a small power. It was not asked to help maintain the balance of power in Europe, and from the mechanism of European statecraft the Dutch people turned in aversion. During the next century the Dutch developed the small-power policy to a point little short of perfection.

The determination of the Dutch nation to play a passive role in world politics was so strong as to amount almost to an obsession. For any participation in what was regarded as power politics, no matter how minor the part, foreign ministers were quickly rebuked by the States-General and by public opinion. When, for example, Foreign Minister van der Maesen de Sombreff at the time of the Polish Rebellion in 1863 joined the Great Powers in sending individual notes to Russia expressing disapproval over the ruthless manner in which the rebellion was suppressed, he was bitterly attacked for this departure from the policy of isolation and was nearly unseated. When, a little later, the Foreign Minister accepted the invitation of Napoleon III to attend a congress on the Polish question, the budget for the Foreign Office was rejected, and Van der Maesen de Sombreff resigned.

In spite of its firm national resolve not to participate in international politics, and notwithstanding the meticulous care with which this policy was pursued, the Netherlands suddenly found itself in the center of world politics in the "Luxemburg Affair." The nation was shocked to learn that the actions of its sovereign and its foreign minister had nearly precipitated a general war in western Europe. Napoleon III, envious and afraid of the expansion of Prussia as the result of the Austro-Prussian War in 1866, demanded some compensation for France. He approached King William III as Grand Duke of Luxemburg, for the cession of Luxemburg to France in exchange for a monetary indemnity. Though small, the country would be of considerable strategic value to France. King William and his Foreign Minister, Count van Zuylen van Nyevelt, thought they had obtained the approval of Bismarck for the deal, but when the plan became known in Germany there followed an outburst of German national sentiment so strong that Bismarck could not have resisted, even if he had wanted to. In north Germany sentiment was for war, if that were necessary to prevent annexation. Great Britain now called a conference of the Great Powers as a way out of the impasse. The conference agreed upon the demilitarization and neutralization of Luxemburg as a solution of the problem. Though King William III and his government got out of a bad situation in a very fortunate manner, the Foreign Minister did not escape a parliamentary storm. The

States-General was critical of the treaty settling the Luxemburg crisis. It disliked the "collective guarantee" of the neutrality of Luxemburg embodied in the convention, fearing that it might involve the Netherlands in the politics of Europe. Although the Prime Minister claimed that his efforts in the crisis had saved the peace of Europe, the States-General expressed emphatic disapproval of his role in the affair by rejecting the Foreign Office budget a few months later.

Resolved as the Dutch were to adhere to a policy of independence and neutrality, they found this attitude challenged in the crisis of the Boer War. The Dutch had a lively, sentimental interest in the Boer republics. As descendants of Dutch colonists, the Boers were closely related to the Netherlanders, and the cultural and ecclesiastical kinship between the two peoples was strong. Many Dutchmen, and foremost among them the powerful popular leader, Abraham Kuyper, had taken a professional interest in the republics, and the Boer governments had drawn a relatively large number of Dutchmen into their administration and diplomatic service. Tension first became acute when it was known that the Boer republics had not been invited to the First Hague Peace Conference in 1899. The Dutch Government found itself in a very embarrassing position, for if it extended an invitation to the Boer republics to send representatives to the conference the British Government would not have participated in the conference and it would have been useless to proceed with plans for convening the international gathering which was to grapple with the problem of armaments. The Dutch Government was confronted with the decision either of being hosts to the conference or of refusing to have it held on its territory. Dutch national sentiment, however, was deeply offended, and a powerful opposition in the States-General, under the leadership of Kuyper, sought to force the ministry's hand. The entire Dutch press, regardless of party affiliation, was angry at the omission of the South African republics from the list of states invited to the conference and all were highly critical of Foreign Minister de Beaufort. The ministry came near falling on the issue. But the Kuyper Ministry, which came to power in August, 1901, found itself as impotent as its predecessor to help the Boers. By this time the cause of the

Boers had become practically hopeless. On January 25, 1902, the Dutch Government offered its good offices to the belligerents, and this act led indirectly to the peace negotiations which brought the Boer War to a close, but also brought an end to the independence of the Boer republics. The result of the episode was an antipathy toward Great Britain for a decade or more.

The adherence of the Netherlands to the North Sea Declaration in 1908 led to a series of events which were extremely disturbing to a small state determined on keeping out of the main current of world politics. In the Declaration all the states bordering on the North Sea declared they were firmly resolved "to preserve intact and reciprocally respect the sovereign rights" which their countries then enjoyed. The signatory states further agreed that if one of the parties should be of the opinion that the existing territorial *status quo* in the region were menaced they would consult one another on measures to be taken to maintain the *status quo* of their possessions. The purpose of the Declaration, the initiative for the negotiations of which came from Germany, was veiled in mystery and was the subject of much speculation. Some members of the States-General saw in it a departure from the traditional policy of strict neutrality, but Foreign Minister de Marees van Swinderen was able to allay such fears. However, a storm was raised in the Netherlands and abroad when a member of the First Chamber, Baron van Heeckeren van Kell, after having repeatedly urged the Foreign Minister to obtain from the German and the British governments a further statement that in event of war they would respect the territorial integrity of the Netherlands, declared that the reason for his insistence was the fact that years ago the German Emperor had made it known to the Dutch Government or to court circles that he would be compelled to occupy the Netherlands if the Dutch Government did not take the necessary measures to place the country in a proper state of defense against England.

The reason why the affair caused such an uproar was that at about the same time the Dutch Government announced plans for strengthening its coastal defenses. French and Belgian papers were very critical of the Dutch plans, especially because they gave priority to the fortification of Flushing, insinuating that the plans were the result of German pressure. It was contended that the purpose of strongly fortifying Flushing, which controls the mouth of the Scheldt, was to prevent a British fleet from going up the river to the aid of Antwerp should the Germans invade Belgium. The fact that the plan included no provision for strengthening the eastern defenses, which were said to be notoriously weak, caused suspicion and distrust. Foreign Minister van Swinderen vehemently denied that the coastal defense bill had been introduced under pressure from Germany. The proposed defenses were not directed against any power or group of powers. The Dutch Government, so Van Swinderen declared, "was determined to place the defenses of the Netherlands in such a state that their neutrality might be defended against all comers." Nevertheless, the coastal defense plans were greatly reduced in scope before they were approved by the States-General. In the meanwhile, Colijn, who had become Minister of War, prepared and guided through the States-General a bill for the reorganization and strengthening of the militia; this bill was given precedence over the Coastal Defense Bill, thus balancing the defense plans in order to provide equal protection against possible attack from the land or the sea.

The crowning achievement of the Dutch policy of independence was its success in keeping the country out of hostilities in the First World War. Although hostilities were threatened by Germany no less than three times, and although Dutch shipping suffered considerable losses—while the Allied blockade and German export control measures caused serious difficulties, if not acute distress—the country was spared the horrors of war. The good fortune of the Netherlands in keeping out of the war may be ascribed to a number of factors. The Netherlands had no minorities to disturb relations with its neighbors. Both belligerent groups had confidence in the sincerity of the Government's determination to remain neutral in the struggle, and in its foreign policy which was in strong and skillful hands.

However, these were not the determining factors. The Netherlands was able to stay out of the war for the reason that the Central Powers and the Allies both thought it was to their interest not to force

Holland into the war. Germany wished to keep Holland open as a channel through which to receive urgently needed imports from abroad, and Great Britain had no desire to see Germany occupy the Dutch coastline and be free to use Dutch ports and Antwerp as submarine bases.

The Hague as a peace laboratory.—Many Netherlanders were aware of the fact that their policy of neutrality, or of independence, as they preferred to call it, was largely passive. Toward the end of the century they began to see an active role in world politics for their country, as the center of peace movements and internationalism. In the Netherlands, so it was argued, the German, French, and Anglo-Saxon cultures met and this fact gave the Dutch the opportunity and the duty to serve as a mediator between the great western European peoples. It is interesting to note that Abbé de Saint Pierre in his plan for a "permanent and perpetual union" suggested either Utrecht or The Hague as the seat for his proposed world organization, on the ground that because the Dutch carried on a wider and more active commerce than any people on earth they had the greatest interest in preserving the peace.

Beginning in 1891 with the Conference for the Codification of International Private Law, The Hague became the seat of numerous international conferences, both official and unofficial. The conference of 1891, which met under the leadership of the great Dutch jurist, T. M. C. Asser, was followed by a series of conferences on the same subject. The Hague Peace Conferences followed in 1899 and in 1907 and a third was to have been held in 1915. If the war had not intervened, these periodic conferences might have developed into a strong permanent international organization. Out of The Hague Peace Conferences came the Permanent Court of Arbitration with its seat likewise at The Hague. After the First World War, The Hague was selected as the seat of the Permanent Court of International Justice, with its quarters in the Peace Palace which had been built out of funds granted by Andrew Carnegie. A Netherlander was the first president of the Court. The Hague became the seat of such unique institutions as The Hague Academy of International Law and the

International Intermediary Institute. Between the two wars numerous important international conferences were held there, such as the Conference for the Codification of International Law in 1929. Dutchmen played a leading role in these conferences, as they also did in those held elsewhere. That the Dutch attached much importance to the effort which came to be known among them as "the work of The Hague" can be seen from the statement by former Premier Pierson in the Second Chamber, that "because of this there develops among civilized peoples the view that there where the Court of Arbitration is established certainly is not the place to wage war." He expressed the conviction that the location of the Court of Arbitration at The Hague gave the Netherlands more security than would have been possible in a collective guarantee of her neutrality.

Relations with Belgium.—The Dutch people accepted the separation from Belgium without regret, and even with some relief, for it enabled them to live their own national life free from external complications. Nor did the Belgians harbor bitterness. Indeed, it was not long before there were movements for closer relations between the two countries. These movements generally came at periods of great political tension in western Europe. In the late 'sixties of the last century, when the relations between Germany and France were tense, Frère Orban, leader of the Belgian Liberal party, promoted a movement for a military alliance and a customs union between Holland and Belgium. Just after the turn of the century the desirability of closer military and economic relations between the two countries was again widely discussed. The Boer War had caused profound disquiet in Holland, and the growing tension between Great Britain and Germany and the development of the Franco-British Entente Cordiale caused grave concern in the two small countries. An unofficial Dutch-Belgian Commission, composed of leading members of the parliaments of the two countries, held a series of three meetings, but nothing came of its work.

The Belgians developed much greater enthusiasm for these movements than the Dutch. The latter feared that a Dutch-Belgian alliance would be regarded with suspicion in Germany as part of a movement of diplomatic and military encirclement. The Dutch also feared that the combined military strength of the two countries would not be enough to deter Germany should she decide to attack or to pass through Holland or Belgium; furthermore, they felt that the chances of the Netherlands staying out of war would be lessened in an alliance with Belgium, as Belgium was directly on the military highway between France and Germany. Too, many Netherlanders were confident that Germany would not want to draw the Netherlands into a war involving Great Britain, for so long as Holland remained neutral much needed grain from overseas could be imported through Dutch ports. Finally, many Netherlanders opposed a Dutch-Belgian alliance because they feared it might draw their country into the French diplomatic and military orbit, and thus into the full current of world politics.

The Netherlands was able to stay out of the First World War whereas Belgium suffered the cruel ravages of invasion and the torture of four long years of German occupation. In spite of Dutch hospitality extended to thousands of Belgian refugees these diverse experiences tended to alienate the two peoples. The fact that among these refugees there were some Flemish activists did not improve relations. Moreover, as a result of her war experiences Belgium's relations with France had become very close. Relations between the two small countries reached their lowest point at the close of the war, when the Belgian Government expressed a desire for the rectification of Belgium's frontiers with Holland in order that her economic and military position might be strengthened. The Belgian Government contended that the configuration of Belgium's territory was very unfavorable and should be modified now that Belgium was to be freed from all limitations upon her sovereignty. Though the Belgian representatives did not demand the annexation of Dutch Limburg and Dutch Flanders, they suggested this as a possible solution, with compensation to the Netherlands from German territory on the Dutch border. The Peace Conference, although recognizing in general the justice of the Belgian demand for a revision of the Treaty of 1839, rejected this solution. It referred the problem of the revision of the treaty to direct negotiation between the two countries, but stipulated that the revision should involve neither the cession of territory nor the creation of servitudes.

A treaty acceptable to both parties was nearly completed when the issue of the sovereignty of the Wielingen Channel was at the last moment injected into the negotiations. Agreement on this issue could not be secured and it was not until 1925 that negotiations were resumed. Representatives of the two countries succeeded in reaching an agreement, but unfortunately the treaty was rejected by the First Chamber of the Dutch Parliament in April, 1927. The chief issue on which the treaty fell was a provision which would have granted Belgium the right to construct a large waterway along a direct route between Antwerp and the Hollandsch Diep near Moerdyke. Many Netherlanders, especially the people living in and near Rotterdam, feared that this grant would give Antwerp an unfair advantage over Rotterdam in the competition for the transit traffic with the German industrial hinterland.

For some years after the rejection of the treaty, relations between the two countries were somewhat less than cordial. However, the two governments finally resumed negotiations and although a general settlement on the complex issues between them was never reached, a number of issues were satisfactorily solved, one at a time. In spite of certain differences the two countries have so much in common and have so many similar interests that closer relations between them are as inevitable as they are desirable. In a noteworthy little speech to a Dutch delegation King Albert once described the fundamental nature of these relations as follows: "Inheritors of the glory of the ancient Low Countries, equally rich in artistic treasures, Holland and Belgium are united by intellectual and economic ties which date from the early times of their history and will operate to bind them closer in the future. The public and the private life of the two peoples is founded on a love of liberty, zealous labor and commercial honesty. The geographic situation of the two states makes them, so to speak, solidary, and it is difficult to see how one of them could keep its freedom, if the other were enslaved. My compatriots fully understand this community of interests, created by nature, and their ardent desire is to see the Kingdom of the Netherlands develop daily in power and prosperity."

In the decade preceding the German invasion great progress was made in developing closer relations. In 1932 the two countries entered into an agreement—the Ouchy Agreement—to extend progressive tariff reductions to each other's products. A new orientation in Belgian foreign policy at this time made closer relations with Holland possible. There were several causes for this change, but not the least among them was the growing influence of the Flemings in Belgian political life. After Hitler's re-occupation of the Rhine, the Belgian Government announced the termination of the Franco-Belgian military alliance and the adoption of a policy of neutrality and independent action. King Leopold, announcing the shift of policy, in his speech of October 14, 1936, made to those who doubted the possibility of such a foreign policy, pointed out "the steadfast and resolute example of Holland and Switzerland."

The annulment of the Franco-Belgian alliance removed the last serious barrier to closer relations between the two states. Belgium now began to take a more active part in the Oslo States Movement, in which Holland was a moving spirit, and the Dutch and Belgian royal families were on friendlier terms than ever before in the history of the two states. Although the two countries did not form a military alliance they did unite in a diplomatic front. On November 7, 1939, Queen Wilhelmina and King Leopold made a joint offer of their "good offices" to bring the war to an end. In December of that year, when it was feared that Germany would attack Holland and not Belgium and thus seek to cut the Netherlands off from the aid of the Franco-British armies in northern France, Foreign Minister Spaak of Belgium reaffirmed the solidarity of interests of the two countries and declared that it would be "madness" to suppose that an attack on Holland "would leave us indifferent."

The Netherlands and the League of Nations.—The idea of an international organization for the maintenance of peace was not new in the Netherlands in 1919. Van Vollenhoven and the others had for years carried on an active advocacy for plans of this nature. Interest in the general idea of a world-peace organization mounted as the war slowly moved to its final stage. The Netherlands Government entered the League of Nations without hesitation, yet for years it was chided by many sections of the public and by many members of the States-General for not being enthusiastic enough in its participation in the League activities and for being too cautious in its League policies. Some Netherlanders saw in the League membership a departure from the traditional policy of neutrality and independence, but Foreign Minister van Karnebeek insisted that it did not involve a change in Dutch foreign policy but merely a shift in emphasis. The Netherlands had always been willing to coöperate in the interests of peace and international welfare but had been opposed to entering one-sided political agreements and military alliances. Membership in the League of Nations did not violate the latter principle.

In the early days the Netherlands delegations to the League Assemblies expressed some fear of the provisions regarding sanctions in the Covenant and joined other small states in insisting upon interpretations which would make the obligations less automatic. However, as time progressed this attitude changed somewhat and the Netherlands Government took a leading part in demanding sanctions against Italy in the Ethiopian affair and vigorously supporting the application of sanctions against her. The Dutch delegation consistently opposed the enlargement of the Council, on the ground that the changes were not made in the interests of the League as an institution but to meet ambitious claims of particular states. During the two years of its membership on the League Council (1926–1928) Netherlands representation stressed the importance of the preventive character of Article 2 rather than the repressive character of Article 15.

With the failure of sanctions against Italy the Netherlands joined the former northern neutral states in a precipitate flight from the League. The League had proved itself powerless to protect a weak state from wanton aggression and the situation had become extremely dangerous for small states, and especially those situated near or between the Great Powers. On July 1, 1936, the former neutrals issued a public declaration at Geneva that so long as the Covenant as a whole was applied only incompletely and inconsistently they no longer felt bound by the coercive provisions of Article 16 of the Covenant. Foreign Minister Patyn declared in 1938 that the situation had changed so greatly that it was no longer a matter of supporting the international community in taking action as a whole against an aggressor but of taking sides in the quarrels of the Great Powers which the Netherlands had no desire to do. If the world was going to return to the policy of the balance of power, the Netherlands would resume its former policy of independence and neutrality. The Dutch Government now advocated making the Covenant more flexible through interpretive resolutions, thereby hoping to induce the return of the Great Powers which had withdrawn from the League.

Germany, after the outbreak of the war, sought by a press campaign to frighten the Netherlands into breaking with the League. The German press declared that neutrals attending League meetings were guilty of unneutral acts, because the League had become an "Anglo-French organ," but the Dutch refused to heed such an accusation. When the Dutch National Socialists in the States-General reverberated these accusations, Foreign Minister van Kleffens in a speech on January 25, replied that the Netherlands would not resign membership in the League of Nations until all hope of realizing the League's noble ends was gone; that it would not lightly contribute to the wrecking of an institution which it had welcomed as a magnificent attempt to achieve that organization of the community of states which alone offered mankind hope of achieving peaceful international coöperation.

The active participation of the Netherlands in the varied activities of the League of Nations is evident from the number of leading positions in the organization which its representatives and its nationals filled. Van Karnebeek was honored by being selected as the president of the Second Assembly, and Loder as the first president of the Permanent Court of International Justice. Lorentz, the great physicist and collaborator of Einstein, served as the second chairman of the

Committee for Intellectual Coöperation. Van Rees and Van Asbeck were for many years members of the Mandates Commission, the former serving as vice-chairman until his death. Van Eyzinga presided over the Conference of Jurists, which examined reservations of the United States to its proposed adhesion to the Permanent Court, and later he was elected a justice of the court. Colijn was a leading figure at the Economic Conference and was chairman of one of its commissions. Van Pelt headed the Information Section, and Sevensma was at the head of the League's magnificent library. Numerous other Dutchmen, such as Nolens, Van Hamel, Zimmerman, Rutgers, Loudon, and Limburg held important League posts.

Final failure of neutrality.—With the failure of collective security the Netherlands fell back on its traditional policy of neutrality. If Britain and France had given decisive leadership in the early 'thirties to the building of a European system of mutual aid, Holland probably might have followed a different policy, but it is doubtful. The Dutch had no illusions about Nazi Germany's intentions, but it was natural in view of Holland's good fortune in staying out of European wars for a century to hope that the miracle could happen again. The developments in warfare and the ideological character of the gigantic struggle, however, made it extremely unlikely. After the German reoccupation of the Rhineland there was little else that the Dutch could do. It was too late to adopt another policy. After that date any move in the direction of a political or military alliance with France and Great Britain would have been the signal for a speedy invasion of their country. Nor did the Dutch feel that an alliance would add anything to their security. In the event of an attack, they were certain of French and British aid, which in all probability would not have been adequate.

The Netherlands refused to be drawn into the German net in any fashion. The Dutch Government rejected Hitler's offer of a guarantee of Netherlands' territorial integrity. When a little later Hitler sought to induce the Netherlands to conclude a nonaggression pact, the foreign minister curtly let it be known that Holland considered its inviolability to be axiomatic and that it could not be the subject of any treaty. In spite of repeated, solemn assurances by Germany that she would respect the integrity of the Netherlands, Ribbentrop on the morning of May 10th, when the attack on the Low Countries had already begun, summoned the Belgian, Dutch, and Luxemburg ministers to read to them statements advising them of Germany's determination to safeguard the neutrality of their countries "by military measures." This announcement, in the typical, cynical Nazi style, brought to a tragic end a century of successful Dutch diplomacy. Neutrality was no longer possible in the world of 1940.

The Dutch face a complete re-orientation of their foreign policy. They have shown by their work in the League of Nations, and outside it, that they are equal to this stupendous task. In the midst of the war the Dutch Government is giving leadership in laying the solid foundations for an international order in which states small and large shall enjoy security and be free to live their own national lives.

Part Four

Economic and Social Development

CHAPTER IX

The Growth of Netherlands Economy

BY HENDRIK RIEMENS

ONE OF THE STRONGEST elements of Netherlands commerce and shipping, with its spectacular and turbulent history, has been the location of the country at the mouth of the Rhine and the junction of several smaller rivers leading into the interior of western Europe, exactly opposite the southern and most highly developed part of Great Britain. The Rhine was important even before the days of the Roman invasion, and the Romans added to this importance by founding two of their outposts on the main arm of the lower Rhine, the sites of the modern towns of Utrecht and Leyden. These towns were certainly more than mere military outposts, for even at that period a great deal of trading was carried on with England. There is also Nijmegen, which was in existence then, the first town to be built on the main branch of the Rhine delta after the river reaches the Lowlands.

The last centuries of the Roman Empire cast a dark shadow upon the Netherlands history. Yet, even under its domination, several new communities, like Tiel and Dorestad on the arms of the lower Rhine, came into existence as trading centers. These towns flourished especially during the Merovingian period, in fact, until the Viking invasions abruptly ended their prosperity. On the banks of the Meuse, Maastricht became a center of the overland trade from Cologne to Quentavic, on the Channel coast near Boulogne—another link in the active exchange of merchandise with Britain.

Charlemagne restored some importance to Nijmegen by choosing it as one of the temporary residences of his traveling court. Although in the century following, sea trade disappeared from the countries along the Mediterranean, a fact which the distinguished Belgian historian Pirenne attributed to the spread of Islam, there is no reason to believe that shipping or commerce vanished from the Low Countries which were so far from the Mediterranean. Indeed, Frisian cloth was then already well known in many countries other than Britain. And the continued arrival of Christian missionaries from the British Isles to the remotest parts of Holland indicates the maintenance of contact by way of the sea.

By the year 1000 an extraordinary development was in process in the Netherlands, particularly in Flanders—the birth of the modern towns—admirably described by Pirenne. Starting merely as military or ecclesiastical centers, conducting occasional trade, these half-rural communities attracted a concentration of industry and commerce which, in turn, transformed them into townships; soon they were larger and more numerous than in any other part of Europe north of the Alps. And in their growth lay the seed of a great social change, because they were comparatively rich and strong, and their citizens were imbued with a sturdy independence which made them ever more resistant to the control of the local aristocracy.

The struggle for freedom is never easy. In the Netherlands it was fought with the utmost tenacity, greatly aided by the existence of the new towns. For, even though the landed gentry apparently had assured revenues from its rural property, in reality those incomes were slowly declining. On the contrary, with the growth of the towns and the rise in prices, the profits of the town merchants and, therefore, their power, were steadily increasing. Both the King of France and the German Emperor would have liked very much to extend their influence over the thriving Low Countries towns, but the distance was too great for easy conquest, and each ruler was having difficulty in maintaining his own power. This state of impasse enormously pleased the King of England, since he naturally preferred to see the mouth of the Rhine free of any powerful monarch; in fact, sometimes he even defended the Flemish towns from attack. Later, when the Netherlands had become the Dutch Republic and was struggling for independence from Spain, Queen Elizabeth proceeded along the same course.

The two leading cities of Flanders—Bruges and Ghent—came into their flowering late in the Middle Ages. The woolen industry, for which the two cities were famous, bought raw wool in England, wove it on Dutch looms and sold the product back to England. The northern part of the Low Countries profited from the thriving fisheries where herring was prepared for shipment to the Baltic countries, to England, and to France. In the course of their evolution, the southern towns became meeting places for traders of many countries. The northern seaport towns had less trade, but had their own shipping.

Commercial prosperity and enterprise, however, were not the only foundations on which the development of the Low Countries rested. The spirit of independence and of democratic city government, and, generally speaking, the vitality of a civilization based on relative freedom, as well as on trade and cultural exchange overseas, have all been tremendously important. As early as 1400, a century before the Catholic Church had been challenged, an architecture and a whole civilization sprang up in Flanders, eloquent of the *tiers état*—over which neither the nobility nor the clergy held domination. This is all the more remarkable because in France the bourgeoisie attained only by the revolution of 1789 the freedom that the burghers, or *poorters,* of the Low Countries had enjoyed for several centuries. In Germany some form of serfdom had existed until 1848.

The new political and cultural ideas current in the rest of the world reached the Dutch seaports more quickly than the landlocked towns of the continental interior. This contact with the outer world accounts, in part, for the profound differences in outlook and in behavior between the Netherlanders and the citizens of neighboring countries. And their independence, born of long freedom from oppressive overlords, stirred the Dutch to indignant revolt when the dukes of Burgundy were followed by Charles V with his program of a strongly centralized government. The empire of Charles V, comprising Spain and the new colonies, the Low Countries and Germany, was the mightiest that Europe had known since the fall of Rome. It was not surprising, therefore, that when an uprising in Ghent was quelled by the powerful government machinery no further attempts were made to throw off the reign of Charles V in the Netherlands. The Dutch spirit was not dead; it was merely quiescent. Then Philip II of Spain succeeded his father and, from the seat of government in Madrid, imposed an even sterner rule on the Netherlands. The causes for revolt multiplied. Rebellion flamed in many hearts, but only a small minority, the persecuted Calvinists, were the most actively militant.

Bruges was no longer accessible to seagoing vessels and like Ghent had lost most of its prosperity. Antwerp was now the most thriving metropolis and, throughout the fifteenth and sixteenth centuries Amsterdam in the north had steadily grown as a shipping and trading center. Even so, the western part of northern Netherlands, called "Holland," did not rival the economic might of Flanders and Brabant, although its sea captains and traders were able to secure a growing part of the northwest European commerce for themselves. The woolen industry of Leyden had begun to compete with that of Ghent and of Ypres, and in Zeeland, the province lying between Flanders and Holland, Veere and Middelburg took a share in the trade of the Scottish mart. Then Dordrecht and Rotterdam, situated near the mouth of the Rhine, and the towns on and near the IJssel in Overijssel and Gelderland enjoyed varying degrees of importance. The duchy of Gelderland, to the east of the sea provinces, had rather close ties with the German Empire, and its towns of Kampen, Zwolle, Deventer, and Zutphen, which were members of the Hanseatic League, were important in trade toward the close of the Middle Ages.

During the Renaissance, the rich merchant colonies of the Genoese, Venetians, and Lombards in different Flemish towns were instrumental in disseminating new, progressive ideas in the world, in the same way that ideas were interchanged in shipping relations between France, England, and the Baltic states and Holland and Zeeland. The rigid pattern of medieval life was too limited for modern demands of commerce; guilds or corporations, with their restrictive protection of local industries, were inadequate to supply foreign markets on competitive terms. The laws of the Church, which forbade the payment of interest on loans, hindered both the money lenders and the enterprising merchants who needed additional capital. Medieval restrictions were felt still more keenly when the Spanish Inquisition began to enforce them. This was at a time when scientific discoveries and progress in art were making great advances everywhere and when the study of the Bible had led both Luther and Calvin to denounce many of the traditional dogmas.

Another factor contributed to the unsettled mental condition of the Netherlanders during this period. It was the imposition of new, high taxes to support the troops who maintained the alien rule which had supplanted the local freedoms so dear to the people. Heretofore, when a count of any province had needed to raise new revenue he had had to submit his proposal to the councils in a form called *beden* or, literally, prayers. Thus the burghers effectively had kept control of their counties.

In 1572, the flame of revolt actually burst in several towns of the northern Netherlands. William of Orange began the long struggle for independence which, in its bloody course, highlighted the inherent characteristics of the Dutch nation. When the definite separation of the northern and southern provinces became inevitable, the south remained under Spanish rule and swung back to the exclusive domination of the Catholic Church. After a period of nearly complete success for the insurgents, the Spanish armies took Brussels, Bruges, Ghent, and finally Antwerp (1585). As the Republicans firmly held Zeeland, they could and did stop all sea trade with Antwerp, and the greatest trading center of the times became a dead city. Now the northern ports, particularly Amsterdam, succeeded Antwerp. Many thousands of Protestant refugees, streaming into the country from southern Netherlands and also from France, contributed toward the building of the young Republic.

During the entire conflict, economic warfare against Spain worked toward the eventual success of the rebels. The seafarers of the northern provinces were excellent fighters as well as sailors, and were not afraid to attack the Spaniards in their home waters, in South America and, later, in the Indies.

In 1602, Oldenbarneveldt, Grand Pensionary of the States of Holland, a title comparable with that of secretary of state in this country, brought about in the United East India Company a merger of all merchants then trading in the Indian Ocean. This group is highly interesting from the economic-historic point of view because it was the first great joint stock company. Every year it sent out huge fleets of merchant ships and soon extended its coastal establishments to the Malay Archipelago, to Burma, India, Malaya, Formosa, Mauritius, and to South Africa. The Company maintained exclusive trade relations with the Japanese through a "factory" at Nagasaki, and, through royal decrees secured from the Shah of Persia and the Sultan of Turkey, opened trade routes to Persia and Arabia. After the defeat of the Portuguese, the United East India Company tried to rid itself of English competition, because the British were then poorly organized and meagerly provided with both capital and ships.

It is now difficult to realize that at that time Britain was largely dependent on Netherlands shipping for even its own trade. Ships flying the Dutch flag dominated Baltic waters. The Hollanders traded wines from France against wheat from Poland, and through the East India Company held a monopoly on the spice trade in Europe. Also in the inter-Asiatic trade they were important carriers, taking copper from Japan to India and cotton goods from India to the Malay Archipelago, trading spices from the Moluccas for Persian silk, and shipping deerskins from Formosa and Cambodia to Japan. And the largest profits came not from the glorified spice trade, but from this general exchange of Asiatic goods.

The East India Company was a source of great wealth. During the one hundred and ninety-three years of its life, it paid out over 186,000,000 guilders in dividends, or twenty-eight times its capital. Colenbrander, one of the leading Dutch colonial historians, estimates moreover that three times that amount was taken home as savings by retired employees. Some five thousand men a year sailed from Holland on East India ships, and all provisions for the voyages were bought at home. The vast fleet necessitated, too, the maintenance of large shipyards. Still, the European trade of the Republic must have been even more important, because the East Indian trade paid in only a twelfth of the total Dutch import and convoy duties during the seventeenth century. This astute trading system was emulated by other countries.

In the Netherlands, a monopoly on trade with the West Indies and the Americas was given to the West India Company, chartered in 1621, but the dividends of the new trading group could not compare with those of the older company. The West India organization, taking over the New Netherlands from an earlier company, founded New Amsterdam on Manhattan Island, and obtained through exploration a foothold on the northeastern shore of Brazil in the rich sugar district of Pernambuco. The company's men, however, spent a great part of their time raiding Spanish vessels trading between Colón, Havana, and Seville. But this was, of course, an unstable source of profits and it disappeared in 1648 on the making of peace with Spain. At that time the West India Company had a great number of bases along the African coast, most of them conquered from the Portuguese, which gave the Dutch control of the lucrative slave trade. In fact, Holland had commercial colonies almost everywhere, although she lacked vast overseas territories such as Spain possessed.

A curious banking institution, the *Amsterdamsche Wisselbank* (1609), was instrumental in promoting trade organization. Merchants of every western nation kept accounts there, and in paying with "bank guilders," or drafts, on the *Wisselbank,* eliminated the previous discrepancy between the numberless coins, of varied weight and composition, then in use.

The scope of the Netherlands trade of those days may be inferred from the source material recently published by J. G. van Dillen. It may be learned, for instance, that modern principles of accounting were in general use in Holland. Simon Stevin, the mathematician, even applied them to state finance which, in other countries, included the income and expenses of the royal household. The comparative economic stability of the Republic of Holland made it possible for the Government to raise loans whenever money was needed for war. Not until 1700 was England in a comparable position. Also, cumulative profits from the wide network of Dutch trade increased state economic stability and made of Amsterdam the leading financial center of the world; Amsterdam remained in this position during the greater part of the eighteenth century, at which time the general trade connections of the country as a whole had lessened in importance.

Dutch commerce did fall off then, although to set a date for the actual beginning of its decline would be difficult. Its decline was preceded by a lowering of the high artistic and scientific standards of the country. To a certain degree, also, it resulted from the Anglo-Dutch wars waged during a short period of twenty years, which culminated in the third war, that of 1672. In this conflict the powerful British fleet, in combination with the still more formidable French armies of Louis XIV, failed to destroy the Republic. But the fleet of ships built by England to end her dependence on Dutch carriers remained active on the seas after the war and were responsible for cutting down the volume of Dutch trade. Then there were the protective measures of Colbert in France and of Cromwell in England, measures to exclude Hollanders from any trade in goods produced in the two countries.

Both England and France increasingly outstripped Holland in overseas trade in the eighteenth century. The British colonies in America, with their rapidly growing population and trade were no longer separated from one another by the New Netherlands, which the British had seized. The rivalries between France and England in India and in Canada had ceased to offer openings for Netherlands enterprise and trade; in fact, the Dutch had few footholds in India and none in North America. When the American colonies rebelled against the British, the Dutch profited for only a limited time. Dutch-American trade in arms and tobacco, shipped by way of the *Gold Rock* of St. Eustatius in the Dutch West Indies, proved to be political dynamite. When, in 1780, England declared war on Holland once again, the Dutch no longer had any fleet with which to challenge English might; indeed, they did not have even an army large enough to coöperate effectively with their French and American allies. The British overran many Dutch settlements in both the East Indies and the West Indies and inflicted serious damage. Actually, the Republic was the only loser on the allied side, because the French obtained some small gains and America won its independence.

Infinitely worse for Holland were the economic consequences of the French Revolution. The country was invaded by French troops and suffered in a protracted war of blockade with England. It lost all its overseas colonies. No foreign ships entered the harbors of Rotterdam or Amsterdam. Rotterdam, with a population of 200,000, was still the second largest city of western Europe, but one-half the inhabitants were on relief. In 1650 Amsterdam had about the same population as Rotterdam, which was for that period a huge figure; then, for the next two centuries the city did not grow at all.

Although the Netherlands regained its independence in 1815, it did not enter what may be called the "modern" era until much later. In 1815 many new developments were perceptible in both England and France, particularly changes in industry and trade resulting from the industrial revolution. But in the Low Countries the repercussions of this industrialization were felt only in the southern provinces which were united with the northern part by the Congress of Vienna. Although William I, son of the last stadholder of Holland and the first king of the United Netherlands, had many progressive ambitions for his country, the north responded slowly. The Netherlands Trading Company, organized in 1824, could assemble sufficient capital only when the King had guaranteed their payment of a certain minimum of dividends each year. Yet both of the old companies had ended in failure, and it was absolutely necessary that some large commercial organization help to reconstruct what was left of the overseas empire. The new company was formed to work with the Government in developing the Indies, in exporting colonial products, and in importing cotton goods.

These cotton goods came from the industrially awakened south, where the *Société Générale,* a banking institution established by William I, inaugurated not only in the Netherlands, but also in the world, the practice of giving industrial credits. When Belgium separated from the rest of the Low Countries, the Netherlands Trading Company looked for cotton manufacturers in northern Netherlands, but found none. All that the north had salvaged from its prosperous past were certain shipyards, pottery and porcelain works, and the old hand looms, relics from the seventeenth century, still used in the rural sections of Brabant and Overijssel.

The weaving industry was the first to be revived and modernized, but although some of the former shipping trade returned to the Dutch ports, few other progressive achievements were apparent. The spirit of enterprise seemed to have died. At this time Europe was going through an interesting evolution in both politics and economics. The staggering public debt, inflicted on Holland by the Napoleonic occupation, hampered the Dutch Government and brought about in Java the unfortunate Culture System, or government exploitation for profit.

The change was gradual, but it did come. Through Thorbecke, the liberal movement in England and France began to infiltrate the consciousness of the Hollanders. Schools were modernized. The harbors of Amsterdam and Rotterdam benefited from extensive improvements. About this time the Suez Canal was opened and numerous steamship companies for East Indian trade were organized. Liberal legislation replaced the culture system with private enterprise, with government protection of the rights of the Indonesian population (1870). The sugar industry developed substantially in Java, and in Sumatra newly cultivated areas such as Deli brought to the market new crops—for instance, the famous Deli Sumatra tobacco.

To continental Holland, also, new prosperity came through the markets in the young industrial districts of the Midlands and the Tyne in England, the Ruhr and the Rhine in Germany. Once more the country enjoyed a brisk transit trade, based on the waterway of the Rhine.

But more important than any single manifestation of progress was the new spirit of energy which followed the long period of depression and indifference. The liberal movement found a parallel in the early socialism of the 'nineties. This slow evolution was nonetheless re-markable because Holland, which had looked backward for so long, was gradually turning its face to the future. The Hollanders became intensely aware of both material and intellectual developments in other countries. After the Civil War, Amsterdam loaned money to the southern American states for reconstruction. Capital accumulated once more, and was placed in the Indies, in Russia, in central Europe, and particularly in the expanding United States.

The industries of the Netherlands were the last elements in the country to regain their former eminence, although the merchant marine, which participated in the growing volume of world trade, regained some of its old ground. This was partly the result of the prin-ciple of free trade, maintained for almost a century. Meanwhile agri-culture was almost entirely coördinated with world trade. Because the Dutch wheat farmers could not compete with the vast new crops of the middle western United States and of Canada, they turned instead to dairy farming for export, and developed specialties in horticulture, such as shrubs and flower bulbs.

On the whole, the Netherlands seemed to have established itself well in the pattern of prosperous western Europe. If there was none of the old commercial glory for Dutch citizens, there were at least good general living conditions which, moreover, improved rapidly. Holland successfully stayed out of the First World War, but had to adapt itself as far as possible to the menacing political instability which followed. Dutch export industries, still principally cotton, but including also machinery for overseas colonies, suffered drastically from Japanese competition. Then there were the imperial preferences and the fall of the pound in Britain. Too, unlimited German competi-tion threatened to ruin the home industries which had been injured considerably by a lack of trade barriers, and Germany's new policy of self-sufficiency in food deprived Dutch farmers of their Rhineland markets. This policy, by the way, helped the Germans to prepare for their next war of conquest.

Immense housing projects and other public works, such as the reclamation of the Zuiderzee, brought only partial relief from increasing unemployment. The higher standard of living established on the basis of prewar prosperity made competition abroad difficult. The subsequent currency devaluations in France, Belgium, England, northern Europe, and finally in the United States, made competition almost impossible. Like the other western nations, the Netherlands committed the costly error of contributing to the reconstruction of Germany with loans, and Germany, while defaulting on all its foreign obligations, gave credit terms to foreign countries with which no private industrialist, Dutch or otherwise, could compete. And the political uncertainty Germany caused in the rest of Europe was the most destructive factor of all.

Nevertheless certain new industries built up the reputation of Dutch products—rayons, for example, and the manufacture of radios and electrical appliances, and the chemical and fertilizer industries. Holland was at a disadvantage in heavy industry because it lacked all the minerals except coal. The Limburg coal mines, however, under excellent government management, were developed extensively during the First World War and steel and iron works were created and subsidized at IJmuiden, on the North Sea coast.

Prosperity did return to the country, but never at the prewar level, and from 1929 on, depression made itself felt heavily in the land. For one thing, the considerable total of investments in American interests, which represented the savings of many small investors, made the Amsterdam stock exchange very sensitive to events in Wall Street. And the low prices for agricultural commodities which prevailed before the depression had diminished the resources of many corporations with plantations in the Indies, even though their war profits in the colonies had been great. These causes had put almost every Netherlands enterprise, industrial or agricultural, on a basis where losses exceeded profits.

The Dutch Government had no choice but to return to the principle of protecting the home market, particularly after the conspicuous failure of the London Economic Conference of 1933. The president of the Conference, the well-known Netherlands statesman Hendrik Colijn, appealed in vain for a "return to normalcy." And indeed normalcy, meaning sound public finance and stable currency, was maintained in Holland even when higher import duties and quotas were introduced. It was even maintained too long and too well, because unemployment kept some four hundred thousand Dutch workers idle, and that is a tremendous figure in a total population of eight or nine million. Finally in 1936 the Government dropped the old gold parity of the guilder and moderately devalued it some 22 per cent. The very next year saw a revival of export trade and of business in general.

Holland in 1938 came under the long shadow of imminent war. Government orders for armaments alleviated a great deal of the unemployment and probably this course should have been followed much sooner. When the war broke out in September, 1939, the naval construction program was far from completed. During the courageous defense of the Indies in the early part of 1942, ships were sorely needed and their lack is a bitterly ironic reminder of the wasted manpower of the unemployed shipyard workers in depression times.

In spite of the great difficulties of the past decade, when the Germans assaulted the country on May 10, 1940, they found in Holland a house as well ordered and stocked as that of any painting by Vermeer of Delft. The destruction and looting and the grief brought to every Dutch heart will not be wasted. During this time of trial the true spirit of the Netherlanders has shown itself proudly. When the Dutch are free again, at the end of this unequal struggle which they undertook without hesitation, they will prove their right to honor at home, in the Indies, and abroad.

CHAPTER X

Holland's Role in World Trade

BY J. ANTON DE HAAS

To TELL THE STORY of Dutch commerce is to tell the story of world trade. The opening of new commercial opportunities, the effect of industrialization upon the struggle for raw material resources, the commercial and industrial battle between the established industries of Britain and the awakening of industry on the continent of Europe—all were reflected in the economic life of this little country. And Holland played an active part in the continental drama of economic development and governmental policies.

The population, the most complex of Europe, has always been a restless one, a population of adventure. After the Netherlands had thrown off the Spanish yoke, the land became an asylum for the oppressed and persecuted. Artists, philosophers, scientists, the forward-looking men from every country of Europe established themselves in that haven of freedom. And all blended into a unified population with racial characteristics which differentiated sharply even from those of their nearest neighbors.

It would have been a miracle if such a group had been satisfied to remain within the narrow confines of a country approximately 13,000 square miles in size—one and one-half times the size of the state of Massachusetts. Until this day the inhabitants have waged a relentless battle against water; but they have learned to control water and to make it serve their economic life. They turned an enemy into a servant. And their fishermen at an early date learned a lesson that some continentally minded people have not yet fully learned, that oceans and rivers are not barriers but are highways. Where there was water, ships could sail. To them who had always lived surrounded by water, oceans held no terror.

Thus they became navigators, explorers, and the carriers of products for all Europe. Their red, white, and blue flag was seen on every ocean of the world, and there were some towns in the Netherlands where the inhabitants owned a greater number of ships than houses.

The Portuguese especially sought to procure the services of the skilled navigators of the Low Countries. They had developed a lucrative commerce with the Far East where they bargained for the products formerly brought by the Arabian traders into the Mediterranean across the narrow strip of sand which today is cut by the Suez Canal. But they had been unable to obtain the necessary crews for their ships. As a consequence, many Netherlanders settled in Lisbon as merchants and even intermarried with the Portuguese.

When the Eighty-Years' War with Spain had placed the Netherlands outside the family of Catholic nations, however, the relationship changed somewhat, although it did not greatly affect trade. The violently Protestant Netherlanders, when in Portuguese waters, kept their opinions to themselves. And seldom indeed did the Portuguese authorities interfere with the trade of the heretics, nor did the war destroy the trade with Spain. Both southern countries needed the products which could be imported from the north—the grain, the salted fish, and the lumber. And they could not afford to close the most important avenue for the distribution of Dutch colonial products, nor of the wine, salt, and olive oil of their own lands. Trade continued in the early years of the conflict. But before long the war in the north was intensified and when, in 1585, the plans of Philip II to build an armada to attack both England and the Low Countries became known, the States-General followed the leadership of Queen Elizabeth and forbade any further trade relations with the enemy.

The destruction of the Spanish Armada destroyed the prestige and power of the merchant fleets of Spain and of Portugal. The opportunity had come for the Hollanders to put into practice the lessons in distant navigation learned from the Portuguese and in 1595, the first trip around the Cape of Good Hope to the far Indies was undertaken. Of the four ships only three returned in 1597; and only 89 men survived of the original crew of 284. Commercially the trip was a failure, but the mere fact that an independent voyage had been accomplished fired the imagination, and in the following year the race for the Indies started. Individuals organized companies to trade with India and many of the cities built municipally owned ships. In 1598, eight ships left for the Far East; these soon were to be followed by other fleets. This competition proved unprofitable and the constant danger of attack by the Portuguese who tenaciously defended their erstwhile monopoly on the trade made coöperation inevitable.

Thus in 1602, was created the United East India Company (*Vereenigde Oost Indische Compagnie*). This company continued to exist until the British, under the pretext that Holland was about to join the league of neutrals favoring America, attacked its possessions and destroyed a substantial part of the empire it had built. But during the period of its existence the Company brought great wealth to the mother country. Its captains drove the Portuguese out of the Far Eastern lands, and acquired the islands which later became the Netherlands East Indies. These islands alone covered a territory of 800,000 square miles, or more than sixty times the area of the mother country. The Company captains established trading posts at Ceylon and on the coast of Bengal, and founded an agricultural colony on the Cape of Good Hope. They landed on the Australian coast in 1606 and called the continent "New Holland." They made repeated voyages to this continent of the south and continued to explore and to survey the coast. In 1633 Abel Tasman discovered Tasmania, and sailed along the south coast in 1642. But the resources of the Company were limited, and the new continent did not offer the inducements for trade that were to be found in the tropical islands under the equator.

On the contrary, Japan and the coast of China offered more attractive opportunities. As early as 1609, one of the Company's vessels reached Japan. It was from the Dutch that the Japanese first learned the science of cartography and became acquainted with Western medical science.

In the light of recent events, it is interesting to note that the first Netherlander to visit Japan was a gunner named Dirk Gerritsen. He reached Japan on board a Portuguese ship and spent seven years in that country before returning home. It was his account of the wealth of that unknown land which inspired the expedition to Japan by ships of the United East India Company.

In 1609, the Dutch were allowed to open a trading post or "factory" in Hirado, and the most important articles of importation were guns and ammunition. The Hollanders also established a factory for the manufacture of guns in Hirado. Trade relations with Japan were maintained even after the closing of the country in 1638, for under the decree of that year (Sakohu) exempting the Chinese and the Dutch, the Dutch remained the sole representatives of European commerce and culture in Japan. This is all the more remarkable because these representatives of the West were merchants, a class held in deep contempt by the Japanese, for as the Japanese ruler stated in 1623, "Merchants are fond of gain and given up to greed, and abominable fellows of this kind ought not to escape punishment." This close relationship between the Netherlands and Japan had never been disrupted until the present war. In 1857 the Netherlands Government presented the Mikado with a steamship which became the first Japanese man-of-war. Netherlands naval officers and engineers became the instructors of Japan's first naval cadets.

When Commodore Matthew Perry was dispatched to Japan in 1852 to negotiate a treaty opening Japan to American commerce, the Netherlands Government was requested to use its good offices with the Japanese Government through the Netherlands representative of Desima "to do anything that may be in his power toward promoting the object of this amicable visit to the Japanese islands." Thus the trade relations established by the United East India Company became the means of opening up Japan for American commerce.

The ambitions of the traders of the Netherlands were not limited to the far Pacific. A West Indies company was formed to exploit the commercial possibilities of the Western world; it established colonies in North America (New Amsterdam), drove the Portuguese out of northern Brazil, acquired control over Dutch Guiana and certain of the islands in the Caribbean. The "Half Moon" (*Halve Maen*) on which the English explorer Hudson in 1607 traveled the river which now bears his name, was equipped by merchants of the Netherlands.

Holland in the seventeenth century became the center of training in maritime science. Tsar Peter the Great of Russia visited Zaandam (near Amsterdam) in order to learn the science of shipbuilding and of navigation. When the Russian navy was created, a Hollander became its first admiral. Russian naval terminology is full of Dutch words and terms.

Such maritime activity placed the Netherlands at the head of all nations. By the middle of the seventeenth century, the English had approximately 300 vessels in the Baltic trade, whereas the Hollanders had more than 3,000. Colbert, the French statesman, wrote: "The sea trade of Europe is carried by 25,000 ships. Of these, 14,000 or 15,000 belong to Holland and only 600 to France." It is not surprising, therefore, that the Netherlands became the most important trading center of Europe and remained so during the entire "Golden Age of Dutch Commerce."

Products brought from every corner of the world were stored in huge warehouses to await auction to buyers from other countries. And with this commercial development came also a corresponding financial growth. The great confusion which reigned in the monetary world and the desire to establish a more reliable system led to the establishment of the Amsterdam Bank in 1609. In order to make the monetary function of the bank its sole aim, all credit activities were prohibited. This prohibition was so great a restraint upon normal banking activities that the bank paid little attention to it. When in 1790 it became known that the bank had granted large loans to the city of Amsterdam and also to the United East India Company, public confidence was weakened, and in 1791 the bank closed its doors. But during its almost two hundred years of existence, the bank had assumed an important responsibility in the financial life of the country and of the world. The Netherlands had become known as a place where it was possible to secure funds for promising undertakings.

In 1611 the "Old Exchange" was opened by the municipality of Amsterdam. On this exchange, products, shipping space, and securities were traded. But long before the officially recognized exchange building was built, transactions were conducted in the street, in coffee houses, and even in a church. As early as 1530 Amsterdam not only had undertaken to regulate the brokerage business but also had placed the brokers under oath.

The stock market was active and the shares of the United East India Company were the most active, selling at times for 500 guilders for a share issued at par for 100 guilders. But the list was not limited to domestic shares. Foreign shares and foreign government issues were also traded on the floor. About the middle of the eighteenth century, nearly one-third of the shares of the Bank of England and of the English East India Company, and nearly 50 per cent of the English debt had been sold to Hollanders on the Amsterdam exchange. The war of the American colonies against England was in part financed by money from Holland. Later, hundreds of millions of guilders aided in the construction of American railroads and in the financing of farm mortgages.

The favorable economic position of the Netherlands was not based entirely on the enterprise of its people. Geographically that section located at the mouth of the Rhine and the Meuse, important highways of commerce, was destined to become the place where goods moving to and from the rapidly developing hinterlands of Germany and France would be transshipped. The trade of the country was still further augmented by both the important fishing industry and the highly developed dairy industry. The products of these industries found ready acceptance in the markets of the world. Gradually, also, there developed industries based upon the raw materials imported from abroad.

The monopoly in the trade with the Orient was undermined by expansion of the English in India and Africa. Increasing competition came not only from England but also from ports like Hamburg which gradually began to draw to themselves a substantial part of the German trade. More and more the industrializing countries of

Europe began to establish direct connections with their markets and their sources of supply. Thus transit trade decreased in relative importance. And, moreover, as industry developed, England gained an advantage in freight rates by offering a welcome return cargo of coal to the ships that brought raw material to its shores. The rapid growth of population in the British Isles still further increased the importance of English trade at the expense of the Netherlands.

To all these unfavorable factors must be added the growing tendency of European governments to put into effect mercantilistic economic policies. Finally the Netherlands suffered a very serious setback when in 1795 the French invasion for the time being ended the country's existence as an independent state.

The opening years of the nineteenth century found commerce and trade in the Netherlands in a depressed state. During the years of Napoleonic rule, London had taken the place of Amsterdam as the largest trading center of Europe. For many years, it seemed as though Holland would not be able to recapture her position. The conservatism of the Dutch merchants who dreamed of reëstablishing "normalcy" and who adhered strictly to the methods of trading that had prevailed in Holland during the years of prosperity, greatly retarded the rehabilitation of Dutch business.

In the period of European industrialization, the Netherlands were distinctly handicapped by the fact that the natural resources were not of a character to encourage the development of industry. There was no coal, no iron ore—none of the other natural raw materials upon which modern industry must be built.

Fortunately for the country, the King was a man of vision with progressive ideas. It was largely under his leadership that the Government gradually undertook the directing of Dutch commerce into new channels. William I had lived in England during the French occupation and had had an opportunity to study the modern economic policies that had given English trade its impetus. His program of freedom, of minimum port charges, and development of both sea and land transportation was immensely practical. His policy finally won against that of the conservative merchants.

Thus the use of the Netherlands as a transit country for the trade of the Rhineland and that of northeastern France with the rest of the world was restored, and a gradual revival of trade began to take place. Holland had not followed the example of its continental neighbors; instead it had accepted the principle of free trade. The import duty on manufactured goods was only 8 per cent of its value, whereas no duty was paid on semifinished goods or on raw materials.

Gradually the Netherlands began to regain its former prosperity, and in 1928 the per capita international trade, excluding transit shipments, amounted to $244, exceeding that of all other countries. Belgium could show only $218, England $215, and the United States $78 per capita.

The port of Rotterdam was greatly improved by the completion of the "new waterway" which consisted of a canalization of the mouths of the Rhine and the Meuse and afforded a wide and deep channel to the sea. The port facilities were greatly expanded to accommodate the growing traffic. Before the Second World War many of the products that passed through the port, such as wheat and ore, were unloaded into barges in midstream for transportation to the German hinterland which extends as far south as Basel; and coal and other export products traveling downstream similarly were transferred directly from the Rhine barges to ocean-going vessels. In addition to this traffic, there was also developed a very large *entrepôt* business. Products from the Indies and from other overseas sources were stored in the warehouses of the port, awaiting sale and reshipment. Thus the port had grown in size until it had become the most important port of the European Continent. In number of ships cleared, Rotterdam exceeded all ports of the world with 110,406 cleared in 1935 compared with 92,032 cleared through the port of New York. In terms of net registered tonnage of the ships using the port, Rotterdam ranked fifth among the world ports exceeded only by New York, London, Kobe, and Yokohama. The port of Amsterdam enjoyed a similar expansion although on a smaller scale. This port became the principal *entrepôt* for products of the Netherlands Indies which were auctioned off to buyers from every corner of the world.

As a result of this growing trade, the merchant marine expanded rapidly. By 1929 it had reached 2,939,000 gross tons or .380 tons per 1,000 inhabitants as compared with .102 tons per 1,000 inhabitants in the United States. It ranked eighth in the world's merchant marine, exceeded by England, the United States, Japan, Germany, France, Italy, and Norway. Before the war the Netherlands, after Belgium, was the most densely populated country of Europe. The 8,639,595 inhabitants (1940) lived in an area of 12,704 square miles. As a natural consequence, the country depended to a large extent upon imported foodstuffs; agricultural development was of an intensive type. Of the 5,563,960 acres given over to agriculture 50 per cent consisted of holdings of less than 12 acres. Vegetables and fruits constituted the most important products of agriculture, and the production of flowers, bulbs, and dairy products added greatly to the national wealth.

In recent years, industry had also expanded. Operations in the relatively unimportant coal mines in the province of Limburg had increased to the point of supplying a major portion of the needs of domestic industry and transportation. In fact, notwithstanding the almost total lack of raw material, industry had given employment to a larger number of persons than any other economic activity. Of all the persons employed in trade and industry, 39 per cent were engaged in manufacturing as against 20 per cent in agriculture and 25 per cent in trade and transportation.

Many of the raw materials for these industries were supplied by the Indies. The fact that the country was the most important transit country of Europe enabled it to draw upon the flow of ore, coal, and other raw materials that passed through its ports.

A very large percentage of the manufacturing industry operated principally for export. The percentage of industrial products in the total exports of the country before the war had reached 60 per cent, approximately twice that of the exports of agricultural products.

These industrial products were of a varied character. Some depended directly upon local agriculture. Beet sugar, potato flour, straw board, and canned fruits and vegetables ranked high among the manufactured exports. Chocolate, quinine, and diamonds added their quota. But most significant in the life of the country was the increasing importance of such manufactured products as chemicals, textiles, steel, superphosphates, and machinery.

A leading role in the industrial development was played by the Philips concern. This manufacturing enterprise which produced radios, incandescent lamps, and other electrical equipment, had become one of the most important concerns of its type in Europe, employing approximately 30,000 workers. This development is typical of the country for it has been said that "the only materials of real Dutch origin used in the production are the vacuum of the lamps and the energy of the founders."

Dutch energy also found a field for activity outside the mother country. The most important enterprise of world-wide importance was the Royal Dutch. This company, founded in 1890 with a capital of 5,000,000 guilders, to develop the oil resources of the Indies, in forty years had expanded its capital to 500,000,000 guilders. In combination with the English Shell company, of which the Royal Dutch owned a goodly portion of the shares, the Royal Dutch Shell was the largest oil concern in the world, with properties in all the oil-producing countries of the world. Its average daily production exceeded 344,000 barrels. The nearest competitor was the Standard Oil of New Jersey, with an average daily production of 215,000 barrels.

The growth of the oleomargarine industry was another evidence of the commercial enterprise of the country. The oleomargarine producers of the Netherlands were the chief partners of the Continental Oleomargarine Cartel and controlled the production and sale of the products on the Continent. Through combination with the British firm, Lever Brothers, the Unilever also controlled the oleomargarine business of the British Empire.

An important role in the economic life of the country was played by the territory overseas, the Netherlands East Indies. With a population of more than 70,000,000, this string of islands along the equator seemed destined to remain one of the wealthiest and most productive sections of the world.

Before the war scientific experimental stations had been established in the Indies and a school for tropical agriculture was maintained in Holland. All that modern science could offer was employed in the development of the agricultural resources of the country. In fact, most of the products that constituted the principal wealth of the Indies were introduced by the energetic colonizers of the Netherlands. Tea was brought from the mainland of Asia, quinine, rubber, and vanilla from South America, tobacco from North America, and many other agricultural products were acclimatized through scientific cultivation. Thus the people of the Netherlands created much of the wealth of the Indies. The tin, bauxite, and petroleum resources were developed, and with it all an open-door policy, with very few restrictions, allowed the nationals of other countries free access to the economic possibilities of the islands.

Under this efficient management, the Indies produced 91 per cent of the world's Peruvian bark; 75 per cent of the world's kapok; 53 per cent of the pepper; 37 per cent of the rubber; 23 per cent of the coconut products; 19 per cent of agava fiber; 16 per cent of the tea; 10 per cent of the sugar; and 20 per cent of the tin. This phenomenal development of export products created a huge purchasing power. But this market was not reserved for the products of the Netherlands. Holland provided only 18 per cent of the total imports, only little more than Great Britain which supplied 13 per cent, whereas the United States shared in the purchases to the extent of 10 per cent.

In recent years an enlightened policy on the part of the Government contributed to the gradual but undeniable improvement in the standards of living of the large native population. Epidemics were practically unknown, education was made available in the native language. The University of Batavia, as well as the technical college at Bandoeng, were open to natives and these constituted the majority of the student body.

Since 1932 the name "colony" no longer has been employed; the Indies are referred to as the "Netherlands Indies." This change was made in anticipation of the establishment of full "dominion status" which the islands will enjoy after the close of the war.

Gradually the way was being prepared for self-government through the establishment, in 1916, of the *Volksraad,* a legislative assembly. Originally intended as a purely advisory body, the *Volksraad* later had legislative powers and all decrees issued by the Government were approved by the Assembly before they could become effective. Before the present war the Assembly was composed of sixty-one members, only twenty-five of whom were citizens of the mother country. The people of both the Netherlands and the Indies look toward the future with confidence and courage.

The present war has already proved costly to the people and the ultimate price to be paid for victory cannot be estimated. The world's economic life already has undergone fundamental changes and the years following the close of the war will present many problems. Economic adjustments will be required. The Netherlands in Europe as well as the Netherlands Indies will feel these effects with exceptional severity. Geared to the world's economic life as exporter and middleman, economic changes in the rest of the world will necessitate fundamental adjustments. But as one representative of the Netherlands Indies Government said: "We created the wealth of the home country and of the Indies. We still have the intelligence and the energy of our ancestors. What was done in the past can be done again. Holland shall rise again."

CHAPTER XI

The Social Structure
of the Netherlands

BY BARTHOLOMEW LANDHEER

AT FIRST IT SEEMS RATHER REMARKABLE that there are relatively few studies which investigate the various aspects of the social structure of the Netherlands. On second thought this absence of sociological interest—sociology as a science was represented in only a few of the Dutch universities and not at all in the Indies—is not so remarkable as it seems in the beginning. Compared with the large European countries and with the United States, the social life of Holland has not been very complicated or dynamic in character in the past. Its development has been rather gradual since the last century, and only a sudden shock now and then has severely disrupted the tranquil flow of events. This absence of sudden social change has confined social thinking chiefly to group ideologies; it has not created a need for a sharp analysis of the national and social situation as such.

Although in reality every society consists of a hierarchy, this will not be admitted by social thinking for numerous reasons. Social thinking is seldom purely analytical because in itself it constitutes a most powerful social force. It represents trends rather than realities, ideals rather than analytical studies of behavior. Thus, analytical sociological study in the Netherlands has been underdeveloped; even Dutch literature has failed to give an accurate description of the social organization of the country. Detailed studies were far more numerous than general ones, because the Dutch did not analyze themselves in national terms. Indeed, it should be pointed out that a typical national party did not exist in Dutch political life.

In order to understand Dutch life in any of its aspects one must always return to the period of Holland's struggle for independence in the seventeenth century. The rift with Spain was created by a desire for unity, but it was unity on a small scale and with limitations. The growth of town economy into metropolitan economy was the factor which prompted the Dutch to break away from the centralistic rule of Spain, under Philip II, with its feudal and absolutistic tendencies. This struggle was manifest chiefly in the form of religious conflict because the world was passing through a period when social thinking, although definitely turning toward the rationalistic, was expressing itself primarily in religious forms. Compared with the ascetic attitude of the Middle Ages, the growth of Protestantism in its various aspects was reflecting a trend toward a more positive form of culture. This mixture of practical and religious attitudes, which is typical of Protestantism, especially in the Netherlands, has left its lasting mark on Holland; it has created a dualism which can be traced through the entire period of Dutch history to the present day.

Protestant ethics demanded, in the first place, a great amount of individual responsibility; in the second place, an active life rather than a contemplative and ascetic one. This led to the contention that an active, acquisitive attitude could be reconciled with religious ideas only if wealth were desired for the sake of others. Invariably, however, economic expansion led to more luxurious living which was condemned in principle but condoned in practice. This, in turn, led to a conflict between the groups who professed religious principles but tended more toward a purely formal adherence.

In the Netherlands, this difference made it possible to distinguish between the great masses of the people, who were often supported by members of the nobility, and the so-called class of the *"Regenten,"* the *"mynheers,"* the leaders of Dutch industry and commerce. This latter group, having grown from the artisans and traders of the small cities, became the leading burghers when the Dutch towns rose to prominence in the sixteenth and seventeenth centuries. In these groups were to be found the energetic traders and shipbuilders whose accomplishments not only had amazed the world of that time, but had also aroused the jealousy of other powers. Immortalized by the paintings of a Rembrandt or a Frans Hals, these traders organized the companies which sent their ships across the Seven Seas and established the Dutch flag in all parts of the world. They were proud and highly cultured; in fact, far more cultured than their modern compatriots who cannot boast of a Vondel, Huygens, Hooft, Boerhaave, or Spinoza as contemporaries.

The life of seventeenth-century Holland was one of overflowing abundance for this group. The robust spirit of plenty was apparent also among the other classes who, to a certain extent, participated in the unprecedented prosperity of the Netherlands. But later, when prosperity had waned, and when the owning groups had begun to show an attitude more conservative than expansionist, the contrast between the classes became more marked. When the differences between rich and poor, although always great, had become more static, the upper classes became self-conscious and pedantic about their position.

The merchants created the burgher-oligarchies which gradually occupied a dominating position in civil life. A "haughty patrician class," consisting in each town of a very limited number of families, closely interrelated, little by little had possessed itself, as a matter of hereditary right, of all the offices and dignities of the town, of the province, and of the state. Within their own town this class reigned supreme, filling vacancies in the town council (*vroedschap*) by co-option, exercising all authority, distributing among their relatives all posts of profit, and acquiring great wealth. Their fellow-citizens were excluded from all share in the affairs of state, and were regarded as belonging to an inferior caste. French fashions and manners, as well as English clothes, furniture, and food, had become the vogue of the patrician class.

The great traditions of the seventeenth century had been forgotten and Holland had changed into a conservative power which abhorred war because it interfered with trade. This change developed aspects of Dutch society which, until then, had been latent. Especially was this true of the conflict already mentioned between theory and practice in Puritanism, when the lower classes began to feel that the upper classes professed a philosophy which they did not follow.

It should be realized that in the modern sense it is impossible to discuss the national and social life of the seventeenth and eighteenth centuries. Differences among the various groups were far greater than they are today, and frequently there was no unity among the provinces nor even within their borders. The function of state and municipality was underdeveloped, and there was very little feeling of social responsibility. Public safety was often poorly enforced, and rowdyism, thievery, and roguishness prevailed. The luxury of the patricians was in strong contrast to the misery of the masses. Indeed, the masses had few sources of pleasure other than taverns, kermesses, and county fairs; their simple philosophy continuously wavered between religion and superstition. A more pronounced national feeling did not develop until late in the eighteenth century. At that period it was artificial and superficial in nature, an imitation of French and English nationalism, not yet deeply rooted in Dutch character.

Holland, in the eighteenth century, was an aristocratic republic in which local commercial interests dominated. Its oligarchic and plutocratic tendencies, however, very often overshadowed the truly aristocratic aspects of Dutch life and gave to it, instead, a conservative, reactionary, and materialistic appearance. In the seventeenth century, Holland produced many great men who broke the shackles of provincialism, although often at a cost of intense suffering and persecution at the hands of their fellow citizens. Not only has this been especially true of great artists and philosophers, who have frequently won little appreciation during their lifetime, but it has also been true of some of the eminent political leaders, like the De Witts, whose undeserved fate bears witness to a period of national mental instability.

At the same time, it should not be overlooked that Holland was one of the most enlightened countries of this period, and that the defects mentioned were equally as strong, if not stronger, in other countries. But the seventeenth and eighteenth centuries formed a period in which light, as well as shadow, was intense and in which progress, lauded now, was tortuous, difficult, and troublesome. The ventures of the human mind into hitherto unknown regions were full of obstacles, relapses, and hesitation, in constant conflict between desire to analyze the existing world, and fear of the metaphysical—a fear which has been such a tremendous force in human history.

This conflict gave a dualistic aspect to life in all countries in the new era but particularly in Holland, where the process of rationalization found one of its focal points earlier than in any other country. Later this process became more intense in France and England. Holland's contribution to the freeing of the human mind has been most significant, not only through the medium of thought and scientific discovery but also through painting which, for the first time, took its objects from daily life. The spiritual development of Holland has been typically individualistic. Only in times of great stress has it been possible to weld the people into unity, first during the struggle for independence, then during the Napoleonic period and, finally, during the present German occupation. The first two of these national emergencies brought changes in Dutch life which otherwise might have remained dormant over a long period, or which might not have challenged the conservative forces which oppose change—forces of the kind which so often have contributed to the outbreaks of violence characteristic of history.

The war against Spain molded the Netherlands into a political unit, although on a federal basis, and gave Dutch culture the depth, brilliance, and national feeling which it might not have acquired otherwise. Struggle lifted the Dutch spirit high above any of its earlier or later manifestations. However, it did not become a group spirit— rather it was individual, sometimes aloof and apart from the events of the day, but always moved by them to greater achievements.

The Napoleonic period transformed Holland into a national state in the modern sense of the word. It did away with the petty rule of local officials and the spirit of conservatism which had come over the Dutch nation. And the ideas of the French Revolution influenced

Holland so deeply that they were to provide the pattern for the political development of the nineteenth and twentieth centuries. Indeed, in the social structure of Holland may be found a reflection of all the social forces which had molded Holland into the country it was before the Second World War.

Holland does not have a strong monarchical tradition. The relationship between the House of Orange and the people of Holland has always been of a strong personal character, similar to that between a leader and his followers. In normal times political life in Holland has been a monopoly of academic and political circles; it has had little or no connection with the common people who have never considered politics a matter of personal concern. Religion, in its relationship between the individual and the universe, took the place of politics in the life of the Dutch who were more interested in deciphering their place in the world than in politics.

In times of stress, when political problems have become paramount, the Dutch nation automatically has turned toward the House of Orange—always the traditional leader of the Dutch people. No figure in Dutch history has ever even approached the position held by William of Orange, who possessed not only those qualities which the Dutch admire, but also an unusual talent for leading a stubborn, individualistic, and often unruly people. Today again, the thoughts of the people in the occupied territory, as well as those of the Dutch elsewhere, turn toward Queen Wilhelmina who is the symbol of the Dutch spirit and its renewed struggle for freedom.

Holland was a monarchy of a feudal and absolutistic type when it was established in 1815, but the feudal tradition has now been firmly broken for a long time. Because the nineteenth century was dominated by the struggle for political democracy, it was more a problem of how far the power of the monarch could be curbed than whether it would be curbed.

According to constitutional law the king has the executive power of the Dutch government, whereas the legislative function is in the hands of the king and the States-General together. According to the traditions of parliamentary government the king is not free in the choice of his cabinet, which, in general, must be in accordance with the political party structure. This complicates the institutional structure which is based upon a combination of the democratic and the monarchic principles. It is not quite possible to find a common basis for these two principles, although it can be assumed that Holland is a "crowned" republic in which the will of the people unites two originally divergent principles. However, it must be realized that in the social structure of Holland static and dynamic principles are interwoven which, for instance, are not to be found to the same extent in a country like the United States.

This means that considerable weight is given formally to the hereditary principle which naturally influences Dutch society as a whole; among the middle and lower classes, there has always been a natural tendency to emphasize kinship relations. There is no doubt but what a static element in national life satisfies the Dutch temperament which is of a pronounced quiet, conservative (*bedaard*) type. It cannot be denied, however, that inasmuch as the hereditary principle has also penetrated the business and professional world it often has led to nepotism and stagnancy.

Political democracy in western Europe has shown a strong tendency toward the development of a middle-class society which can benefit only from an intermixture with aristocratic elements.

At the top of the social structure of Holland was the "official group," which in itself comprised many different elements. The hereditary principle did not dominate the composition of this group. The group recruited its members from among the nobility, the upper and middle bourgeoisie, the professional groups, and those individuals who, by ability only, succeeded in attaining high positions. For certain positions some preference for the nobility was shown, but it was not by any means exclusive for any position in the recent past. On the whole, positions were granted on the basis of ability, although it cannot be denied that preferential tendencies existed in the educational system. This official group constituted the upper class, together with the leaders of finance, industry, agriculture, business, the top-ranking professional men, and the leaders of the arts and sciences.

Although it was not easy to enter this group, it would be quite possible to cite numerous examples of people who have made a career without having had any preferential status at the start. This occurred in business, as well as in the world of officials, although the influence of nepotism and clannishness should not be underestimated. Unfortunately there has been a tendency in the recent past to make more difficult promotion on the basis of achievement only.

In general, the upper classes also fell into the higher income strata, although income in no way determined social status. In 1938–1939, according to income-tax statistics, the income distribution in the Netherlands was as follows:

Guilders . . .	800–	1,400	643,649
(Value of guilder	1,400–	2,000	369,295
approximately	2,000–	3,000	183,599
54 cents)	3,000–	5,000	100,474
	5,000–	10,000	46,169
	10,000–	20,000	14,641
	20,000–	30,000	3,319
	30,000–	100,000	2,921
	100,000 and higher		341
	Total		1,364,408

Property-tax statistics gave the following picture of the distribution of property:

Guilders . . .	16,000–	30,000	84,920
(Value of guilder	30,000–	50,000	42,924
approximately	50,000–	100,000	31,662
54 cents)	100,000–	200,000	14,262
	200,000–	300,000	4,212
	300,000–	500,000	2,858
	500,000–	1,000,000	1,755
	1,000,000 and higher		816
	Total		183,409

Wealth and power have always been more concentrated in the Protestant north than in the Catholic south. Considerable progress has been made by the Catholics in recent times, however. In part this may be explained by their increasing share in the total population. A comparison of the birth rate of the different confessions gives the following picture:

	1909–1910	1935
Roman Catholic	286.9	208.8
Protestant	215.9	133.4
Jewish	157.1	85.2
No religion	88.2	69.2

(Number of legitimate births per 1,000 women)

Although this table shows a decline in the birth rate for all groups, it is noticeable that the decrease in the Catholic group is relatively smaller. In politics and business a growing influence has been exercised by the Catholics; in fact, the group constitutes the strongest political party in the Netherlands.[1]

In general, the Netherlands before the Nazi invasion was somewhat similar to the United States. Economic progress had been accomplished chiefly by a small group of liberals who had succeeded in creating for Holland an impressive economic position in the world. When the negative aspects of unrestrained capitalist production had become more and more pronounced, this group gradually had begun to encounter opposition from many directions. In Holland this resistance came from two sides: from the Socialist parties of the Left and from the Catholic and Protestant parties of the Right. Among the large number of political parties in Holland, practically all were in favor of an evolutionary process of change. Only the Communist party and, in the last fifteen years, the Fascist parties could be termed revolutionary from the democratic point of view, although they stated repeatedly that they expected to gain power by obtaining a majority of the votes. During the invasion days the Fascist parties showed that they were fully prepared for direct action.

The other evolutionary parties to a marked degree succeeded in taking the sharp edges off capitalism and in making Holland a well-balanced country with pronounced middle-class tendencies. Throughout the past decade there could be observed the same phenomenon,

---

[1] See Chapter VII, "Political Parties" by David Friedman.

which is to be found in many countries, of skilled labor approaching a middle-class status. This gave to Holland a substantial middle group of small farmers, laborers, and tradespeople who held a moderate outlook. On the contrary, in a society which placed too much value on a high standard of living, the cleavage within labor of a fully employed group, with a decent income, and the unemployed never found a satisfactory solution. Only a great feeling of social responsibility and a far-reaching system of economic control could solve this problem which, in Holland as elsewhere, was patched up, but not really dealt with in a satisfactory manner.

Contrary to popular belief, Holland is not an agricultural country. Before the Second World War, according to recent statistics, not more than 22 per cent of the working population was engaged in agricultural pursuits which accounted for about 12 per cent of the national income. In 1939, 48.4 per cent of the population lived either in towns of less than 20,000 inhabitants, or in rural communities. This gives the same picture of urbanization which may be observed in other countries.

Nevertheless, before the war, Holland differed considerably from other small western European countries. Through its overseas territories and its world-wide trade and commerce it was more "world conscious" than many of the other smaller countries. It is not accidental that Holland has played such an important role in international law. From the days of Grotius it has had to live with nations in all corners of the world. This fact has given an opportunity to those people in the Netherlands who preferred to leave and to carve a life for themselves in remote corners of the earth, where initiative and energy were often more appreciated than in the conservative home country. Those citizens who returned from remote sections of the Empire, together with those of the widely traveled leisure class of Holland itself, created the international atmosphere that existed before the Second World War.

On the whole, the average Dutchman has not been particularly empire-conscious. He has been too individualistic to regard the Dutch role in the overseas territories as an achievement of the community as such. But he has taken a pardonable pride in the achievements of his fellow countrymen, and this has aided him in overcoming the inferiority complex peculiar to citizens of many small countries, a reaction by no means alien to the Dutch. Particularly have the middle classes been likely to show a sense of inferiority when traveling in other countries; this, in turn, has often prompted them to copy, in a manner not always dignified, the behavior of their larger neighbors.

Holland has been a prosperous, well-balanced, conservative country, perhaps inclined to be too materialistic and individualistic, but nevertheless fundamentally sound. The dissatisfied groups in the Netherlands were small in size. Some of their grievances were real, while others seemed to express a social neurosis. Holland was perhaps not sufficiently dynamic, but then it could hardly be expected to be dynamic when it had enjoyed peace for more than a hundred years.

The small Fascist group consisted mostly of ill-adjusted and frustrated elements which had been unable to find their place in life, and of intellectuals and lower middle-class people who had been influenced by a new ideology. The Fascists received some support from business leaders who wanted to keep labor in its place. In Holland, too, were certain individuals who thought that a more "heroic" attitude would solve both social and economic problems. Overindividualism in times of peace is hard to prevent in an independent nation, but since the Nazi occupation Holland has united to organize and efficiently direct its underground activities.

Dutch life has always resembled that of the English in its love of the sea, its relationship with vast overseas territories, and its stoicism. As a small country, Holland has been less formal and more neighborly, and perhaps has had an attitude more of "live and let live" than Britain. On the contrary, Holland has often shown a certain pettiness and a "living-room" (*huiskamer*) culture not displayed by its neighbor across the Channel. The family structure in Holland has often been too strong and has exercised too great a pressure on the grown-up members. However, there have been many positive aspects to this dominant family life, one of which has been its ability to prevent the political excesses often observed in larger countries.

France has always exercised considerable influence on the cultural life of the Netherlands, particularly in the field of law. It is known that Holland adopted the Napoleonic codes and that Dutch constitutional law has been influenced by the thinkers of the French Revolution to a considerable extent. Holland, as a country of civil law, has seen more formalism in its legal life than during the period of Roman-Dutch law which preceded it, and of which important remnants have remained.

Apart from this legal influence, French thinking and French literature have had a much greater influence on the so-called "better" classes in the past than in recent times. Germany has never enjoyed great popularity among the masses in Holland, because the Dutch and German characters are diametrically opposed to each other. The Dutch are individualistic, stubborn, and unruly, while the Germans excel in love of discipline and regimentation. In military and scientific circles, however, Germany has had considerable influence, especially before 1933, when German achievements were greatly admired. To a somewhat lesser degree engineering, and the fields of German philosophy, music, and literature have won their share of admirers but not to the exclusion of the achievements in these fields by other countries.

The systematic patterns of German political thinking—Marxism, for instance, became considerably less rigid and abstract when interpreted by Dutch political thinkers. Even Dutch national socialism was of a much milder type, at least in the beginning, than its German prototype. The Dutch were undoubtedly far ahead of Germany in genuine feeling of social responsibility, although they were less articulate and verbose about it.

Perhaps the most serious problem which Holland faced before the war was that of increase in population. It has been estimated that the resources of Holland could support a population of approximately 10,000,000 people under normal conditions. Because the population before the war had already passed the 9,000,000 mark, and because the excess of births over deaths had amounted to 100,000 annually, this problem would have demanded great attention and will, indeed, after the war if it again occurs. A regulation of the increase in population will undoubtedly prove necessary. This may be accompanied by a policy of emigration, should that prove feasible. The overseas territories of the Netherlands, such as the Netherlands East Indies, are capable of absorbing a far greater part of the Dutch population than they have in the past. A wise general policy will undoubtedly investigate these possibilities which were neglected before the war.

Holland has had every reason to be proud of its past. It will also have every reason to be proud of its future if it realizes that strict regulation of economic and social relations will be a matter not of progressive philosophy alone, after this war, but one of strict necessity. The leeway which a prosperous Holland had before 1940 has been curtailed severely, but common suffering has strengthened the social ties and has created a greater feeling of unity than ever before. Also, ideological differences may have to be taken less seriously in order that a practical policy may be carried out much more easily.

There can be no doubt, as one views world-wide changes, that political democracy will need a firmer social and economic foundation than it has had in the past. Trends in that direction were noticeable before this war, and there is every reason to believe that the war itself, will prove to have been a powerful stimulus for these tremendously important developments.

CHAPTER XII

Labor

BY MARINUS MICHIEL LOURENS

THE PROCLAMATION OF October 5, 1798, by authority of the Executive Directorate of the Batavian Republic, ordered the dissolution of the guilds. In 1813, after the Netherlands again had become independent, many efforts were made to restore some form of guild organization. The energetic King William I, who was half a century ahead of his times, decided by Royal Decree of October 23, 1818, that a limitation of the number of enterprises in any municipality would be equivalent to a return of the guild system and "this could not be considered in these times."

Between 1860 and 1870, the development of modern industry on a large scale began. The amassing of great numbers of workers in the Netherlands had the same effect as in England, Germany, and France—the organizing of laborers in like industries and trades. Religious convictions exercised greater influence upon the workers than in other countries. The freedom of organization and assembly was guaranteed by the law of April 22, 1855. The way was now open for the workers' unions.

The close relation of an Amsterdam tailor, J. W. Gerhard, to the leaders of the International Workmen's Association, especially with the Belgian members, led to the formation of a Netherlands section of the First International at Amsterdam on August 30, 1869. Sections of the International were established in The Hague and Utrecht and, in 1871, the three sections were united in a Netherlands Labor League. The violence of the Paris Commune in 1870, the struggle for mastery between Marx and Bakunin within the International, the unsavory methods used by Marx to expel his opponents from the Congress of the International at The Hague in 1872, had divided and weakened the Netherlands sections. After the dissolution of the International in 1876, only isolated clubs of working men were to be found in Amsterdam, in The Hague, and in Haarlem, which claimed to adhere to its principles. In 1871 the General Netherland Workers' Association, neutral as to religion and politics, was organized.

On February 27, 1873, Samuel van Houten introduced his child-labor law in the Second Chamber. It was coupled with a compulsory-education regulation. The discussion, beginning after April, 1874, made it clear to proponents of the law that it would not be passed if the compulsory-education clauses remained. Therefore, the clauses were dropped. The law in its final form forbade the hiring of children under twelve years of age, except for personal and domestic services and for certain forms of farm labor. In 1886, under the leadership of Goeman Borgesius, a parliamentary inquiry was undertaken to determine the results of the Van Houten Child Labor Law. A report was published in 1887, which revealed such miserable labor conditions that, in 1888, the Ministry of Ruys de Beerenbrouck introduced a new draft which became the Labor Law of May 5, 1889. All prohibitive clauses of the Van Houten Child Labor Law were retained. The working time for women and persons under sixteen years of age was limited. Such persons were not allowed to work in dangerous occupations. Women and young persons were not allowed to work longer than eleven hours per day and not at all between 7 p.m. and 5 a.m. Mealtime had to be not less than one hour. All Sunday labor for women and children was forbidden, and in confinement cases no woman was allowed to return to work sooner than four weeks. All agricultural labor was excluded from the working of this law.

The orthodox Protestant union movement started with the National Workmen's Association (*Vaderlandsche Werklieden Vereeniging*) in 1871, at Amsterdam and Utrecht. This attempt to unite the orthodox Protestant workers was a dismal failure. The dissatisfaction with the educational policy of the General Netherlands Workmen's Association, which favored public rather than denominational schools, and the hatred of the principles of the International, stimulated the formation of a trade union, "on the conviction, that God's Word and the traditions of our people are reliable foundations for a Christian society."

In the organization, Heritage of the Fathers (*Patrimonium*), sponsored by the Amsterdam mason, Klaas Kater, and three of his closest friends, the workers were the regular members and the employers the "extraordinary" ones. The organization developed great activity in arranging popular lectures and in founding numerous small libraries. The liberation of the people from social misery was to be attained through a complete Christianization of the nation. No pure trade-union was contemplated, no coöperative effort made, and no social legislation planned. Concerted action with the employers, the establishment of sick benefits and pension funds for old age, and even for funeral expenses were clauses in the work program of the Heritage of the Fathers. In general, this organization followed the leadership of the Anti-Revolutionary state party, at the same time disavowing all independent political action.

The Roman Catholic trade-union movement began comparatively late in the history of the Netherlands. Associations of St. Joseph were formed at Bergen-op-Zoom and at Amsterdam in 1868. The first Catholic trade-union was organized by the carpenters at Arnhem in 1872. The antireligious attitude of the Socialists was the great stimulant. Independent associations of St. Joseph were organized in North Brabant and in Limburg. In 1885, in Friesland, a St. Boniface Society was founded which later joined the League of Roman Catholic Workmen's associations in the archbishopric of Utrecht.

In 1877 an organization composed of manual and brain workers was denied admission to the General Netherlands Workmen's Association for the sole reason that its majority was socialistic. This rejected organization constituted itself as a Social Democratic Union in 1878. J. W. Gerhard and Klaas Ris became its principal leaders and in the following year an exodus of socialistic members from the G.N.W.A. led to the formation of Social Democratic clubs in The Hague, in Haarlem, and in 1881 in Rotterdam. Toward the end of that year all Socialist organizations merged into a Social Democratic League. Gerhard became its president, but soon had to yield the leadership to Frederik Domela Nieuwenhuis. Nieuwenhuis had been a Lutheran pastor who, in 1878, had left the ministry, convinced that his increasing radicalism was incompatible with the doctrines and social theories of that denomination.

In 1883 the Social Democratic League began the publication of a weekly paper, *Justice for All* (*Recht voor Allen*), of which Nieuwenhuis became the chief editor. At its first congress in 1882, the Social Democratic League adopted the "Gotha Program," a compromise between the views of Marx, that Socialism was the inevitable, historic product of the contradictions in capitalism, and the opportunistic propaganda of the agitator, Lasalle. After 1883, the number of Socialists increased rapidly. The economic depression caused widespread unemployment and was felt acutely in the farming districts. The demand for general suffrage became stronger and in 1885, at The Hague, a suffrage demonstration took place which culminated in the passing of a revolutionary resolution threatening that the parade would be the last peaceful one.

Disturbances by the distribution of Socialist literature, and riots at Socialist meetings became frequent. A tension resulted from the dismissal of socialistic government functionaries; many lawsuits for personal insults followed, as did complaints about bodily attacks, destruction of property, and limitation of individual liberty. *Justice for All* published an article entitled "The King Comes," on the occasion of the yearly visit of King William III to the capital, Amsterdam. The author expressed his astonishment that so elaborate a celebration had been organized and so much homage had been given "to a man, who made so little of his job." Nieuwenhuis, as responsible editor, was prosecuted for *lèse-majesté*, received a sentence of two years solitary confinement, but appealed.

The High Court reduced the sentence of Nieuwenhuis to one year and he was incarcerated in January, 1887, to the satisfaction of an overwhelming majority of the Dutch people who were irritated by his flamboyant propaganda campaign pending his appeal.

The universally respected Professor Allard Pierson published an article on May 1, 1887, advocating the release of the rebel. Prominent persons presented to the King a petition for his liberation and a royal act of grace gave to Nieuwenhuis his freedom on August 31st, the birthday of the Crown Princess Wilhelmina.

In the International Socialist congresses at Brussels in 1891 and at Zurich in 1893, Nieuwenhuis defended his antiparliamentary thesis, but was defeated by the German Social Democratic representatives. In 1891, Nieuwenhuis was not reëlected to the Second Chamber. He had never expected anything from parliamentary action, but he considered himself obligated to introduce a law regulating the eight-hour day, which was rejected. Realizing that his antiparliamentary action was a failure he resigned from the Socialist League in 1898; he had completed the metamorphosis from Christian to Anarchist.

The International Socialist and Trade Union Congress at Brussels in 1891 had recommended the formation of labor secretariats in every country. Two years later the National Labor Secretariat was organized at Amsterdam. The principal aim was the amalgamation of all labor associations into one labor group. In the beginning political parties were included, but the constitution and by-laws were revised in 1901 and political parties were henceforth banned. Under the leadership of G. van Erkel, the National Labor Secretariat leaned toward semianarchistic and syndicalistic principles and tactics. The powerful General Netherlands Diamond Workers Union, organized in 1894 at Amsterdam, did not join the National Labor Secretariat. Under the capable leadership of Henri Polak, this union became a purposeful, splendidly administered society of workers which educated its members to militant, aggressive action. Dues were made high from the outset in order to form a large strike fund, to confer benefits, and to improve labor conditions. Apprenticeship was made exclusive as protection against an influx of the semiskilled. The union built magnificent headquarters and conducted educational courses. It wrung many concessions from the employers. The majority of the diamond workers either were Socialists already or became members of the organization.

The continuous struggles within the Socialist League between the parliamentarians and the disciples of Nieuwenhuis led to the desertion in large numbers of advocates of political action. After an incubation period of months, there was founded on August 26, 1894, at Zwolle, the Social Democratic Labor party (*Sociaal Democratische Arbeiders partij*) by twelve men who thereafter were referred to as that party's "apostles," their leader being the well-known Frisian lawyer, Pieter Jelles Troelstra. Later the Marxist "Erfurt Program" of 1902 was accepted as its own "program of principles." An avalanche of abuse poured in from *Justice for All,* the Socialist League, and from Nieuwenhuis who pronounced his anathema on the "heretics."

The advent of the Ministry of Goeman Borgesius with its progressive liberal program promised much for labor. Dr. Nolens, Roman Catholic leader, hailed it as the "Ministry of Social Justice," but impatient Troelstra cried out, "social procrastination." The year 1895 had seen the passing of a law concerning safety measures in factories, the limitation of hours of adults in dangerous occupations, and an extension of labor inspection (further intensified in 1909). A prohibition of the use of white phosphorous in the fabrication of matches followed in 1901. On January 2, 1901, the first Accidents Insurance Law was placed on the statute books. The law had been introduced in the Second Chamber in the spring of 1898, but its public discussion began only in the autumn of 1899. The first draft was rejected by the First Chamber, because the projected compulsory insurance was to be administered by a "State Insurance Bank." It was contended that in this manner the relation between employer and employee was changed from a private to a public juridical relation. The law was passed after a concession to the employers who individually, or in a group, were allowed to carry the risk. Better housing, stricter inspection of child labor, and public hygienic measures were introduced.

Since 1891 the railroad workers had protested against bad working conditions and low wages. A Union of Railroad and Tramway Employees had been organized with Jan Oudegeest as leader. Insistence on voluntary discipline and concentration of power in the executive committee had built this union into a powerful organization. A partial strike in one of the warehouses in the harbor district of Amsterdam on January 28, 1903, made all stored goods "tainted." Railroad employees refused to move or shunt cars containing these goods. One yardman was discharged on that account and immediately workmen of other yards stopped work. The strikes spread like wildfire to all railroads between Amsterdam, Rotterdam, and Utrecht. The railroad companies appealed to the Government, but Kuyper sent only small military detachments as a precautionary measure. On January 31st, the railroad companies capitulated and all strikers were reinstated in their jobs, including those in the warehouses. No wage demands had been made. The complete victory resulted from a phenomenal solidarity among the workers.

The press clamored for laws prohibiting railroad strikes. The unions countered by threats of a general Netherlands transportation strike. Municipal employees in Amsterdam took a menacing attitude toward the city government. The Government in The Hague called out militia reserves. Kuyper introduced three laws on February 23, 1903: one prohibiting strikes in public services; another creating an "emergency railroad brigade"; still another legalizing an inquiry into the working conditions of railroad workers. A Committee of Resistance was formed, representing Socialists, Anarchists, and radical trade-union members. The confessional unions organized what were known as "committees of order." It became clear that a sharp difference of opinion prevailed in the Committee of Resistance regarding the feasibility of a general strike against the laws. On the night of April 5th to 6th, the railroad unions called a general strike. The Government occupied all stations with military units. Confessional unions ordered their members to keep on working. Only in Amsterdam did the strike have a measure of success. The diamond workers struck to a man; stagnation followed on the railroads and in the harbor works. Confusion reigned on the communications to Haarlem and Utrecht. All employers in Amsterdam answered with a complete lockout. The strike laws had been passed on April 2d in the Second Chamber over the votes of the Socialists and Liberal Democrats. The First Chamber was certain to approve. The strike furor began to wane on

April 8th, and the Committee of Resistance finally called off the strike on the night of April 9th.

Thousands of railroad workers lost their jobs. They were supported by the diamond workers and remained loyal to their union. The Anarchists, the followers of Nieuwenhuis (now called "Free Socialists"), the leaders of the National Labor Secretariat and the Ultra-Marxists accused the executive of the S.D.A.P. of treason. Vitriolic language was used against Troelstra, who had written for *The People* an editorial warning "What Now!" against continuing the strike after the passing of the laws. Within the S.D.A.P. the division between the orthodox Marxists and the "revisionists" widened. All confessional unions gained large numbers of adherents. The National Labor Secretariat turned definitely anarchistic. Many left its jurisdiction. At the initiative of the diamond workers a new association of workers was organized on January 1, 1906—the Netherlands League of Trade Unions, a federation of trade-union leagues, with strong centralized power in administration and finances. The initial membership was eighteen thousand. The general strike encouraged state interference and strengthened the advocacy of government ownership. A fierce hatred against Kuyper flamed up in Socialist and Liberal circles. The slogan became "Down with Kuyper!" and in the elections of 1905, he was defeated by a coalition of all leftist parties. After 1903, Nieuwenhuis was forced into the background and became a lecturer for isolated groups.

The Marxian theorists were mostly intellectuals who formed a group of contributors to the monthly periodical *New Time*. In 1906 the Marxists refused further coöperation with the Executive of the S.D.A.P. and founded a weekly, the *Tribune,* and thus a dissident faction was born, with Wijnkoop as leader and the poets Gorter and Henriëtte Roland-Holst as members. An extraordinary party congress at Deventer in 1908 voted discontinuance of the *Tribune.* Its editors refused to yield and were expelled. Some nine hundred members left the S.D.A.P. and organized the Social Democratic party which joined the Communist Third International in 1919 as the Communist Party of Holland.

Labor legislation under both Kuyper and his successor, De Meester, may be summed up as follows: in 1902 a law was passed defining
all occupations included in the Accidents Insurance Law. A greater
number of occupations were included in the revision of 1909; accident compensation, fixed in 1903, resulted in the organization of a
State Insurance Bank; in the same year a state pension law for public
servants reached the statute books. In 1904 a mining law regulated
for the first time the length of the workday for mature laborers—no
underground work was permitted for boys under sixteen years, nor
for men over sixty years of age; protective timbering was ordered
and methods for protection against explosions and rules for ventila-
tion given. In 1905 a caissons law limited the working hours in caissons and provided medical examination for all underwater workers.
In 1907 the civil code was revised to protect all workers against any
possible breach in private contracts. Finally, in 1908, the Netherlands
signed adherence to the Bern Convention, prohibiting all night work
for women and all uses of white phosphorous. The victory of the
confessional coalition at the polls, in 1908, brought A. S. Talma
into the Ministry of Th. Heemskerk, as Minister of Agriculture,
Industry, and Commerce. Talma possessed a great capacity for work,
a refreshing idealism and was imbued with magnificent consecration
to his task as a Christian social reformer. He made the Labor Law
of 1911 apply to all women and children. He introduced a stonecutters'
law, giving protective measures against stonedust and providing
periodic free medical examination of lung conditions. This law was
made more strict in its application in 1921. He failed in the passing of
a draft of a law regulating the working time of bakers. His crowning
achievement was a sick-benefit insurance law revised as to the size
of the benefits in 1929. The States-General extended still further the
range of compensations in 1930.

Since 1911, universal suffrage had become the paramount issue.
Every year the Socialists and the radical unions had organized mon-
ster parades and meetings on a certain Tuesday. These so-called "Red
Tuesdays" became increasingly significant. On September 11, 1912,
Troelstra proposed that in the *Answer to the Address from the*

Throne a demand should be inserted for the speedy introduction of universal suffrage. The proposition was voted down, "Right" against "Left." In 1913, the Liberal Democratic coalition won at the polls and the Socialists gained eighteen seats. The Queen entrusted the formation of the new ministry to D. Bos, a capable, well-balanced Liberal Democrat, who promptly offered three cabinet posts to the Socialists. A special Congress of the Social Democratic Labor party, after a heated discussion, declined the offer. Bos withdrew and the Queen called Cort van der Linden, who formed an extraparliamentary ministry. A revision of the Constitution had to open the way for universal suffrage. A committee was appointed in November, 1913, to consider the matter. One month later another committee was given the task of devising a revision of the elementary-education law, in order to give the private confessional schools equal rights and equal financial benefits. The Socialists approved the aims of both committees, the Catholics followed, the Christian Historicals approved a short time later and, lastly, the Anti-Revolutionaries overcame their aversion to suffrage for the masses. All laboring men and women were to have a voice in the government.

The first of August, 1914, saw the German hordes violate the neutrality of Belgium. War was brought to the very doors of the Netherlands. The Second Chamber met in extraordinary session on August 3d. Troelstra rose to declare, "The national idea overrules all national differences," and accepted a political truce under condition that the workers of the nation should share on equal terms in the distribution of food and clothing.

The revision of the Constitution making possible the granting of suffrage to all men and women appeared in the statute books on November 29th, and on December 12, 1917, the public proclamation took place in every municipality.

Under the first two coalitions, the Ministries of Ruys de Beerenbrouck, the Portfolio of Labor was entrusted to the capable hands of the Roman Catholic, P. J. M. Aalberse, who built on the foundations laid by the Liberal, Goeman Borgesius and the Anti-Revolutionary, A. S. Talma. Aalberse is responsible for the Old Age Benefits

Law (passed in 1919 and revised and extended in 1929), which covered insurance for all Netherlands subjects, even for those residing in foreign countries, against old age, death, and funeral expenses. The law provided for benefits of five to twenty-five guilders per week at the age of fifty-five to sixty-five. Seamen were protected by the Maritime Accidents Law of June 27, 1919, which provided for 70 per cent of the daily wage in event of incapacity for work, for twenty-six weeks ashore, and benefits for widow and orphans and surviving blood relations. The greatest achievement of Aalberse was the new Labor Law of 1919 (latest revision in 1930), covering both sexes and all ages and regulating work in stores, restaurants, hotels, manufacturing establishments, and home industries, in spaces detrimental to health; regulating nightwork; providing free Saturday afternoons and prohibiting Sunday work, with exceptions; regulating overtime and stipulating working time in pharmacies, bakeries, building trades, offices for post-telegraph and telephone services; determining labor conditions in inland shipping, fisheries, railroads and trams; in drafting rooms; for musicians; and in hospitals. Scarcely a single business was left untouched. Rest days for special religious sects, other than Sundays, have been specified for Jews, Sabbathists, Seventh Day Adventists, and Mohammedans.

Aalberse extended accident insurance to agricultural and horticultural workers; this was the first time that farm labor had received full benefits from legislation. In 1923 a law concerning labor conflicts provided conciliation measures. Referees appointed by the State or by the contending parties themselves, decided the issue. If no agreement could be reached, the Minister of Social Affairs could set up a commission to investigate the causes of the conflict. The Government could take measures to prevent or to conclude strikes and lockouts. The institution of a High Council of Labor was prepared by Aalberse in 1919, but was legally established in 1927 by his successor, Dr. J. R. Slotemaker de Bruine. This body gave advice to various government departments. The Council consisted of at least thirty, and at most sixty members. One-sixth were functionaries appointed by the Queen. The remainder were also appointed by the Queen on nomination of the Minister of Social Affairs. Three-tenths to one-third of the members were appointed on the advice of employers, and the same number on the advice of the most important associations of trade unions. At least one-sixth of the members were to be persons who had made a special study of social-economic problems or of social legislation. The term of members who were not functionaries was four years. The chairman was to be elected by the Council and was to serve not more than two years.

An important work, done by the Council in 1933, on its own initiative, was research concerning the influence of the wage scale on the prices of commodities. In the same year collective labor contracts were regulated by law. Such contracts are agreements, arrived at by negotiations between the organizations of employers and those of employees, both having the same legal position.

The Christian Historical, Slotemaker de Bruine was succeeded by the Roman Catholic T. J. Verschuur. The flow of labor legislation continued: in 1931 laws were passed determining the legal status of traveling salesmen, and regulating the use of X-ray machines in order to prevent detrimental consequences.

The most important work done by Verschuur was the formation of industrial councils by the Law of April 7, 1933. Such councils regulated collective labor contracts, advised on subjects relating to labor in industry, made special rules for vocational schools, took measures against unemployment and for work expansion, collected statistical data, and encouraged conciliation between workers and employers. The law provided that the Crown may institute in every industry, for the whole or for a part of the country, a council of industry.

The succeeding four coalition ministries, under the leadership of Hendrik Colijn, embraced a period between May 26, 1933, and August 10, 1939. In May, 1933, a Department of Social Affairs was established with Slotemaker de Bruine as its first Minister, followed by M. Slingenberg (Liberal Democrat) and C. P. M. Romme (Roman Catholic). In this department are divisions for labor, workmen's insurance, labor inspection, labor expansion, etc. The amount of labor legislation in this period was extensive.

The Domestic Labor Law of November 17, 1933, determines which localities may be used for doing work outside an industrial plant, the minimum wages for such work, and the protective measures against "sweaters." In 1934, a law was passed regulating the purchase and sale of foodstuffs and commodities through automatic machines; the law contained stipulations about worktime and hygienic conditions in stores using automats. In the same year the Factory Safety Law revised a similar one of 1911, and contained strict stipulations for workshops on lighting, temperature, clothes closets and toilets, covering of machine parts, electric conductors, fire prevention, and prophylactic hygiene.

In 1935 the working time in automatic pane-glass factories was brought into accordance with the agreements reached by the International Labor Conference at Geneva in the previous year. The Sickness Benefit Law was radically revised; benefits were increased and the application liberalized.

Two laws concerning labor of women reached the Statutes in 1937: one regulated their work in mines and another restricted nightwork. Organization of workers' insurance bureaus was simplified and the workers themselves were protected against the worst consequences of the depression. Millions of guilders were poured into the treasuries of the labor unions for unemployment benefits.

The councils of labor organized public bodies to execute social insurance and to coöperate in the application of legal regulations which concerned labor insurance. Each council was to be composed of a chairman, appointed by the Queen, and two members each representing employers and employees and providing for four substitutes. The members were all to be appointed by the Minister of Social Affairs on recommendation of the most important organizations of employers and employees. Their term was three years.

On the tenth of August, 1939, the first two Socialists entered the ministry: J. W. Albarda, mechanical engineer and leader of the Social Democratic Labor party since Troelstra's retirement, as Minister of Waterways and Communications, and J. van den Tempel, whose biography might bear the title "from house painter to the

Queen's advisor," as Minister of Social Affairs. The conditions created by the Second World War at once demanded measures to protect the workers against its economic effects. A new stevedore's law and elaborate regulations and laws concerning unemployment were planned. The lot of the seamen was to be further improved. But, on May 10, 1940, the dark, ominous shadow of slavery crept over the land.

Part Five

Cultural Aspects

CHAPTER XIII

Philosophy and Religious Trends

BY DAVID FRIEDMAN

IN ITS SPIRITUAL DEVELOPMENT Holland appears to have been a land of theology rather than philosophy. However, if it is correct to say that during the seventeenth century, the "Golden Age of the Netherlands," the rigid discipline of the Dutch Reformed Church performed an indispensable social and intellectual function, it is equally true that it did not dominate integrally the national life of this period. This age was in reality characterized by an antithesis between the dominant Calvinist Church and the "libertines," or free-thinkers. Or, to put it in other words, an antithesis between the theocratic principles of the Reformation in its Calvinist form and the humanistic-individualistic principles of the Renaissance which in Holland have never blended into one harmonious whole. On the contrary, both the Renaissance and the Reformation in the Netherlands were the full realization of that liberation from the shackles of medievalism which made man's return to himself possible, and free inquiry into religious and philosophical concepts and values imperative. This development had its antecedents in the mystic, subjective, and individualistic-humanitarian tendencies of the late Middle Ages. In the midst of the ecclesiastical decline of the late medieval period when scholasticism—essentially a blend of the philosophies of Plato and Aristotle applied to Christian theology—had deteriorated into a rigid complex of quibbling and logical hair-splittings, a Christian Renaissance made itself manifest in the Netherlands which found a striking expression in the Brotherhood of the Common Life, the *Devotio Moderna,* founded by the philosopher, Geert Groote (1340–1384).

The *Modern Devotion* had its roots in the mystical spiritual trends which rose and flourished in opposition to the pedantic scholastic wisdom of the time and the worldliness of the Church. Contemporary of Geert Groote was Jan van Ruusbroek or Ruysbroeck, the "Miraculous" (1294–1381), a friend of birds and flowers, like a second Francis of Assisi, and immersed in the mysterious realm of the contemplative life. Inspired by the writings of the great German mystic, Eckehart, and by the tender and fervent prose and poetry of the Flemish poetess, Sister Hadewijch (about 1250 A.D.), who extolled in her letters and visions the divine love and the mystical union with God, Van Ruusbroek, the "good prior," gathered around him in the beautiful surroundings of Groenendaal, near Brussels, a group of devout men whom he roused to a true brotherhood in God, a pure inner life and a practical imitation of Christ. Van Ruusbroek's writings, occasionally deviating from the accepted doctrines of the Church and exerting a great influence, contained the seeds which some 150 years later would blossom into the spiritual movements of the Renaissance and the Reformation.

This mystic school, this revival of inner Christian life came to the northern provinces of the Netherlands through the magnetic personality of Geert Groote. Together with his friend and disciple, Floriszoon Radewijnsz (1350–1400) he founded around 1380 his community of the Brethren and Sisters of the Common Life which became established in the cities of the IJssel Valley (Deventer, Zwolle, etc.) and from there spread throughout the country. The brotherhood was essentially a lay-community although after 1381 monasteries and convents were established at Windesheim, Diepenveen, and elsewhere. The Brethren and Sisters aspired at a realization of truly Christian ideals in daily life. To serve God in love and charity, but also in wisdom and knowledge, was their heartfelt desire. Hence, the community became a famous center of learning and education where not only much energy was devoted to the spiritual training of the members and of schoolboys but where also much attention was given to the study of the great classical and medieval authors. The Brethren undertook a correction of the *Vulgate* as well as a translation of parts of the Bible into the vernacular. Through their charitable deeds and their work for the general good, through their adverse attitude toward decadent scholasticism, but, above all, through the illustrious men who rose from their ranks, this movement became the predominant precursor of the Protestant Reformation and of humanistic learning in the Netherlands. Prominent among these men was Thomas à Kempis, credited with the composition of the *Imitatio Christi,* a precious jewel among the religious scriptures of the world, translated into every conceivable language, and always a source of spiritual consolation and elation.

Other great humanistic scholars who were directly inspired by this movement were Wessel Gansfort, Rudolf Agricola, Hegius, Beatus Rhenanus, the great theologian and scholar Cardinal Nicolaus Cusanus (1401–1464), and above all Desiderius Erasmus (1466?–1536), who received his early education at the famous Latin school of Deventer. Different from his great contemporary and opponent Luther, Erasmus tried to realize a regeneration of Christianity within the Roman Catholic Church. His piety and love of God blended harmoniously with his classical erudition and marvelous learning and gave rise to that Christian biblical humanism which became a real Dutch reformatory movement, stimulating freedom of thought and religious tolerance. Through his critical edition of the New Testament, based on a study of the original texts, through his stoic conceptions, as well as through his numerous writings revealing a broad-minded criticism, humor and universal understanding he imbued many great scholars and reformers, both within and outside the Roman Catholic Church, with that undogmatic spirit which centered in the purity of faith and morals, the Brotherhood of Christ, and the enlightenment of reason.

Although his ideals were superseded by those of the Protestant Reformation, the Erasmian trend lived on in those fighters for religious freedom and tolerance, who, from the middle of the sixteenth century, favored a sacramentarian, biblical-evangelical, tolerant, anti-confessional form of religion and apart from their theological conceptions won renown through their firm attitude against the persecution and killing of heretics. After these "Evangelicals," as well as the followers of Luther, Zwingli and the Anabaptists, had first formed a nucleus of reformers, Calvinism rapidly asserted itself in the Netherlands, without being able to supersede fully the more tolerant rational trends. This fervent religious movement was, in the first period of the Eighty-Years' War, the principal inspirational force of the Dutch people in their fight for religious and social freedom. Through its direct spiritual and realistic appeal to the individual, as well as through its moral grandeur and puritanical principles aiming at a Christian regeneration of life and society, it kindled the fire of intense faith in the hearts of its followers, which gave them the strength to suffer great hardships and persecutions. However, after Calvinism had practically obtained the position of a State Church, its sad fate was to grow increasingly intolerant. This was partly because of its still precarious position, and because certain of its confessional doctrines, emphasized by the specific orthodox dogma of the Reformed Church, and presenting the Calvinistic creed as sole repository of ultimate religious truth, did not allow different points of view.

Above all those who, in humanistic Erasmian spirit, opposed this trend must be mentioned Dirk Volkertszoon Coornhert (1522–1590), the convinced champion of a nonconfessional Christianity and of religious freedom. Of patrician descent he suffered persecution, imprisonment, and temporary exile for his humanistic convictions which brought him into conflict with the Roman Catholic Church, to which he nominally belonged, as well as with the Calvinists whom he considered too intolerant. Moreover, the Calvinistic deterministic conceptions of original sin and predestination were irreconcilable with his own views regarding the moral dignity of man, giving him the right to determine independently his own fate and conscience under the guidance of inner faith and human reason. Coornhert, whose activities were manifold, was strongly influenced by the moral conceptions of the Stoics. He gave excellent translations of Cicero, Seneca, and Boethius. Like Erasmus, he believed that the great "pagan" authors of classical antiquity were moved by God's spirit, as much as were the Christians. Viewing Christianity as the purest revelation of that universal inner truth which the truly sage and pious of all ages have shared, he aspired to a natural, rational, tolerant religion transcending the mutually conflicting dogmatical reasonings. He published several works of which the treatise *The Art of Ethics, i.e., the Art to Live Well (Zedekunst; dat is Wellevens-kunste*, 1587) was the most important. In it he expressed the idea that true happiness is based on virtue. Man could aspire to the highest, for in his soul dwells a spark of the divine light. On the contrary, man is hampered by the human passions. The task and significance of moral Christian life are contained in the mastering of these passions. In his fight for the rights of the human personality, Coornhert's ideals greatly contributed to the establishing of those traditions of tolerance and freedom which in later years became characteristic of the Dutch philosophy of life.

At the beginning of the seventeenth century the Calvinist Reformed Church, rather than the Netherlands population as a whole, became divided into two main parties, the Remonstrants and the Counter-Remonstrants. Their followers were irreconcilably divided on theological questions. This dissension was in reality determined by the old controversy which had kept Calvinism divided into two schools since its introduction into the Netherlands from Switzerland and France. There were the Reformed, the strict Calvinists or Precisionists, who rigidly adhered to Calvin's and Beza's doctrines, professing the absolute sovereignty of God, original sin, and the total depravity of man, predestination and election through divine grace, and determinism of the will. Their tenets were embodied in the *Netherlands Confession of Faith (Confessio Belgica)*, composed by Guido de Bray (1559 and 1566) and the *Heidelberg Cathechism* (1563), to which all would be required to conform on pain of being deprived of their rights as citizens. They advocated the autonomy and democratic organization of the Reformed Church without interference on the part of the states. At the same time they aspired to the creation of a State Church entailing a supremacy of the Church over the State. These Calvinists comprised the larger masses of the Protestant people. On the contrary, there were the Evangelicals and Libertines to whom belonged the majority of the wealthy ruling burgher-regents of Holland, the most influential province. In the main they adhered to the anticonfessional and undogmatical tolerant principles as preached by Veluanus, Coornhert, and others. At the same time these humanistic, classically minded Republican Liberals were in favor of the rights of the State to interfere in ecclesiastical affairs.

The ever-smouldering conflict between these groups became acute in 1604 when Jacobus Arminius (1560–1609), Professor of Theology at the University of Leyden, an eloquent preacher, affiliated by marriage to the "regenten" of Amsterdam, launched his attack on the doctrine of predestination, claiming that Christ died for all men and not for the select few, and that men, even after sincere repentance might still fall from grace. Arminius subsequently defended his liberal views in a public debate with his colleague Franciscus Gomarus (1563–1641), a rigid Calvinist. In 1610 the Arminians presented their *Remonstrance,* a religious apology, composed by Johannes Uytenbogaert (1557–1644), in which the tenets of reprobation and predestination were once more rejected and from which they henceforth derived their name of "Remonstrants." This religious dissension which swept the country and which essentially was concerned with freedom or compulsion in the matters of conscience ultimately culminated in the coup d'état of 1618 of Prince Maurice of Orange and in the execution of Johan van Oldenbarneveldt, who was Lord Advocate of Holland and a staunch upholder of the hegemony of this province in the United Republic, supporter of the Remonstrants and defender of the rights of each province to regulate its own religious affairs. The controversy was settled at the famous Synod of Dordrecht (1618–1619) where the Counter-Remonstrants triumphed. Calvin's *Institutio* became the accepted cue, the Remonstrants were repudiated in five articles and the old national principle of freedom of religion had to yield temporarily to the Genevan spirit of absolute authority. In short, "supranaturalism" gained a seeming victory over the rational trends prevalent among the Remonstrants, Arminians, and Socinians. This, however, did not impair the status of the Catholics, Jews, and the nonconformist Protestant groups.

One of the most distinguished men who fell victim to these quarrels was Hugo Grotius (Huig van Groot, 1583–1645) who became famous as a jurist, historian, philologist, theologian, philosopher, and diplomat. At the age of fifteen he finished his studies at the University of Leyden, the seat of classical learning and humanistic trends, which through its illustrious scholars (Scaliger, Salmasius, Heinsius, Vossius, among others) had laid the early foundations of modern philology, jurisprudence, and science. Urged on by Oldenbarneveldt he became involved in 1613 in the fervent religious controversies which led to his imprisonment for life in the castle of Loevestein. In 1621 he succeeded in escaping to France. From 1635 to 1645 he was Swedish ambassador at Paris. Grotius' ideal was the reunion of the hopelessly divided Christian nations and Christian churches on the basis of a rational, tolerant free confession which would restore the pristine "apostolic" principles of the early Christians. Both in his theological and stoical conceptions and his critical-historical-philological approach he tried to realize Erasmian-humanistic ideals. Independent of theological postulates and religious prejudices, he aspired to a new order of society based on the principles of reason and law and transcending the nonfundamental religious conflicts. In his various publications, above all in his *De jure belli ac pacis,* he outlined the principles of a general jurisprudence as well as the fundamentals of natural and positive law. He became the preëminent founder of international law, which in his opinion should be the infallible foundation of social, religious, and international peace. His book entitled *Freedom of the Sea,* won world-wide fame. Grotius was a typical exponent of that mighty period of cultural efflorescence which marked Holland's "Golden Age."

Theology as a primary, and philosophy as an auxiliary science, the humanities in all their diverse aspects, as well as the exact sciences received a great impetus from the founding of the universities, although many of the most outstanding scholars remained outside their ranks.[1]

It was the Frenchman, René Descartes (Renatus Cartesius, 1596–1650) who greatly furthered the cause of philosophy as the art of

---

[1] See Chapter III, "The Seventeenth Century: the Golden Age," by Adriaan Jacob Barnouw.

free and autonomous thinking, detached from the arbitrariness of phantasy, the one-sidedness of some particular experience or the duress of transmitted dogmas and traditions. Born in La Haye in Touraine, Descartes received his early education at the Jesuit school of La Flèche, followed by studies at the University of Paris. Dissatisfied with the uncertainties, prejudicial fallacies and wrong methods of the scholastic systems he decided to gain truthful knowledge by seeing for himself lands and peoples, or in his own words "by reading the great book of the world." This brought him in 1617 to the Netherlands where he volunteered in the well-trained army of Prince Maurice, the great patron of the exact sciences. After a period of extensive travel throughout Europe, he lived from 1629 to 1649 in Holland, where he engaged in the writing of many philosophical and scientific treatises which gave him the name of "father of modern philosophy."

Descartes' writings were primarily the *Essais Philosophiques* containing the *Discours de la Méthode* (1637); the *Meditationes de Prima Philosophia* (1641); the *Principia Philosophiae* (1644); and the *Traité des Passions de l'Âme* (1649). The significance of Descartes for the history of human thought lies in his rational methodical approach, his theory of knowledge, his overcoming of doubt and uncertainty through self-consciousness, as well as in his mathematical publications. In his philosophical investigations Descartes wished to emancipate himself from the contradictory opinions and theories of the numerous philosophical systems in order to discover the "Archimedean point" of absolute certainty. So that he might achieve this, he methodically applied absolute doubt as a severe test for whatever claimed to serve as the sure starting point of knowledge. Reasoning that everything can be doubted but doubt itself, he inferred that at least an "ego" who doubts, and therefore thinks, exists. "*Cogito, ergo sum*," or "I think, therefore I am." This was the Archimedean point of absolute certainty, an axiomatic truth, self-evident to the intellect and therefore a sufficient guarantee of its validity.

Descartes was a dual personality. In spite of his being a mathematical genius who tried to apply a system of "universal mathematics" to all kinds of scientific investigation, he remained a loyal

Catholic, genuinely attached to a certain traditional theology. Most of his publications, however, met with disapproval by the Roman Catholic Church. During his stay in Holland he made many friends, among whom were the well-known mathematician Isaac Beeckman (1588–1637) and the poet and statesman, Constantijn Huygens (1596–1687). Although he led a hidden life (*bene vixit, qui bene latuit*) he exerted an immense influence, which brought him into conflict with Gisbertus Voetius (Voet) (1589–1676), a former pupil of Gomarus, a devout champion of the Dordtian brand of Calvinism, a preacher of penitence, a fierce anti-Catholic, who was Professor of Theology in the University of Utrecht. Voetius saw clearly that the Cartesian doubt inevitably would lead to the questioning of the authority of the Scriptures, and the articles of the confession of faith, thereby strengthening the nonconformist attitudes of the Arminians, Socinians and other dissident groups. The religious-philosophical disputes which ensued throughout the country ultimately induced the municipal government of Utrecht to denounce Descartes' philosophy as atheistic. Descartes thereupon accepted Queen Christina's invitation and left for Sweden, where he died in 1650.

Among his many prominent followers in the Netherlands must be mentioned Henricus Reneri (Henri Renier), Professor of Philosophy, and Henri le Roy, Professor of Medicine in the University of Utrecht; the famous Johannes Coccejus, Professor of Theology at the University of Leyden; also Abraham Heydanus and Balthasar Bekker, a minister of the Church and a great scholar who was celebrated for his original and humane publications against superstition and trials for witchcraft. Above all there should be remembered Arnold Geulincx (1625–1669), who originally was attached to the University of Louvain but who became a lecturer in Leyden after his conversion to Calvinism. Like Descartes, Geulincx maintained the sharp distinction between mind and body, bridged by divine intervention. On the contrary, he assumed that this intervention occurred only occasionally. Because of divine laws there was a general correspondence between mind and body, to be compared with two synchronized clocks adjusted by the same watchmaker. His system is therefore called "occasionalism." His best-known works are *Gnothi Seauton* or *Ethica* (1665), and *Metaphysica Vera* published in 1691.

The rigid dogmatism of the Reformed Church, with its emphasis on orthodoxy rather than on inner devotion, found its reaction in the rise of several pietistic, ascetic, and mystic movements, which were partly nonconformist and aspired at higher Christian experience through regeneration and sanctification, repentance and faith as an attitude of heart.

One of the most remarkable sects was formed by the followers of Jean de Labadie (1610–1674) who was a devout mystic, an eloquent homilete and a learned theologian. In 1666 he went from Geneva to Middelburg where he was minister of the Walloon Reformed Church. His ideal was the creation of a holy community, which should substitute living piety for dead orthodoxy and should strive for moral and religious perfection. His refusal to submit to the accepted confession of faith and discipline brought him into conflict with the Walloon Reformed Church which caused his suspension. Labadie then formed a free community at Veere and at Amsterdam which attracted many followers and interesting personalities in spite of the fact that they were time and again expelled and forced to look for more hospitable refuges in Herford (Westphalia) and Wieuwerd (Friesland).

The Labadists had certain spiritual affinities to the Quakers. Penn, Fox, and Barclay visited the community in Wieuwerd. Their ideals were ascetic and puritanical. They emphasized prayer, which they considered as listening to God, renunciation, and mystic contemplation. They also introduced community of goods, and new marital conceptions in which they dispensed with all formalities. One of the most devout members of the community of Wieuwerd was Anna Maria Schuurman (1607–1678) an exceptionally versatile and talented character who excelled in many arts and sciences. She was an exceptional linguist who mastered the classical as well as Oriental languages, and who wrote beautiful poems and learned theological treatises. She also became a famous sculptress and musician. Among these nonconformist sects mysticism flourished and the writings of Böhme and other mystics were widely read. Especially was Jan Luyken (1649–1712) the famous engraver and moral poet, strongly influenced by Böhme's mystic-pantheistic doctrines.

A similar sect was formed by the so-called *Rijnsburg Collegiants*. It developed during the Remonstrant wrangles as an independent group which became renowned for its liberalism and breadth of thought. In their meetings which were, for the most part, private and were patterned after the style of the early Christian *Collegia profetarum,* every member had the opportunity to speak or rather prophesy freely, as enunciated in I Cor. 14. Through their anticlerical and anticonfessional principles, as well as through their ideals of tolerance, philanthropy, freedom of thought and inquiry, and undogmatic piety, they were able to form rallying centers throughout Holland for all those who were dissatisfied with the tenets and methods of the official churches. In their social conceptions the *Collegiants* were, to a certain extent, precursors of Tolstoi. Although most of their followers were among the more simple people, many prominent and famous men joined their ranks. Descartes frequently visited their meetings. The most typical representative of this group was the poet Dirk Rafaelszoon Camphuysen, who, by preference, preached to all those who suffered the persecution of the established churches.

It was in this tolerant and irenical sphere of the *Collegiants* that the Netherlands' greatest philosopher, Baruch de Spinoza (1632–1677), found a refuge, although he rose far beyond their religious and philosophical convictions. In Spinoza the philosophical rationalist thinking of the seventeenth century came to full maturity and perfection. His life, characterized by unselfishness, true understanding and sincere religious feeling, was certainly the reflection of the moral and ethical implications of his own philosophy. He was the grandson of Portuguese crypto-Jewish immigrants who had found a refuge in the Netherlands. In his early years he attended the school for Jewish boys led by the eminent scholars, Saul Morteira and Manasseh ben Israel. There he received instruction in the Old Testament, the Talmud, the Hebrew Codes, the works of Ibn Ezra, Maimonides, Crescas, and others. Outside the school hours, Spinoza acquired a sound knowledge of secular subjects and many languages.

From Hebrew books which dealt with the exact sciences, he obtained an early knowledge of mathematics and physics. Already as a young student he had proved to be an exceptionally gifted and independent thinker. Although educated in strictly orthodox Jewish trends, he gradually came into inner conflict with the traditionalism and supernaturalism of the accepted Jewish dogmas, and followed in the footsteps of his unfortunate rationalist predecessor, Uriel Acosta, who suffered excommunication for his independent convictions. It was especially his acquaintance and friendship with several prominent *Collegiants* who were greatly interested in the philosophy of Descartes, and more in particular his association with the ex-Jesuit Cartesian scholar, Franciscus van den Ende, which led to his estrangement and ultimate excommunication from the synagogue.

The same tendency to revolt against mere tradition and ecclesiastical authority which kept contemporary Dutch Protestantism divided, became also manifest in Spinoza. Since his attitude was considered to be as anti-Christian as they believed it was anti-Jewish, the religious leaders of the Portuguese community greatly feared that their still precarious position would be strongly endangered. Hence, they formally reported the fact of his excommunication to the civil authorities of Amsterdam, in order to absolve the Jewish community from all responsibility for Spinoza's heresies. Spinoza subsequently left Amsterdam and later moved on to Rijnsburg where he lived in close touch with the *Collegiants*. From there he went to Voorburg and finally to The Hague, where he died of tuberculosis. While studying and writing in spiritual solitude and carrying on a correspondence with the greatest scholars of his time, he partly supported himself by grinding lenses, at which he was expert. The fact that he refused a professorship in philosophy in Heidelberg because he did not want to endanger his freedom of thought and speech, was characteristic of his independent attitude toward life.

Although Spinoza came under the influence of Descartes, he derived his philosophic inspiration from the Neoplatonic and Jewish mystical writings as well as from early medieval Arabic philosophers. The monistic conceptions of Giordano Bruno also seem to have contributed to Spinoza's philosophy. During his lifetime he published only two works: a book on the philosophy of Descartes entitled *Principia Philosophiae Cartesianae,* which he clearly expounded, yet repudiated, and his *Tractatus Theologico-Politicus.* When one realizes that this book was referred to as "having been forged in hell by the apostate Jew with the aid of the devil," it need cause no surprise that it created a true sensation, in spite of the fact that it was published anonymously. In this book Spinoza advocated the theory that the State should grant freedom of religion and scientific inquiry, the more so, because otherwise the Church inevitably would gain supremacy over the State. Since every exclusive state-religion must be based on divine revelation, Spinoza reasoned that the Bible should be submitted to higher criticism in order to establish or repudiate its rightful authority. No wonder this book aroused a storm of indignation among the orthodox Calvinists. But, it also focused definitely the attention of many philosophers and free thinkers on Spinoza. Nevertheless, his other works had to be published posthumously. They consisted of the *Ethics (Ethica),* the *Political Treatise,* the *Treatise on the Improvement of the Understanding,* the *Letters* and a *Hebrew Grammar.*

Spinoza's rationalistic-mystic system of monistic philosophy, especially as demonstrated *ordine geometrico* in his *Ethica* cannot be adequately described in a short article. During and after his lifetime it was denounced as sheer atheism and only a few disciples came under its influence in the Netherlands. Nevertheless, it gave rise to fervent religious and philosophical disputes just as did the philosophy of Descartes. The true greatness and value of this philosopher, who towered so high above the prevalent thinking of his time, was not discovered until the nineteenth and twentieth centuries.

When compared with the "Golden Age," the eighteenth century was a period of decline and recapitulation. Politically, the Republic lost its leading position; culturally, its life was determined by talent rather than by genius; the religious quarrels greatly subsided. The fierce disputes around Descartes, Geulincx, and Spinoza lost their strength; liberalism and tolerance, verging on indifference, prevailed;

and Methodism, Pietism, and Quakerism flourished. On the contrary, the new trends of the time, rationalism and enlightenment, coinciding with a great interest in natural science made much headway. Philosophy became subservient chiefly to science. In the beginning of the eighteenth century little attention was given to German philosophy. Leibniz and Christian Wolff exerted some influence as may be seen from the work of Nicolaas Engelhard, professor in Groningen who wrote on the preëstablished harmony in the universe. The French philosopher, Pierre Bayle (1647–1706), forerunner of the later French encyclopedists, lived, just as Descartes, the greater part of his life in Holland, where he became Professor of Philosophy and History at Rotterdam in 1681. Through his numerous works he greatly stimulated the principles of enlightenment, reason, and religious freedom. The combination of exact science and philosophy was excellently represented by the famous Professor of Medicine, Herman Boerhaave (1668–1738) who was wrongly "accused" of Spinozism, and by Willem Jacob van 's Gravesande, who taught physics, astronomy, ethics and philosophy at the University of Leyden. Following the scientific doctrines of Newton, he strongly opposed the fatalistic determinism of Spinoza and Hobbes.

The rising materialistic trends found a strong opponent in Franz Hemsterhuys (1721–1790) the most significant Dutch philosopher of the late eighteenth century. His position as a government official gave him sufficient time for scientific and philosophical studies. His friendship with Princess Adelheid Amalie Galitzin, his *Diotima* brought him in personal contact with Goethe and Herder. H. F. Jacobi came under his influence. Hemsterhuys, who was the son of the famous classical philologist Tiberius Hemsterhuys, based his philosophy primarily on Plato and Socrates, although he eclectically adopted many views of Locke, Shaftesbury, Leibniz, and others. In his system he tried to reconcile rationalism with sensualism. His works, written in French, were mostly in the elegant style of dialogues and letters.

The philologist Daniel Wijttenbach (1746–1820), also showed in his works close affinity to ancient Greek philosophy, having been strongly influenced by Leibniz and Wolff. He became especially known for his bitter antagonism to the philosophy of Kant which, from the end of the eighteenth century began to make great headway in Holland.

The same controversy between "Idealism" and "Naturalism," between "Pure Reason" and "Common Sense" or between "Critical Philosophy" and "Orthodox Theology," which dominated the thinking of the nineteenth century, made itself also manifest in the Netherlands. It is a remarkable fact that nowhere, outside Germany, was Kant's significance sooner realized than in Holland. Like Descartes and Spinoza in earlier times, this philosopher caused a true philosophical "conflagration." Early protagonists were Paulus van Hemert (1756–1825) and Johannes Kinker (1764–1845). The former, a Remonstrant Professor of Philosophy in Rotterdam, wrote an excellent treatise on the principles of the Kantian philosophy and tried to popularize Kant in a magazine, *Literature at Breakfast and Tea.* Kinker, the poet, linguist, and philosopher wrote, among others, several articles on the *Critique of Pure Reason* which, through their French translation, exerted considerable influence on contemporary philosophical thinking. In an allegorical play in verse, in which the dramatis personae symbolized Kantian ideas, he created propaganda for a moral-rational religion. The famous orientalist Taco Roorda, eulogized Kant in Latin verse. More important was the fact that these men founded the *Magazine for Critical Philosophy,* which obtained the collaboration of prominent intellectuals who really attempted to initiate a new era of philosophical thinking. No wonder this caused a reaction among orthodox circles who considered Kant's moral rationalism dangerous to orthodoxy and who recognized in his followers the spirit of Remonstrants, Baptists, and other nonconformists.

Typical of contemporary Dutch situations was the way in which the controversy was conducted. The poet who wrote for children, Hieronymus van Alphen, admonished like the proverbial Dutch uncle, but was soon refuted by Van Hemert, who also became engaged in a bitter dispute with Wijttenbach. The latter considered the *Sancta rectaque doctrina Platonis metaphysica et moralis* as the only true philosophy. Moreover, he greatly objected to the obscure terminology and involved style in which Kant phrased his philosophy. The sentimental romantic poet Rhijnvis Feith, was very much opposed to a purely rational belief in God which deprived "supra-naturalist revelation" of its *raison d'être*. In his *Letters to Sophie (Brieven aan Sophie)* on the spirit of the Kantian philosophy he maintained that Kant destroyed Christianity. These letters were answered by Kinker, whose satirical *Letters from Sophie to Mr. Feith* revealed Feith's ignorance. The famous Willem Bilderdijk (1756-1831), father of the new religious awakening—known by the name of the *Réveil*—gave vent to his anti-Kantian feelings in satirical rhymes, in which he prayed God to deliver the Netherlanders from the Kantian "fad." Kant's doctrine of moral autonomy he ridiculed as follows:

> "Perfect—that is man uppermost.
> There is no higher—no divinity, no 'Ghost.'
> Yet, our grandeur, should constantly higher move.
> Just read Kant and Fichte, that is what they will prove."[2]

The controversy between Van Hemert and Wijttenbach terminated the early Kantian movement in Holland. The impression that it was dangerous to religion and morals, along with the vicissitudes of the Napoleonic period and a lack of interest in speculative idealistic philosophy, caused its premature expiration.

More in keeping with the prevailing trends was the "common sense" philosophy of Ph. W. van Heusde (1778-1839), a pupil of Wijttenbach, and the most influential philosopher of the early nineteenth century. In 1803 he became Professor of History and Classical Philology in the University of Utrecht. In contrast to Bilderdijk he was called the father of the Neo-Humanistic *Réveil*. Van Heusde was greatly influenced by Hemsterhuys, as well as by German romanticism. Dissatisfied with the arid materialism of the time, he turned to Hellas—the land of beauty—wishing to imbue the people of the nineteenth century with ancient Greek ideas, particularly with the philosophy of Socrates and Plato, which he believed contained the

---

[2] H. Y. Groenewegen, "Kant in Nederland," in Kant, *Beteekenis voor de Wijsbegeerte*, Amsterdam 1924, pp. 7-20.

true principles and method of philosophizing best suited to the character of the Dutch people. The "common sense" philosophy of Van Heusde gained power over the rationalism of the end of the eighteenth century, which attempted to prove everything. It was related to the philosophy of faith and immediate experience of Jacobi, which taught that God had created in man common sense, which gives him a direct knowledge of God and the external world.

Van Heusde wanted to reconcile philosophy with Christianity. Philosophy should accept a special revelation but should examine it according to its own standards of the divine and holy. Christ was not, in the first place, the Redeemer of fallen mankind, but rather the ideal and divine example to humanity. Man was imperfect but he aspired to self-perfection. The essential characteristic of his nature was will to love, not to sin. God revealed His order in history, nature, and in inner conscience by which He educated humanity in conformity with Himself. All great men, the most outstanding of whom were Socrates and Plato, and particularly Jesus Christ, were the great educators of man. Life, persons, and facts were more than mere doctrine.

Van Heusde's system was eclectical. His influence was considerable, the more so because he voiced to a certain extent the rising post-French-revolutionary ideas and sentiments of the people. His ideas gave rise to the so-called "Groningen School" of theology, which taught an evangelical form of Christianity, based on the motto: "Not a dogma, but the Lord." This cultural, optimistic trend was in keeping with the views of Lessing and Schleiermacher and was prominently represented by Hofstede de Groot, Pareau, Van Oordt, and others.

In general, the study of philosophy occupied only a minor position in Holland during the first half of the nineteenth century. In his book, *Philosophy in the Netherlands,* Professor Land observed: "Among capable students a general impression prevailed that philosophy was too difficult as a pastime and not profitable enough as a serious occupation."

Theology, on the other hand, flourished. The *Réveil* led partly to a renewed orthodoxy of various shades and in later years to Neo-

Calvinism as propagated by Dr. Abraham Kuyper and others. The ethical school of Professor D. Chantepie de la Saussaye emphasized the religious-moral nature of Christianity which should be realized by regeneration and conversion through heart and conscience.

J. J. van Oosterzee and J. T. Doedes were the chief representatives of a supranaturalist theistic trend. They came forward as apologists of Apostolical and Historical Christianity and opposed both the "Groningen School" and the "Modern Theology," which had come into being around 1860. This new movement wanted to adjust its own conception of Christianity to contemporary scientific thought. It derived its chief impetus from C. W. Opzoomer (1821–1890), who was undoubtedly the most original and significant philosopher of the nineteenth century in Holland. After having studied law at Leyden, Opzoomer at the age of twenty-five became Professor of Philosophy in Utrecht, "from recruit to marshal" as he himself observed. He was originally influenced by the idealism of Krause, Schelling, and Hegel, but turned soon to the empiricism of Auguste Comte and others, which gave him the name, "Dutch John Stuart Mill." In his works he emphasized the belief that man should become reconciled to himself through philosophy, which opposed the supranaturalist belief of revelation. The way of experience only, led to true knowledge in both philosophy and theology. Although he opposed the Kantian *a priori* factors of knowledge and emphasized experience and feeling through the senses, he nevertheless assumed a separate religious, ethical, and esthetic feeling, through which he thought he could establish a synthesis between science and the belief in a personal God, moral freedom, and immortality. Another prominent scholar in the school of "Modern Theology" was J. H. Scholten who gradually arrived at a pure spiritualistic monism on deterministic grounds.

During the second half of the nineteenth century, philosophy became increasingly emancipated from theology. Geulincx, Spinoza, Kant, Hegel, and the other creators of great philosophical systems began once more to engage the attention of Dutch scholars. Allard Pierson (1831–1896), a pupil of Opzoomer, and one of Holland's greatest prose writers, tried to arrive at a synthesis of Darwinist empiricism and Spinoza, criticizing from this point of view the Kantian doctrines. M. H. van Voorthuysen, able critic of Kant, pointed out how difficult were the problems of a satisfactory theory of knowledge.

Critical philosophy, in the form of Neo-Kantianism, on the other hand, was ably reintroduced by C. Bellaar Spruyt (1842–1900) and J. P. N. Land (1834–1897). The former, a professor in Amsterdam, was originally a follower of Schopenhauer. In later years he became one of the best Kant scholars of his time, as may be seen from his work on "innate ideas" (1879) in which he explained that the mind gives *a priori* objectivity to its knowledge. J. P. N. Land, in particular, was a versatile scholar who greatly stimulated the study of philosophy. Apart from being an eminent historian and orientalist, he wrote an excellent treatise, *Introduction to Philosophy,* in which he ably interpreted Kantian ideas. His outstanding achievement, however, was his critical first edition of the works of Geulincx. Professor Land also coöperated in the edition of Spinoza's *Opera* (first edition, Amsterdam 1882–1883) which ushered in a new period of Spinoza research in Holland. His coeditor was Johannes van Vloten (1818–1883), one of the best contemporary Spinoza interpreters. It was the good fortune of the latter to rediscover a large collection of letters written by Spinoza, which he ably edited and used for his excellent monographs. The first short biography written, in 1705, by the Lutheran pastor, Johannes Colerus who lived in Spinoza's house in The Hague, repudiated his system as atheistic, but gave a truthful picture of his life. Van Vloten's description, however, was the first objective biography to reveal a deep admiration and true understanding for this philosopher. A statue of Spinoza was erected in The Hague. Spinoza societies, with their own periodicals were founded. The houses in Rijnsburg and The Hague, where Spinoza had lived were dedicated to his memory and became centers of Spinozistic learning. Among the many scholars who greatly contributed to this must be mentioned Dr. W. Meyer and Dr. J. D. Bierens de Haan (1866–1943), one of the most outstanding of contemporary Dutch thinkers. The philosophical system of the latter is a synthesis of Spinoza's ethics and Hegel's dialectical idealism with a strong bearing on esthetics.

Another prominent philosopher was Professor B. H. C. K. van der Wijck, who taught a spiritualistic monism, reminiscent of Fechner. From the end of the nineteenth century there was an increasing tendency in Holland to emancipate philosophy from the natural sciences. Two scholars in particular should be mentioned: G. Heymans (1857–1930) and G. J. P. J. Bolland (1854–1922). Heymans succeeded Van der Wijck in the chair of philosophy in Groningen in 1890. His starting point was empiricism which he applied to an analysis of mind, consciousness, and character. This led him, in agreement with Kant, to the adoption of *a priori* principles of knowledge. His doctrine of spiritualistic monism became the basis of his applied psychological research, which has been of the greatest practical interest. Following Wundt, he created in Groningen the first laboratory for experimental psychology which became a model for similar institutions in Amsterdam, Nijmegen and Utrecht. His work was continued among others by his pupils, Leo Polak and the psychologist H. J. F. W. Brugmans.

Bolland was the outstanding representative of pure speculative philosophy. No other contemporary thinker exerted during his lifetime such a great influence. In philosophy he was an autodidact with all the fervent enthusiasm of such. From the status of teacher of English in Batavia, he became in 1896 Land's successor as Professor of Philosophy in Leyden. Starting with the philosophy of Eduard von Hartmann he turned in later years to that of Hegel, of which he became one of the best European experts. He was a brilliant stylist and orator. His lectures which gathered crowds, attracted the fine flower of Dutch intellect. He did not teach only philosophy but rather how to philosophize independently. As may be seen from his numerous publications, he was a scholar of such wide interests as esthetics, philology, and theology. Especially are his studies on the origin of the early history of Christianity a landmark in this field. Interesting also are his books on Freemasonry. According to Bolland, religion originated in philosophical thinking—philosophical thinking did not originate in religion. His independent and forceful personality brought him many prominent pupils but also many enemies. His followers founded the "Bolland Society" and issued the periodical *De Idee.* Prominent among his followers were J. Hessing, the brothers Van den Bergh van Eysinga, J. G. Wattjes, and Esther Vas Nunes.

Recent decades have revealed a picture of lively philosophical interest, which did not leave a single important trend out of discussion. Be it Hegelianism, Neo-Kantianism, Empiricism, Critical Realism, Behaviorism, Phenomenology, Nietzsche or Bergson, they all had their excellent representatives. The names of B. J. H. Ovink, A. J. de Sopper, Tj. de Boer, H. J. Pos, H. J. Jordan, G. Mannoury, Ph. Kohnstamm, J. A. der Mouw, G. A. van den Bergh van Eysinga and many others must be mentioned. Neo-Calvinism (H. Bavinck, D. H. Th. van Vollenhove, H. Dooyeweerd), and Neo-Thomism (C. V. de Groot, R. R. Welschen, J. Th. Beysens, and T. Brandsma) also greatly flourished. Whereas in earlier centuries theology was the starting point for philosophy, in modern times liberal Protestantism, in particular, increasingly applied philosophy, psychology, and sociology to its religious and social conceptions.

Over the entrance of Spinoza's house in Rijnsburg appears a little poem, written by the pious preacher Camphuysen. It reads:

> Oh! if only mankind just were wise
> And acted also well
> This earth were then a Paradise
> Now it is most a Hell.

The Netherlanders under German occupation realize fully the truth of these simple words. Their present behavior, under the strain of Nazi deviltry, once more brilliantly manifests their inherent natural wisdom and their basic Christian faith—characteristics which pierce the applied philosophy of Nazi propaganda, and are essential to Dutch thinking.

CHAPTER XIV

Education

BY BERNARD H. M. VLEKKE

THE HISTORICAL EVOLUTION of Netherlands society over many years and the political development of the Netherlands State determined the outward form, as well as the inner purposes, of the Dutch educational system. In this, as in the other departments of public life, the concepts of the French Revolution brought not only an almost complete break with the traditions of the past but also a fresh impetus to progress.

Before the fifteenth century, education in the Netherlands paralleled the lines followed in the rest of western continental Europe. Primary instruction was to be had in parish schools, which were maintained by chapters of the prominent churches, and in the towns by public schools supported by town councils. As for higher education, there were no facilities in the Netherlands until 1423, when Philip II of Burgundy founded the University of Louvain partly to offset the growing trend of young scholars to attend foreign universities, especially those of Paris, Orleans, Montpellier, Cologne, Erfurt and some of northern Italy. But for centuries, the Grand Tour through France, Italy and, whenever possible, also through England and western Germany, remained one of the principal requirements of a good Dutch education.

After the turn of the fifteenth century, education within the country was greatly influenced by the congregation of the Brethren of the Common Life. This community was founded by Floriszoon Radewijnsz of Leerdam, a follower of the religious leader, Geert Groote of Deventer, for the promotion of study and for the instruction of youth. In their methods of teaching Latin, the Brethren emulated the Humanists of their own era rather than their medieval predecessors and inasmuch as there was scarcely a town in the Low Countries without a school under the Brethren or the Sisters of the Common Life, their progressive approach to education had, at the beginning of the sixteenth century, according to Erasmus, brought the general level of learning to a high standard. In spite of this, there were very few prominent scholars among their pupils.

For some two hundred years the Netherlands kept its place among the nations in the vanguard of progressive education. With the Reformation, the influence of the Dutch Reformed Church replaced that of the Roman Catholic faith. This strengthened the lay element in the school system because the town schools increasingly were maintained partly from funds of the Dutch Reformed Church and partly from revenue derived from secularization of former church holdings, and because of the custom of combining the schoolmaster's office with that of the sexton. But in the committee appointed by the town councils to control the schools, ministers of the Reformed Church exercised a dominating influence.

Town schools were commonly called "Dutch schools" because all instruction was given in the idiom of the country. There were also French schools which were organized by private teachers who taught French. Private schools were strictly supervised. For instance, a private school could be established only with the permission of the town council, given solely to teachers who professed the Reformed religion. One reason for such restrictions was the fear that competition of the private schools, if too strong, might diminish the income of the public schoolmaster, which came from fees paid by the parents. There was some provision for the education of the poor, such as the free schools maintained by the United East India Company for children of Batavian slaves.

Besides the Dutch and French schools, there were the Latin schools, which prepared students for the university, teaching a great deal of Latin, some Greek, and some mathematics, with history and geography included in the Greek and Latin courses. These were public schools, maintained by the town councils. Many of them were simply a continuation of schools which had been established by the Brethren of the Common Life.

In the northern Netherlands, the first university came into being in Leyden, in 1575, primarily intended as a theological seminary for the new Reformed Church, and endowed with part of the land of the monastery of Egmond. The University of Leyden rapidly became one of the most important centers of Humanist learning of the period and, in the eighteenth century, of the study of physics and medicine. Inevitable rivalry between the provinces promoted the founding of numerous schools of higher education, some of which flowered into full-fledged universities as in Utrecht and Amsterdam, some of which were in time reduced again to the status of Latin schools, but with enlarged curricula.

The theory of education was never of such great interest to Netherlands teachers as the actual practice of it until the twentieth century. In the eighteenth century, which was a period when most of the neighboring countries were experiencing a flowering of pedagogic thought, the educational system of the Netherlands remained somewhat static in concept. Near the close of the century, the Dutch scholarly societies, recognizing the need for study of educational methods and aims, formed in 1784 the Society for Public Welfare (*Maatschappij voor het Nut van het Algemeen*) for this purpose. The principal function of the society was to reform methods in the primary schools and to replace the old books, which had been changed very little since the late Middle Ages, with suitable textbooks. Its work was considerably influenced by the school reforms of Austria and of northwestern Germany.

When the French army marched over the frozen rivers into Holland in January, 1795, the French Revolution had already brought the institutions of the old Netherlands to an end. The invasion was followed by a revolution in Holland, whereby the aristocratic government of the Republic of the United Netherlands was discarded in favor of the democratic government of the Batavian Republic. The new regime held it to be one of the State's duties to educate its citizens in democratic principles, in their obligations toward their fellow men, and toward the Supreme Being. Thus general and public education became one of the principal cares of the State.

Among the other changes wrought in Dutch public life by the revolution was one which also had an effect on the educational system. Before 1795 the Dutch Republic had been a federation of states, with the provinces exercising sovereign rights and the power of the central government strictly limited by law. When, after that date, it became a political unity with a centralized administration, the provincial universities were doomed. Although most of these universities had been decaying for a long time and their disappearance would be no great loss, the extent to which the Government should interfere in school affairs remained a moot question.

A Department of Education, probably the first of its kind in the world, was created under the Constitution of 1798 with J. H. van der Palm at its head. And three years later the first law regulating the school system of the whole country was issued. Van der Palm was imbued with the principles of the Society for Public Welfare. He set out to reform the entire Netherlands educational structure, even the private schools, according to those precepts. The law of 1801 provided that schools would be organized in all the communities of the Republic, and where the existing schools were adequate, they must conform to the new regulations. A committee was appointed to supervise both public and private schools as to general standards of instruction and the appointment of teachers, but without control over methods of instruction or textbooks used in the private schools. Teaching posts were open to anyone who could meet the rather lenient requirements and who, in addition, had permission from the local authorities.

This law was not thorough enough to suit Van der Palm and, as soon as he could, he had it modified. In 1801, when a new Constitution was adopted for the Batavian Republic, the power of the central government was further strengthened and that of the legislative body diminished at the direct request of the dictatorial Emperor Napoleon Bonaparte. The Department of Education, merely a section of the

Department of the Interior, now was ordered to supervise the schools more strictly. Van der Palm, who remained in office, issued new regulations which practically deprived the private schools of any independence in their methods of teaching (1803).

Naturally, under the Napoleonic influence, the reorganization of the Netherlands State had a reactionary character. The elements, which had ruled the country before 1795, regained part of their former power. Van der Palm reluctantly had to leave school inspection to the regional administrators of the department, and this, under the circumstances, made it possible for the Reformed Church to recapture some control over the education of a large majority of Dutch youth.

The actual work of supervision was entrusted to the secretary of the Board of Inspectors, Adriaan van den Ende, who had long been interested in the school reforms of various parts of Europe and knew from personal experience the work of Frederick E. von Rochow, reformer of the Prussian schools. Van den Ende was able to implement more of his ideas as a result of a completely new law, that of 1806, in which state supervision of education was further strengthened, so far, in fact, that education became a virtual state monopoly.

By now, however, the State had broken with the purely rationalistic ideas of the revolutionary period. Napoleon had made his peace with the Roman Catholic Church in France, so that when he installed a monarchical government in Holland (under the Grand Pensionary, Schimmelpenninck in 1805, and under his brother, Louis Bonaparte in 1806), he pressed the Government to come to an agreement with the Reformed Church. Consequently, under the law of 1806, education was to be governed by the principles of Christianity, as interpreted by the State. Necessarily, the Jews had to have their own schools. Their textbooks occupied a separate part of the list of school books decreed for the use of teachers by the Government.

The incorporation of the Kingdom of Holland into the French Empire in 1810 produced only a few changes in the existing school system, with the exception of the Latin schools and the universities which were drastically reduced in number. Of the universities only Leyden was allowed to continue and that under the vigilant eye of the *Université Imperiale,* or Board of Control, instituted by Napoleon. The other universities, such as that of Utrecht, were reduced to secondary schools.

Many important aspects of the Dutch school system of today date from its reorganization during the French period. The transfer of education from the local governments to the central authority of the Dutch State was accomplished then, as well as control of the subjects taught, the method of their teaching, and especially of teaching appointees by requirement of certain qualifications.

When Holland regained her independence in 1813, the existing laws regulating education were retained, as were many other institutions of the French period, but excessive control over the subjects and methods of teaching was lessened. The University of Leyden immediately regained full freedom for its scientific activities, the University of Utrecht was restored and, shortly after, that of Groningen.

But whereas before 1795 the universities had been divided into four faculties, those of theology, law, medicine, and arts and sciences (the latter was called, in medieval times, *artes liberales*), in 1815 a fifth was created by splitting the arts faculty into two, that of letters and philosophy and that of the philosophy of nature, or science. This quintuple faculty was confirmed by the law of 1876 and still exists in Netherlands universities. Strangely enough, Latin was reinstated as the language of instruction in the beginning of the nineteenth century, when in most of the other European universities the vernacular language was replacing it.

Access to Dutch universities was gained through graduation from the Latin schools. But these were not yet organized to be uniform, so that preliminary instruction, or *propaedeusis,* was for some time an important part of university work. During the nineteenth century, however, this situation was remedied by the return of preparatory work to the Latin and other secondary schools. The curriculum of the Netherlands universities can, since then, be compared in large part to graduate work at American universities.

But the grammar schools remained subject to the regulations made law during the French period for another fifty years, and secondary education continued to be rationalist-Protestant in character, to the growing dissatisfaction of the more orthodox Protestant groups, as well as to many of the Catholics. This discontent was particularly strong in Belgium, united between 1815 and 1830 with the Netherlands into one state, and contributed to the Belgian revolt against the rule of King William I. The Protestant historian and political leader, Groen van Prinsterer, voiced the prevalent feeling to such an extent as to leave no doubt of its strength and depth.

The Constitution of 1848 introduced, along with other liberal reforms, the freedom of education. Immediately two trends of thought on the future development of the Dutch school system became vocal. One group insisted that education should be completely free, without intervention from the State except to supplement inadequate private initiative. The adherents of Groen van Prinsterer and most Catholics belonged to this group because they planned denominational schools to be maintained by their churches or by organizations of parents. Some liberals supported this solution, too, believing it would remove unnecessary interference by the State in public affairs.

The other group held that the State must provide nondenominational instruction for the whole country whether the parents of the pupils wanted it or not, and that the strict state supervision of the laws of 1806 and later should be enforced. A compromise between these two opinions was reached in the law of 1857, which regulated primary instruction. It placed the institution of public schools under the purse strings of the State, and gave to those who wished it freedom to establish denominational schools, but at their own expense. However, like most such compromises, the measure satisfied nobody. There were constant complaints from many parts of the country that people were given schools they did not want, and were forced to pay extra for the schools they did have.

The political struggle between these two groups filled parliamentary history for the next sixty years. It was ended only by the Constitution of 1917, which gave equal rights to both public and private schools and secured to them all equitable support from the public funds.

In the meantime, however, educational processes had not stood still. The normal schools had been brought to a much higher level of scholarship, examinations had become more difficult and grammar-school curricula embraced a larger number of subjects. The law of 1879 was particularly important in these reforms, and in 1901 attendance at grammar school until the age of thirteen was made obligatory.

The secondary schools also have undergone improvements, brought about by the laws of 1862 and 1876. Johan R. Thorbecke, the great Liberal leader, was responsible for the former, with his plan of a system of secondary education for the benefit of the whole population through the organization of the inappropriately named middle-class schools or *burgerscholen*. These *burgerscholen,* with their curricula of three years, were to be equivalent in the Dutch system to the high schools of America. In addition to *burgerscholen,* Thorbecke proposed *hoogere burgerscholen,* a more highly developed school to prepare students for the Academy of Technology in Delft (founded in 1843, organized in 1905).

Some changes occurred in the execution of this plan. For instance, the *burgerscholen* were ill-attended, whereas the *hoogere burgerscholen* were a great success; this is understandable because the latter, with a five-year course, include many subjects taught in college in this country. Before 1940, there was discussion about extending the course to six years. Later, graduates of the *hoogere burgerscholen* were eligible for further work in university faculties of medicine and science.

The Latin schools were finally organized in 1876 and were then called *gymnasia*. Their graduates were eligible for college entrance and their curricula were twice modernized, first in that same year, and again in 1921. As the *gymnasia* taught many subjects usually reserved for university study, preparatory work at the universities diminished in importance. Eventually most preparatory examinations were abolished.

The gradual formation of grammar schools with expanded curricula, of vocational and business schools completed the system. An Academy of Agriculture (*Landbouwhoogeschool*) at Wageningen, a School of Business at Rotterdam, both ranking with the universities, rounded out the higher educational facilities. Also, the law of 1876 recognized the Amsterdam Atheneum as a university. And when that law was modified in 1904, the privately endowed universities of the Reformed and Catholic churches, founded in 1880 and 1923 at Amsterdam and Nijmegen, received the same recognition.

Now the Netherlands has six universities, the state universities of Leyden, Utrecht, and Groningen, the Municipal University of Amsterdam, the Reformed University of Amsterdam with four faculties, and the Catholic University of Nijmegen with three faculties. Amsterdam University has installed economics as a sixth faculty, and Utrecht made a sixth faculty out of the Veterinary School, which had been a separate institution. The total number of students at the combined universities in 1938 was 9,470, of whom 1,901 were women. More than one-third were enrolled in the medical courses. Then there was the Academy of Fine Arts in Amsterdam, with 84 students.

The following institutions rank equally with the universities: The Academy of Technology at Delft, the Academy of Agriculture at Wageningen, founded in 1917, the Business School at Rotterdam, founded in 1913, and the Roman Catholic School of Business at Tilburg, founded in 1927. Together these institutions had 3,035 students in 1938, of whom more than half attended the Academy of Technology.

In the same year there were 52 *gymnasia* in the Netherlands, 136 *hoogere burgerscholen,* 56 *lycea,* which were created after 1917 and combined two sections with the curricula of *hoogere burgerscholen* and *gymnasia* respectively under joint leadership, and 22 secondary schools with enrollment of nearly 60,000 students. Of the 242 preparatory schools, 96 were denominational. They graduated 2,980 students in 1938, and 1,600 of these actually took up further work at one or another of the universities.

From these figures it is clear that the selection in Dutch preparatory schools is very severe. It is not unusual for one-third of the girls and boys in the first year in a gymnasium or *hoogere burgerscholen* to fail in their first examinations and many such students then go over to one of the vocational schools to prepare for a different sort of life. Of the 1,498 students who took the final examinations in 1937 at the *gymnasia* and the *burgerscholen,* 220, or approximately 16 per cent, failed to pass.

At the beginning of university studies, another severe test confronts the prospective student. About one out of every three freshman students in law and medicine failed his first examination in 1937. The preparatory studies are thus kept at a very high level. And this is necessary as the Dutch system does not know the college as an intermediary between preparatory and graduate schools. It may be that, on the contrary, the Dutch system overemphasizes the acquisition of knowledge at the expense of the formation of character. It has been realized that in preparing students for graduate work at the universities in all faculties, secondary school curricula have been overburdened with additional subjects; a reform of the whole system has frequently been considered.

A gymnasium student is required to have a rather thorough knowledge of five languages besides Dutch—Greek, Latin, English, French, and German. He is also obliged to study history, geography, physics, chemistry, mathematics, biology, astronomy, drawing, and the history of art. Only in the last two years before the invasion was he allowed to chose between curriculum A, which included more Latin, Greek, and history, and curriculum B, which focused on mathematics, physics, chemistry, and biology.

The *hoogere burgerscholen* include courses in mathematics, physics, and chemistry as principal subjects, with Dutch, English, French, German, history, geography, biology, mechanics, and bookkeeping, all obligatory subjects. Here, also, a choice is possible in the last two years of study, curriculum B centering all studies around the sciences, while curriculum A devotes most of its schedule to languages, literature, and business. Although in most countries the schools have tended to reduce the amount of Greek and Latin required, and sometimes to omit them altogether, in Holland, shortly before the German invasion, a bill was introduced in the States-General to make the study of Latin obligatory in all *hoogere burgerscholen.*

Dutch vocational schools totaled 716, including those for naval engineers and officers of the merchant marine, with an enrollment of 143,066. The grammar schools numbered 7,021 in 1938, when the population was 8,727,321. Of these 4,457 were private schools, nearly all denominational. Grammar-school enrollment was 1,143,181, of which 785,429 were students of private schools. Although private schools were 63.5 per cent of the total number of schools, their enrollments were nearly 69 per cent of the total number of students.

The State no longer passes on the textbooks of private schools and even leaves their selection in the *hoogere burgerscholen,* maintained by the State, to the discretion of the teaching staff. The selection of subjects, however, is strictly prescribed as are the number of hours devoted to their teaching. Graduation from both *hoogere burgerscholen* and *gymnasia* requires an examination before a board of examiners who are appointed by the Minister of Education. Private schools, as well as public, must conform to these rules and also to periodic government inspection. The growing refinements of the educational system have required so much government time, a separate Ministry of Education has taken over since 1918.

It is reasonable enough that there should be government control of the educational structure, because almost all expenses of private and public schools are paid out of public funds. Eighty per cent of secondary-school costs are met by the State and part of the remaining 20 per cent is usually provided from other public funds, such as those coming from the provinces and communities. Buildings for these schools are constructed at the expense of the founding association, but the cost is gradually refunded by the State, and grammar schools, private and public, are fully supported from state and community public funds. The total cost of education from public funds, according to the latest available figures, those of 1934, amounted to 189,363,000 guilders—about 22 guilders per capita. Of this amount, 124,406,000 guilders were paid by the central government, out of a total budget of 698,839,000 guilders for the same year.

The Dutch contribution to the theory of pedagogics has not been of any major importance. Although new trends originating abroad have been studied with interest and have sometimes been followed, there are few Dutch names among the great educators. There are two exceptions. Jan Ligthart (1859–1916), the principal of a grammar school at The Hague, was one of the men who inaugurated the period of Dutch education in which the excessive severity of the old system was mitigated by a sense of love and responsibility of teacher toward pupil. The second exception is that of Dr. J. H. Gunning, born in 1859, and who is still living.

Practicality characterizes the Netherlands system of education, aiming as it does at preparing the young for the tasks that await them in life, and aiming to develop in them intelligence and knowledge. Many reforms were under discussion when the German invasion interrupted national development. Once the war is over, these and other reforms will probably be realized more rapidly and radically than would have seemed possible before.

CHAPTER XV

Art

BY JOEP NICOLAS

THE INFLUENCE OF TWO DISTINCT TRENDS is perceptible in tracing the early Christianization of the Netherlands: the late Roman civilization which came from southern Europe in the wake of the imperial legions, and the later Celtic civilization which was brought into the Low Countries from Ireland.

The roots of Dutch art.—Although the Dutch are indebted to the Romans for their earliest architectural and sculptural activity, particularly in the southeast in towns like Maastricht, the oldest remaining relics principally of Byzantine conception with a somewhat rough provincial touch, date from a period close to the Carolingian era. Around the year 650, Irish Benedictine monks settled along the North Sea coast as far as the Frisian Islands. From their principal center, the abbey of Egmont in the Bishopric of Utrecht, their members went forth into all parts of Holland to promote science, art, the crafts, and the building of churches. The influence of Roman Merovingian culture was strongest in the southeast, along the Meuse, the Rhine, and the IJssel, as well as in Brabant.

Art in the Netherlands before the fourteenth century can hardly be spoken of as Dutch. The archives of the old monasteries and cities frequently mention collaboration of Rhenish and northern French artists, but the many illuminated manuscripts of those early days give no clue as to the identity of their designers. Then came a period when the artists of the Netherlands migrated to those neighboring countries whose greater wealth offered wider opportunities and higher rewards for creative talents.

[238]

The first great Dutch sculptors, Claus Sluter, Claus van der Werve, and Jan Baerze, among others, worked for the dukes of Burgundy; before the German invasion, their works were to be found in Dyon, Champmol, Beaune, and Bourg en Bresse. Melchior Broederlam and Jean Malwael, whom the French call Malouel, were early miniaturists who won international fame and left many wonderful illuminated manuscripts. The three Van Limburg brothers were unique in their triple endowment of talent. Two of them were the authors of the masterpiece "The Very Rich Hours of the Duc de Berry" (*"Lès Très Riches Heures de Duc de Berri"*); the third brother was the court painter of the counts of Holland. So far as is known, the brothers were born in Limbricht, on the Meuse, opposite the township of Maeseyck, the birthplace of the two Flemish masters, Jan and Hubert van Eyck. The Van Eycks belong to the second classification of Dutch artists— the painters who left their native Dutch regions for the wealthy Flemish cities of Bruges, Ghent, Louvain, and Brussels.

Many of the so-called Flemish primitive painters were really born in northern Netherlands. Petrus Christus came from Baarle, near Bois le Duc. After 1444, he worked in Bruges as did Gerard Janszoon David, from Oudewater. Dirk Bouts of Haarlem settled in Louvain and Hugo van der Goes, a native of Goes in Zeeland, worked both in Ghent and in Rougecloitre, near Brussels.

Court life in northern Holland lacked the riches and pageantry of the Flemish and other Dutch courts, and in the cities the burghers had not yet acquired the wealth that was to be theirs through the United East India Company. In fact, Holland was then a rather isolated stretch of European land, still divided politically by the complicated heritage of the medieval system. It was not yet the republic of the Seven Provinces, and would not be until the Union of Utrecht— it was only a conglomeration of disparate political units. So, it was natural that many Dutch artists who had attained more than provincial stature should leave to seek fortunes in Burgundy or in Flanders.

Some of the most original "talents," however, did not leave, but contented themselves with local commissions from nobles, clerics, important burghers, corporations, and confraternities. It is important

to the history of the Dutch that these indigenous masters, comparatively unpolished by international classicism, and more or less indifferent to cosmopolitan fashions, were, nevertheless, steadfast in
keeping the conception and technique of their work to a faithful
reflection of the inherent Dutch character. Their unstinting love of
life as it was in that period made their idealistic, mystical contemplation the more poignant. Because of their aversion to idealization and
their frankness in expressing human emotions, their art intimately
touches the beholder. In their hands, ugliness, wonderfully composed,
psychologically delineated, and never glossed over or hidden, came
to have an element of intense and piercing beauty. When the painting "The Entombment of Christ," as conceived by the Dutch master
of the "Virgo inter Virgines" (Liverpool, Walker Art Gallery), is
compared with the composition of Roger van der Weyde, there is
found essentially the same contrast as between the later exponents of
Dutch and Flemish psychological thought: Rembrandt and Rubens.

There are scattered over Europe some twenty works by this unknown, undoubtedly Dutch, primitive painter. His work is identified
by a panel in the Amsterdam Rijksmuseum, showing the Virgin
Mary with the Christ Child, surrounded by the saints, Barbara, Cath-
erine, Cecilia, and Ursula, in a cloister garden. In every panel he
painted, this artist was inspired directly by the typical Dutch faces
of the day, sober and impassive.

The most challenging personality among the early Dutch artists
is Jerome Bosch, who painted in Bois le Duc some time from 1488 to
1516. His painting—for instance in such panels as "Christ's Betrayal,"
"The Wedding at Cana," and "The Prodigal Son"—more than the
painting of any other artist marks the contrast between the stark,
unadorned conception of the northern Netherlands and the suaver
tradition of Flanders. In his later works, greatly sought after by Spanish grandees, Bosch applied his powerful skill in imbuing with reality
a fantastic visualization of nightmares, temptations, and deviltries.
Seldom, in the scope of creative art, has such great and prolific beauty
been attained through the medium of terrifying triviality.

Never has a profound study of nature been utilized so thoroughly

in picturing the unnatural, or perhaps one should say the super-
natural. No modern surrealist has surpassed this great and persuasive
master of imagery—Jerome Bosch. There is a strong Bosch influence
apparent in the paintings of Peter Breughel the elder, who was born
in Breughel not far from Bois le Duc some seventy years after Bosch.
Breughel, working in Brussels, became the greatest of the realistic
interpreters of life, as well as the most eloquent accuser of the Spanish
oppressors of the Netherlands.

Two great painters, Albert van Ouwater and Geertgen tot Sint
Jans, worked in Haarlem at about the same time. Because most of
Ouwater's works have been lost, he is known principally through the
records of the day. Early critics called him the first landscape painter;
it is recorded that in 1521 Cardinal Grimani of Venice was proud to
possess some little landscape panels by "Alberto de Olanda."

Geertgen tot Sint Jans, so called because he worked in the cloisters
of the Friars of St. John, died when only twenty-four. Not more than
thirteen of his paintings have been located; the most important of his
works, the main altar of the Knights of St. John, was destroyed by
Protestants during the siege of Haarlem. But the known paintings
of Sint Jans's creations are filled with a deep religious devotion and
profound mystical vision, and the two wings in the Vienna *Kunst-
historisches Museum* which have survived the years are among the
most beautiful of compositions. Sint Jans's artistic aim was to glorify
his subject, and in painting scenes from the life of Christ or of the
saints, he bent his mind to that end in a preoccupation with the intensity of action portrayed, and the psychological reasons prompting it.
Although Sint Jans must have produced until the last few years of
the fifteenth century, neither in his conception nor in his technique
is there a single foreshadowing of the Renaissance which was to revo-
lutionize art, religion, and science. The isolation of the Dutch provinces may account for this delayed conception of the Renaissance; it
may even justify the fact that the Dutch considered the fifteenth
century the end of the Middle Ages in Holland.

The Dutch Renaissance.—The first indications of the Renaissance
are seen in the work of such men as Jan Mostaert, Corneliszoon

Engelbrechts and, even more, of the great Lucas of Leyden. Until he was called to the service of Margaret of Austria and lived with the court either in Malines or in Brussels, Jan Mostaert worked in Haarlem. Whereas in his earlier work he was very much influenced by Geertgen tot Sint Jans, in Flanders his work reflected the new fashion of painting antique architecture against a landscape background. His portraits are intensely limned, most of them half-figures projected on a background of spacious landscape. One panel, a scene depicting the discovery of America, in the Amsterdam collection of Goudstikker, must have originated at the Austrian court when Mostaert heard stories of the conquests of Columbus and Pizarro.

Corneliszoon Engelbrechts was the founder of the Leyden school. In his work there is seen for the first time in the Netherlands what was later called the "painter's touch," as differentiated from the skillful superimposing of transparent coatings, the typical method used during the fifteenth century. His pupil, Lucas van Leyden, born in 1492, is the most famous Dutch master of the sixteenth century, and one whom Vasari places higher than Dürer. Besides his magnificent triptychs and portraits, Lucas painted certain remarkable profane pieces; in fact, he may be considered the originator of genre painting. His "Fortune Teller," which was in Paris, his "Chess Players," in Berlin and, in the Philips collection at Eindhoven, the panel of a man and woman playing cards, are representative of the Renaissance tendency toward secularizing the art of painting.

It was a long time before the Dutch artists of the day could digest the riches of the Italian masters manifest in the tremendous effervescence of classicism of the sixteenth century. Jan van Scorel and many others came back from Italy as skillful designers and painters, employing an international, humanistic language of crowded compositions, of counterpoint, anatomy, perspective, architectural drawing, and billowing draperies.

In Gouda, a unique creation was taking place—a series of unrivaled stained glass windows in the St. Janskerk. The brothers Crabeth, Dirk and Wouter, by their technique, were probably pupils of Jean Cousin, and by their draftsmanship, related to such Flemish masters as Van Orley. These two brothers collaborated with Lambert van Noort of Amersfoort, Van Zyl, and others, in completing the fifty-five huge Renaissance masterpieces, which put the art of glassmaking as far ahead of medieval methods as sixteenth-century painting was superior to primitive miniature work. These artists achieved something much greater than that which could be accomplished by an expert copying after an imported pattern, for they developed entirely new processes in their own studios in Holland.

Besides the group portrait, which has oftentimes been considered the most typical expression in art of Dutch democratic solidarity, a new category of painting, the still life, came into being in Holland, possibly through the influence of Pieter Aertszen, a native of Amsterdam who had, however, absorbed the Rabelaisian style of painting prevalent in Antwerp. Although Aertszen had never painted an actual still life, he produced many scenes in which he treated the foreground in that manner. The kitchen interiors of this artist are strongly suggestive of still life. When he was commissioned in 1533 to do a triptych for the main altar in the Oudekerk in Amsterdam, he employed the realistic method in its execution.

The coming of absolute realism.—With the beginning of the seventeenth century, the world seemed ready to enjoy for the first time an absolute realism, a combination of high mastery of craftsmanship and skill with a contemplative love of everyday life. It is not quite clear whether the Reformation, by emasculating the Church, brought about the end of idealism in painting, or whether, on the contrary, the common people caused the sterility of the Church by their aversion to picturesque unreality, and the answer is not particularly important. The result was that the Church was no longer the principal patron of art, but was supplanted by a growing class of burghers whose appetite for luxury and beauty, and financial means by which to possess them, provided the painters with new opportunities.

Frans Hals (1581–1666).—Portrait painting then, at this period, was a matter of commercial production, executed with great ability, but with a certain uniformity. The Van Mierevelt's studio at Delft produced thousands of highly respectable portraits of princes, dignitaries, patricians and officers. They seem to be of an infallible exactness and of a conventional elegance. It was, therefore, all the more remarkable that Frans Hals could develop a highly personal style, with the artistic accent on skill for its own sake, a style which inaugurated the virtuosity of later modern painters. Perhaps more than any other, Hals, was a "painter's painter," secure in the professional understanding of all who prefer the astonishing beauty of vital, personal pronunciation to mere smoothness and sumptuousness. His observation of human nature was not always profoundly psychological, but in contrast to the closely observed portraits of the sixteenth century, his glory was achieved in the freshly natural rendition of a smile, a free movement, the almost stenographic recording of flickering daylight on a face, a velvet coat, a lace collar. A rapid worker, Hals completed some of his portraits in an hour, and if he was the first modern painter, he was also the cleverest. He has been called superficial, but many of his portraits, and especially two painted when he was eighty-four, of the governors and governesses of the Old People's Almshouse—with which he paid for his own board—place him among the greatest of the psychological analysts.

The Flemings who had come to Amsterdam had adopted a technique which is somewhat reminiscent of Breughel, but the Dutch artists achieved greater directness and realism. They enjoyed painting scenes of frolicking peasants, of merrymakers, of military men. They formed a school of "painters of gay life"; among them were Frans's brother, Dirk Hals, as well as Pieter Codde, Anthonie Palamedesz, Jan Steen, and Adriaan Brouwer.

From this time on there was no end to the specialization in subjects and, naturally, the best methods of expression. From the kitchen interiors of Aertszen a magnificent group of still-life painters developed, each a master in his own subject: the breakfast table, the fish still life, the fruit and flower piece, the game and fowl arrangements. The most important men among them were Kalf, Van Beuren, Heda, d'Hondecoeter, and Weenix.

Landscape came into its own with Esaia van der Velde, and his pupils, Jan van Goyen and Solomon Ruysdael. The painting of architecture likewise reached a high level of accomplishment with Van Bassen, Emmanuel de Witte, and Saenredam.

The old classical idealization did not quite disappear. It did, however, take a new turn and must not be forgotten in understanding Rembrandt's romantic realism. Bloemaert and Honthorst, both of whom had enormous followings, interpreted the Italian influence.

Rembrandt van Rijn (1606–1666).—At the time when Rembrandt was born in Leyden, Dutch realism was thoroughly established. When Rembrandt began to paint in Van Swanenburgh's studio, Hals had already achieved such masterpieces as the "Archers of St. George." In 1623 Rembrandt went to Amsterdam to study with Pieter Lastman, but returned in six months with his fellow student, Jan Lievens. Living at his father's house beside the mill on the Rhine, outside the city of Leyden, Rembrandt painted for several years, studying as an independent artist. He was interested primarily in portraiture, but was also attracted to historical subjects. From this period he has left the paintings, "David with Goliath's Head," and "St. Paul in Prison."

In 1631, when he was twenty-five, Rembrandt returned to Amsterdam where he was acclaimed a finished master. He had indeed earned his place with the marvelous portrait of his father, and the etchings he had made in Leyden, which surpassed anything previously accomplished in this medium. One of his first important commissions was executed in the depiction of the anatomical lesson of the surgeon, Tulp. It was in this painting that Rembrandt rose head and shoulders above all the other group portraitists.

With his marriage to Saskia, a whole new series of charming, somewhat romantic dress portraits came from his brush. Probably under the guidance of Saskia's father, the wealthy art dealer, Van Uylenburg, Rembrandt began his collection of antiques. Most of the self-portraits and figure pieces of these years reflect the painter's love for colorful fabrics, precious brocades, and curious jewelry.

The great physicist, Huygens, obtained from the Stadholder in 1633 a momentous commission for Rembrandt. All five of the paintings which resulted from that commission are now in Munich: "The

Erection of the Cross," "The Deposition," "The Entombment," "The Resurrection," and "The Ascension." In 1639, after some years of prosperous activity, Rembrandt bought the large house in the Jodenbreestraat. The year 1642 was a milestone in his career, the peak of his glory, when he was considered by his contemporaries as one of the greatest of living painters.

Rembrandt's most famous canvas, the "Night Watch," was also the freest interpretation of a group portrait ever known. The commission was merely to paint the officers of the civil guard under Captain Banning Cocq. The men who sat for the picture must have been somewhat astonished to see what a masterly and unusual composition was born of their simple desire for perpetuity in paint.

But Saskia died in the same year and only Titus survived of the several children. The light of great happiness became gradually dimmer in the master's life. His many pupils now paid him liberal fees, but there were too many of them to live in his house. He rented a storehouse for them on the Bloemgracht, in the outskirts of Amsterdam. Although after Saskia's death, material prosperity no longer came to Rembrandt with the same prodigality, his artistic power greatly increased and his most beautiful canvases, as well as his most powerful etchings, took shape.

After his bankruptcy, Rembrandt fell into a humble sort of life, bereft of glamor, full of humiliation. His commissions still came in, but he could not earn a proper living. His second wife, Hendrikje Stoffels, and his son, Titus, opened an art shop where his paintings were the regular stock. In these reduced circumstances Rembrandt painted his most sublime works, like "Claudius Civilis" (Stockholm), "The Syndics," "The Prodigal Son," and "The Jewish Bride." Perhaps no artist believed more in his own qualities and received less of official appreciation than did Rembrandt during this period. His "Fabius Maximus," his "Moses," and the "Claudius Civilis," which he painted for the new City Hall of Amsterdam, were refused.

The "Golden Era."—Beginning sometime around the year 1630 an outpouring of art of such tremendous richness made the last decades of the seventeenth century in the Netherlands an era not to be compared with any other in history. To find so many great painters, all producing at the same time, in a country of no more than a million inhabitants, is a phenomenon. It may have come from one of several causes. The burgher class, which was steadily gaining in wealth, encouraged the production of luxurious beauty for its homes. Also there were many gifted artists working in the shops of the various masters. They instinctively exploited their personal qualities, splitting up their production in well-realized specialization. Then, too, this period was only the beginning of a still greater era of wealth, because, as yet, the artists' manner of living had not risen in proportion to their aspirations or their abilities to create.

Rembrandt, at the peak of his career, Frans Hals still producing wonders, and Vermeer, in Delft, beginning his career around 1653— these are the three great masters of Holland, each so different from the others and each unsurpassed in his own style.

Behind the three giants comes a legion of excellent painters, any one of whom would have been a leader under any other circumstances, who were somewhat eclipsed by the brilliancy of Rembrandt, Hals, and Vermeer, and reduced to the rank of "little masters." The perfection of a Jan Steen, a Van Ostade, a Pieter de Hoch, a Metsu, or a Terborgh, compared with the high accomplishments in other countries, however, shows that a Dutch "little master" of that time stood above the most highly estimated leaders elsewhere.

Vermeer lived in Delft from 1632 until 1670 and was registered in St. Luke's Guild there in 1653. His first paintings were colored by Italian idealism but he achieved his greatest mastery in the painting of small realistic panels treating such silent and intimate subjects as a girl reading a letter, the painter himself at work, a girl at the clavichord, among others. The painting of a view of his own house and one of the city of Delft make him a master of architecture painting far superior to the Venetians, Canaletto and Guardi. Vermeer's followers, or rather the men who worked in a somewhat similar style include Hoogh, Terborgh, Metsu, Ochtervelt, and Brekelenkamp.

Jan Steen was born in Leyden in 1626, just in time to be fully productive during the "golden" period. He studied at Utrecht and at

The Hague, where he married Van Goyen's daughter. He was at the same time a master of still life and of figure composition, and a painter of interiors and landscapes. His technique is not easy to describe, but he can be said to combine the refinement of the Vermeer school with the dashing realism of Hals. Before him no one had dared to criticize and evaluate objects and events of the day, good and ugly alike, making of them all colorful subjects of painting. Psychologically Steen is rather superficial, with none of the great Rembrandt emotion, but he was far more correct in picturing circumstances and surroundings.

Some of Rembrandt's pupils did remarkable work and achieved fame, among them the best known was Nicolaas Maes, whose genre pieces show the closest relationship to Rembrandt's technique. Later in his life, Maes was taken in by the fashionable baroque style of portrait painting. Carel Fabritius was the most talented, but this Rembrandt student died as early as 1654, in an explosion that ruined his studio and probably most of his paintings. Of all the pupils of Rembrandt, the most faithful was Aert de Gelder, who carried on in the master's style for a long time, and many of whose canvases might actually have been made in collaboration with Rembrandt himself, or made from one of his sketches.

The masters of landscape.—The highest skill in depicting Holland's dark foliage under cloudy skies, of endless perspectives and lighted horizons belonged to Solomon van Ruysdael, Jan van Goyen, Aert van der Neer, Paulus Potter, Adriaan van de Velde (marines), Albert Cuyp, P. H. Koninck, Jacob van Ruysdael, and Meindert Hobbema. Van Berchem and Wouwerman were more romantic in their concepts. Of the other branches of painting, Willem Kalff and Abraham van Beyeren led in the field of still life, Dou and Van Ostade headed a phalanx of outstanding genre painters, and De Witte (Emmanuel), Saenredam, and Jan van der Heide were representatives of architecture painting at its best.

So, when the seventeenth century drew to a close, little Holland with one thousand prolific artists had written the most glorious page in the history of painting, a page of revolution and of evolution— depicting the strongest of movements toward the liberation of the human spirit. A sentence of Rembrandt's quoted in a letter by one of his friends explains the strength and beauty of this evolution. He said, "Whenever I try to give relaxation to my mind, it is not honor I seek, it is liberty."

The eighteenth century.—The Holland of the eighteenth century was rich, pretentious and given to cosmopolitan elegance. With money easy to come by, a high standard of living was taken for granted. The native artists' concentration on indigenous subjects yielded to a desire on the part of the younger generation to assimilate the fashionable mannerisms of Italy and France, in particular the rococo style which was pervading Europe from Naples to St. Petersburg, from Prague to Amsterdam. Principally concerned with interior decoration, the rococo school produced some superb artists, Tiepolo, Watteau, Lancret, and Boucher, but aside from them the style was impersonal and superficial.

The nineteenth century.—By the end of the eighteenth century there was a tendency toward neo-classicism and, as a result of the French influence of David, a growth of the academic trend. Native Dutch made a poor showing in the first part of the nineteenth century, except for a few landscape painters like Van Troostwijk and Van Os, and two historical painters, Pieneman and Kruseman.

Nearly three-quarters of a century had passed before the Dutch awakened again to the consciousness of their national virtues. Their appreciation of the art of the "Golden Age" finally came to them through the eyes of the English and the French. Gainsborough and Constable both highly valued Ruysdael and Hobbema.

The French realists of the Barbizon school then took over and reached a new level in poetical interpretation of landscape and figure. It was chiefly because of them that vitality returned to Dutch painting. Bosboom, who grew up under the romantic tradition, turned to a sound realism. Israëls, Mauve, and Mesdag rediscovered the beauty in Holland's vistas of land and sea, rediscovered, too, the infinite lights and shadows of the Low Countries. Soon a whole new group of artists joined them. Because they met in The Hague, the movement they created is known as "The Hague school."

In Joseph Israëls' work may be traced the development from romanticism to realism, as is shown in early canvases, like "After the Storm" (1858), with its strong theatrical and sentimental touch. Israëls was a pupil of the historical painter, Kruseman. Matthijs Maris was a member of the group, although he spent many years in London. He never departed from the romantic influence. But his two brothers, Jacob and Willem Maris, became uncompromising realists and the chief representatives of The Hague school. Jacob excelled in landscape as much as in figure painting. His views of Dutch cities from a river bank under a cloudy sky are his most admired genre, but his portraits in interiors have an equally broad touch. Jacob Maris worked for some time in France and his paintings reflect some influence of Corot, although each of his canvases is immediately recognizable as his own. His brother, Willem, specialized in meadow scenes; cattle, sheep, and geese near ditches and shaded by willow trees are characteristic of his work. Roelofsz, Weissenbruch, Begriel, Mauve, Neuhuys, and De Bock are the best known masters of this group.

If in Israëls romanticism was lost to realism, elsewhere it preceded Neo-Gothic tendencies in architecture and in painting. It seems undeniable that this love for a lost beauty, akin to romanticism, was a compensation for the new ugliness created by industrialization in the nineteenth century, and because of which mechanical means began to be used to obtain the effect of hand work. Cast-iron balustrades with flowers, chandeliers and inkstands in *cuivre poli* were the highest expressions of this industrial art against which the Neo-Gothicists revolted. The "church style" which swept the realm of architecture naturally compelled the decorators, too, to absorb something of the medieval style. Throughout Holland the architect Cuypers built Gothic railway stations, Gothic museums, and Gothic châteaux. He designed sculpture, and among other things, the stations of the Way of the Cross for St. Patrick's Cathedral in New York. He also designed furniture, and a variety of other objects to be realized by dreamy young artisans, who had no more idea of what was happening in their own time than they had of the Middle Ages. It was escapist art, prompted by nostalgia for the beauties of the past.

From the stirrings of so deep-rooted a craving for artistic style, a new school of symbolists and lineal composers emerged in Der Kinderen, Toorop, Roland-Holst, Torn Prikker, and Van Konijnenburg. Their paintings were intended to be more or less two-dimensional mural decorations, somewhat reminiscent of Puvis de Chavannes, Klimt, Hodler and Burne-Jones. Starting from a rather academic preoccupation with composition, their works became more and more ecstatic, finally reaching a high tension of geometric counterpoint which directly prepared the way for modern abstract painting.

The twentieth century.—During the first years of the twentieth century, the counterpart of The Hague school came into existence in Amsterdam, and made of the city a center of Dutch art. The painters of The Hague group might be called the Dutch impressionists, although in their choice and use of color they differed so greatly from their French contemporaries that their work could not be anything except Dutch. Such masters as Breitner, Dijsselhoff, and Verster of the later Amsterdam school, came a little nearer to French impressionism. But the only painter who possessed the "light touch" was Joseph Israëls' son, Isaac.

While the followers of these two schools were developing along their chosen lines, the most powerful and original genius of modern painting had been developing in Holland, Vincent van Gogh. This painter, a martyr to his own artistic truth, was never in all his life able to sell a single picture except to his brother. He is the true prototype of the *fin de siècle* genius, craving pure and uncompromising beauty, and enduring an agony of revolt every day of his too-short life. In tracing the development from his early, often Rembrandt-like drawings to the dramatic orgies of color and texture of his later works, painted under the blazing sun of southern France, it is clear that the tortured man fought heroically for freedom of expression, and in the struggle suffered as few artists have.

Van Gogh's style has tempted many a young artist. But he was a great individualist who could be followed only through adoption of surface mannerisms. So there has never been a Van Gogh school. However, an indirect Van Gogh influence, as well as a trace of

Cézanne, is discernible in Dutch art of the early twentieth century. A group of young painters who followed them, but with distinct indigenous characteristics, settled in the village of Bergen, north of Amsterdam, during the First World War. Their figure painting, landscapes, and still lifes reflected the new tendency toward a more geometrical construction, a simplification of line and color. In a fresh, poetic contemplation of Dutch life, they absorbed the international era of "isms." Painters like Sluyters, Mathieu and Piet Wiegman, Colnot, Gestel and Charlie Toorop, strove for direct personal expression unshackled by traditional treatment. They are the voices of an outspoken modernism.

Another group, of abstract painters and decorators, worked with a more international scope around the new architectural movement of the early 'twenties. Within the limitations of *de Stijl,* the Dutch equivalent of the German *Bauhaus,* such names as Mondriaan, Van Doesburg, and Van der Lek rank with men like Klee, Jeanneret, Leger, and Arp.

Meanwhile the later disciples of The Hague school were still producing actively. In Holland, as in all democratic countries, individualism was the strongest basis of art, but the highest attainments in sculpture were achieved by men who adapted their talent to modern architecture in a less free and more angular style. Krop, Zijl, Raedeker, and Polet are the four leaders who are not unrelated to Bourdelle, but who lean toward compact primitivism.

CHAPTER XVI

Architecture

BY PAUL BROMBERG

RCHITECTURE OFFERS a rich picture of the manifold happenings of the historical, social, and
cultural life in the Netherlands. Whereas
other forms of art may appear only sporadi-
cally, works of architecture must, of necessity, be produced at all
times because they are rooted in daily life. This being true, it is possible to judge the fertility of an era by the architectural works it has
produced; whether these are inspired or are dull may be taken as a key
to the cultural life of the particular times.

There has been some dispute about the date which can be ascribed
to certain of the earliest works of architecture in the Netherlands.
Some authorities believe that the Chapel Valkhof in Nijmegen, the
only remaining part of a large stronghold, was built by Charlemagne.
It is definitely known, however, that the chapel was rebuilt in 1155
by Frederick Barbarossa.

The oldest part of St. Servaas Church, in Maastricht, built about
900 A.D., shortly after the Norman invasion, and considered as proto-
Romanesque in architecture, has stood through many periods and
has been affected by many different styles of building—Romanesque
as well as Gothic. The Church of Our Dear Lady, in Maastricht, is
another example of the Romanesque in the Netherlands. The general
characteristics of this style are extreme sobriety, a striking absence of
sculptural ornamentation, and heavy walls with little window space.
Tympani, rich in sculpture as they are in France, cannot be found in
the Netherlands at this time. Another deviation from the usual are
the churches in Groningen and Friesland whose towers are often

topped by a roof rather than a spire. In general, it may be said that
the architecture of the Rhine had greater influence on Dutch architecture of this period than had French Romanesque.

The transition from Romanesque to Gothic architecture came
about slowly.

The technique of war and the technique of building influence each
other constantly. The ingeniously constructed city gates of the early
towns served as the locks of the town. Where the rivers crossed under
the city walls, water gates were built. In civilian architecture, however, new technical possibilities of building dominate. In these early
towns, as soon as construction changed, architectural expression also
changed, as is exemplified by the immense influence of the new
building system of vaults. The solid and massive appearance of the
Romanesque building made way for the "open" wall which, in turn,
made possible the rich development of stained glass windows.

One of the transitional churches is the Münster Church in Roer-
mond, typically Romanesque in its floor plan, with Gothic influence
apparent in its pointed arches and ribbed vaulting. In earlier times
German examples of architecture had been followed, and so they were
in the later Gothic period. There are only two churches in the
Netherlands in which French influence can be seen and which are
comparable in their magnificence to the great cathedrals of France—
the Domkerk in Utrecht and the St. Jan Cathedral in 's Hertogenbosch. The shallow ground of Holland could hardly support the
great and lofty structures of the Gothic period and made necessary
a simplification in architecture. Although the buildings usually are
not very large, they are very wide; most churches have five aisles,
while some, like the Buur Church in Utrecht, have seven. Another
striking feature of the Netherlands Gothic is the absence, in general,
of flying buttresses. Even in buildings such as the St. Bavo in Haarlem, where provision has been made for flying buttresses, they were
never added to the completed work.

Mention must be made here of the secular buildings of the Gothic
period. The best of these are to be found in the province of Zeeland
where Flemish influence predominated. The most outstanding work

is the Town Hall of Middelburg, or rather *was* the Town Hall of Middelburg, for this magnificent Gothic structure was ruined by German bombardment. Netherlands Gothic is represented further by the Hall of the Knights in The Hague, the Gates in Amersfoort, Zutphen, and in other towns, in numerous churches, castles, and in the City Hall of Gouda.

When the power of the Burgundians reached its culmination (about 1450), the first Renaissance motifs appeared in the Netherlands. They were on gold and silver work, however, whereas architecture remained Gothic. It was not until after the Reformation (1517), that Renaissance architecture began to develop. The growth of architecture must not be regarded as an isolated phenomenon. In the fine arts and the decorative arts everywhere, a great upswing took place. The technique of oil painting unfurled a rich palette, the art of book printing brought education to broader strata of society. Architecture followed the creative renewal, but in those days planning and building took more time than at the present. The first signs of the Renaissance architecture are to be seen at the castle in Breda (1525). Some of the oldest Renaissance motifs are preserved in the chair benches in the St. Vitus Church in Naarden (1531). For homes as well as for public buildings, the essence of the building style remains the same as in the Middle Ages. The Renaissance influence may be observed as a decorative addition. This was stimulated by a new building code for the towns where wood building, because of fire danger, had been prohibited. For instance, there was no longer a tendency to divide the façade—now built in stone—into rectangular spaces, formerly dictated by the construction of beams and wooden panels. With the placing of windows permissible wherever they were needed, a more decorative style became possible. Italy and Holland became equally important centers of Renaissance architecture. A paramount influence was exercised by the painter-craftsman-architect, Hans Vredeman de Vries, born in Leeuwarden in 1527. His influence penetrated even to Germany and to the Baltic Sea region. During this time—the latter part of the sixteenth century—Holland was engaged in a serious war. Consequently, new ideas of architecture could not be carried out. This may be the reason why so many Dutch Renaissance buildings have been constructed in Denmark, Sweden, and Germany. At the turn of the century the intensity of warfare lessened. The founding of the East and West India companies brought economic prosperity. Cities became prosperous and merchants grew rich. Architecture came into full bloom.

One of the greatest Dutch architects of this period was Hendrik de Keyser, whose work, the Zuiderkerk in Amsterdam is one of the most important Protestant churches ever built in Holland. The ground plan of this building is of the basilica type, with three aisles combined under one roof. Although the building itself is closely related to medieval structures, the magnificent tower shows many Renaissance motifs. The tower is built on a square base, but instead of an immediate transition to the octagonal part, there is one story which, though it is really octagonal in shape, appears square by means of four columns encircling it. These columns have ionic capitals and are topped by a vase-shaped ornament. There is a niche between the columns bordered by a balustrade. This niche was probably intended to hold a statue, but in the first heat of the Reformation the reaction against statues of all types was so strong that the niche was never filled. The clock follows this section and is topped by a beautifully simple roof built in the form of a pediment. Out of this part rises the slender octagonal section which, in turn, supports an even narrower and open section containing the carillon. The pear-shaped spire which completes this tower is a late Gothic motif, found on most of the churches of this period, which adds considerably to the charm of the structure. The tower of the Westerkerk is very similar in shape to the Zuiderkerk tower, but is even more simple and severe architecture. It is a tower which does not belong to the period of the Dutch Renaissance.

Another great architect of this period was Lieven de Key. The Butchers' Hall, for which he was architect, is an excellent achievement, especially in the structure of the gables. The doorway is done very simply, but this simplicity is entirely obliterated by the wealth of decoration in the gables. Especially are the three side gables heavily

ornamented and each corbiestep is topped by a spire. The front gable
is less ornate, displays the simpler, stepped style usually associated
with the architecture of Holland.

As Holland grew more prosperous, the wealthy sons of merchants,
who had favored this simple and intimate style, wanted something
more distinguished and elegant and so a style, more closely resem-
bling the Italian Renaissance, was developed. The great builder of this
classical period (1630–1700) was Jacob van Campen, who had studied
in Italy. Van Campen was a member of the Dutch intelligentsia and
a friend of Pieter Hooft and Constantijn Huygens. His commissions
came from the circle of Stadholder Frederik Hendrik and Johan Mau-
rits van Nassau. This gave him the opportunity to build in the lavish
style he had learned in Italy. The Coymanshuis in Amsterdam, the
Mauritshuis in The Hague, the former City Hall of Amsterdam,
now the Royal Palace, are all examples of his works. The façade of
the Mauritshuis is made into a unit by the pillars which extend over
the entire two stories, while in the Coymanshuis the pillars begin
anew at each story, thereby showing the interior division on the
façade. A typical device used by Jacob van Campen, which may be
seen in the Mauritshuis, is the high roof.

Other important architects of the period were Pieter Post (1608–
1669), Daniel Stalpaert (1615–1676) and the two Vingebooms, whose
many houses at the Amsterdam canals are still standing. In the neighborhood of the large cities many summer houses arose which became
a tribute to Dutch fame. The eighteenth century was dominated culturally, and therefore architecturally, by France. The Huguenots,
who found shelter and safety in the Netherlands, brought French
influences to the Netherlands. Daniel Marot (1661–1752) was the most
important and influential artist of this time for exteriors, as well as
for interiors. The architecture of the second half of the eighteenth
century is ruled by the influence of the French Louis XVI style.

With the Napoleonic invasion of Holland a temporary stagnation
came over Dutch cultural life. French culture increasingly dominated
the Netherlands, and disruption of trade prevented the building of
large projects. The only work built during the early and middle

nineteenth century worthy of mention is the Palace of Volksvlijt in Amsterdam, built in 1855 and destroyed by fire in 1929. This was one of the first buildings in which glass and steel construction was used in order to achieve architectural design.

Mechanized production began to influence the life of the times. It is especially worthwhile to stress that, in spite of new building materials, such as construction iron and reinforced concrete, architecture passed through a period of dullness. The architect failed to meet his task with a fresh approach to construction, an approach which might have served a functional purpose. Instead he tried to attain a pleasant general impression by applying architectural fragments of the past. Problems of urbanization developed with the rapid growth of industrial centers. It was possible to benefit from the use of steel construction, and this new development could not fail to act as a stimulant to architecture as a whole. The new era began in the latter part of the nineteenth century with the English country-home style of Voysey, Baillie Scott, and the outstanding work of Frank Lloyd Wright in America. Another influence came from France where Viollet-le-Duc drew the attention of the public to French indigenous architecture, the Gothic. He wanted the French to discard classical style, and to develop their own architectural inheritance.

This Neo-Gothicism was brought to Holland by Dr. P. J. H. Cuypers, who had studied under Viollet-le-Duc, and was a great admirer of the trend introduced by him. The Central Station and the Rijksmuseum in Amsterdam are examples of Neo-Gothicism in the Netherlands, but important for Cuypers, as an architect, was the strong revival of Catholic faith which followed the restoration of the Catholic hierarchy (1850). A need arose for churches to be built, and he could give vent to his ideas in the construction of new cathedrals, although Cuypers never strove for slavish imitation of Gothicism in the Neo-Gothic style. He made use of new building materials and his work shows honest construction at all times. It cannot be said that he founded a new architecture, but he did help Dutch architecture to become a craft again, an achievement which ultimately led to one of the greatest architectural periods in Dutch history.

The new era opened—unstable social conditions led to new ideologies such as liberalism, democracy, and socialism. At the same time, architects began to believe that these philosophies would be the foundation of a new world.

A manifestation of this idealism, coupled with a realistic view of the function of building, may be found in the work of Berlage (1856–1934). His buildings show honest construction—a contrast to the nineteenth century, when architecture had been completely blurred by style imitations. His greatest architectural work was the Stock Exchange (1893–1903) on the Damrak in Amsterdam; natural stone was applied to the solid and colorful brick wall in a functional and yet decorative manner. K. P. C. de Bazel (1869–1923), whose last work was the Netherlands Trading Company's building in Amsterdam, and W. Kromhout (1864–1940), who built the Hotel American in Amsterdam (1898), may be considered, along with Berlage, among the forerunners of a new and vigorous school of architecture.

The rational trend of building begun by Berlage did away with senseless style imitations and gave the architect an opportunity to create works which conformed to the needs of his own time. Because all building in the Netherlands conforms strictly to contemporary demands, the term "modern architecture" has no significance, as there is no contrasting tendency, no style that can be called "old" as compared with "modern." The reaction, an inevitable consequence of Berlage's movement did not, as might be expected, bring about a reversion to "Period building"; instead it represented a departure from the strict principles put forth by Berlage which tended to restrain truly imaginative creation.

It is quite understandable that the new movement, called the "Amsterdam school," because it had been founded by a group of young Amsterdam architects, swerved too far to the other extreme in abandoning Berlage's austerity. The leader and inspirer of this school was an architect of real genius, M. de Klerk (1884–1925). He built settlements in Amsterdam which by their fantastic shapes and great expanse—manifold houses united to one street façade—drew the attention of architects throughout the world. Unfortunately, however, this architecture was purely ornamental and the houses were not ideal as living quarters. The bridges designed by P. Kramer with this same masterful *élan* amazed the world; yet the bridges built by the architect-engineers D. Rosenburg and A. J. van der Steur, on government commission, are of greater import because they are more than expressions of temporal manifestations. An outstanding product of this movement, however, is the Shipping Building (1911–1914) designed by J. M. van der Mey. In this structure bricks are placed against a concrete skeleton to provide an intriguing and picturesque means of decoration.

The overwhelming admiration shown by foreign countries for this rather artificial, fantastic, and overly decorative toying with building materials, as practiced by the Amsterdam school, is easily explained in the striking difference between this expressionistic way of building and the unimaginative styles used by other countries at that same time. This admiration is justified so far as this new building style was a reaction to endless monotone and characterless rows of houses, of which there were far too many in Amsterdam. However, problems of housing cannot be solved on a purely decorative basis; though the work of Berlage was too dogmatic and austere it solved the essential architectural problems of the twentieth century. Houses in the shape of a ship, such as were found in the villa park, Meerwijk, in Bergen, were more reminiscent of prehistoric times than of the twentieth century. This movement proved to Holland and the world at large that the vitality and imagination of Dutch architects had not been obliterated even by a long period of stagnation.

Purification came out of this chaos and brought with it some of the most brilliant creations of modern architecture. Contemporary with the Amsterdam school was another movement which came into being under the influence of the abstract painters, Th. van Doesburg, Piet Mondriaan, B. van der Leck, and V. Huszar. Although their philosophical theories about the rendering of space did not directly create a new architecture, indirectly the abstractionists did help Dutch architecture to develop and to reach a point of greater maturity. It was not long before architects such as J. J. P. Oud, G. Rietveld, C.

van Eesteren, J. W. E. Buys, J. A. Brinkman, Van der Vlugt and many others took the abstractionist philosophy out of its theoretical sphere and transformed it into a concrete reality. The resultant architectural movement was closely connected with the international trend called "Fitness for Purpose." The building in The Hague, the Volharding, which housed the stores and offices of this coöperative, built by Buys in 1929, and the Van Nelle factory in Rotterdam, built in 1929, in collaboration, by the architects Brinkman and Van der Vlugt are some of the first fruits of these new ideas. This movement not only resulted in outstanding architectural works, but it also had a beneficial influence on other Dutch architects who were not yet ready for these new theories and their consequences. The expressionism of the Amsterdam school had been conquered, the romanticists had to curb their imagination, for the functionalists were fighting passionately for their ideas, not sparing anyone or anything with their ruthless criticism.

The periodical, the *8 en Opbouw* (1926) united those Rotterdam and Amsterdam architects who felt themselves called upon to aid this new architecture. Now, indeed, the Netherlands saw the creation of architectural works more than worthy of the praise of foreign countries. As early as 1924 came a strong urge to bring air, light, and sun into the home, for it was in this year that G. Rietveld built his revolutionary villa in Utrecht. Later he built middle-class housing blocks in that same city (1931–1934) and a movie theater. J. J. P. Oud designed the settlement Hoek van Holland and the settlement De Kiefhoek in Rotterdam, which served as an example for housing problems all over the world.

Berlage must be considered the precursor of these functionalist architects, even though their work no longer bears any Berlagian characteristics. It must be remembered that Berlage was the one to purify and simplify Dutch architecture and to make consequent developments possible. Berlage emphasized construction which should be honest in its form of expression at all times; the functionalists on the contrary accent the function of the building and each part thereof. They naturally taboo all false construction; the architecture must be controlled entirely by the floor plan, and the façade must be the result of the interior.

Another striking quality of this architecture was its "open" character. An attempt was made to unite the outside with the inside. This manner of building was especially popular in the construction of the type of unattached houses built by A. Komter, one of the gifted young architects. It was ideal for buildings such as the sanatorium Zonnestraal in Hilversum, where it enabled the patients to get all the necessary fresh air, in schools such as the open-air school in Clio-straat in Amsterdam (1930) built by Bijvoet and Duiker, and the Montessori School in this same city by Van Tijen. Because the new ideas of progressive education met with great response in Holland, a vast new field was opened for the architect—the building of schools to fit the needs of modern pedagogy (H. Groenewegen, Montessori School in Bloemendaal). This great desire for large windows and the wish to open the houses as much as possible was brought about by the rather dreary climate, and the need to utilize all the sunlight possible.

The acceptance of functionalism as an irrefutable starting point lends to each building those characteristics which correspond to the purpose the building must fulfill. The principle "fitness for purpose" has been generally accepted in Holland for office buildings and factories. Architect and engineer began to work together, not only in Holland, but also in the United States, and some of the finest architectural works have resulted from this collaboration. The beautiful bridges, such as the one in Vianen designed by the Department of Buildings and Roads, are evidence of the value of such a partnership.

In the first *élan* of the functional movement, many of the architects stripped their designs of every semblance of beauty; architecture, in the recent past, had been so overburdened with superficial ornament that these young revolutionaries felt it their duty to renounce every feature even reminiscent of the decorative or the picturesque. In the same way that Berlage and his disciples at times overemphasized the constructive element, the functionalists were often carried to extremes in stressing the point of utility. But such extremism was not always carried out because the artist in every architect urged him to express in his creations individual character-istics. This need for expression was sometimes so strong that the goal of utility fell short.

"Fitness for purpose" became a symbol which blocked the way for the essential purpose. Architects who had found it difficult to part with the picturesque or the decorative manner of building, were attacked so vehemently that they had to admit the importance of function in architecture. On the contrary, the functionalists fell under the influence of the picturesque architecture produced by their colleagues, who were often very talented persons. This reciprocal effect resulted in the exceptional maturity of Dutch architecture. In the last few years, before the invasion, the dogmatic principles which had been worked out by the functionalists became less oppressive. Much credit for this achievement must be given to S. van Ravensteyn.

This architect, a man of outstanding technical ability and of great esthetic refinement, was one of the leading figures of functionalism. As architect for the Netherlands Railroad Company he designed numerous buildings and also signal boxes, all of them following the principle of "fitness for purpose," without any romantic features at all. In his later works, however, in the stations in Arnhem, in Rotterdam, and in Utrecht, as well as some renovations, and the design of the royal yacht "Piet Hein," he was not satisfied with the purely functional solution of the building problem, but added to this some playfully bent forms which broke the chain of the "fitness for purpose" dogma completely. Several members of the functional school followed him in this, and his point was proven when the rationalist, J. Duiker, in his masterly work, the Hotel Gooiland in Hilversum, did not shy away from the decorative either.

Still, a great difference remained between the work of the functionalists with an inclination toward the decorative, and the work of the romanticists who did not neglect to consider the function of their buildings. Function remains the dominating factor for the functionalists, whereas achievement of the picturesque remains the primary purpose in the work of the romanticists.

Catholic church architecture has been less influenced by these new movements. Much of the heaviness has been retained, as may be seen in such works as the Abbey Egmond by A. J. Kropholler, Cloister Egmond and a church in Scheveningen built by M. van Moorsel, or the churches in Zuidbroek and Eindhoven by B. H. Koldewey, which still express the Berlagian conceptions. The architects of this group are united by their belief in the Catholic way of life. They have attempted to create a modern sphere of church and cloister and to retain, at the same time, typically Dutch characteristics.

In contrast to these Catholic architects and the functionalists, both of whom felt it their duty to carry into effect an international style movement, the great majority of Dutch architects have wished to maintain their individual ideas of form. The internationalists felt congenial with modern architects throughout the world for they shared their spiritual and social views. In 1928 they held the first of their annual meetings of the International Congress for the New Way of Building, but although the functionalists attempted to support an international movement, Dutch characteristics crept into their work, for the true artist can never entirely sacrifice his individuality or deny his environment. Among the individualists the Netherlands has many great builders whose style, closely connected with the Dutch landscape, possesses a truly Dutch character. Foreign influences on their manner of building cannot be denied, but this does not lessen the individuality of their work.

Romantic block-architecture is dominated by the architect M. Dudok, and the greatest example of this style is his magnificent City Hall in Hilversum (1928–1930). Dudok was influenced by Frank Lloyd Wright, but he cannot be considered an imitator. His manner of fitting geometrical building elements into a design is always dependent upon his personal interpretation of the needs of the building and its environment.

The rural tradition of architecture was upheld by Professor Granpré Molière who built the garden-village *Vreewijk*, in Rotterdam in 1929. Others of this school were Professor Landsdorp, and J. F. Berghof who not only built houses of the rural type of architecture but also was one of the prize winners of the contest for the design of a new city hall in Amsterdam. A very remarkable architect who has built a number of country homes, which are worthy examples of Dutch rural architecture, is A. Eschauzier. Other great architects of this time are J. van der Steur whose Boymans Museum in Rotterdam is an unequaled creation and G. Friedhoff who gained fame with the City Hall he built in Enschede and the Christian Science Church in Amsterdam.

The rich picture of modern Dutch architecture presented here, and Holland may be considered one of the leading architectural centers in the world today, has to its credit numerous public-utility buildings erected by J. Emmen, factories by S. H. van Rood, schools, such as the lyceum, built by J. Baanders in Amsterdam, and additional works of architects too numerous to mention. The development of urban settlements, even those of small communities, is guided by experts; unplanned building is avoided at all times. Every town, even the smallest hamlet, is built under the strict supervision of a planning commission whose task it is to see that esthetic norms are maintained. A unique expansion plan for the city of Amsterdam arose under the direction of C. van Eesteren; this plan, which comprised the world's largest park plans, has already been partly executed.

The influence of good architecture upon a population as a whole should not be underestimated as a cultural factor. A single example will suffice to illustrate the foregoing statement. Thousands of people come into daily contact with the mighty New Amstel Station in Amsterdam built by H. G. J. Schelling and are impressed by its power and cheered by its magnificence. This building, situated opposite the Berlage bridge, is a product of the same architect who, in an earlier period,—to be seen in the station in Bussum—was close to the conceptions of Berlage, but was strongly influenced by the purpose of functionalism in its later development.

It is an undeniable fact that a noble architecture which has left its mark throughout a country influences the life and thus, also, the interiors and home furnishings of the people. It would be boastful to contend that each Dutch interior is a perfect example of good taste, comfort, and cultured living, but it is no exaggeration to state that

Dutch interior decoration, on the average, is of an admirably high standard. Interior decoration has been guided by the same movements that have influenced exterior architecture, and the development of the two has been closely related. The explanation of this lies in the fact that many prominent architects have done the interior decoration for their own works. The interior decorator, on the contrary, always has tried to make his interiors fit the style of the house. He realizes the interrelation of the exterior and the interior and tries to combine both into a harmonious unit.

Architecture, both interior and exterior, is an interpretation of the living culture of a people. In the Netherlands its variations have reflected periods of simplicity, of wealth and superficiality, of somberness, and finally, the period of modern functionalism. And in its successive steps, architecture in the Netherlands has reflected, also, qualities of great vitality and strength.

CHAPTER XVII

Literature

BY JAN GRESHOFF

I N DUTCH LITERATURE two features are conspicuous from the beginning and are noteworthy,
particularly because they assert themselves
during the entire period of literary develop-
ment. From this continuity it may be concluded that these features are
connected with essential components of the Dutch national character.

The first is the power of appropriating foreign material. Hendrik
van Veldeke (1171) adapted his legend of *Sint Servaes* from the Latin,
his *Eneide* from the French. And after him the influence of intellectual life beyond the boundaries of the Netherlands asserted itself
without interruption. The rich epic-dramatic literature of the Middle
Ages consists exclusively of adaptations. Only of the play *Karel ende
Elegast* is no foreign prototype known. But, with a single exception,
those translations, free translations, adaptations, and limitations received a completely Dutch character. The most singular example of
this intellectual imperialism is *Van den Vos Reynaerde,* which constitutes one of the high points of Dutch literature in the Middle Ages.
No historian of literature doubts for a moment that the author,
Willem die de Madoc maakte, borrowed his material to a considerable extent from the French epic *Le Plaid,* but this does not alter the
fact that *Van den Vos Reynaerde* came to be known as one of the
most intimate and most genuine works of Dutch literature.

Even in the Middle Ages, and particularly in the period of humanism and the Renaissance, can the influence of the classics be
ascertained. Hooft was influenced by Italy, Vondel by France. In the
eighteenth century French classicism gave the tone; at the end of

the eighteenth century and the beginning of the nineteenth count-less influences may be detected—of Goethe (Werther), or Ossian, Byron, Scott; at the end of the nineteenth century those of Shelley, Keats, Platen. And, to conclude with the present, a man like Slauer-hoff (1899–1932) harks back to Tristan Corbière, Alfred Jarry, and Paul Verlaine. But it cannot be asserted emphatically enough that from the Middle Ages to modern times all Dutch authors have fully assimilated these influences and have transformed them into a strongly personal style in which one hardly recognizes the original elements. Here there takes place in the intellectual realm the same process that occurs daily in the material: from the animal and plant world are derived all the elements required for the building and main-tenance of the human body; alien material is ingested and digested in order to form human flesh and blood.

The second feature in Dutch literature is truly no less character-istic—a combined tendency to moralize and to indulge in lyrical flight. Dutch lyric poetry forms the escape valve of a life which is dominated by strict moral laws and an almost slavish adaptation to traditional customs. Although medieval life had not as yet given much occasion for it, the first indications of this phenomenon were visible at that time. But it was to attain its full significance only after the victory of the Calvinistic idea, which for centuries had deter-mined the mental attitude even of those who believed they had dis-carded the faith of their forefathers.

The epic, as the synthesis of the lyric and the didactic, may be found in the Middle Ages (*Van den Vos Reynaerde*), at which time Catholicism did not exclude a strong worldly passion; it may be found again in the twentieth century (in the form of the modern novel), at which time Protestantism, in its preponderance, has lost much of its absolutism.

In the early Renaissance, in the "Golden Century" (the seven-teenth), and in the period of decadence the same irresistible urge toward both didacticism and lyricism may be found in Dutch litera-ture. These two tendencies found expression in the work of every author of any importance of those days, more clearly in Vondel, who perhaps is not the greatest poet, in the strict sense of the word, but is, as a man and as an author, the greatest figure in Dutch literature.

In the Middle Ages is a truly great masterpiece, *Van den Vos Reynaerde,* a number of important dramatic specimens, *Karel ende Elegast, Lancelot van Denemarken,* several famous stories (*Beatrijs*), and a countless number of splendid short poems. This period, one of unprecedented richness and variety, closes with rhetorical poetry, in which there is very little of permanent value.

It took some time to free Dutch literature from the influence of rhetoricism. Even in the great poets of the "Golden Age" traces of it may still be found. Freedom in part came from popular poetry which, though not always of pure content, had the incalculable advantage of genuineness; but primarily deliverance came from the intellectual renovations of the Western world, an influence which made itself felt strongly and lastingly in the Netherlands, because the Reformation came to be an inseparable and gradually predominating factor in that renovation process.

"Humanism" and "Renaissance" are technical terms which are so often used and misused that they have gradually lost their contour. The somewhat childish conception that periods succeed one another in such a way that one can fix a date for the end of one and the beginning of another has finally been given up. The world has come to the realization that all changes are successive manifestations in an orderly flow of events, and that an intellectual and social movement has been prepared long in advance and is in a latent state before it becomes outwardly manifest.

That transition period in which the medieval spirit was still producing powerful after-effects and in which the new mode of thought was developing with still greater power, produced in the Netherlands a number of important figures, but not a single great literary work of art in the Dutch language. Even the universal humanist, Desiderius Erasmus, of Rotterdam (1466?–1536), who, however incalculable may be his importance as a thinker, not only for the Netherlands, but for all of western Europe, can be mentioned only in an indirect connection in a summary of Dutch literature, because he wrote in Latin.

The new popular art in which, it is true, traces of rhetorical style may be detected, developed with a joyous enthusiasm and produced at least one sound masterpiece, the "Wilhelmus," which was the battle hymn and hymn of solace of the Protestants about 1572, just as in these days it is the battle hymn and the hymn of solace of the Netherlanders within and outside of the Fatherland. The text of the hymn has been attributed to Marnix van St. Aldegonde (1539–1598), "probably rightly so" according to Dr. J. Prinsen; he gives, however, no further reasons for this statement. Marnix, who surpassed himself as a poet, if the "Wilhelmus" is by him, was one of the strongest figures of the young Reformation in the Netherlands. He crowned his studies with a course in Geneva, which center he left in 1561 as "a Calvinist to the back-bone."

The beginning of the great conflict of the Netherlands against Spain furnishes proof of the belief that arts, letters, and sciences have never attained their highest florescence in times of civil strife and war. Art is preëminently a fruit of peace. Art is luxury, even though in an exalted form. Great art, therefore, has flourished in the Low Countries only when religious conflict and the wars for freedom have lost their violence and their immediate importance for the existence of the nation, and when, instead, commerce and industry have provided the means for a full and carefree life.

The four figures who dominated the literature of this period, the greatest that the Netherlands had experienced until the second florescence about 1880, are P. C. Hooft (1581–1647), Gerbrand A. Breero (1585–1681), Joost van den Vondel (1587–1679), and Constantijn Huygens (1596–1687).

Among these, Hooft was a pure lyric poet gifted with a strange poetic power; Breero touches one by his deep human accents; Vondel is the person who because of his unusual dimensions dominates the entire period; and Huygens, witty, wise, and keen, is the man who represents intellectual passion. If, in order to round out the picture of this rich period, the name of Jacob Cats (1577–1660) is added, then in conclusion there are also the qualities of good-natured common sense, simple faith, and the animal spirits of the common people.

Of these artists who enriched the Netherlands with an enduring literary treasure, Hooft and Huygens were, as human beings, surely the most agreeable and most highly cultivated. They were traveled and well-read, men of captivating manners, conversant with the secrets of statecraft. Vondel, on the contrary, was and remained a man of the people, with all the good and bad connotations of that epithet. Although Vondel did not possess the refinement and the lyrical tension of a Hooft, nor the noble intellect of a Huygens, yet he had enthusiasm, an intellectual driving power, an inexhaustible wealth of thought, and above all an imagination which were lacking in Hooft and Huygens. Vondel's effervescing artlessness, his simplistic power of faith, both before and after his shift to the Roman Church, his surrender to inspiration, and his guilelessness make a medieval impression in the midst of his Renaissance contemporaries. A typical representative of the Baroque, Vondel proves that there is an inner relationship between the medieval and the Baroque, that, whether above the actual Renaissance or below it, they are adjacent. The periods in which feeling is supreme are related, no matter how different the forms of expression, and form a contrast to the periods in which the intellect predominates. This does not mean that the Middle Ages were devoid of intellect and the Renaissance devoid of feeling; the concern here is merely with the period of greatest emphasis.

Breero, a youth of the people, had a greater resemblance in type to Vondel than to Hooft. He was the first Bohemian in Dutch literature; of unbridled nature, now living in wild intoxication, and then urged by regret to a deep and sincere repentance. And both sides of his nature, the sensuous and the pious, he has depicted in a number of unforgettable poems.

What a period in the Netherlands! A period in which there originated the sonnets of Hooft, some fifty sound masterpieces; the best lyrical poems and the best lyrical dramas by Vondel; the songs of Breero, now engagingly full of the love of life and then again pathetic; the intellectual descriptions of Huygens. And besides them are the authors Jacob Reefsen, Heiman Dullaert, Jeremias Decker, Johannes Stalpaert van der Wielen—all of whom must be rated as secondary figures, but who, nevertheless, have accredited to their names some of the finest poems ever written in the Dutch language.

Although the eighteenth century was not so completely empty and unimportant in the Netherlands as former historians of literature have made it appear, the Netherlands did not possess, during this period of quiet and agreeable life, any writers or works of art important and universal enough to be presented to a foreign public.

After a century of sluggish life there arose a new interest in art and literature. The truly genuine poet of the beginning of the nineteenth century was A. C. W. Staring (1767–1841). He is in many respects related to Hooft, both in his attitude toward life and in his purely lyrical nature. After having completed his law course, he finished his education at a foreign university, as did Hooft, and just like Hooft he later led—not indeed at a castle, but at a stately country-seat in the province of Gelderland—the noble life of a poetic, wise, refined, cultured man. Staring's poetry is certainly inferior in quality, less penetrating and stately than that of Hooft, but he had the same sensitiveness and sharpness, the same liking for a jaunty arabesque, and he is equally lovable as an artist and as a man. When, at the end of the nineteenth century a new criticism, with ruthless severity and not always with due justice, rejected practically the entire production of the preceding hundred years, an exception was made of Staring. His exemplary worthiness as an artist and his gifts of spirit and mind proved to be unassailable.

What Staring was for poetry, Jacob Geel (1789–1862) was for prose. He was a witty, capable, careful stylist, a versatile scholar, and the first man in the Netherlands to state clearly the problems involved in the concepts of romanticism and classicism and to treat them in an illuminating way. Geel was and remains the greatest essayist, in the strict sense of the word, that Holland has produced. He wrote only one volume of prose, but it is so alive and so significant for the readers of today that the volume might have been written at this time.

E. J. Potgieter (1808–1875) dominates the entire middle of the nineteenth century. He was the founder and editor of the paper *De Gids,* which still exists and is now in its one hundred and sixth year. He was regarded as the perfect prose writer, the inexorable yet just critic, and the pure poet—in short he was the central figure and the embodied ideal of all who were liberal between 1840 and 1880 and who cultivated Belles Lettres, or took a genuine interest therein. The importance of Potgieter as a leader and a literary figure can hardly be overestimated. But a part of his writings is now accessible only by very great exertion. It is his critical work that has best withstood the passage of time; in addition, a number of his great poems, such as *Florence,* and *De Nalatenschap van een Landjonker,* of which the conclusion *"Gedroomd Paartrijden"* forms a separate unit, have survived with proud positiveness. Together they form the most monumental body of poetry in Dutch literature; they are significant, abundant with learned views and human considerations, exemplifying truly grand design and structure.

It is impossible to gain a clear picture of Dutch literature in the nineteenth century without including the noble, serene person of Anna L. G. Bosboom-Toussaint (1812–1886), and her stately, voluminous works which consist preponderantly of historical novels in which, with a single exception, material of Holland is treated. Present-day readers are wont to call her novels tedious. On the contrary it may be said that all works of lasting and substantial importance are and must be tedious for the general public, which asks only for a story, for an anecdote. Madame Bosboom-Toussaint has a broad, quiet, dignified narrative style; she finds no difficulty in a detailed description and elaborates her ideas on an extended scale. For those who have not yet been affected by the contagious disease called "haste," her austerely constructed novels (for instance, *De Delftsche Wonderdokter*) form a source of calm and intimate enjoyment. Madame Bosboom-Toussaint, endowed with an undeniable and convincing epic talent, is one among few novelists in the strict sense of the word, and of these she is probably the most gifted.

But, however much the many-sided merits of a Potgieter, a Huet, and a Bosboom-Toussaint may be enlarged upon, and however gladly they may be accorded the praise that is their due, it must be asserted that the nineteenth century in the Netherlands actually produced only one truly brilliant artist—Eduard Douwes Dekker (1820–1887), known by the characteristic pseudonym of "Multatuli." In Dekker's nature, and therefore also in his strangely rich and lively prose, may be seen the complete and harmonious synthesis of the two national characteristics: the tendency toward moralizing—the old-fashioned urge to preach, with pleasure in preaching—and, as the sole means of escape therefrom, lyric flight. Dekker is the lyrical moralist, the moralizing lyric poet. His life-work consists of essays which, in reality, are rather effusions—aphorisms, maxims, and fragments, animated without exception by a dark glow and formulated with cutting sharpness. Even his two books, *Max Havelaar* and *Woutertje Pieterse,* are composed of a number of fragments brought into a union which is often very loose. They dispense altogether with the rigid traditional structure which characterizes the genuine nineteenth-century novel. They are none the worse for that. On the contrary they derive their value and their charm from their freedom and their moral laxity, their whimsicality, their swift surprising turns, and their inexhaustible wealth of ideas and emotion.

Dekker's life was one of passionate conflict. His vitality, his conviction, and his interests were so great and so many-sided that he was unable to remain impartial with respect to any problems of importance. The best period of his life was dominated entirely by the tremendous problem, of greater national interest than any other, regarding the relation between Netherlanders and Indonesians in the Dutch Asiatic domain, for which he invented the poetic name "Insulinde." Both by his acts and by his writings he brought about an entirely new conception regarding that relation. At first this was opposed sharply and not always fairly. But eventually the ideas championed by Multatuli with such intense ardor were elaborated upon in great detail, and were generally accepted as the basis of the maintenance of loyal coöperation.

Before him there had but rarely been any writing in the Dutch language so fervent, with such tempo and conviction. Multatuli's influence persists even to the present day, because he rehabilitated the spoken language and, in counterdistinction to the extremely solemn exaltation which was characteristic of his best contemporaries, he not only defended the "ordinary word," but elevated it into a serviceable, charming, and insinuating literary means of expression. It is no wonder that Multatuli found such ardent admirers among the young writers (Menno ter Braak and E. du Perron) around 1930; they defended, with equal assurance and emphasis, the rights of sober language and natural style, as he had in his time.

Of all the authors of the nineteenth century Multatuli is the only one whose work has remained alive and current for more than half a century. On a Potgieter, a Huet, a Carel Vosmaer, time has impressed its stamp, and their works are read in the constant realization of the past. But Multatuli's swift, mobile, penetrating prose gives the impression of having been written today. It is therefore not absurd if Multatuli is regarded as the precursor of the intellectual renovation which occurred in the Netherlands between 1870 and 1880. He was not the only one who proclaimed this renovation but, among those in whom were displayed the first possibilities of a radical revolution, he was by far the greatest and most striking figure.

The "Movement of the Eighties," originating from premonitory indications given by the predecessors that have been named, was a thoroughgoing desire for a deepening and a purification of the concept of art on the basis of its conscious rehabilitation and a concomitant glorification of personality. This desire arose not only in literature but likewise in painting, architecture, and philosophy, and was coupled with passionate criticism of the immediate past.

It is not an exaggeration to speak here of a second Renaissance, particularly because the character of the new movement was also determined primarily by a renewed florescence of individualism and a conscious ideal. From this it follows logically that criticism had necessarily to occupy an important place in this movement, and that actually proved to be so.

By far the most important lyrical poet was Herman Gorter (1864–1927), the author of *Mei,* a lyrico-symbolic story, which in a very short time has become one of the classics of Dutch literature. In the same period Gorter wrote a number of short poems which were collected

under the title *De School der Poëzie*. In these, poetic individualism
finds its richest and most glorious expression. Later, after his acces-
sion to the then still young tonalistic movement, Gorter wrote two
philosophico-lyrical poems, *Een klein Heldendicht* and *Pan* (the latter a very lengthy work). These still comprise a number of fragments
of incomparable beauty, but as a whole they no longer satisfy, because
in them the thinker and the politician too often dominate the poet
and impose silence upon the individualism of his earlier poetry.

Willem Kloos (1859–1930) was the theorist of the new movement,
and he illustrated his principles by means of a number of truly human, deeply moving poems. However, he did not fulfill the high
expectations which had been originally and very rightly entertained.
At the close of a period of intense intellectual life he suddenly collapsed. After a serious illness there was nothing left of his former
passion, his old energy, his former lucidity of mind. During his long
life he occupied himself with studies in the history of literature, which
were of secondary importance; he also wrote numerous criticisms
which were without motivation or discrimination, and a series of
1500 completely unreadable sonnets under the title *Binnengedachten*.
Young Kloos, who is honored as one of the masters, wrote a hundred
poems which have withstood the passage of time, and a volume of
theoretical essays which have as yet lost little of their value and none
of their beauty. In 1883 Kloos established a periodical, *De Nieuwe
Gids,* which was for a decade the focus of intellectual life in the
Netherlands, but which lost all its importance after Kloos's collapse.

Frederik van Eeden (1860–1932) was one of the editors of *De
Nieuwe Gids*. The first period of his life was so strongly influenced
by Thoreau that he gave the name of "Walden" to the countryseat
where he carried on his experiments in coöperative agriculture. He was
a versatile man: a physician greatly interested in the new psychiatry,
a poet, novelist, dramatist, sociologist, and practical reformer. He
concluded his life and his career as a Roman convert. Frederik van
Eeden was richly talented, but he lacked self-criticism, and a characteristic of indecision again and again interrupted his work, making
it deficient in contour and cohesiveness. During his lifetime he was

involved in so many controversies that public opinion and the critics did not succeed in forming a correct picture of his nature and value. Now that all the storms he aroused have subsided, it is generally beginning to be realized that he enriched Dutch literature with a number of works of the first rank. To begin with, is his allegory in three parts, *De Kleine Johannes,* of which the first part is the best known and by far the weakest; next his drama in verse, *De Broeder,* grandiose in intention, rich and splendidly variegated in execution; his psychological novel, *Aan de Koele Meeren des Doods;* his comedy, *De Heks van Haarlem;* several profound philosophical studies and a small number of excellent poems; and these are only the high points of his extensive and varied production.

In the school of the "Eightiers" must also be included two prose writers of importance, Van Looy and Couperus. Jacobus van Looy (1855–1930), who was at the same time a highly meritorious painter, is a man of description, of plastic prose, and of this he supplied several small masterpieces; but his true significance as a man and an artist appears only from his *Wonderlijke Avonturen van Zebedeus* (in three volumes), a book which is unique in Dutch literature and which resembles no work known in any foreign literature. If one wishes to find a vague parallel, one must compare it with one of the liveliest, most whimsical books of German romanticism, *Kontraste und Paradoxen* by Friedrich von Sallet. *Zebedeus* is a book filled with delicious inventions, rich in unexpected variegations and changes, poetic, satirical, humorous. One who knows Van Looy's life and his environment discovers amusing allusions again and again, and one who studies the history of the "Movement of the Eighties" and is able to fathom Van Looy's playful symbolism finds a wealth of material in the *Zebedeus.* Another document of value is W. A. Paap's novel *Vincent Haman,* a caustic caricature of the artists who grouped themselves in and around *De Nieuwe Gids.*

The second of these prose writers, Louis Couperus (1863–1933) was the first born story-teller in the Netherlands. His writing was very uneven. In addition to novels of great importance and lasting value he wrote hasty hack-productions planned for a cheap temporary success. But Couperus at his best constitutes a pinnacle in this new literature. His books have been translated into numerous languages. The English translation, prepared by Teixeira de Mattos, is highly praised. His works consist of "modern" and "historical" novels. In general, the former are more personal in tone, stronger in character delineation, and more deeply felt.

In his books there lives forever an atmosphere and a state of mind, strongly affected by Indian influences, which were characteristic of life, particularly in The Hague, around 1900. Of all his contemporaries—the so-called "Eightiers," Louis Couperus, in his somewhat mannered, but nevertheless genuine refinement, was the most picturesque phenomenon, and, at the same time, as a man certainly the most lovable and the noblest.

When *De Nieuwe Gids,* after a fortunate existence of ten years, lost its importance and influence, there arose at the same time a reaction against the slogans proclaimed by that periodical. Impressionism, subjectivism, sensitivism, simultaneously with naturalism and realism, began to lose their charm and meaning for the groups of younger writers in the Netherlands.

In the "First Transition" usually four authors are mentioned—lyric poets, who although originally greatly influenced by the "Movement of the Eighties," had developed for themselves a new attitude toward life and a new style of writing. These are J. H. Leopold (1865–1925), P. C. Boutens (1870–1943), Henriëtte Roland-Holst (born 1869), and J. A. der Mouw (1863–1919). Of these, J. H. Leopold is the most moving poet, sophisticated and naïve at the same time; P. C. Boutens created what is, viewed in its entirety, the most impressive lyrical ensemble in Dutch literature, noble, pure, and cool; Henriëtte Roland-Holst, nee van der Schalk, influenced and impelled like Gorter by a profound social passion, wrote a number of intense, compassionate verses, countless theoretical writings, and several excellent biographies (among others, those of Garibaldi and of Tolstoi).

To this "First Transition" there belongs likewise Arthur van Schendel (born 1872), in whose work the contrast with *De Nieuwe Gids* finds its sharpest expression. Arthur van Schendel is rightly regarded as the greatest prose writer in the Netherlands. He has never expressed himself critically or theoretically. His complete rejection of naturalism is evident from the character of the extensive lifework that he has produced.

It is customary to divide Van Schendel's production into two periods. The first comprises the books which treat of historical and, for the most part, Italian material. The most important and certainly the best-known work of this period is the novel of the *Zwerver,* written in two parts, *Een Zwerver verliefd* and *Een Zwerver verdwaald.* The two central features of Van Schendel's nature are already clearly present in this youthful work—the problem of fate and the problem of solitude. The second period is characterized by Dutch motives and by a greater interest in the present day. Like all subdivisions, this one also has only partial validity. In spite of an undeniable turn which took place around 1930, the work of Arthur van Schendel constitutes a closely knit, natural unit. To the second period belongs the trilogy *Een Hollandsch Drama* (renamed *A House in Haarlem* in the English translation), *De Rijke Man,* and *Grauwe Vogels.* Van Schendel has written altogether some twenty novels, all of which are of interest and importance. Slight differences in value can probably be discovered, but his work knows no declines nor failures. This writer has now maintained an impressively high level for forty years. Mention must be made of *De Waterman,* a sound masterpiece. It is also necessary to call attention to Van Schendel's countless fantastic stories, of which five volumes have now appeared. These stories reveal an entirely different side of his nature and talent; they are playful, wise, witty, surprising, and disclose unlimited power of invention. Arthur van Schendel remains the greatest prose writer of the Netherlands and one of the greatest Dutch authors of all time.

It is customary to designate a group of writers who came to the fore after the "First Transition" by the name "Generation of 1905," after the year in which they first began to flourish. Although they are, in fact, contemporaries, it is hardly possible to discern in them a profound internal identity of nature. But they are all, if not exclusively, yet chiefly, lyric poets. Epic prose was hardly cultivated by this generation. By far the most captivating and important figure among them is A. Roland-Holst (born 1888), and mention may be made also of J. C. Bloem (born 1887), and P. N. van Eyck (born 1887).

Holst is the poet of sea and wind, of the dreamed-of islands, of Elysian passion, and cosmic desire. But even in his most unworldly poems he always preserves an undertone of deep, genuine humanity. Bloem's work is dominated by bitterness over lost illusions, over misfortune, over solitude. He compares daily reality with an idealized glory of youth and feels himself defeated. His three volumes constitute a moving testimony of human weakness, which is transmuted by the miracle of poetry into greatness and power. P. N. van Eyck, Verwey's successor as professor at Leyden, wrote, particularly during the years just before the invasion, a number of penetrating essays. And he also produced a fairly extensive body of poetical works, which is not always rated at its true value. The most important prose writer of this generation is J. Gronlöh, who wrote only three novelettes, of which two are perfect in their conciseness.

The "Second Transition" is represented by four poets of undeniable importance, J. W. F. Werumeus Buning (born 1891), Victor E. van Vriesland (born 1892), M. Nijhoff (born 1894), and Herman van den Bergh (born 1897), of whom M. Nijhoff, who wrote very little, is unquestionably the greatest. He introduced a wholly new accent into Dutch lyric poetry, succeeded in realizing in it a strange sort of ecstatic objectivity, and exerted a decisive influence on the younger poets. These younger poets united in the publication of a periodical, *De Vrije Bladen,* which in turn gave prominence to three lyric poets of great importance: J. J. Slauerhoff (1898–1936), H. Marsman (1899–1940), and Hendrik de Vries (born 1896).

If an introduction for foreign readers must be limited to essentials, H. Marsman must be chosen as representative of the most recent literature. His name is chosen primarily because of the intrinsic value of his work, and because of his many-sidedness, his marked influence on older and younger contemporaries, his contagious enthusiasm, and his unassailable personality. More than any of his contemporaries, Marsman was the modern poet and the poet in modernity.

When the periodical *De Vrije Bladen* had performed its important work, there originated, partly as a reaction against the inferior successors of Marsman and Slauerhoff, the movement which crystallized in the monthly *Forum*. Poetry of metaphysical enthusiasm was followed by conscious disillusionment; what was too exalted was followed by what was too free, which ran aground in a thin, vacuous Gongorism. There came of its own accord the desire for a poetry of confession and understanding. One of the men of the *Forum,* or rather the soul of that periodical, Menno ter Braak (1902–1940), spoke of the rehabilitation of the common word. People spoke "heart to heart"; they rejected "form," which had become autonomic and thereby meaningless, and called for "confession" and the human element. In years of fighting about principles, distinctions were frequently too sharply drawn, and opinions formulated too apodictically. The essential differences between *De Vrije Bladen* and the *Forum* proved to be less than was originally anticipated, and very soon Marsman, Slauerhoff, Hendrik de Vries and others who were classed with the group of *De Vrije Bladen,* belonged among the faithful collaborators of the *Forum*.

To the *Forum* group there belongs, in the first place, Menno ter Braak, an acute and witty critic, merciless if necessary in order to pillory mediocrity or falsehood, but understanding, guiding, humane when he discovered honest intent and sincere talent. Menno ter Braak wrote a philosophico-literary treatise in three volumes: *Het Carnaval der Burgers, Politicus zonder Partij,* and *Van Oude en Nieuwe Christenen,* five volumes of articles and essays, two novels, the value of which has been systematically underrated, and one drama. Between 1930 and 1940 he devoted an important part of his time and energy to the fighting of Fascism in all its forms and disguises. When, on May 10, 1940, the Germans invaded the Netherlands, he knew that there was no other outcome for him than voluntary death.

E. du Perron (1899–1940), Menno ter Braak's associate in the founding of the *Forum,* was a curious, whimsical person, originally rarely gifted, ardent and enthusiastic withal, ready to fight, but at the same time of captivating heartiness. Du Perron, born in Java, came only comparatively late to Europe, where he remained for about twelve years from his twenty-fifth to his thirty-seventh year, mostly in Paris and Brussels. He was driven back to the Indies by an irresistible urge. And shortly prior to the invasion, after a stay of three years in the Indies, he returned to the Netherlands. Two days after the invasion he died of an attack of angina pectoris. He contributed to Dutch literature three books of unprecedented, almost excessive wealth of emotions and ideas. The first was his novel *Land van Herkomst,* unequaled in the Netherlands in its tone, form, and substance, a book of flesh and blood, of oppressive genuineness and directness; then a volume of short stories, *Nutteloos Verzet;* and, finally, a volume of essays, *De Smalle Mens.* Furthermore, du Perron devoted four works to E. Douwes Dekker (Multatuli), to whom he felt himself related and for whom he had unbounded admiration. An extensive series of short notes and diary pages, extremely curious and enthralling, has not yet, in so far as is known, been issued in book form.

Finally, mention must be made of S. Vestdijk (born 1898), essayist, poet, and novelist, of undeniable genius and of amazing productiveness. Now that so many of his contemporaries have met an untimely death, he represents his generation and, although still comparatively young, because of his richness, his variety, his singularity, and his wealth of invention he is one of the greatest writers of Dutch literature. His chief works are a trilogy of child life, *Sint Sebastiaan, Surrogaten voor Murk Tuinstra, Ina Damman,* together forming the novel *Anton Wachter's Jeugd;* and an impressive historical novel using the figure of El Greco, *Het Vijfde Zegel.*

The critico-humanistic spirit of the *Forum* had again to be succeeded by a new turn. Under the influence of three currents, which are characterized by three names, Freud, Bergson, and Breton (surrealism), there arose in the Netherlands also a fundamentally irrational tendency, which produced two poets of importance, G. Achterberg (born 1906) and Ed. Hoornik (born 1910).

There are insufficient data concerning literary activity during the occupation to offer a definite opinion. The issues of periodicals and the books which have reached the outer world by a circuitous route give the impression that the arts are developing normally in accordance with their own laws, without being greatly influenced by the horrors of the time. From what has come out of the Netherlands it would appear that Dutch authors have remained conscious of the incontrovertible fact that intellectual life proceeds in a different world and on a different plane from the material, and that material life can exert only a superficial influence upon it. The Dutch writers of importance, young and old, without exception have remained aloof from a *rapprochement* to the usurper; on the earthly plane they have remained faithful to their nation, and on the heavenly to their destiny, namely poetry.

CHAPTER XVIII

Music

BY HENRI EMILE ENTHOVEN

FOR THE HISTORIOGRAPHER of Dutch music the most important date is to be found, strangely enough, in a period which had promised to be of very little importance to Dutch musical life. When the year 1826 opened, all signs pointed to a continuation of the unproductive state of music in the Netherlands which had existed in the preceding twenty-five years. And yet, in 1826, in almost every other European country music flourished as never before.

In Vienna, Beethoven and Schubert, whose last string quartets are the expression of this upsurge, were writing their immortal masterpieces. In this same year, on the shores of the Thames, London reveled again in her old glory as a musical metropolis, with Drury Lane Theatre witnessing the world première of an opera in English, Weber's *Oberon,* the unrivaled masterpiece of the romantic school. In Paris, Liszt and Paganini reigned as emperors of the concert stage, whereas Hector Berlioz built the foundations of the modern orchestra. At the same time, on the shores of the Amstel and the IJ, and in the proud royal residence, The Hague, the old proverb *"Frisia non cantat"* threatened to become a reality. And then, quite suddenly, a new dawn broke!

The Royal Institute of Arts and Sciences (*Koninklijk Instituut voor Kunsten en Wetenschappen*) published the prize-winning essay of a contest and, significantly, through the collaboration of a Frenchman and an Austrian in this contest, the solution to the dilemma of Dutch music was found. In their essay, Fétis and Kiesewetter had lifted the veil of obscurity which had hidden the extraordinary and

unique meaning of those great Dutch masters who had dominated
the sacred and secular music of the civilized world for two and a
half centuries.

In the years following this revelation, real and pseudo musicolo-
gists tried to introduce the old timeworn antiphons and missals into
modern scores. A short time later the masterworks of these early composers were made available to anyone who was interested in the
spiritual trends of the Netherlands at the end of the Middle Ages.
The first of these composers, noteworthy enough to be included in
a short survey, was Guillaume Dufay (1400–1474), one of the creators of the "organically built Mass." Following this master a second
generation of composers, led by Johannes Okeghem (1420–1495),
and that great citizen of Bergen-op-Zoom, Jacob Obrecht (1430–
1505), raised polyphonic music to a remarkable virtuosity. How completely Okeghem had mastered the technique of counterpoint is
clearly demonstrated by the fact that he composed a canon for thirty-
six voices. It is also noteworthy that his Masses for four voices are
often based on a secular *cantus firmus,* as, for instance, on the French
folk song so well known in those days, *"L'Homme Armé."* Obrecht's
most important work, written in part for the Guild of Our Dear Lady
in Bergen-op-Zoom, is the Mass *De Beata Virgine* in which the *cantus
firmus* in the soprano "Sub tuum praesidium" is combined with five
successive Maria songs, all of which retain their original texts. His
St. Matthew Passion, the first of a rich literature of similar *motet-
passiones* built on the Gregorian *cantus firmus,* also deserves mention.

The third school, or generation, of Netherlands masters was
founded by Josquin des Prez (1450–1521), (also known as Jossé de
Prés), who, as a composer, is usually included among the sixteenth-
century masters. Josquin des Prez brought his music into greater
accord with the text than did most of his forerunners. His ability of
adjustment was of a deeply psychological character; he was, for many
years, a singer in the Sistine Chapel in Rome, but later his field of
activity was transferred again to the Low Countries. He strove for
an absolute evenness and sameness of voices so that, from this time
on, church music became purely vocal. His contemporaries were so

acutely aware of the great difference between his work and that of his predecessors, they gave his style a special name *"Musica Reservata."* Another member of this school who deserves mention is the Dutch master Noel Bauldewijn, composer of a four-voiced Mass, based on the unequivocably secular song "My Love's Brown Eyes" (*"Mijn liefkens bruyn oghen"*).

The next generation—the fourth Netherlands school—was composed of masters who, at the court of Charles V, retained or further developed the Gothic traditions of their precursors. Lupus Hellinck and Jacobus Clemens (1510–1556) (known also as Clemens non Papa), were the most important representatives of this generation. In his two hundred and thirty *motets* and in other works, also, Clemens achieved a euphoniousness only to be equaled and surpassed by Palestrina. Adriaan Willaert, another worthy exponent of this generation, was born in Bruges between 1480–1490, and died in Venice in 1562. Although he was educated according to the precepts of Josquin des Prez, he was less renowned for the development of Dutch music than for the creation, in Venice, of the double choirs (*chori spezzati*) in which two four-voiced choruses interchanged—an application of the antiphonic concept to four-voiced music.

A combination of Renaissance and Gothic elements was characteristic of the fifth, and last, generation of these fifteenth- and sixteenth-century Dutch masters. At this time, the center of music shifted more and more to Italy where the great figure of the Maestro Palestrina (Giovanni Pierluigi, called "Palestrina") began to show itself on the horizon, yet this era was destined to produce one of the most brilliant representatives of Dutch musical genius—Orlando di Lasso (1532–1594), actually Roland de Lassus, born in Hainault and educated in Italy. He was the most prolific, the most universally gifted and, next to Josquin des Prez, probably the greatest of the Dutch composers of this generation. The music of this period seems to have attempted to recreate all that had been achieved in the last century.

A text often inspired De Lassus to create tone pictures in the fullest and truest sense of the word; he must also be credited with having introduced the chromatic element into church music. His greatest masterpieces are, without doubt, the *Penitential Psalms*. De Lassus was the last of the great counterpointists of the Netherlands. Dutch leadership of European music ended in this period. In reaction against their polyphonic music, an opposite style gained favor—the solistic. Man as an individual emerged from the group. A solo voice now was accompanied by instruments. Drama and reciting both made use of music, the renewed figured bass, recitative, and the aria gained in prominence and, gradually, instrumental music became independent.

Dutch participation in this development was of little significance; Italy and England assumed the role of leaders. Yet, music was by no means unimportant in the life of seventeenth- and eighteenth-century Holland; the paintings by the great Dutch masters, Rembrandt, Hals, Judith Leyster, Ogtervelt, Jan Miense Molenaar, and Terborch testify to that statement. The many music colleges bear witness to the fact that the playing of musical instruments was an integral part of the life and education of the Dutch.

The Netherlands produced a composer of great fame in the first half of the seventeenth century in Jan Pieterszoon Sweelinck (1562–1621). Although born in Deventer, Sweelinck went to Amsterdam at a youthful age where, for many years, his father was the organist of the Oudekerk. Sweelinck himself held this position for forty years, a function which was undoubtedly the most important any musician could fill in the young, prosperous, commercial city. Sweelinck's compositions have been made available in a ten-volume publication by the Society for Dutch Musical History (*Vereeniging voor Nederlandsche Muziekgeschiedenis*). His psalms and chansons for mixed voices belong to the most beautiful compositions of the seventeenth century. It was in organ music, and he composed many works for this instrument, that he truly thought instrumentally. He may, in fact, be considered the creator of the organ fugue which was later perfected by Johan Sebastian Bach.

Among the organists in Holland Cornelis Schuijt, organist of the Pieterskerk in Leyden, and composer of exquisite madrigals should also be mentioned as outstanding in the field.

Gradually a generation of composers emerged who composed

solely for the instrument. Of first importance was Jacob van Eyck, a native of Utrecht, who published *Flute's Paradise (Der Fluiten Lusthof)* in 1649.

A new phenomenon in the musical life of the Netherlands appeared in the eighteenth century. The colleges of music placed their orchestras and concert halls at the disposal of foreign artists. A real concert life now began. The famous Italian composer Pietro Locatelli, pupil of Corelli, spent a great deal of his life in Amsterdam, where he died in 1764. To a certain degree he may be considered the father of modern virtuoso violin music. The most important event in the eighteenth century was the visit of the Mozart family to The Hague in 1765–1766, where young Wolfgang Amadeus wrote various works for the coronation of Prince William V of Orange.

The first decade of the nineteenth century was not a period on which musical Holland can look back with pride. One may truthfully say that not one really great figure was produced at that time. The observation, made in those days by a foreigner, that the only music appreciated by the Dutch was the tinkling of church bells and ducats, contained some essence of truth. This statement fails to imply, however, that a great number of foreign composers and virtuosos celebrated their triumphs in the Netherlands even at that time.

A change took place in the latter part of the nineteenth century. At the court, the gallant King William III became actively interested in the royal pensionnaires, and the gracious Queen Sophie, also an author of note, gathered about her many well-known contemporary artists. This was the time of J. J. H. Verhulst (1816–1891), the first musician of real significance in Holland; a pupil of Mendelssohn and a friend of Robert Schumann—the latter composer dedicated his Overture, Scherzo, and Finale for orchestra to him—he held a truly eminent position. The great music festival, held at the time of the twenty-fifth anniversary of the Society for the Encouragement of Music (*Maatschappij tot Bevordering der Toonkunst*) in Rotterdam in 1854, grew into a national demonstration of hero worship of Verhulst by a people who, after two hundred years, again had a truly Dutch composer. It is evident now that such great hope for a Dutch composer was not fulfilled. Verhulst's influence as conductor and music teacher was exceptionally great; but as a composer he was never able to free himself of the influence of his teacher, Mendelssohn, and in his fervent conservation against the performance of the music of Berlioz and Wagner, the eccentric Verhulst outlived his fame.

The first composer who was able to write really Dutch music was a younger contemporary, Richard Hol (1825–1904). Utrecht was the place of Hol's activity, and in him is to be seen the father of the so-called "Utrecht school" which has had an integral part in the development of Dutch music. This is easily understood, if one considers the fact that it was Richard Hol who formed Johan Wagenaar, Willem Mengelberg, and Catharina van Rennes; that it was, in turn, Johan Wagenaar to whom musicians such as Peter van Anrooy, Bernhard Wagenaar, Willem Pijper, Alexander Voormolen, Henri van Goudoever, and Henri Emile Enthoven owe their musical education; and that this chain of influence was continued by Willem Pijper, the teacher of a third generation of musicians including Guillaume Landré, Piet Ketting, Bertus van Lier, and Henk Badings.

In The Hague in the 1860's and 1870's musical conditions were only fair, whereas in Amsterdam they were abominable. In 1883, when Johannes Brahms went to Amsterdam to introduce his *Second Piano Concerto,* three cellists began to play, simultaneously, the famous solo from the third movement, each cellist having considered himself a soloist, reluctant to cede his rights to a colleague! But a factor which led to the establishment of the Concertgebouw orchestra in Amsterdam was the concert tours of the excellent Meininger Hofkapelle under the direction of Hans von Bülow, and of the orchestra of Bilse, which gave to the public an inkling of real orchestral playing. The Concertgebouw orchestra, which was to gain world fame within such a short time, performed in 1888, with Henri Viotta as conductor of the first concert. Its establishment coincided approximately with the rebirth of Dutch literature under such leaders as Jacques Perk, Willem Kloos, Frederik van Eeden, and others.

A few years later a generation of Dutch composers arose who were able to write truly native music. The father of these was the Amsterdammer Bernhard Zweers (1854–1924). Although educated in Leipzig he was, nevertheless, entirely Dutch in character, as may be understood from his symphony *To My Fatherland* (*Aan Mijn Vaderland*), his *Ode to Beauty* (*Ode aan de Schoonheid*) based on the text of Boutens, for soloists, mixed chorus and orchestra, his cantata for the coronation of Queen Wilhelmina, his overture "Saskia" written for the Rembrandt tricentenary, and his "incidental music" for Vondel's *Gijsbrecht van Amstel*. Zweers is another composer who created a school. Among his pupils may be mentioned Sem Dresden, Bernhard van den Sigtenhorst Meyer, Anthon van der Horst, and Willem and Hendrik Andriessen. Here, too, a second generation may be mentioned, for Dresden proved to be a pedagogue worthy of his master, to whom young and talented composers like Henriëtte Bosmans, Henk Badings, Willem van Otterloo, and others owe their musical education and encouragement.

Julius Röntgen (1855–1932) also received his musical education at Leipzig. He was a son of the violinist Engelbert Röntgen, originally from Deventer, then concertmaster of the famous Gewandhaus orchestra. Julius Röntgen came to the Netherlands at a youthful age, occupied a leading position in the musical life of Amsterdam for many years as composer, pianist, and teacher, and in this last function held the position of director of the Amsterdam Conservatory of Music. Röntgen was at home in every field of composition. In his younger years, his work was unmistakably influenced by Brahms; in later years his great friendship for Edvard Grieg left a definite mark on his development as a composer. In the last period of his life Netherlands folklore held a profound attraction for Röntgen and, consequently, he wrote typically Dutch music, certainly more nationalistic in character than that of many composers who had been born within the Netherlands. Röntgen had an extraordinarily productive talent. His works embrace many symphonies, piano concertos, the operas *The Laughing Cavalier* and *Agneta,* and many works for chamber music. Among his shorter works a ballad based on an old Norwegian folk song and an old Netherlands suite merit special mention. One of his strongest compositions is a piano quintet entitled "Swansong."

Gerard von Brucken Fock (1859–1937), composer and painter, is to all intents and purposes entirely autodidactic, even though he worked for a short time under Richard Hol. He did not hold an official function, but worked for many years for the Salvation Army in Paris. His compositions disclose a poetical late-romanticism. He is the Dutch Frederic Delius. These compositions embrace two symphonies, several suites for orchestra, besides an oratorio, *Christ's Return*, and many songs and pieces for the piano.

An entirely unique place in the music life of the Netherlands is occupied by Catharina van Rennes (1858–1939). Her special strength centered in the miniature genre. She was able to create an absolutely individualistic style in Dutch children's songs. In these songs in both text and music, she caught the spirit of youth. This is said without any intention of slighting the artistic value of popular music. Her "Hymn to the Sun" (*"Zonnelied"*), "Cradle Song" (*"Wiegenlied"*), and her "Short Poems" (*"Kleengedichtjes"*), based on the texts of the contemporary Flemish poet Guido Gezelle, could easily be accepted as folk songs and that, indeed, is high tribute.

Johan Wagenaar (1862–1941), also a native of Utrecht and from the school of Richard Hol, was able to unfold his talent to the fullest degree as organist of the Domkerk in Utrecht and later as director of the conservatory, first at Utrecht and later at The Hague. A great many Dutch composers, Peter van Anrooy, Willem Pijper, Bernhard Wagenaar, Alexander Voormolen, Emile Enthoven, and Henri van Goudoever, received their musical education at his hands. The most striking characteristic of Johan Wagenaar's compositions is his pronounced sense of humor which often becomes rollicking, as exemplified in his cantata *The Shipwreck* (*De Schipbreuk*), his parodistic operas *The Doge of Venice* (*De Doge van Venetie*), and *Le Cid*. Yet Wagenaar was also able to create tone poems of a much more embracing nature, found in the overtures "Cyrano de Bergerac" and "The Taming of the Shrew"; and in the tone poem "Saul and David" which holds a remarkable obligato for the harp, written for the Rembrandt Memorial of 1906. His orchestral coloring is strongly influenced by the scores of Hector Berlioz and Richard Strauss, yet a freshness and robust humor stamp Wagenaar's composition as a product essentially Dutch in character.

One of the most interesting figures of this generation is Dr. Alfons Diepenbrock (1862–1921), who, for many years, was a teacher of classical languages at the college in 's Hertogenbosch. It is not surprising that Diepenbrock emerged as a decided mystic; he came from the Roman Catholic intelligentsia of Amsterdam, and had lived for many years in Den Bosch within proximity of the superb Gothic St. Jan Church. In his musical education he was almost entirely autodidactical. Naturally, he felt the influence of Wagenaar, and in later years his friendship with Gustav Mahler and with certain of the outstanding French masters left its traces on his work. Two elements are the genesis of Diepenbrock's works: the vocal and the literary. They point the way to the serene *missa* in "Die Festo" and to the glorious "Te Deum," both of which are ornaments of European choral literature of the last century. These elements also make it understandable why Diepenbrock chose the texts of Novalis and Hölderlin on which to base his songs and hymns with orchestral accompaniment which in many instances grew into symphonic works. In the last period of his life he wrote stage music for Aristophanes' sprightly comedy *The Birds,* for Sophocles' *Electra,* and for Goethe's *Faust.* Important, too, are his many songs, as well as his excellent works for A Cappella chorus, in which he often escapes into Gregorian chant. Since his death, twenty years ago, the greater part of Diepenbrock's works continues to live on. Yet, the unbiased critic cannot deny that his compositional technique and his orchestral scoring show, at times, traces of amateurism, the inevitable result of his autodidactical education.

Jan Brandts-Buys (1868–1933), is, without doubt, the most important of a large family of Dutch musicians. His work, however, took him to Austria at an early age, where he remained. His most outstanding work is the opera *Die Schneider von Schönau* which was included in the repertoire of many central European opera companies at the beginning of this century.

One of the most important and most national figures of this time is the composer Cornelis Dopper (1870–1939). Dopper, schooled in

Leipzig, is one of the few Dutch composers who has lived in the United States for any length of time as conductor of a traveling opera company. He was the conductor of the famous Concertgebouw orchestra for nearly twenty-five years, and it was here that most of his works received their first performance. Dopper, perhaps, knew more about the modern orchestra than any of his contemporaries, and he may also be considered the greatest expert on counterpoint among the modern Dutch composers. His sixth symphony, *Amsterdam Symphony*, catches the spirit of this city quite as well as Sir Edward Elgar's overture "Cockaign" catches the spirit of London. In his seventh symphony, *Zuiderzee Symphony*, he presents a colorful medley of old Dutch songs, as well as of folk tunes of a more recent date. He has succeeded in welding all this into a marvel of sound coloring. Among his most important works may also be mentioned *Ciacona Gotica*, a concerto for cello and orchestra; a concert piece for viola and orchestra; and a concertino for trumpet, tympani, and orchestra. There is also the excellent, but almost unknown, incidental music for Vondel's *Lucifer*. Especially noteworthy, too, are a number of Dutch songs for boys' choir and orchestra which have been seldom performed. Cornelis Dopper is really one of the last of the older generation of Dutch composers whose influence is felt, to this day, within as well as outside the Netherlands.

Bernhard Zweers, Julius Röntgen, Gerard von Brucken Fock, Alfons Diepenbrock, Johan Wagenaar, and Cornelis Dopper all have, in their way, had a part in making possible a school of industrious native composers in the Netherlands. The younger generation is now too far removed from these masters to permit a definite opinion about the deeper significance of their works; but the conclusion may be reached that, if indications do not deceive, a great deal of the work of the "big six" will remain.

One cannot say that the second generation of modern Netherlands composers has brought forth figures as great in stature as those of the first generation. Nevertheless, there should be mentioned certain men who have shown outstanding possibilities.

Dirk Schäfer (1873–1931) was one of the ablest pianists ever to have come from Holland. Among his compositions for orchestra are the "Suite Pastorale" and the "Rapsodie Javanaise," into which gamelang melodies have been woven. Willem Landré (born 1874), was a pupil of Bernhard Zweers. He was, however, more active as a critic than as a composer, although some of his compositions, among them the opera *Beatrijs* and a "Requiem for Orchestra" have attracted attention. Peter van Anrooy (born 1879), after his successful debut at the age of twenty as composer of the brilliant and fresh "Piet Hein Rhapsodie" for orchestra, has devoted himself exclusively to conducting.

Sem Dresden (born 1881) was one of the most profound, if not the ablest theorist among living Dutch composers. In recent years he has performed an excellent job as director of the Amsterdam and The Hague conservatories of music. Dresden was founder and conductor of the Netherlands Madrigal Society. Jan van Gilse (born 1881), for many years conductor of the Utrecht Municipal Orchestra (*Utrecht-sche Stedelijk Orkest*), was entirely under the influence of the Central European school. Four symphonies, and two great works for full choir and orchestra, both based on German texts, *Eine Lebensmesse* and *Der Kreis des Lebens* deserve attention.

Although born (1882) and bred in Holland, Richard Hageman must be considered an American composer. Dirk Fock (born 1886) is one of the few Dutch composers who has settled in the United States. He is known for his *declamatorium* "Ein hohes Lied." Among his other compositions is a *mysterium* "Von Eon zu Eon." Willem Andriessen (born 1887), today imprisoned in one of the many concentration camps, is an excellent pianist. He also has been director of the Amsterdam Conservatory. Among his few compositions may be named a definitely pianistically conceived sonata for piano and a praiseworthy Mass. Bernhard van den Sigtenhorst Meyer (born 1888), a pupil of Zweers, has proven to be a delicate painter of tone coloring in many songs and pieces for the piano. A work for full choir "The Temptation of Buddha" and incidental music for Tagore's *The Letter from the King* have attracted attention.

Hendrik Andriessen (born 1892), like his brother Willem, comes from the school of Zweers. His music is of a contemplative character.

He has also been one of the few Netherlanders who has enriched organ literature. Among his outstanding contributions is his sonata "da Chiesa." Rudolf Mengelberg (born 1892) has been equally attracted by the mysticism of the Roman Catholic Church. Among his most important works are a violin concerto, a cantata, *Weinlese,* for chorus, and the hymn "Op Amsterdam," based on the text by Vondel. Bernhard Wagenaar (born 1894) for many years has been a resident of the United States. An outstanding teacher of theory and composition, he is also known for three symphonies and many other works for orchestra, an opera, and for songs and piano music. An amazing mastery of all the intricacies and problems of musical theory is one of Bernhard Wagenaar's most outstanding qualities.

For many years, Willem Pijper (born 1894) has been the man who has commanded the most attention among the young Dutch composers. With his sharp pen he has won a place in the extreme Left Wing of the revolutionary elements in Dutch musical life as a writer, and composer. His work includes three symphonies, many pieces of chamber music, one piano concerto, six epiphonic epigrams for orchestra, incidental music for *Sophocles, Antigone, Euripides,* and for Shakespeare's *Tempest.* He is also composer of the opera *Halewijn.*

Alexander Voormolen (born 1895) is another figure of this period. A pupil of Johan Wagenaar and later of Albert Roussel, Voormolen is known for a consummate mastery of the problems involved in presenting typical rococo music in modern style. Works like "Sarabande-Fagel," "Rondo Wolfenbuttel," "Air Willem V," the overture "Viva Carolina," and the ballet *Diana* have a definitely universal appeal despite their essentially Dutch character, as has his remarkable concertos for oboe and orchestra.

The opus of Henriëtte Bosmans (born 1895), also a pupil of Pijper, contains several works for cello and orchestra, a violin concerto, a piano concerto, and chamber music. Marius Monnikendam is imbued with the spirit of Roman Catholic Church music. The massive sound of choir has had a peculiar attraction for him, as is apparent in his seven Penitential Psalms. His symphonic movement *Toil,* however, is too strongly reminiscent of Henegger's *Pacific 231.*

Henri Emile Enthoven (born 1903), composer, and historian on the faculty of the University of Leyden, wrote among other compositions, three symphonies and romantic variations; also four suites for orchestra, incidental music for the Egyptian pageant *Ichnaton,* an orchestral hymn "Sol Justitiae," music for a pageant for Princess Juliana's wedding, songs with orchestral accompaniment, and piano music. He came to the United States in 1939. Guillaume Landré (born 1905), son of the above-mentioned Willem Landré, received his musical education from his father and from Willem Pijper. Besides several works for chamber music, a violin concerto, a suite for string quartet, and one symphony, he wrote the opera *The Pike.* Piet Ketting (born 1905) and Bertus van Lier (born 1906), both products of Willem Pijper's teaching have won renown, the former for his incidental music for Aeschylus' *The Eumenides,* the latter for his chamber music, two symphonies, and one concertino. Van Lier is also a very able theorist, but his love for experimentation has been his undoing at times.

The most talented figure among the younger generation is undoubtedly Henk Badings (born 1907) who is a skilled engineer and geologist as well as an eminent musician. Badings, whose *oeuvre* is outstanding by its great variety, wrote among other compositions three symphonies, one violin concerto, a great number of works for chamber music and full choir, variations for orchestra, and incidental music for the greatest of all Dutch classical dramas—Vondel's *Gijsbrecht van Amstel.* Exceptionally sound musicianship is Badings' greatest asset, whereas his technical ability is not to be excelled. Many of Badings' works[1] belong to the regular repertoire both in Europe and in the United States.

Among the younger composers, whose works have been played the following also deserve mention: Leo Smit, Robert de Roos, Julius Hijman, Jan Feldehof, Léon Orthel, Hans Osieck, and Johan Franco and Felix de Noble, both of whom reside in the United States.

In the realm of music the Netherlands not only has produced great composers, but also outstanding performing artists. First among the

---

[1] In October, 1943, word was received from Holland of Badings' ballet, *Jeanne d'Arc.*

latter is Willem Mengelberg (born 1871), for more than forty years conductor of the Concertgebouw orchestra. In this capacity he has been of paramount importance to the Netherlands and Europe, and also to the United States. It is an irrefutable fact that Mengelberg's constructive work has been a source of encouragement and inspiration to musical creation in the Netherlands.

Among the Dutch conductors Willem Kes (1856–1935), the first conductor of the Concertgebouw orchestra, deserves a salute of honor for his ability to achieve the seemingly impossible in the seven years that he worked with the orchestra. The work of Henri Viotta is of extremely great importance, in as much as Dutch musical life has dominated the Dutch operatic world for many years, particularly through his founding of the Wagner Society. In 1904 he created the Residentie orchestra so that under his leadership The Hague again became a music center, worthy of the days when Mozart visited the Royal Residence.

The two previously mentioned orchestras, the Wagner Society, and the different choral societies founded by the *Maatschappij tot Bevordering der Toonkunst,* with the Amsterdam group as its foremost exponent, have contributed toward making Holland during the last forty years that unique center of the musical world where Grieg and Reger, Mahler and Strauss, Debussy and Ravel, Stravinsky and Prokofieff, Respighi and Schelling, Hindemith and Milhaud, all came personally to conduct or to perform their latest compositions. The younger generation of Dutch conductors has given ample proof of its ability to uphold the traditions established by its predecessors; a few of these younger conductors have already been mentioned among the Dutch composers. To these may be added the name of Eduard van Beinum who has replaced Willem Mengelberg as conductor of the Concertgebouw orchestra in late years. Despite his youth, he has given evidence of belonging to Holland's most outstanding conductors.

Mention must also be made of the excellent instrumentalists who have held Holland's name high all over the world. The names of the pianists Dirk Schäfer and Willem Andriessen have already been given. Without any claim to completeness, there now must be added the names of the eminent violinist Henri Petri (1856–1914), and his equally talented son, the pianist Egon Petri (born 1881), who at present is located at Cornell University, Ithaca; also the outstanding cellists Joseph Hollman (1852–1934), and Hans Kindler (born 1892), the latter having been more active as conductor of the National Symphony Orchestra at Washington, D. C., during the last few years. Among the singers who have left their stamp so indelibly on their generation are Johan Messchaert (1857–1922), the unexcelled interpreter of baritone oratorio parts, Jacques Urlus (1867–1933), for many years the Lohengrin, Tristan, and Siegmund of Bayreuth and of the Metropolitan Opera in New York, and Anton van Rooy (1870–1931), who also for many years has sung the baritone role of Wagner's operas in Bayreuth as well as in the Metropolitan Opera.

Furthermore, mention must also be made of those two great interpreters of the *Lied,* Julia Culp (born 1880), and Tilly Koenen (born 1873), and the two great soprano oratorium singers, Aaltje Noordewier-Reddingius (born 1868), and Johanna Vincent (born 1898). The latter are both magnificent interpreters of the soprano parts of the entire oratorium literature. The courageous Johanna Vincent is at present a hostage in the hands of the Germans.

One other category of Dutch music still must be mentioned—the Dutch singing towers. These famous carillons, located on the towers of innumerable Dutch Renaissance buildings, which year in, and year out have sung their glad songs of courage and gallantry, are now silenced. But the day will soon come when the stately strains of the National Anthem, and the strains of other songs of courage and victory will ring out again from the singing towers of Holland.

Part Six

Netherlands Overseas Territories

CHAPTER XIX

Races and Peoples of the Indies

BY RAYMOND KENNEDY

FIVE HUNDRED THOUSAND YEARS AGO ape men roamed the Indies. Most of their bones have long since disappeared, but a few remains have been discovered, enough to show that these islands were among the earliest haunts of man. No older human remains than those of Java Man have ever been found anywhere in the world. The Indies are the anthropologist's Garden of Eden.

No one knows what went on in the islands between this remote beginning and perhaps twenty-five thousand years ago. The ape men somehow disappeared, and the next inhabitants about which knowledge exists are the ancestors of the present Australian natives, most primitive of all existing human beings. They lived in the Indies, and then passed on to the great continent lying southward. The only signs that they once dwelt in the Archipelago are a few preserved bones and some living people of Australoid type found in the islands of Timor and Flores, in the eastern Indies near Australia.

Three other ancient races succeeded the Australoid, although the order of their arrival is uncertain. One of these was the ancestral stock of the woolly haired Oceanic Negroes who now live in the Melanesian Islands of the Pacific far to the east—the Bismarck Archipelago, the Solomons, the New Hebrides, and New Caledonia. Their race has almost vanished from the Indies, but it is known that they must have passed through, for they could have reached the Pacific islands by no other route. Moreover, in certain unfrequented parts of the Archipelago, especially in the vicinity of Timor, the bushy-haired, sooty-skinned Melanesian Negroid stock still survives.

The other two archaic races of the Indies still live there. But only a few are left and these are seldom seen, for they have retreated to the most remote and inaccessible places. Both are dwarfish and frail: the one a pygmy Negroid type, called Negrito; the other a small, wavy-haired, weak-chinned variety, called Veddoid, which looks as though it might be a stunted hybrid of Malay and Australoid. Negritos are found in certain sections of the vast swampland of Sumatra, in some of the eastern islands, such as Timor, and in the mountains of New Guinea. Outside the Indies, there are groups of them in the Andaman Islands, Malaya, and in certain isolated parts of the Philippines. Remnants of the Veddoid race inhabit the east Sumatra marshlands, parts of Borneo and Celebes, and certain islands of eastern Indonesia, notably Ceram. The Veddoids of the Indies have anthropological relatives in Ceylon, Malaya, and in the Philippines; and in all these places, as in Indonesia, they live a furtive, primitive existence far from the centers of civilization.

Perhaps ten thousand years ago, a new migration into the Indies began. It came from southeastern Asia—southern China, Burma, Siam, and Indo-China—and brought to the islands the first tribes of Malay stock. When the earliest Malays arrived, the islands were probably thinly populated by Negrito, Veddoid, Oceanic Negroid, and Australoid groups. Then, for thousands of years, successive waves of the new race of Malays, who were finally to inundate the Indies almost completely, poured into the Archipelago from Asia.

The earlier Malays were of a less Mongoloid appearance than their racial kinsmen who came later. Despite their short stature and dark skin, their facial appearance more closely resembled Caucasoid, or "white," than later Malay. They lacked the exceedingly wide and high cheekbones, the slanting eyes, and the coarse, straight hair of the Mongoloid race. They looked more "European" than the later comers and, as a matter of fact, they were more closely related to the white race than to the yellow. The reason for this interesting fact is that originally Southeast Asia was inhabited by tribes who were dark and distant outliers of the European peoples. These early Malays, thus, belonged to a dusky branch of the white race.

With the passage of time, an ever-increasing movement of Mongoloid peoples from the north invaded Southeast Asia, and, mixing with the old inhabitants there, gradually changed the racial type in the Malay homeland from predominantly Caucasoid to predominantly Mongoloid. Thus the later arrivals in the Indies from this region were progressively more Mongolized, showing this in their wider faces, higher cheekbones, straighter hair, and more slanting eyes.

The great bulk of Indonesians at the present time are of the Malay race. The branch of this stock which came into the islands first is now found mostly in the remoter districts of the Indies, whither they were pushed by the later arrivals. This type may be appropriately named the "Earlier Malay," or, in technical terminology, the "Proto-Malay subrace."[1] The other subdivision of the Malay race may also be called by either of two names: "Later Malay," or "Deutero-Malay." Peoples of the Later Malay type predominate in the coastal regions of the large western islands. This is where one would expect to find them, because they are the most recent arrivals in the Archipelago, except for the Hindu, Chinese, European, and other historic immigrants.

To the person untrained in fine anthropological distinctions, both Earlier and Later Malay types look quite similar. Both have brown skin, very short stature—averaging about 62 inches for males—broad and flat faces, and straight or wavy black hair. But the differences noted above are easily perceptible on closer examination, and are sufficient to warrant the subdivision.

One other racial type is found in the Indies, far to the east, in New Guinea and in neighboring islands. This is the so-called Papuan stock, whose origin may be traceable to crossbreeding between the Australoid and the Melanesian types. Their bodies are lanky and long-limbed, their skin dark, and their faces narrow and angular, with thin lips and long noses, the latter often full-fleshed and hooked at the tip. They are hairy, many of them having full beards; and the hair is frizzy. In the Moluccas, a transitional area from the racial

---

[1] Some American and British anthropologists refer to the Earlier Malay subrace as "Indonesian," an unfortunate usage because, properly speaking, all inhabitants of the Indies are Indonesians.

viewpoint, intermixture of the Papuan and the Earlier Malay types has produced the so-called Alfur hybrid, characterized by medium to tall stature, slender build, medium to dark brown skin, straight to wavy hair, a relatively hairy body, and features ranging from the broad-faced, flat-nosed Earlier Malay norm to the narrow-faced, "semitic-nosed" Papuan conformation.

Broadly speaking, therefore, five general racial zones in the Indies may be indicated: (1) the coastal regions of the large western islands (Sumatra, Borneo, Java, Celebes), where the Later Malay type predominates; (2) the interior sections of the large western islands, inhabited primarily by peoples of Earlier Malay stock; (3) the middle zone of the Lesser Sunda Islands, stretching east from Java (Bali, Lombok, Sumbawa, Sumba, Flores, Timor, etc.), peopled principally by the Earlier Malay race; (4) the Moluccas (Ceram, Ambon, Halmahera, Buru, etc.), where the Alfur hybrid of Papuan and Earlier Malay predominates; and (5) New Guinea and neighboring islands, the habitat of the Papuan type. In remote nooks and corners of these main zones live the scattered remnants of the four archaic stocks: Australoid, Melanesian Negroid, Negrito, and Veddoid.

If exceptions of detail are slighted, it is possible to make an even broader racial division of the Indies into western and eastern sections. The western islands are almost solidly Malay in stock, and the eastern region Papuan, whereas in between, in the Moluccas, various combinations of these two principal strains are found. Temperamentally, too, the eastern peoples of the Archipelago differ from those of the western section. The Malays are, generally speaking, very sedate and reserved, almost stoical. The Papuans, however, are excitable, noisy, and aggressive. The traveler on a ship voyaging eastward in the Indies sees this change occur as he leaves the Malay zone and enters the area of the Papuans. The natives become progressively less restrained, louder, and more loquacious until, in New Guinea, the entire "human atmosphere" reaches almost a polar extreme from the lands of the serene Malays and Javanese. Whether this temperamental divergence is racially or culturally determined is a question undecided by anthropologists. Probably it is more a matter of training.

The primary physical traits of the Malay race, and the distinguishing characteristics of its two subdivisions have been described. Some further remarks may be made which apply to the Malay peoples in general. Men and women are not only small, but delicately and beautifully built. Their bodies are almost always symmetrical, neither too fat nor too lean, and their limbs are round and "well turned." The beauty of the Malay body tends to be somewhat spoiled, from the white person's viewpoint, by the facial appearance. Most Malays are flat-nosed and rather thick-lipped, and their customs of filing off their front teeth and chewing betel nut, which stains the mouth and lips dark crimson, make an ugly impression on Europeans and Americans. In manner they are remarkably dignified and well-poised. They move slowly and gracefully, and speak softly. Finally, most of them are exquisitely polite. The poorest Javanese, receiving a stranger in his pitiful, little thatched hut, acts the gracious gentleman naturally and effortlessly. It is difficult to think of any place in the world where one meets more genuinely charming people than in the Indies.

About two thousand years ago, foreigners with an eye to conquest and profit began to invade the Indies. The first alien adventurers were the Hindus, from India, who came to dominate all of Java and the coastlands of the other western islands. For long centuries, until about five hundred years ago, Hindu civilization flourished in this part of the Indies, and great empires rose and fell in slow progression. The Hindus have left marks of their racial type in many parts of the western Indies, especially in Java among the upper-class families. Although Mohammedanism replaced the Hindu civilization of the medieval period, it brought no new racial strains into the islands— except for a small immigration of Arabs—for it came from India, by way of Malaya.

For hundreds of years Chinese have been coming to the Indies, until in 1940 their number exceeded 1,200,000. They have scattered widely over the islands, and have interbred freely with native women. Their physical effect can be noted only in an accentuation of the Mongoloid racial characteristics of the Malay peoples in some regions. Asiatic immigrants other than the Chinese have come to the

Indies in relatively small numbers. Their combined population in 1940—the largest groups being Arabs and Hindus—slightly exceeded 100,000. Finally, about four hundred years ago, Europeans, principally Dutch, began to arrive but the white population in 1940 totaled only about 250,000, and most of these were of mixed European and native ancestry. Moreover, they were heavily concentrated in one island, Java, and in a few places in other sections of the Archipelago, principally Sumatra.

Thus, of the total population of 70,000,000, over 68,000,000 are natives. The largest single tribe, or nation, is the Javanese, who number close to 30,000,000. They inhabit most of the island of Java, with the exception of the extreme western section, where dwell the Sundanese, with a population of almost 10,000,000, and the northeastern coastal region, which is peopled by Madurese from the neighboring island of Madura. The Madurese in Madura and Java total almost 5,000,000. Two other small groups live in the mountain fastnesses of western and eastern Java, respectively: the Badui, with a population of only 1,200, and the Tenggerese, numbering about 10,000. The great majority of the people of Java belong to the Later Malay stock, the more Mongoloid division, but among the Sundanese, and indeed in most of the interior districts, the Earlier Malay type is almost as prevalent. In Java, also, the effects of Hindu blood admixture are more noticeable than elsewhere in the Indies, for this was a center of Indian civilization in past centuries.

Sumatra and adjacent smaller islands, although not nearly so densely populated as Java, contain several very large tribes. Most numerous are the 3,500,000 Malays, whose territory extends over the entire eastern coast of Sumatra. The northern coastland is occupied by the Atjehnese, numbering 750,000; and the interior of Atjeh is the home of two quite primitive mountain tribes, the Gayo and the Alas who, together, have a population of 50,000. The central mountain districts are inhabited by two very large groups, the Batak and the Minangkabau, who total 1,000,000 and 2,000,000, respectively. The southern end of Sumatra is peopled by 500,000 natives belonging to a complex of several related tribes, called the Redjang-

Lampong group. Then, as a final group in this listing of the population figures of the island of Sumatra are the very primitive nomads who roam through the remote and forbidding areas of the eastern

NETHERLANDS EAST INDIES

swamps known as the various Kubu tribes, whose combined population would add to approximately 25,000 inhabitants.

The racial affiliations of the peoples of Sumatra show a distribution similar to that in Java: the coastal groups—Malays and Achinese—are chiefly of Later Malay type; the interior tribes—Gayo, Alas, Batak, Minangkabau, and Redjang-Lampong—predominantly Earlier Malay in stock. The primitive Kubu are Veddoid, and one of their divisions, the Akit, displays strong Negrito characteristics. Thus the racial distribution reflects the history of the peopling of Sumatra, the older races dwelling in the interior districts, and the later comers inhabiting the coastland. The smaller islands off Sumatra's west coast, as might be expected, are occupied by groups of the Earlier Malay racial type: Nias, with a population of 200,000; the Mentawei Islands, with 10,000; and Engano, with only 300. The Enganese are among the very few peoples of the Indies whose numbers have declined since the coming of the white men.

Virtually the entire coastal margin of the vast, though thinly populated island of Borneo is inhabited by mixed Malay, Buginese, Macassarese, and Javanese settlers, who have driven the aboriginal tribes back into the interior. This hybrid population of the seacoast and lower river courses, of Later Malay stock, numbers about 1,000,000. All of the inland tribes belong to the Earlier Malay racial group.

It has become customary to lump together all of these natives under the general name "Dyak," but the author has worked out a more precise classification which combines the hundreds of little tribes into six tribal complexes, distinguished from one another by cultural differences, even though all of them are Earlier Malay in physical type. The largest complex is that of the Ngadju peoples of southern Borneo who, together, total 400,000. The Bahau tribes of the central area and the Klamantan groups of northwestern Borneo number about 300,000 each. The Iban or "Sea Dyak" people in the middle portion of Borneo's west coast have a population of 200,000. Finally, the wandering Punan hunting bands of the deep interior number close to 50,000. Inland Borneo, thus, is inhabited by tribes of the Earlier Malay type, surrounded on all sides by mixed coastal groups of Later Malay stock. The entire island is one of the most sparsely populated parts of the Indies, its enormous bulk of 290,000 square miles supporting only about 2,500,000 people.

The grotesquely shaped island of Celebes, east of Borneo, is only one-fourth the size of the latter, but has a much larger population. Over half of the 4,000,000 total are included in the Macassarese-Buginese group, whose center of population is the southwestern

peninsula of the island, around the city of Macassar. This large combined nation numbers about 2,500,000. The northern peninsula, too,
contains a sizable tribal complex, that of the Minahasa-Gorontalo
peoples, whose total population is 500,000. The interior tribes of
Celebes are sometimes classified under the single general heading of
Toradja, but this name is more properly applied to the mountain
groups of the central region, who number together around 200,000.
South of the Toradja dwell the Sadang tribes, in the upper districts
of the southwestern peninsula. Their population is close to 500,000.
The eastern and southeastern peninsulas are inhabited by the Loinang
and Mori-Laki tribal complexes, numbering 100,000 and 200,000,
respectively. All of the groups so far mentioned are of Earlier Malay
racial type, with the exception of the Macassarese and Buginese, who
belong to the Later Malay stock. One purely Veddoid tribe, totaling
only about 100, has been discovered in an isolated mountain district
of southwestern Celebes. This minute and archaic fragment of the
ancient Veddoid race, the Toala, are famed as the only surviving
cave-dwelling people of the Indies, but already they are rapidly mixing with and disappearing into the surrounding Buginese nations.

Whereas western Indonesia comprises the four large islands of the
Greater Sunda group—Java, Sumatra, Borneo, and Celebes—eastern
Indonesia is an area of innumerable small islands, lying between the
Greater Sundas and New Guinea. There are several different ways of
grouping these islands, but perhaps the most convenient classification
can be made by dividing them into two sections: the Lesser Sundas
and the Moluccas.

The Lesser Sundas stretch east from Java to Timor in a long chain,
separated from each other by narrow straits. They include, from west
to east: Bali, Lombok, Sumbawa, Sumba, Flores, Savu, Roti, the
Alor-Solor Islands, and Timor. Although their total population is
3,500,000, over a million of these live on the island of Bali. Lombok,
Flores, and Timor are peopled by 600,000, 500,000, and 700,000
natives, respectively. Sumbawa has a population of 300,000; Sumba,
100,000; Savu, 27,000; Roti, 60,000; and the five islands of the Alor-
Solor group (Solor, Adonara, Lomblem, Alor, and Pantar), 150,000.

The peoples of the Lesser Sundas are predominantly of Earlier Malay stock; but toward the eastern end of the chain—in Timor, Flores, and the Alor-Solor Islands—the racial situation becomes highly complex, for this remote corner of the Indies has functioned as a *cul de sac,* where several racial strains have piled up in an astonishing potpourri of physical types. Here the Earlier Malay strain is easily discernible, but, in addition, there are Melanesian Negroid, Papuan, Australoid, and Negrito elements. This area is indeed a kind of living museum, exhibiting specimens of virtually every racial type that has lived in the Indies since earliest times. From the viewpoint of physical anthropology it is one of the most interesting regions in the world.

The Moluccas are a vast array of islands—some rather large, but most of them small—lying between Celebes and Timor on the west and New Guinea on the east. Population is sparse in most of them, the total being only about 425,000. Ten islands or island clusters comprise the southern Moluccas, stretching eastward from Timor to New Guinea. The largest ones include Wetar, with a population of 7,500; the Tanimbar Islands, with 25,000; the Aru Islands, with 20,000; and the Kei Islands, with 30,000. The smaller ones are Kisar, having 9,000 inhabitants; the Leti-Moa-Lakor group, 15,000; the Luang-Sermata Islands, 5,000; the Nila-Teun-Serua chain, 3,000; and the Roma-Damar cluster, 3,000.

The northern Moluccas, situated between Celebes and New Guinea, include three quite large islands: Ceram, with a population of 60,000; Halmahera, with 50,000; and Buru, with 20,000. Three of the smaller island groups here have fairly large populations, namely, the Ambon Islands, with 60,000 inhabitants, the Ternate-Tidore pair, with 35,000, and the Batjan Islands, with 35,000 also. The remainder of the northern Moluccas are mostly small, and sparsely settled: the Ceramlaut Islands, having 6,000 inhabitants; the Goram Islands, 6,000; the Watubela group, 2,500; the Banda Islands, 6,000; and the Sula Islands, 15,000. Obi, a rather large island of the northern Moluccas, has lost its aboriginal population, and now supports only a few transient fishermen and gatherers of forest products.

The peoples of the Moluccas are mostly of the so-called Alfur racial type, which, as previously mentioned, is a hybrid of Earlier Malay and Papuan. The inhabitants of the islands nearer New Guinea are more Papuan in physical type, while those nearer Celebes and Timor show more Earlier Malay characteristics. The Moluccas are, thus, a zone of transition between the western Indies, the Malayan racial area, and New Guinea, the great center of the Papuan stock. In certain remote parts of the Moluccas, notably eastern Ceram, Veddoid remnants still survive.

Dutch New Guinea and adjacent islands have an estimated population of 500,000, but this region is largely unexplored, and anthropologists have yet to work out the tribal divisions. Nearly all of the inhabitants, however, belong to the Papuan race, although in the interior mountains numerous tribes of dwarf Negrito stock are found.

Two principal conclusions emerge from the foregoing analysis of the races and peoples of the Indies. The first is that the racial divisions follow quite regular lines of geographical distribution, with the most archaic strains (Australoid, Melanesian Negroid, Negrito, Veddoid, and Papuan) pushed back into absolutely the most remote sections of the Archipelago, the tribes of the Earlier Malay subrace occupying intermediate locations in the interior districts of the western islands and most of the central zone of the Indies, and the Later Malay racial stock dwelling chiefly in the coastal areas of western Indonesia. The cultural differentiation runs parallel with these racial and geographical lines. Thus the old "remnant" stocks, living in the most inaccessible regions, possess very simple cultures; live principally by hunting, gathering wild products, and by rudimentary agriculture; know little or nothing of such material arts as metalworking and weaving; seldom rise above the level of the primitive band in social organization; and are almost totally pagan in religion.

The peoples of Earlier Malay stock, inhabiting the somewhat less remote islands and districts, are still largely pagan in their religious beliefs and practices, only partially influenced by Hindu civilization or Mohammedanism; lack many of the advanced techniques of material culture; preserve ancient features of social organization; and, although they live principally by agriculture, many of them have yet to progress beyond the hunting stage, or, at best, to employ even the simplest methods of cultivating the soil. The groups belonging to the Later Malay subrace, living chiefly in the coastal sections, have undergone strong Hinduist acculturation, with nearly all groups now Mohammedan in religion; they possess a wide repertory of manufacturing techniques; have long since adopted centralized state forms of government; and are expert agriculturists, with remarkable skill in irrigation engineering.

The other conclusion, pertaining more specifically to the tribes or nations than to the races of the Indies, is that the native groups in this part of the world are unusually large. Even though the Dutch policy of protecting and preserving indigenous culture has fortified the traditional civilization of the Indies against alien inroads, sheer force of numbers has undoubtedly operated as the strongest single bulwark against cultural disintegration under the impact of foreign colonization. The beliefs and customs of tribes with populations ranging into the hundreds of thousands and millions do not yield easily to change, and for many centuries the peoples of Indonesia have withstood successive and strong intrusions of Hindu, Chinese, Mohammedan, and European Christian civilizations without losing their own cultural and social identity. Indeed, there are few other places in the world where native cultures have remained so nearly intact, even up to the present time, as in the East Indies. It is unlikely, therefore, that the violent upheavals of our day will affect the people of the islands either profoundly or permanently.

CHAPTER XX

History of the East Indies

BY BERNARD H. M. VLEKKE

AT THE BEGINNING OF THE CHRISTIAN era the islands of the East Indian Archipelago, vaguely known to the ancient Greek geographer Ptolemy as the "Gold and Silver Islands," were a thinly populated territory where an indigenous civilization was slowly unfolding. The Indonesian tribes had advanced far beyond the stage of primitive life when, with the arrival of scattered groups of Hindu immigrants, a new period of their history began.

The immigration of the Hindus, which for the next fifteen centuries shaped the outward forms of Indonesian life, continued from the first to the seventh century A.D. It certainly never took the form of a conquest of Indonesia by the Hindus, nor of a mass immigration. Probably a thin but uninterrupted stream of immigrants, merchants, and an occasional group of political refugees moved into the island world. The Hindus brought their script, their art, and their religion to the Indonesians, and these elements were quickly assimilated into the Hindu civilization.

The economic connections of Indonesia with China must have been almost as old as those with India. The Chinese chroniclers noted carefully the embassies, sent to their emperor by Indonesian princes, who arrived, bearing gifts which varied from wild animals to spices. Chinese merchandise was given in exchange for these presents and, thus, a profitable trade was developed by the Indonesians. The Chinese emperors themselves were greatly pleased by the yearly arrival of the envoys who were considered to have come to do homage on behalf of the Indonesian princes.

[313]

It is still not known how far the Hindu immigrants and the Hindu influence—which also has been spread by Hinduized Indonesians—penetrated into the eastern part of the Indies. Traces of Hindu-Indonesian civilization have been found in the southern Celebes and in Sumbawa. The oldest inscriptions have been discovered in eastern Borneo north of Muara Kaman, in a now sparsely populated area. The inscriptions probably date from about 400 A.D. and prove the existence of a small Hindu-Indonesian state in which the Brahman religion prevailed. Nevertheless, in consequence of the Hindu immigration, only in Sumatra and in Java were more stable political formations established in early history. It is known there was a kingdom of Çrivijaya on the island of Sumatra, with a capital at the site of the present city of Palembang. In Java there existed in the seventh and eighth centuries a kingdom, Kaling, the capital of which was probably not far from the present Djokjakarta. Here the oldest Hindu temples of Indonesia and the enormous "stupa" of the Boro Budur disclose by the purity of their architectonic forms and of their sculptures that their builders and artists must have been Hindu-Javanese. Although the oldest temples—on the Dieng plateau—are dedicated to Çivaitic deities, the Boro Budur and the Tjandi Mendut, built in the same half-century, were erected in honor of Buddha.

Between 400 and 700 A.D. a change of religion undoubtedly took place in both Hindu-Indonesian kingdoms, in the Sumatran Çrivijaya as well as in the Javanese Kaling. The history of this early period is necessarily very obscure, but it seems quite probable that future discoveries of inscriptions may throw more light upon the sequence of events. At the time of the construction of the Boro Budur the name of Çailendra both in Sumatra and in Java appears as that of the ruling dynasty, but it is not known whether this indicates a conquest of Java by the Sumatran kings (where the name Çailendra seems the older one) or simply a temporary union of the two states.

From middle Java the center of Hindu-Indonesian culture shifted after 900 A.D. to eastern Java and, at the same time, Çivaism again became predominant. It is not known whether or not there was an outspoken hostility between the adherents of the two creeds in Indonesia. Of such hostility there is no proof whatsoever, whereas evidence does exist that both religions flourished side by side for many centuries. Both creeds were strongly influenced by Indonesian religious concepts and, finally, were blended into one philosophy and system of religious ceremonies in which magic played a predominant part.

The shifting of the center of culture and government from middle to eastern Java probably was accompanied by a migration of a large part of the inhabitants of the island. This may have had something to do with the increased interest of the Javanese in naval affairs and overseas commerce. King Dharmavangça, the organizer of the eastern kingdom (around 1000 A.D.) directed maritime expeditions against the Hindu-Indonesian states of western Borneo and Malayu (Djambi) in central Sumatra. This prince was overly ambitious, and caused the temporary ruin of his state, but after its reorganization by King Airlangga, who died in 1042, Javanese influence spread rapidly to the east as well as to the west. In the twelfth century Javanese vassal states existed in the Moluccas. Bitter struggles kept Java divided; in the twelfth and thirteenth centuries the most important kingdoms were those of Kediri and Janggala, each of which was forced to recognize the overlordship of the princes of Singhasari (1222–1292) and that of Pajajaran in west Java. At the same time the Sumatran realm of Çrivijaya passed through a series of ups and downs in which expeditions to Ceylon and even to distant Madagascar were as common occurrences as invasions of Sumatra by Hindu and Ceylonese kings.

Foreign commerce became increasingly important. The immigration of Hindu merchants really never came to an end. Merchants from Gujerat (north of Bombay) could be found in all ports of the western islands and of the Malay Peninsula. Since the Javanese had undertaken the interinsular traffic from the Moluccas and Timor—the sandalwood island—to east Java and from there to Sumatra, the Gujerats only occasionally penetrated farther to the east than west Borneo. In the Hindu-Indonesian world their presence passed unnoticed until in 1196 Gujerat was conquered by Mohammedan invaders. The immediate effect was the arrival of Mohammedan merchants in Indonesia and the beginning of the spread of Islam.

In 1292 Marco Polo visited northern Sumatra on his trip home from the court of Kublai Khan, ruler of Asia. At Perlak (in the present Government of Achin) Marco Polo found Islam predominant. The oldest Mohammedan tombstones of Indonesia have been found at Samudra, a hundred miles north of Perlak, and by their characteristics they betray their origin from Gujerat. A new wave of Western influence seemed imminent, coinciding with a renewal of political pressure from the north.

Kublai Khan had decided to establish his authority over the whole of Southeast Asia. Indo-China was conquered but the King of Singhasari refused submission. A Chinese expedition sailed southward, conquered and destroyed the principal cities of east Java but had to withdraw before a counterattack of Prince Vijaya, who became the founder of the city and kingdom of Majapahit. The first direct interference of the Chinese with Indonesian affairs was a failure and before the introduction of Islam and European invasions changed the aspect of Indonesian life, the Hindu-Indonesian civilization was permitted a last period of glory. This was the period of the kingdom of Majapahit (1293–1478).

Majapahit was a naval empire. The fleets of King Hayam Wuruk (official name, Radjasanagara, 1350–1389) forced all coastal states of the Archipelago, even far-away kingdoms, like Brunei, on Borneo's northern coast to recognize the overlordship of east Java. The kingdom of Çrivijaya was conquered and Palembang became the residence of a Javanese governor. The real founder of this mighty empire was Gajah Mada, the *patih,* or Prime Minister of the King. The most famous of all medieval Javanese chronicles, the *Nagarakertagama,* composed around 1365, is in reality the epic of Gajah Mada. After Hayam Wuruk's death the empire foundered. Internal strife destroyed the power of its kings. The local potentates of Borneo and Sumatra sought the protection of China, powerful again under the emperors of the Ming Dynasty. All over the western archipelago Chinese ambassadors intervened in the internal affairs of the Malay kingdoms. Under their protection a new Mohammedan princedom came to power, that of Malacca.

The port of Malacca was founded by a Javanese nobleman at the end of the fourteenth century. It rose rapidly to prosperity because of its excellent geographic position. Once the inhabitants had gone over to Islam they became the principal promoters of that religion in the islands. In the beginning of the fifteenth century there were already numerous Mohammedan communities in some of the ports of east Java. The princes of Ternate in the Moluccas turned Mohammedan around 1440.

At the beginning of the sixteenth century Islam predominated in most of the coastal districts of Sumatra, Java, and Borneo. The interior of the islands, however, remained pagan for another fifty years, as in Java, or perhaps for a century and more, as in Sumatra. In Java, Islam led to another shifting of the center of political and cultural life in which the districts of middle Java regained their importance with the foundation of the kingdom of Mataram.

Islam has never triumphed completely in Borneo even in recent times. The Mohammedan missionaries were merchants or, perhaps, pirates and conquerors, but never priests who fostered the ideal of bringing Truth to benighted heathens. Thus, Islam was spread over all areas usually visited by merchants and skippers. In a few instances, the pagan tribes of the interior, in fear of subjection to the Mohammedan sultans of the coastal districts resisted the Islamitic propaganda. And the people, lead by their kings and strongly influenced by Çivaitic refugees from Java, resisted fanatically all attempts of the Javanese Mohammedans to conquer the island and introduce Islam.

The introduction of Islam was closely followed by that of Christianity (Catholicism), even so closely that in some instances the Mohammedan conquerors could barely forestall the Portuguese missionaries. In the Moluccas the political feuds of the native tribes turned into religious wars between the protagonists of the two creeds.

In 1509 the first Portuguese ship anchored in the roadstead of Malacca. The crew was attacked by the Malays, and to avenge this insult a fleet under the personal command of Alfonso de Albuquerque, Viceroy of the Indies, came and conquered the city (1511). The Sultan fled and transferred his residence to Johore. The first care of Albuquerque was to send a squadron to the "Spice Islands." The Portuguese found the whole island world of the Indies divided between the rulers of the tiny islands of Ternate and Tidore. The Portuguese came in contact with the Prince of Ternate first, which incident decided the final unhappy outcome of their enterprise.

The Moluccan sultans considered the presence of the Portuguese of great advantage. International competition on the spice market made the prices rise. The Sultan of Ternate desired the economic alliance with the Portuguese, but as the protagonist of Islam in the Moluccas he fought savagely all people who sympathized with Christianity. By accepting the alliance with Ternate, the Portuguese became involved in an equivocal position that inevitably led to disaster. The Portuguese missionaries, mostly Italians by nationality, vainly demanded a change in the political system. They saw clearly that their success was wholly dependent upon the political prestige of Portugal. Their mortal enemy, Sultan Hairun of Ternate, was much too shrewd to break completely with the Portuguese governors, although he persecuted the Christians mercilessly. In despair, the governor of the Portuguese fort at Ternate ordered the Sultan to be murdered. This act decided the fate of the Portuguese. A general revolt overthrew their authority. Only Amboina was saved and it was here that all activities of Portuguese political, economic, and religious enterprises were concentrated.

In 1596 the first Dutch ship arrived at the roadstead of Bantam, in Java. One Frenchman, Jean Parmentier (in 1529), and three Englishmen, the gentlemen-pirates Drake, Cavendish, and Lancaster (in 1579, 1588, 1592), had sailed the Indonesian seas before them but their visits had been without further consequence. The route to the Indies was well known to the Dutch. Jan Huygen van Linschoten had sailed to Malacca in Portuguese ships and published in his *Itinerario* (1592) ample details of the route and the countries to which it led. Dirk Pomp of Enkhuizen had given an accurate description of Japan which he had visited twice between 1570 and 1586 on a Portuguese ship. Since 1584 the Dutch had sought the northeast passage to China. Neither fear of Portugal and Spain nor ignorance of the rich field

offered by the trade, but rather the great risks of navigation had prevented the Dutch from venturing along the spice-trade route before
1596. And the famous decree of King Philip II of Spain and Portugal
forbidding the Dutch entrance to all ports of his kingdom, was a
challenge rather than a deterrent to the opening of this trade.

The first voyage of the Dutch was highly unsuccessful because of
deficient leadership, but in the year 1598 alone, twenty-one ships
sailed for the Far East, twelve around South Africa and nine through
the Strait of Magellan. Of the first fleet, twelve returned safely; of
the second, only one, that of Oliver van Noort, the first Hollander
to circumnavigate the globe. Thus, in exploration of the route to the
Far East, the journey around South America was proven to be im-
practicable and was thereafter abandoned.

The fierce competition among the numerous small Dutch trading
companies caused prices to rise by the month. In order to find new
markets the Dutch skippers extended their trading along the entire
Asiatic coast, from Mocha in Arabia to Hirado in Japan. Achin and
Bantam, which between them controlled the pepper trade, gained an
importance and power as never before. Even the "orangkajas" (the
village chiefs) of the tiny Banda Islands in the Moluccas shared in
the general growth of power and importance.

The period of free competition among the Dutch was also one of
relatively peaceful trading. The Dutch skippers were ordered to avoid
conflicts with the Portuguese. But within ten years the prices of spices
had risen to such a high figure that the trade around the Cape seemed
doomed to fail. Only the expectation of huge profits could induce the
merchants of western Europe to risk their ships on the far voyage
half around the world.

Therefore, the Grand Pensionary Johan van Oldenbarneveldt, in
1602, organized all Dutch companies into one privileged United East
India Company to which the States-General of the Dutch Republic
granted a monopoly for all trading and shipping east of the Cape of
Good Hope and west of the Strait of Magellan. Within these boundaries, the Company received the right to act as a sovereign power
representing the States-General.

With a capital of six and a half million guilders the Dutch Company could successfully compete with its English sister company whose capital was only one-sixth of that amount. From the beginning the Company decided to wage war on the Portuguese subjects of King Philip II, the mortal enemy of the Republic, but even so trading remained the chief purpose of the enterprise. The war was considered necessary in order to guarantee freedom of trade in Asia and to eliminate Portuguese competition.

The results of the first ten years of the Company's activities were moderate. Trading posts were founded, and contracts with the princes and village communities of the Moluccas concluded. In 1605 the Portuguese were driven from their sole stronghold in the Archipelago; Amboina, and the inhabitants of that island voluntarily recognized the overlordship of the Company and of the States-General. Thus, the inhabitants of Amboina became the first Dutch subjects in the Indies. A governor-general was appointed in 1609 to coördinate the efforts of merchants and skippers and to direct the naval expeditions against the Portuguese. Yet, a definite organization of the trade was still lacking.

It must be remembered that Europe had little to offer to Asia in exchange for the spices, chinaware, silk, and other specialties of the Far East. In the first years of the trade the Dutch had exported some of their merchandise—the list of items is often amusing—but they had found no buyers except for their firearms, harnesses, and *norimbergerie* (toys and small ornaments). Consequently the Europeans had to pay for their merchandise in gold and silver which could be obtained only from America—in other words—from Spain. In order to make their India trade completely free, the Dutch had to eliminate this economic factor. The trading system devised by Governor-General Jan Pieterszoon Coen (1617–1623 and 1627–1629), not only overcame this difficulty but promised great profits besides.

The amount of merchandise traded between Europe and Asia was a mere trifle compared with that exchanged among the Asiatic countries. Coen's scheme was to found a maritime base in the Indies, midway between India and China, and to make it the headquarters of an extensive Dutch trade in Asia, the profits of which would be converted into spices, silk, chinaware, and other Asiatic specialties to be shipped to Europe. Establishment by force of a trade monopoly in the Moluccas would bring the price of spices down to the level of the Portuguese era and thus double the profits.

Batavia (from Batavi, the name of an old Germanic tribe mentioned by Tacitus as having lived in the Netherlands), on May 30, 1619, was founded as the trading center. For a century it remained a port without a hinterland, and lacked communication with the interior from which it was separated by dense jungles. Coen had planned to entrust the inter-Asiatic trade to free Dutch citizens and to found Dutch settlements in the Far East. The directors of the Company preferred to carry on the trade with their own ships and through their own trading posts. In order to execute this scheme extensive capital was needed. The normal profits were not large enough to provide for this and, at the same time, to satisfy the shareholders. Huge loans were floated among the wealthy people in Holland, and it took more than twenty-five years of financial anxieties and maneuvers before the directors could be assured of their success.

Consequently, the Company sought no political authority or territorial expansion during the seventeenth century, except in the Moluccas where its authority was based upon treaties with the princes of Ternate and Tidore. At Tidore the Spaniards, coming south from Manila, had maintained certain outposts until 1663.

By the middle of the seventeenth century the Portuguese had been driven from the Archipelago. In 1641 their chief bulwark, the city of Malacca, was conquered by the Dutch. The prosperity of the port rapidly declined, and many of the inhabitants migrated to Batavia. Only in the southeast, on Timor and on adjacent islands, a few Portuguese missionary posts remained which, after 1700, were organized under Portuguese administration. In the Moluccas the Company maintained a rigid system of monopoly, and enforced severe restrictions on the cultivation of clove and nutmeg.

The inter-Asiatic commerce continued to flourish until the end of the seventeenth century. Then it began to decline because of the diminishing exports from Persia, the impoverishment of the Moluccas and other areas in the eastern part of the Archipelago, and because of the severe restrictions on the Japanese trade by order of the Japanese Government.

In the second half of the seventeenth century the Company became more and more involved in the political affairs of Indonesia. Competition in the Moluccas led to a war with Macassar, the principal naval power in the eastern section of the Indies. In 1667 Macassar became a vassal state of Batavia. In 1684 the sultanate of Bantam shared the same fate, and after that the port of Bantam rapidly lost its significance. The third naval power in the Archipelago, Achin, was weakened by the defection of its subjects on Sumatra's west coast. By the Treaty of Painan (1663), Achin accepted the protection of the Dutch Company. In the same period the Dutch gained control over the tin deposits of Kedah (Malay Peninsula) and Bangka. Finally, the Javanese empire of Mataram was broken up. The sultans of the seventeenth century had tried to break the power of the district rulers, their vassals, and had fairly well succeeded in this attempt but the universal hatred caused by their harsh rule led to a revolt in which the warlike Madurese saw an opportunity to win a foothold on the eastern shores of Java proper. Expelled from his capital, Sultan Amangku Rat III implored the help of the United East India Company. He was restored to his throne, but the independence of Mataram virtually had come to an end. The Company acquired the Preanger districts in west Java (1679–1705). The remaining part of Mataram was constantly upset by wars of succession until, in 1755, the empire was split into two parts, the sultanate of Djogjakarta and the empire of Surakarta.

The Company was now a territorial power, but at a loss as to what to do with the acquired territory. The burden of military enterprises became increasingly heavier, and the returns of the inter-Asiatic trade lessened. All these difficulties disappeared when the Company turned to agriculture as its principal source of income.

Around 1700 some high officials of the Company were experimenting with coffee culture on their private estates outside Batavia.

The first results were disappointing, and the attempt would perhaps have been abandoned had it not been for the encouragement of Nicolaas Witsen, Burgomaster of Amsterdam, one of the directors of the Company. Witsen, a man deeply interested in science and geography and the author of a most important book on northern Asia, encouraged the Batavian Dutch to continue with their experiments. In 1711 the first one hundred pounds of Java coffee were delivered into the storehouses of the Company by Arya Wiratana, native ruler of Tjandjur, south of Batavia. Twelve years later the output amounted to six thousand tons.

Within a few years coffee became one of the chief export crops of the Indies. The Dutch never undertook the culture themselves, but left it to the native district rulers who delivered the coffee at a fixed and very low price to Batavia. Before 1711 the directors of the Company had considered the territory acquired in the Javanese wars as useless, but with the introduction of coffee culture that territory suddenly gained great value. Coffee remained the principal export crop of the Indies in the eighteenth century, but sugar and indigo were also important. Attempts to introduce tea and cocoa plants into Java were unsuccessful at that time.

Because of this change of trade of the United East India Company, in which agricultural enterprise now gained precedence over purely commercial activities, the years shortly after 1700 are of the greatest historic importance for the Indies. Until 1700 the presence of Europeans in Indonesia had scarcely affected native life and economy, except in the Moluccas. In Sumatra and Borneo only a few sultanates had been forced to become vassal states of the Company, but neither the Company's monopoly of trade, nor the presence of a few dozen Europeans in scattered outposts in the principal towns had any marked influence on the development of Indonesian society. In Borneo strong foreign influence actually was exerted, but it was the result of Chinese and Arabian, not of European penetration. The most remarkable feature of this penetration was the founding of the Chinese settlements near Sambas (northwestern Borneo).

Gold mines had been discovered in the sultanate of Sambas around

1750. The sultans called in Chinese coolies who, within a few years, had become so numerous that they freed themselves from the authority of the sultan and formed small workers' republics. This is the only example of a permanent Chinese settlement in the Netherlands Indies which consisted of an industrial and, after the mines had been exhausted, agricultural character.

In the same decade Arabian traders settled along Borneo's southern and western coasts, and one of them succeeded in founding the sultanate of Pontianak that ultimately became the most important native kingdom of west Borneo (1772).

The acquisition of extensive areas in the interior of Java brought· a new problem of administration. It was decided that Batavia, founded as a Dutch city, was to be ruled according to Dutch law, but that all other territories should be ruled according to the customary laws of the inhabitants. The subjects of the Company were divided into three groups: officials and employees; free citizens, originally Dutch and Portuguese, who in a few generations were completely assimilated by the surrounding native population; and Asiatics. Racial discrimination between Europeans and Asiatics was unknown. Among the Asiatics the Chinese held a special position because they were ruled by their own "captains" according to their own customs.

The Company's officials wrongly believed that the Javanese, being Mohammedans, followed the pure Mohammedan law. Not until the close of the nineteenth century was the importance of the "adat," the customary law of the Indonesians, fully understood. The first person to do serious research work in this matter was Johan Fr. Gobius, resident of Tjeribon from 1714 to 1717, who, in his description of customary law of Tjeribon, clearly distinguished between the religious or Mohammedan law and the Indonesian customary law. Notwithstanding these difficulties, a serious effort was made to follow the general rule that every national group in the Indies should be ruled according to its own national customs.

It was of the greatest importance that the Company decided to carry on the production of coffee through the intermediacy of the Javanese "Regents" (district-rulers). Under this system the native rights to the land were fully preserved. Except in the immediate neighborhood of Batavia, Europeans could not acquire landed property.

The fourth Anglo-Dutch war (1780–1784) caused a crisis in the affairs of the United East India Company. The products of Java could not be shipped to Europe, and, in consequence of the financial policy of the directors, the Company in Europe could not meet its obligations. Bankruptcy seemed imminent. A committee was appointed to prepare a reorganization of the affairs of the Company, but the head of the committee, S. C. Nederburgh, immediately identified his own interests with those of the ruling clique in Batavia. The financial situation of the Company promised to be far from hopeless if only a reorganization could be carried through, but the armies of the French Revolution brought the independence of the Dutch Republic to an end. The existing aristocratic government was replaced by a democratic one, composed of men who were wholly under French influence. Prince William V of Orange fled to England. Here, in the capacity of Director-General of the East and West India companies he requested all governors in the colonies to put their territories under the protection of the British navy.

Most colonies, however, followed the orders from the legal government in The Hague. Then the question arose as to whether the principles of equality and freedom, proclaimed in Holland, should also be applied to the colonies. The new democratic government decided that this could not be done, except in the economic field. On December 31, 1799, the Dutch East India Company ceased to exist and its possessions and debts (more than 120,000,000 guilders) were taken over by the Government.

The system of government of the revolutionary period, as formulated in the Constitutional Act of 1807, differed little from that of the Company. The only important difference was in the principle which proclaimed that the Government should rule the Indies in order to establish the greatest possible welfare in that area. Ultimately this plan also aimed at procuring the greatest possible financial advantages for the mother country.

In the meantime, the British had occupied all Dutch colonies except Java. They did not care to undertake a costly expedition for the conquest of that island, so long as its administration remained in the hands of people more friendly to the British Government than to the government in Holland. This attitude of the British changed when King Louis Bonaparte of Holland sent Herman Willem Daendels to the Netherlands Indies not only to reorganize the administration but also the system of defense.

Daendels governed Java for three years (1808–1811). In this short period he created a new army and built the first highway connecting Batavia and Surabaya. He reformed the administration, and, though he extended compulsory labor, he made it more bearable by abolishing numerous abuses. At the same time, however, he began to sell extensive tracts of "government-owned" land, which led to the building up of large estates on which the Javanese lived practically in bondage. The free play of economic forces proclaimed by the idealists of the revolution, turned wholly to the advantage of the economically stronger individuals. Natives who offered their labor on the estates automatically were reduced to the status of "peons."

In 1810, when the Kingdom of the Netherlands became a province of the French Empire, the French flag was also hoisted in Batavia. This caused the immediate intervention of the British forces. A strong expedition landed near Batavia, defeated the Dutch-Indian troops under Governor-General Janssens and occupied the whole island. Thomas Stamford Raffles, formerly agent of the English East India Company in Penang (Malay Peninsula) was appointed Lieutenant-Governor of "Java and dependencies" (Palembang and southern Sumatra, Bandjermasin, Macassar, and Timor). The Moluccas were formed into a separate administrative unit.

Raffles is one of the most remarkable figures in the history of Europeans in the East Indies. A man of outstanding intelligence and great skill as a writer and a student of Indonesian affairs he, nevertheless, suffered during his whole life from a feeling of inferiority not only because of his humble lineage, but also because of the hard years of his youth. This emotion induced in him a burning desire to accomplish something of importance in history. In his methods to combine imperialistic aims with humanitarian slogans, he was the predecessor of men like Cecil Rhodes. But whatever may have been the underlying causes of his restless activities in the Indonesian Archipelago, the fact remains that he made a thorough study of Indonesian affairs and that he was the first European to publish a full, and still remarkable history of the inhabitants of Java. It was also Lieutenant-Governor Raffles who inaugurated the administrative reforms which, many years later, were to be effective in the abolition of the ill-reputed Culture System.

The principal reform introduced by Raffles was that of the tax system. He instituted the landrent, a tax copied from the administration of Bengal. Raffles declared that, theoretically, the whole soil of Java was the property of the Government and that, consequently, the farmers had to pay rent. As rent he asked a certain percentage of the crop, or its equivalent in money. The idea was to liberate the Javanese peasant from the forced labor on export cultures formerly demanded by the Company through the intermediacy of the Regents. Raffles' system has been maintained, but it did not work well until a complete survey of all lands had been made. This took nearly seventy years! Thus, Raffles could not carry through his own reforms, but had to maintain the compulsory cultivation of coffee. He regained part of the "government lands" sold by Daendels but, on the contrary, did not hesitate to dispose of some of the best coffee-producing districts when he saw that his term of office was expiring and that the British Government was not at all interesed in maintaining its authority over Java, once continental Netherlands had been liberated from French oppression.

In 1813, after the Battle of Leipzig, the Dutch rose against French rule. In 1815 Prince William VI of Orange took the title of King William I of the Netherlands. The British Government showed great interest in the strengthening of the new kingdom and decided to return to it part of the former Dutch colonies. Among these colonies were all former Dutch possessions in the Indonesian Archipelago. In 1816 the Dutch flag once more was hoisted in Batavia.

The Royal Commissaries who took over the administration from

Raffles' successor, John Fendall, were determined to follow an outspoken liberal policy. For the first time in history it was decided that the Indies should be governed for the welfare of the Indies only. But this was a short-lived plan. Under Governor-General G. A. van der Capellen (1819–1824), matters came to a crisis. The income of the Batavian administration was absolutely insufficient to meet the expenses. By hindering the formation of large privately owned estates and by putting an end to the exploitation of the simple Javanese peasants in the "principalities" (Surakarta and Djogjakarta), Van der Capellen made himself hated by Dutch and Indonesian landowners alike. Johannes van den Bosch was appointed Governor-General to reorganize the administration (1830–1834, when he became Minister of Colonies).

Van den Bosch believed in social progress through organization of labor and production. The idle and ignorant should be induced to work, if necessary compelled to work, and once they saw the beneficial results, they would continue of their own free will. The theory was beautiful, but the practice less so. Moreover, there was really no reason to catalog the hard-working, though simple-minded, peasants of Java in that class of people for which the scheme was evolved in Europe.

Through the intermediacy of their native chiefs—the Regents—the Javanese were put to work at the production of export crops, principally coffee and sugar. The results were amazing; for not only did the treasury of the Indies show a large surplus for the first time since the middle of the eighteenth century but there was also a decrease in wastelands. The latter were rapidly brought into cultivation by the fast-increasing population. Encouraged by this success, the Government began to experiment with new crops (tea, cocoa, and cinchona bark among others). Most of these crops did not succeed under the prevailing system, but were destined to become of great importance in the following "liberal" era of Indonesian history.

The Van den Bosch system is generally known as the Culture System (a somewhat awkward translation of the Dutch term *"cultuurstelsel"*). In spite of certain advantages which the system undoubtedly had for both Europeans and Indonesians, it has gained an evil reputation in Dutch colonial history. After a short while, the sole idea of government officials and Javanese Regents was to increase production at all costs. Rice culture suffered under the excessive demands made upon the people for the production of export crops. There was much misery among the workers on the sugar plantations the management of which was usually entrusted to foreigners, Chinese and European. The Netherlands Government, burdened by the financial demands of the war with Belgium (1830–1839), asked no questions so long as the remittances from Batavia increased. Some friends of the people of Java, among whom Wolter Robert, Baron van den Hoëvell was foremost, as early as 1849 vigorously protested against the Culture System, but their protests met with little response among the Dutch people. Eleven years later public opinion was to be aroused by the fierce accusations of Eduard Douwes Dekker who, under the pseudonym of "Multatuli," wrote *Max Havelaar*.

Multatuli's book may have been important in changing public opinion, but it was only one of the many factors that caused the final change in the policy of the Government toward the Culture System. The Liberal party had gained control in the Netherlands, after the revision of the Constitution in 1848, and though many Liberals disliked the idea of giving up the additional income which the State of the Netherlands obtained from the Indies through the Culture System, the majority readily conceded that the system of government exploitation and monopoly, as practiced in the colonies, was not in agreement with the principles of the Liberal party.

Between 1866 and 1870 the course of colonial policy was radically changed. All monopolies came to an end. The Indies were thrown open to private enterprise. The Moluccas, finally liberated from an intolerable burden, regained their former prosperity until, a short time later, the competition of the African colonies dealt a decisive blow to their spice culture. The growing fear that foreign powers might attempt to penetrate into the areas which the Dutch claimed to be under their overlordship, induced the Indies Government to undertake the effective occupation of the Outer Territories. The costly conquest of Achin, achieved by the close of the nineteenth century, completed this development.

The rapid progress of political thinking in the Netherlands finally reversed public opinion on the relations between the mother country and the colonies. After 1900 it was generally understood that the Netherlands could no longer remain content with restoring and increasing the material prosperity of the Indies primarily for the purpose of making them more profitable for the home country. That the Netherlands had "a moral duty to fulfill toward the Indonesian people" was a principle openly proclaimed by the Netherlands Government in 1901. This proclamation inaugurated the period of the so-called "ethical policy." To take care of the people of the Indies and to foster their interests became the principal purpose of colonial administration, but it included, of course, a tendency toward excessive paternalism. That everything ought to be done *for* the Indonesians was common opinion, but that many things ought to be done *by* the Indonesians themselves, was not so readily accepted. However, this idea also gained ground and, consequently, in 1916 the "People's Council" was instituted as a representative body that would advise the Governor-General on matters of legislation.

In the first years of its existence the People's Council was still composed of a majority of Europeans and a minority of Indonesians and "Foreign Asiatics" (Chinese and Arabians). The decisive turn of the development took place in 1922 and 1925 when, with the revision of the Constitution of the Netherlands and the introduction of a new Indonesian Constitution, the period of self-government definitely had been started on its course.

With the revision of the Constitution of the Netherlands the terms "possessions" and "colonies" were abolished and the territory of the Kingdom of the Netherlands was now described as extending over "the Netherlands, the Netherlands Indies, Surinam and Curaçao" thus enumerating its four separate administrative units as four equal parts. The Indonesian Constitution of 1925 transferred the discussion of the annual budget from the Netherlands States-General to the People's Council and made this assembly a colegislative body.

It also introduced local self-government for the provinces of Java where provincial and regency councils were instituted, whose members were elected by the people. Self-government outside Java itself, was also projected at this period.

At the same time, Indonesian nationalism, originating in the last years of the First World War, turned to more constructive ideals. The history of Indonesian nationalism is one of ever-shifting, grouping and regrouping parties under a few leaders. It started as an Islamic mass movement, the organization of the "Sarekat Islam" but later fell rapidly under the influence of Western revolutionary tendencies, especially those directed from Moscow. The Indonesian people understood little of the dialectics of Marxism and Leninism. A part of the people followed the revolutionary leaders because they promised the return of the "good old times of prosperity and happiness" of the empire of Majapahit. Others followed because they considered the newly founded trade unions for Indonesians a strong weapon in the struggle for better conditions of living, and others again out of resentment against European superiority. All these factors together caused considerable unrest in west Java and west Sumatra in 1926 and 1927 which, however, was finally quieted.

This gave more moderate leaders the opportunity to come to the front. Dr. Sutomo, the founder of the "Indonesian study clubs" and Suwardi Suryaningrat (Dewantoro), the founder of the "Taman Siswa" schools, took the leadership of Javanese nationalism which, because of the predominance of the people of Java, means that of Indonesian nationalism.

In the period between 1922 and 1932 the revolutionary Nationalists had taken up Gandhi's method of noncoöperation, which, however, was only applied in regard to participation in representative bodies. It never took the form of refusing to serve the Government in office or to work for the Government. The revolutionary parties did not accept Gandhi's theory of nonviolence either. Although insular congresses were held by the Nationalists and an "interinsular congress" was planned to give leadership to a movement similar to the Indian Congress party, nearly all of the tactics and even the slogans of the early Nationalist movement in the East Indies were taken from the Western world which may have been one of the reasons why revolutionary nationalism after a single decade proved to be a failure.

The Nationalists of the second period, lead by Sutomo and Dewantoro, forsook revolutionary ideals and proclaimed as their sole aim harmonious development and coöperation between the different population groups of the Indies. By performing excellent and constructive work—the organizing of coöperative societies and trade unions, for instance—the Nationalists laid the foundations for a more durable national revival of the Indies. This turn in Nationalist politics made possible the uniting of all sections of the Indonesian people in joint defense against Japanese aggression.

MEETING OF THE REGENTS, NETHERLANDS INDIES

GOVERNOR-GENERAL VAN STARKENBORGH STACHOUWER PRESIDING

CHAPTER XXI

The Dutch in the Far East

BY AMRY J. VANDENBOSCH

THREE CENTURIES OR MORE AGO, the small band of fearless, seafaring people who inhabited the half-submerged deltas of the Rhine, Meuse, and Scheldt rivers, won a vast colonial empire. This was accomplished at the same time that the Dutch themselves were struggling for independence against the mightiest empire of that day. They were late in arriving in the Far East; the Portuguese and the Spanish had preceded them and had already obtained strategic footholds. But, within a few decades, the Dutch had carved out an enormous area of domination.

The Dutch had enjoyed a rich trade in spices and in other Asiatic commodities between the ports of Spain and Portugal and those of western and northern Europe. Philip II, however, stopped this commerce by closing the harbors of the Iberian Peninsula to the Dutch rebels. But the Dutch were not to be so easily thrust out of the profitable business of distributing the products of the Indies. They decided to send ships to the Indies and to engage in the trade direct, thus obtaining even greater profits. From 1595 to 1602 no less than sixty ships, in fourteen different expeditions, fitted out by as many different companies, set sail for the East Indies. The intense competition between the Dutch traders quickly forced prices up in the Far East and drove them down in the home markets. In order to prevent this destructive competition and to secure protection for this trade in distant waters, the States-General, in 1602, incorporated the East Indian traders into the United East India Company and conferred upon the Company divers rights of monopoly and sovereignty. To the exclusion of all other Netherlanders, the Company was given a monopoly of shipping and trade in the area east of the Cape of Good Hope and west of the Strait of Magellan, and also given the power to perform, in the name of the States-General, such acts of sovereignty as the making of alliances and contracts with princes and potentates of the Far East. The Republic retained only a right of control.

It was the United East India Company, with sovereign powers, which secured for the Netherlands its empire in the Far East. In 1605 the Dutch drove the Portuguese from Amboina and from the "Spice Islands," and in 1619 established themselves at Batavia. After their conquest of a British garrison at Amboina in 1623, the English abandoned trade in Japan, Siam, and in the East Indies. When the Dutch captured Malacca from the Portuguese in 1641, they were left alone in the East Indies until the Napoleonic Wars. The Dutch also set up factories or trading posts in Bengal and in Persia. In the period from 1638 to 1658 Ceylon was brought under their control. In 1624 they took possession of Formosa, but were able to retain control of that strategic island for less than forty years. In 1662 they were driven out by the native rebel Koxinga. In 1652 the United East India Company established a victualing station at Cape Town for ships en route to and from the East Indies. The original colony was not large; accessions from the outside were few and ceased altogether in 1707. Almost all of the present-day 1,200,000 Afrikanders, whose Dutch culture has been modified by isolation in a vastly different environment, are the descendants of the approximately 2,500 Europeans who were planted in the colony at Cape Town three centuries ago.

Early Dutch relations with Japan form one of the most interesting chapters in the history of international relations. The Portuguese and the Spanish had already been in Japan for many decades when the Dutch, in 1609, established a trading post at Hirado. The British, who had in 1613 likewise established a factory at Hirado, voluntarily abandoned it a decade later. In 1624, all Spaniards were driven from Japan, and in 1638 the Portuguese traders suffered the same fate. In 1636 the Japanese were forbidden to go abroad with the result that, from 1638 to the opening of Japan by Commodore Perry in 1854, the only intercourse which Japan had with the outside world was through Chinese traders and the Dutch factory on the small island of Deshima, in the harbor of Nagasaki, to which island the factory had been moved in 1641. Except for this small aperture, Japan was hermetically sealed. Yet, through it the Japanese learned much of what was taking place in the outside world. Through it filtered scientific knowledge from the Western world. Many Dutch scientific books were printed and freely circulated in Japan from 1775 on.

A decade before Commodore Perry arrived at the doors of Japan, King William II of the Netherlands wrote to the Japanese Emperor a highly significant letter, warning him that the policy of seclusion could not be maintained much longer and advising him to adopt a policy of friendly, commercial relations as the only method of preventing conflicts with strong Western Powers. It was to the Netherlands Government that the United States Government turned, in preparing for Commodore Perry's mission, to request the good offices of the former in promoting its "amicable visit to the Japanese Islands." During the first few years after the establishment of diplomatic relations between Japan and the Western Powers, Dutch was the common medium of communication. Through the work of the Dutch-born and Dutch-trained missionary Guido Verbeck, Dutch cultural influences operated at a very formative period in the life of modern Japan. Verbeck, sent out by the (Dutch) Reformed Church of America, arrived in Japan a few years after its opening and became the intimate adviser of several of the younger leaders of the Meiji Restoration in 1868. From 1868 to 1878, a crucial decade in the development of Japan, Verbeck was in the employ of the Japanese Government. His influence, especially in the field of educational policy, was considerable.

With the opening of Japan in the middle of the last century, the special position of the Dutch in that country was lost. Even before this loss the Dutch empire in Asia had suffered some diminution. Successively the Dutch lost their small holdings in India. By the Treaty of Paris of 1784, which marked the end of the Fourth Anglo-Dutch War, the Netherlands ceded Negapatam to England. As the result of the Napoleonic Wars, Ceylon and Malabar were lost. In the

Treaty of London of 1824, between the Netherlands and Great Britain, the Dutch relinquished Malacca and their remaining posts in India and surrendered their claim to Singapore in exchange for Bencoolen on Sumatra and for British claims to the island of Billiton. In the settlement after the Napoleonic Wars the Dutch also lost the Cape of Good Hope, the important half-way station to their possessions in the Far East.

It was not the original purpose of the United East India Company to set up a territorial dominion. Its primary objectives were commercial; but the Company was steadily compelled to shift from a commercial to a territorial basis, because it could not successfully trade unless it also governed. The continual warfare among the native peoples and the devious ways of the native rulers forced the Company into greater diplomatic, military, and political penetration. Nevertheless, until 1750, the government of the Company at Batavia stood at the head not of a territory, but of a series of scattered establishments stretching from Japan through the Malay Archipelago and India proper to Cape Town. After 1750 the replacement of the mercantile system by a territorial system proceeded much more rapidly, but the administrative penetration of the entire area which it had staked out for control was never completed by the Company. Indeed, it was not until a century after the Company had ceased to exist that an energetic campaign for the administrative penetration of the last remaining unoccupied parts of the Indies was undertaken.

When the shift to direct governmental control was made, the old Dutch Republic of the United Provinces gave way to the Batavian Republic (1795–1806). Although at the time the Dutch were strongly under the influence of French revolutionary ideas, no sharp break in colonial policy took place. Daendels, Dutch revolutionary patriot and later a general under Napoleon, did institute a number of reforms while he was Governor-General (1808–1811). He removed certain evils and abuses from the system of agriculture and from the delivery of products, and did much to transform the loose, commercial organization into a centralized state administrative system. But the fundamental spirit of the administration had changed little.

After the occupation of the Dutch possessions in the Far East by the British in 1811, "Java and its dependencies" were placed under Lieutenant-Governor Raffles, a subordinate of Lord Minto, then Governor-General of India. Raffles instituted a number of reforms and by reason of his work in the Indies acquired a reputation as one of the greatest of British colonial administrators.

At the end of the Napoleonic Wars, Great Britain restored all of the Dutch colonies in the Far East, except Ceylon which had already been ceded to England by the Treaty of Amiens in 1802. The return by Great Britain of nearly all of the vast Dutch colonial empire in the Far East was prompted, in part, by a desire for a strong Netherlands, enlarged by union with Belgium, to serve as a buffer state against France. On the contrary, the cession of strategic bases to Great Britain formally marked the end of Dutch sea power in the Far East. Henceforth, the Dutch were largely dependent upon the British for the protection of their Asiatic empire.

In the decade immediately following the restoration, plans for opening the East Indies to private initiative and capital were seriously considered by King William I, whose control over colonial policy was practically unrestricted. Mounting deficits in the budget of the East Indies and the influence of his trusted adviser, Van den Bosch, caused the King to return to old practices. The plan proposed by Van den Bosch, and adopted by the King, is known as the Culture System. Under it the inhabitants, instead of paying to the Government a certain proportion of their crops, put at the disposal of the Government a certain proportion of their land and labor-time and, under the direction of the Government, cultivated crops for export. From a fiscal point of view the plan worked very well; for nearly half a century a stream of money flowed into the treasury of the Netherlands. But the system was not one calculated to improve the welfare of the natives, and by keeping out private enterprise the development of the country was retarded.

Beginning with the constitutional revision in the Netherlands, there slowly but steadily developed a more liberal attitude towards colonial policy. A number of liberal principles were written into the

East Indian Government Act of 1854, but a more liberal policy was not immediately put into practice. Impetus to the new movement was given by the publication, in 1868, of the novel entitled *Max Havelaar,* written by a former Indies official, Eduard Douwes Dekker, under the pseudonym of Multatuli. With the passage of the Agrarian Law in 1870, the fight against the Culture System was won. The movement for reform was aided by the rise of the middle class to political power. The middle classes reasoned that the replacement of the system of state exploitation by free private enterprise would result in a more rapid development of the Indies and, likewise, in a greater flow of profit to the Netherlands, although not directly to the Netherlands Government. The East Indies was progressively opened to private exploitation, with the Government increasingly acting as protector of the natives.

The advent to power in 1901 of the Kuyper Ministry, representing a coalition of Christian parties, marked another shift in spirit in colonial policy. In the *Speech from the Throne,* in 1901, there appeared the following significant passage: "As a Christian power, the Netherlands is obligated in the East Indian Archipelago to imbue the whole conduct of the Government with the consciousness that the Netherlands has a moral duty to fulfill with respect to the people of these regions. In connection with this, the diminished welfare of the population of Java merits special attention." This primary emphasis on the welfare of the population of the Indies received the term "ethical policy." In 1905, a forty million guilder advance from the Netherlands treasury was cancelled under the provision that a similar amount was to be spent by the East Indies Government during the course of the next fifteen years for the improvement of economic conditions in Java and Madura.

Until the opening of the People's Council in 1918, the East Indies Government was a highly centralized and bureaucratic organization. The first step in the direction of decentralization was made in 1903, when a number of district and municipal councils were created. A central representative body was established by the Act of 1916 and inaugurated on May 18, 1918, with the name of "People's Council"

("*Volksraad*"). In the beginning, the Council had merely advisory powers and only one-half of its members were elected. In 1927 it was given colegislative power with the Governor-General, and in 1931 the proportion of Indonesian members was increased. The membership of sixty was distributed among the racial groups as follows: Indonesians, thirty; Netherlanders, twenty-five; and Chinese and Arabs, five. Of the total membership, thirty-eight were elected by indirect vote and the remainder were appointed by the Governor-General. In the two decades of its existence, the People's Council became a firmly established institution in the life of the community and developed into a very influential body.

Beginning in 1925, the work of decentralization and democratization of the governmental system was vigorously pushed; Java and Madura, although not large in area, were regarded as having much too great a population to permit the formation of a single intermediate political unit. Java and Madura were divided into three provinces, each with a population of about 14,000,000. At the head of each province was placed a governor who, in the administration of national functions, was responsible to the Governor-General and, for the administration of provincial affairs, was responsible to the Provincial Council. The governor was assisted in the administration of provincial functions by a committee chosen by and responsible to the Provincial Council. That ancient institution, the Javanese autonomous regency, was democratized by the creation of regency councils. Likewise, the urban municipalities were democratized, patterned on Western lines.

After the work of decentralizing and democratizing the governmental structure on Java had been completed, the task of reorganizing the government of the remainder of the Indies was undertaken. All the territory outside Java and Madura was divided into three "governments," as the intermediate units in the outer territories are called, namely, Sumatra, Borneo, and the Great East. The latter included the entire area east of Borneo and Java. These new governments began to function on July 1, 1938. It was planned to add representative bodies to these governments, thus transforming them into provinces as soon as possible. In the meantime, regional councils for areas inhabited by homogeneous ethnic groups would be created. One such body, the Minangkabau Council on Sumatra, by several years of successful operation, had already demonstrated the practicability of the regional council. Then, all these fruitful developments were cut short by the Japanese invasion.

When beginning the active preparation of the Indonesians for full participation in government the Dutch were rather slow, but in the brief span of years between the creation of the People's Council and the Japanese invasion very great progress had been made. The Indies Government had acquired a large measure of autonomy, representative councils at all levels had been created, all with considerable legislative power, and Indonesians were increasingly associated with the Dutch in the administration of this large and economically important country in tropical Asia. Indonesians have held the highest positions in the Indies Government, with the exception of that of governorgeneral. At the time of the invasion, an Indonesian was burgomaster of Bandung, one of the largest cities of Java, the Department of Education had an Indonesian at its head, and two of the five members of the Council of the Indies were Indonesians. After the invasion of the Indies, an Indonesian was made a member of the Ministry of the Dutch Government in London. In the last two decades Indonesians have served as members of Netherlands delegations to the meetings of the League of Nations Assembly and the International Labor conferences. Likewise, Indonesians have represented the Netherlands on important international committees and commissions.

The economic development of the East Indies by the Dutch has evoked admiration from all peoples. Their success was primarily because of their application of scientific methods to the problems of agricultural production. Private enterprise and the Government had joined in the generous support of laboratories and experimental farms for the scientific study of tropical agriculture. Several of the chief products of Indies export, like cinchona and rubber, were not indigenous plants, but were taken to the Indies and there developed to a high state of yield and quality. After a professional tour of the countries of Southeast Asia, Mr. Rafael R. Alunan, Secretary of Agriculture of the Philippines declared, "In Java are found the best-equipped experiment stations of the Orient." He attributed the rapid and spectacular rise of Indies agricultural development to: (1) the liberal policy of the Government in extending help to the industries; (2) complete reliance on the results of scientific methods of production; and (3) the high plane of efficiency of the scientific institutes and experiment stations made possible by the generous support of the Government and private enterprise.

In the years immediately preceding the invasion, the world became very conscious of the Netherlands Indies as a producer of important raw materials, some of which were of strategic significance for rearmament programs. The share by the Netherlands Indies in the world export of a number of commodities was as follows: cinchona, 91 per cent; pepper, 86 per cent; kapok, 72 per cent; rubber, 37 per cent; agave, 33 per cent; coconut products, 19 per cent; tin, 17 per cent; oilpalm products, 27 per cent; tea, 24 per cent; sugar, 11 per cent; coffee, 4 per cent; and petroleum, 3 per cent. The production of bauxite was not begun until 1935, but in 1940 the Indies was supplying 5 per cent of the world's output of this highly strategic mineral. It should also be noted that although the Indies' share of the world's production of oil was not large, there was, in reality, little oil produced in the Far East and, hence, the oil resources of the Indies were of great military importance. The value of the exports from the Indies in 1940 was 931,000,000 guilders, or $493,000,000 in United States money. In 1928, before the World Depression had sent the price of raw materials down so drastically, the value of the Indies' exports was over 1,500,000,000 guilders.

Because of its liberal commercial policy in the Indies, the Netherlands did not enjoy a very large percentage of the foreign trade of its dependency. In 1938, 22 per cent of the Indies' imports came from the Netherlands and about 20 per cent of the Indies' exports went to the Netherlands. In 1933, at the height of Japanese competition, the figures were only 12 and 18 respectively. In the year immediately preceding the war, trade with the United States had increased remarkably. In 1940 the United States took over one-third of the exports of the Indies and tied first with Japan as a source of imports for the Indies; each of these countries supplied more than 23 per cent of the total imports in terms of value.

A large percentage of the huge exports came from Western enterprises. In 1939, over 40 per cent of the total value of exports came from Western agriculture and about 25 per cent from native agriculture. About 30 per cent of the value of exports in the year came from the mining industry, which was operated either by the Government, by mixed corporations in which the Government owned the controlling interest, or by Western corporations. Foreign investments in the Indies totaled between $2,500,000,000 and $3,000,000,000. Of this capital, about three-fourths was Dutch.

For a century after the Napoleonic Wars the Dutch were permitted to develop their vast empire in the East, relatively free from international tension. At the time of the opening of the Suez Canal the Dutch gave evidence of some nervousness. Large parts of the Indies had not yet been brought under effective military and administrative control and, with the new burst of imperialistic activity throughout the world, the Dutch had become apprehensive. For a brief moment they feared foreign intervention in their relations with the Achinese, a fanatic Moslem people in northern Sumatra, at the entrance to the strategic Malacca Straits. Alarmed, they plunged into the costly Achinese War, which engaged much of the energy and resources of the East Indies Government for decades, but which did finally end in an effective occupation of the entire territory. The Achinese War, however, retarded the social and economic development of the Indies, because it swallowed enormous government revenues which otherwise would have been used for education, social services, and developmental projects.

Had China been a united, strong, and aggressive state the million Chinese in the Indies might have caused the Dutch some uneasiness. Except for minor friction between Indonesians and Chinese, some difficulty about getting the Chinese Government and its consular officials to recognize Indies-born Chinese as Netherlands nationals, the numerous Chinese in the Indies gave little trouble; rather, they contributed greatly to the spectacular development of the country.

Dutch fears of Japanese intentions began during the First World War. There were indications that the Japanese were beginning to direct their thoughts southward. Articles began to appear in the Japanese press broadly hinting at the desirability of expansion in the Indies Archipelago, and the imperialistic policy Japan displayed toward China was not reassuring. The acquisition by Japan of the former German colonies in the southwest Pacific, as mandates of the League of Nations, caused further misgivings. The intense international rivalry for oil resources after the First World War and the fact that oil reserves in eastern Asia were meager, as well as the general tension prevailing in the Pacific, accentuated that fear. Dutch anxiety was momentarily allayed in 1922 by the Washington Conference, from which came a declaration by the British, French, Japanese, and American governments that each was firmly resolved to respect the rights of the Netherlands in relation to insular possessions in the region of the Pacific Ocean. Fears arose again, however, at the Japanese commercial invasion of the Indies markets during the World Depression. During those years Japan supplied one-third of the imports of the Indies, but refused to increase materially its meager purchases of Indies exports. This intense rivalry extended also to the shipping business. The Dutch feared that the commercial invasion would be followed by political penetration.

Indeed, the political drive was not long in coming. The Japanese Government requested a commercial conference, which was granted by the Netherlands Government and was held at Batavia in 1934. The Japanese delegation used the conference for political purposes. In his opening speech, the chief of the Japanese delegation stated that the negotiations should be conducted primarily in the interest of the native population. Referring to the vast economic opportunities of the Indies, he hinted at joint Dutch-Japanese exploitation. In every way possible the Japanese ingratiated themselves with the Indonesian population. After six months of fruitless negotiations, the conference adjourned. A Japanese-Dutch shipping conference at Kobe in the following year was likewise abortive. However, during the next few years several issues between the two countries, notably the shipping controversy, were settled by piecemeal negotiations.

In the meanwhile, designs of Japanese aggression in the South Seas were assuming definite form. Articles in the press, speeches and inter-pellations in Parliament, naval and military activities all pointed to the same goal, accompanied, however, by simultaneous official and unofficial goodwill missions to the countries of this area. Then, in May, 1940, came the German invasion of Holland. The Japanese Government immediately began a diplomatic offensive culminating in another commercial conference at Batavia. The conference began in September, 1940, and dragged on until June of the following year; it was abruptly ended by Governor-General Tjarda van Starkenborgh Stachouwer with his polite but firm rejections of the sweeping eco-nomic and political demands of the Japanese delegation which would have made the Indies virtually a dependency of Japan. Six months later came the attack upon Pearl Harbor.

Although the Dutch and the Indonesians, two years before, fever-ishly, if belatedly, had begun to prepare for the expected attack, they had been hampered chiefly by an inability to procure armaments which had to come from abroad. Large and long-outstanding orders were never delivered. The Dutch and Indonesians fought valiantly, but to no avail. Practically all of the Netherlands officials in the In-dies, including the Governor-General, remained at their posts; they now share the fate of the people with whom the Dutch have been associated for over three centuries. In the United States, in Australia, in England, in Surinam, and in Curaçao, Netherlanders and Indone-sians are gathering from all over the world and laboring without pause to prepare the blow which will give deliverance from the enemy on the European continent and in the Pacific.

Before the German invasion of Holland the Indies had become a vital center of Dutch culture. Many Netherlanders had migrated to the Indies to make it their permanent home, to acquire a new father-land. With the invasion of Holland the cultural, political, and eco-nomic autonomy of the Indies ripened with amazing rapidity. The

Indies had become ready for a new status in the Netherlands Empire. This fact has been acknowledged in repeated declarations by the Prime Minister, the Minister of Colonies, and by the Minister of Foreign Affairs, but most notably by courageous Queen Wilhelmina, leader of her people in war as in peace. In a radio address to the Empire on December 6, 1942, she declared that it was her intention after the liberation "to create the occasion for a joint consultation about the structure of the Kingdom and its parts, in order to adopt it to the changed circumstances. . . . I visualize, without anticipating the recommendations of the future conference, that they will be directed towards a commonwealth in which the Netherlands, Indonesia, Surinam, and Curaçao will participate, with complete self-reliance and freedom of conduct for each part regarding its internal affairs, but with readiness to render mutual assistance."

CHAPTER XXII

Indonesian Culture

BY RADEN MOEHAMMAD MOESA SOERIANATADJOEMENA

THE CIVILIZATION of Java,[1] one of the most highly developed parts of Indonesian culture, has a long history. Its origin may be traced to the beginning of the Christian Era when the Hindus from the Indian Peninsula migrated to the Indies, carrying with them their ancient and profound culture.

Little is known about the first Hindu settlements. The earliest indications of the presence of Hinduism in the Indies are the inscriptions which have been found there in several places. More readily recognized as remnants of the Hindu period in Java are the large monuments such as the Buddhist stupa of Boro Budur, and the Çivaitic temple of Prambanan. In the eighth century Çrivijaya, on Sumatra, was a powerful kingdom. It was ruled by the famous Çailendra Dynasty which extended its might over Middle Java well into the ninth century. In later years Çrivijaya and Java were bidding for the supremacy of the Indies. The competition for power ended in the thirteenth century with the founding of the Majapahit Empire in the island of Java.

The ancient Indian culture, brought by the Hindus into the islands, later separated from the country of its origin, passed through stages of development which historians now call the Hindu-Javanese culture. Very clearly the different stages may be seen in the aforementioned inscriptions. The oldest inscriptions are to be found on

---

[1] Inasmuch as it is impossible to describe the various cultures of Indonesia in so limited a space, certain characteristics of Javanese culture have been presented as representative of one of the most highly developed types of Indonesian civilizations.

stones. No date is given on these inscriptions but, because of the script used, they are believed to have been inscribed in the fourth and fifth centuries. The language is Sanskrit, that of ancient India. The oldest dated inscription was from 732 A.D., and was found in Tjanggal (Kedoe, Central Java); here the language is still Sanskrit, whereas the script used is still Pallava, one of the developmental stages of the scripts used for Sanskrit. Later inscriptions showed differences in language and script of a minor character until, at last, the differences were so basic that it must be assumed a new language had been adopted. In about 760 A.D. appeared the first document in Old Java-nese, or Kavi script, still based on Sanskrit. The oldest inscription in Kavi script, and written for the first time, also, in Kavi language, was found in the Dieng Plateau, dated about 809 A.D. The earliest inscrip-tion on material other than stone is the inscription on a silver umbrella from Mandang (Kedoe) dated about 843 A.D. The development in language and script from Kavi to modern Javanese has been gradual. The Javanese people have credited their alphabet to the legendary King Aji Saka. The Hindu-Javanese period ended in the last quarter of the fifteenth century when the supremacy of Java went over from the Hindu-Javanese kingdom of Majapahit to the Islamic rulers of north-central Java.

The Hindu influence on Javanese civilization has been very strong. Up to now remnants of the ancient culture have been found in the Javanese language, in literature, music, sculpture, and in other branches of art. In so far as language is concerned one may safely assume that almost half the Javanese vocabulary can be traced back to Sanskrit. Sanskrit words are still used for titles, for names, and for many other terms. The official title for a regent is *"Bhupati,"* which is a genuine Sanskrit word meaning "lord of the earth." The words *"atmaja," "putra,"* and *"tanaya,"*—Sanskrit words for "son," or "scion," are still used in personal names, as *"Surya atmaja"* ("son of the sun"), etc. Such Javanese terms as *"Sagara"* for "sea," *"nagara"* for "state," and *"pura"* for "city" are pure Sanskrit.

Another remnant of the Hindu influence in Javanese may be the typical division of the language into different classes. This may be a remnant of the division of Indian society into different castes, which must have existed in the Hindu-Javanese period in Java. Such a caste system is still in existence in Bali where the culture may be considered as a continuation of the Hindu-Javanese civilization. It has been proven that in the middle of the fourteenth century the Hindu-Javanese culture from Majapahit was being introduced in Bali.

Roughly speaking, there are the three classes of culture, *Kromo, Madio,* and *Ngoko.* The difficulty is not in the grammar, which is comparatively easy, but in the proper use of these classes. If someone speaks, he must always take into consideration the class of the person to whom he is speaking, or to whom his speech relates. For instance, if a man, who belongs to the middle class, is speaking to another, who is higher in social standing or older, he should use the *Kromo.* There is, of course, no punishment for using words belonging to another class; however, the speaker will stigmatize himself as illiterate, uncivilized, rude, or at least presumptuous if he uses the wrong class of words. If a man is speaking about a person of higher standing, then he should also use the *Kromo.* If, however, he is speaking to someone of his own social standing, then he may use the *Madio.* In speaking to someone of lower social standing, or to a very intimate friend, he may use the *Ngoko.* In learning the Javanese tongue one must know the different classes of words. For example, "to come" in *Kromo* is "rawoeh," but in *Madio* it is "doegi" and in *Ngoko* it is *"teko."* The use of this language division is, of course, rather difficult when speaking at large meetings where people from different social standing gather. A speaker may be in doubt as to the type of language he should use; therefore, Malay is usually chosen as a general language. In later years there has been a trend among the Javanese to abolish this difference in classes; however, because the language is closely interwoven with the various aspects of the Javanese social structure and customs, it is doubtful whether these efforts will have positive results.

The second feature of cultural life which has undergone the Hindu influence is literature. The first productions were pure Sanskrit. The earliest Old Javanese prose literary work dates back to the end of the tenth century and consists of a translation of three *Mahabharata-*

TIN MINING, NETHERLANDS INDIES

parvas by Anantavikrama. As a matter of fact, the two great epics of Sanskrit literature—the *Mahabharata* and the *Ramayana* cycles have always been a source of inspiration for Javanese literature, not only in the past, but even to the present day.

The *Mahabharata* relates the struggle for supremacy between two branches of the royal Bharata family, which culminated in a bitter war between cousins. The story has been compared by Western scholars to the great epic of Homer, the *Iliad*. The *Ramayana* gives the story of King Rama who, because of his father, went into voluntary exile. While Rama wandered through the forest, the wicked King of Langka (Ceylon) kidnaped his wife. In order to rescue his wife, Rama had to wage war against the mighty King of Langka. The adventurous itinerary of Rama led Western scholars to a comparison of his epic with Homer's *Odyssey*.

Of these two epics the *Mahabharata* has enjoyed more popularity than the *Ramayana*. At the beginning of the eleventh century, appeared the first Old Javanese poem, the *Arjunavivaha,* composed by Kanva, the first great poet of the Old Javanese era. This work is based on the *Mahabharata* and relates the adventures of Arjuna, one of the principal heroes of the epic. The flourishing period of the Old Javanese Belles-Lettres, which began with Kanva, ended at the beginning of the thirteenth century, only to undergo a revival in the middle of the fourteenth century under the reign of Emperor Hayam Wuruk of Majapahit.

The *Nagarakrtagama,* a contemporary chronicle rather than a work based on any Sanskrit poem, was composed by Prapanca who was court poet and superintendent of the Buddhist clergy to the court of Emperor Hayam Wuruk. It told the story of the founding of the Majapahit Empire and, what is more important to modern research, it gave a fair picture of the social structure and life in the Hindu-Javanese period. It showed, for instance, that the Majapahit Empire had relations with foreign countries; that once a year a great military gathering took place; that there were Buddhist and Çivaitic monasteries to which several kinds of privileges had been granted, and that those monasteries had been registered. All such items are of the greatest importance to a complete understanding of the different stages of Javanese culture and society.

A later work is the *Pararaton,* written about the end of the fifteenth century. Its language is not Old Javanese, but the type which scholars call the Middle Javanese. It also gave a kind of contemporary chronicle but, according to Dr. Krom, its quality as a source of historical study is less important than the *Nagarakrtagama.* Javanese literature has found its best writers among the nobility and members of the higher social classes. One of the Mangkunagaran princes composed a famous poem on the Javanese view of life, the *Serat Vedatama.*

The greatest Javanese poet of the last century was Raden Ngabehi Ranggavarsita. Before that century, Javanese literature had consisted chiefly of songs and poems. Only recently, under the influence of Western education, has Javanese prose appeared in the literary field.

Closely related to songs and poems is another interesting cultural asset of the Javanese—music which, contrary to Western music, has only five tones in its scale. To what extent Javanese music has undergone Hindu influence cannot be said. It is certain that in the Çailendra Era music had already reached a fairly well-developed stage. One of the three keys is the *Salendro,* which name may indicate its development in the Çailendra Era. This key is used for gay and vigorous melodies. The second key, which may be compared to the Western minor or flat key, is the *Laras Pelog.* This is used for sad and sentimental melodies. The third key is the *Laras Barang-Miring.* According to a Javanese authority on music, it has been stated that this key probably is the oldest in the musical system and is used principally in ancient religious songs and also in many old songs for children.

Of the instruments one may safely assume that the *gamelang,* or Javanese orchestra of today, has passed through the necessary evolutions. The *kemanakan* is thought to be the oldest instrument; it is constructed of bronze bars of varying lengths. Foreign elements, such as the *rebab,* or Javanese violin, are not unusual. Contrary to its Western equivalent, this *rebab* has only two strings. When, and by whom this instrument was introduced in Java is not known; possibly it is of Persian origin.

The *gamelang* is not less complicated than the Western orchestra. According to their tones, and to their function in the musical composition, the instruments may be ranged in the following groups: (*a*) the melody "producers"—the *rebab*, the *gambang*, or xylophon, and the *soeling*, or flute; (*b*) the melody "maintainers," which are played like the piano in accompaniment—the *bonang* (three sets), and the *gener* (also three sets), all of which are made of bronze; (*c*) the rhythm "producers"—the *kendangs*, or drums; (*d*) the rhythm "maintainers"—the *ketoeks, kenongs, kempoels*, and the *gongs*, whose function is to punctuate the several parts of the composition; and (*e*) the melody and rhythm "maintainers"—the different sets of *sarons* and *geners*.

In discussing Javanese literature and music, mention must also be made of the *wayang*, or shadow play. This is the most popular entertainment among the Javanese. In reality, it is more than entertainment. It is also a school for the philosophy of life, and is a harmonious combination of literature, music, and handicraft. The characters of the plays are taken from such literary epics as the *Mahabharata* and the *Ramayana*. The performance is always accompanied by music; and the leather puppets, by means of which the *wayang* is enacted, are the products of a highly skilled handicraft. The number of puppets used is very large—approximately two hundred in all. The stories, or plots, are taken from the Indian epics which, in the course of centuries, have become Javanized. In later times, mostly unknown artists have created new stories which do not really belong to these epics; but through use of the same personalities the necessary link with the epics is made.

Almost all the stories, because they comprise lessons on philosophy and the way of life, may be characterized as "moral teachings." People, for instance, are taught that pride must suffer a fall. When King Nivatakavaca, for instance, dares to attack the *devas* (gods), although he has won invulnerability from them by virtue of his self-chastisement, he must, nevertheless, pay with his life for his pride. The Pandavas, one of the two branches of the Bharata family are considered the personification of goodness. They are always ultimately victorious, even though evil, personified by the second group of the Bharata scions, the Kauravas, in the beginning has inflicted defeat upon them. The chivalrous behavior and gallantry of the principal heroes of the plays are impressed upon the mind of the public. The wisdom of the sages, depicted in the stories, inspire the more philosophically minded among the spectators. Examples are given of faithfulness in marriage, loyalty to the king, truthfulness, and firmness of purpose. In short, all good characteristics are instilled in the minds of the audience, while, simultaneously, constant emphasis is given to the adage that a departure from the right way of life invariably ends in destruction.

The *wayang* performance is always accompanied by the *gamelang*. One performer, called the *dalang,* operates all the puppets. Not only must he be a gifted speaker, a learned man, a capable musician and singer, but he must also be a gifted impersonator because he must speak for the women characters in the play as well. He is, in short, the pivot in the *wayang* performance. He also signals to the musicians to begin or to end the music, to accelerate the tempo—in fact, from that viewpoint he is also conductor of the music.

The *dalang,* the *gamelang,* and the puppets are separated from the spectators by a white screen. Above the head of the *dalang* is suspended an oil lamp with an open wick. The public may therefore see only the silhouettes of the puppets which are directly placed on the screen and which are illuminated by the lamp. The performer and the *gamelang* players who are behind the light circle are not visible to the spectators. Women are supposed to sit at the side where the silhouettes are seen, whereas men are permitted to sit behind the *dalang.* But this rule applies only to invited spectators. If the performance is held near the street where every passer-by may look on, then even women may sit or stand at the *dalang* side. According to Rassers, a Dutch scholar who has made an extensive study of Javanese culture, this segregation in the seating of the audience is probably of ancient Indonesian origin.

The philosophical Javanese compares the whole *wayang* performance to the pattern of life. The spectator sees, on the screen, heroes performing gallant deeds, and villains and traitors executing their foul intentions. All of the characters are moved by the invisible hand of the *dalang*. The screen, therefore, is compared with the stage of the world. The *dalang* is compared with Providence which knows and plans all world happenings, whereas the puppets are the personification of humanity which acts only at the will of Providence. From this point of view it is only logical that the spectators should be at the silhouette side of the stage. That the *wayang* performance also contains a religious element may be recognized in the fact that the *dalang* must always perform a certain rite, as, for instance, the burning of incense while uttering some Old Javanese prayer.

Another feature of Javanese culture, closely related to music, is the dance. Javanese dancing cannot be compared with Western ballroom dancing, but it may be compared more or less with ballet dancing. The sex element is virtually lacking in Javanese dancing. The dancer performs an act which is an expression of his soul, his movements guided by the intricate rhythm of the *gamelang*. When it is said that the sex element is lacking, it does not mean there are no female dancers; it means only that men and women do not dance together. Female dancers perform in groups of four or eight in dances known as "*srimpi*" or "*badaya*." Dances of this type are performed only in the privacy of the *kraton,* or palace, of the Javanese princes.

Comparable, to some extent, with Western amusement dancing is the Javanese *tayoeb*. At a feast where the *tayoeb* is a feature of entertainment, the dancer is one of the guests. He is invited by the host to dance, and usually the *tayoeb* provides an opportunity for him to display his ability. In his dancing he is accompanied by a professional female singer. Of the many styles in Javanese dancing, the two most outstanding are the *Solo* and the *Djogja*. The difference between the two styles is in the way the arms are lifted, and in the foot and leg movements. Whereas the *Solo* style creates a serene impression, the *Djogja* involves more vigorous action.

Comparable with the Western ballet are the dances which are performed by professionals. There are many types, such as the *kiprah,* which is usually performed by men, and the *golek,* which is danced by both sexes. The Hindu influence in the dance is very remote. Having lost touch with India for so many centuries and having changed in religion from Hinduism to Islam, the Javanese have allowed the dance, more than the language, to follow its own development. Only one or two movements of the hands may be traced back to the old Indian religious dance.

Among the nobility, the dance, as well as the principle of the *gamelang,* is considered an art that must be taught to children. It is not unusual in a family gathering for some members to take over the instruments from the professional musicians and begin to play a favorite melody, while one of the older members is asked to dance to the accompaniment.

It is a pity that words can never fully describe the esthetic enjoyment of seeing a Javanese dance performed. One must see it in actuality in order to appreciate its beauty and grace.

Of the subject of sculpture, it must be admitted that in the Hindu-Javanese era the arts of carving and the molding of statues were further developed than in the present era. As an example of that ancient art one may mention the Buddhist stupa of Boro Budur, situated near Magelang, in Central Java. It must have been built in the eighth century during the Çailendra Era. The monument is constructed around and on a hill to make a stupa form. It consists of many galleries. The walls of the galleries are carved in bas-relief and the carvings depict, among other themes, the life story of Buddha—the span from birth to death. The figures are very neatly carved. On the upper galleries are several stupas containing Buddha statues. Scholars regard the Boro Budur as one of the finest examples of Buddhist art in the world. Remarkable, also, is another Buddhist temple, the Mendut temple, situated not far from the Boro Budur. Within a huge niche, a sitting statue of Buddha, phenomenal in size and majestic in appearance, gives the visitor an idea of the art of ancient times. Not only did Buddhism give birth to mighty temples, but also Çivaism, which likewise flourished in Java. The Tjandi Prambanan in east Java is a distinct specimen of Çivaitic influence.

The decline in the art of sculpture in Java proper may be the result of the adoption of the Islam by the Javanese. It is strictly forbidden by the Islam to depict a living being, particularly a human being, lest people should become worshipers of statues. This kind of worship is an act of heresy. As a result of this ban, the people may have lost interest in sculpture entirely. In Bali, on the contrary, where nearly all the people are of Hindu faith and where no such prohibition has existed, sculpture has continued to flourish. As a result, Balinese carving now is the most highly developed carving in the Indies. With the influx of Western tourists, the art has become modernized; before the Japanese occupation it was carried out more and more on a commercial basis which was not always an improvement.

One of the most important items of culture of the Javanese is their philosophy, their attitude toward life, and the means by which they seek to attain happiness as one of life's aims. The Javanese do not pretend to have solved life's problems, but the wise and sage among them have attained the secret of being at peace with themselves. One of the basic teachings is that man is only a tool of Providence. He must and can persevere in his purpose because it is also recommended by the sages that by perseverence he can accomplish nearly every purpose. Nevertheless, if he fails in his efforts, he is not desperate because it then becomes clear to him that it is not his fate to fulfill his wish.

Typical is the teaching about persons whom the Javanese must obey—"*Guru, Ratu, wongatoea karo,*" which means, "the teacher, the ruler, and both parents." These names make up the first category of persons to whom obedience is due.

Another keynote in the Javanese attitude toward life is desire for harmony. Relationships within the family, with the neighbors, with other people, and even with the universe must be harmonious. To be out of harmony is considered the cause of unhappiness. In speaking of a person who is always looking for trouble with other people, it is said that if he is not in harmony with his fellow creatures he is not in harmony with God. As a consequence, he will not be blessed by Him.

The Javanese try to be in harmony even with the universe. An orthodox Javanese would never dare to go on a long voyage or to celebrate a solemn happening in his family without consulting the stars and dates. For instance, in a marriage, first of all, after the usual deliberation of social standing and of other qualifications, an investigation is made about the birthdays of the couple. It is believed that if the birthday of the bride-to-be is not in harmony with the birthday of the bridegroom-to-be, the marriage will be a failure, because every detail must be harmonious in order that the pair may attain happiness. When choosing a day for the wedding itself, the stars must again be consulted.

One characteristic of the sage is modesty. Modesty is a quality which is held in high esteem. A person who likes to display his ability or his cleverness is considered a fool even if he is able or clever. A Javanese will never answer directly in the affirmative a question as to whether or not he is capable of performing a certain act or service. To answer so would not be modest. He will nearly always say that he does not know whether or not he is able. If he is somewhat certain of himself, then he will say, "I will try" or "I beg your blessing." It is no wonder that foreigners, who do not understand the Javanese way of thinking, misunderstand this kind of modesty.

Another typical Javanese attitude is resentment of wealth. There are, of course, rich people among the Javanese. It is, however, not customary in Java to strive for worldly wealth. Unscrupulousness in business is a sin and a man who has shown greediness in acquiring money is never held in high esteem. The Javanese likes to think that everything he has, even his own life and intelligence are possessions entrusted to him only temporarily by God. He is firm in the belief that abuse of power, or intelligence, or knowledge, of which he is only the trustee, will be punished. Unfortunately this attitude toward wealth, power, and knowledge is not universally adopted. Therefore, it is commonly thought that the Javanese does not possess economic insight, that he is docile, and can be easily managed.

It is not known whether or not the happiness of the Javanese would be promoted by a reversal of this attitude against wealth, power, and knowledge. On the contrary, in order to maintain their existence in this far-from-ideal world the Javanese people will certainly need to revise their inherent opinions about the economic side of life.

It would be a serious mistake if nothing were said here about Dutch-Javanese culture. After all, the relationship between the Dutch and the Javanese people has lasted for at least three centuries and it would be surprising if Dutch influence were not to be found in Javanese culture. To speak of colonies is to arouse unpleasant thoughts of oppression and exploitation. It is not strange that, in the past, foreign rulers have superimposed their own civilization on the subject people. However, it must be said of the Dutch that they have dealt very wisely with the Javanese. Instead of superimposing Dutch culture on the Javanese, they have always helped to preserve the Javanese culture from decline.

Literature, for example, has been promoted by the printing of old manuscripts which otherwise might have been lost. A new generation of writers has matured through the endeavor of the Government. When it was clear that the art of sculpture was disappearing in certain parts of Java, sympathetic Dutch Government officials sponsored a revision of the old art. And by introducing children's antiquated songs and games in native schools, not only has a new approach to the educational problem been found, but also a feature of Javanese culture which had long been forgotten. A society for promoting Javanese culture has been set up under the name of the Java Institute, which has rendered valuable service to a better understanding of Javanese civilization. Nowhere in the Far East has such extensive research in native customary laws (*adat* law) been made as in the Indies. The feeling of inferiority which the Javanese felt toward their own culture, as compared with Western civilization which threatened to dominate their minds, was neutralized by Dutch intercedence. Ki Adjar Dewantoro, a Javanese leader, understood very well the importance of the Old Javanese culture as a basis for a healthy and vigorous national life and developed, more than twenty years ago, his own educational system. His schools, called the Pupil Garden (*Taman Siswa*) School, are spread throughout the whole Indonesian Archipelago. His idea is that Javanese, as one of the Indonesian cultures, is not in the least inferior to Western culture. He believes it wrong for a people to take over foreign civilization indiscriminately and, at the same time, lose touch with their own. Foreign elements must be adapted to one's own culture in order to achieve a harmonious whole.

Although there are many and varied cultures in the Netherlands Indies, the Government of the Netherlands has acted as a unifying agent and it is likely that in time a uniform Indonesian culture will take shape. That future Indonesian culture will be a synthesis of the various Indonesian cultures—influenced by Javanese culture. An example of that synthesis may be seen in the *Bahasa Indonesia,* the language that is used in meetings and in journalism. It is basically Malay, the *lingua franca* of the Indonesian Archipelago, but it is enriched by non-Malay elements. The Dutch influence may be seen clearly in the *Bahasa Indonesia,* in words which have been taken over from the Dutch. Besides foreign words, which have been adopted in the past, the people have tried to create words for new ideas. Words from other Indonesian languages, with slight alteration in meaning, are used in the *Bahasa Indonesia.* The word *"kolot"* taken from the Sundanese has acquired the meaning of "orthodox," or "conservative" in the *Bahasa Indonesia.* In the original tongue it means "old" without any thought of conservatism. And so to understand the *Bahasa Indonesia,* it is not enough that one knows Malay; one must know other Indonesian languages as well.

CHAPTER XXIII

The Economic Significance of the Netherlands Indies

BY JAN O. M. BROEK

LONG BEFORE THE EUROPEANS FOUND THEIR way to the Netherlands Indies the islands formed a valuable trading area for the merchants of China, India, and even of Arabia. The penetration by the West led to direct trade and an increase in volume of goods exchanged with Europe; a considerable proportion of the total commerce of the Indies, though, remained Oriental in character and destination. In contrast, the newly discovered "West Indies" became an almost complete adjunct to the European economic sphere and, as far as Europe was concerned, soon outstripped its eastern counterpart in economic and political importance. During the nineteenth century, however, the competitive advantage gradually switched from tropical America to tropical Asia. The instability of the Latin-American governments and the abolition of slavery discouraged European capital investments. Southeast Asia, on the contrary, remained under colonial rule, a rule which, moreover, strengthened its hold on the country as time went on. Slavery, as the New World knew it, was never an important institution here, and the use of native labor thus was not affected by this issue. Besides, China and Japan were opened to Western trade. The gold rushes in California and Australia drew considerable numbers of the white race to the borderlands of the Pacific Ocean. The opening of the Suez Canal (1869), largely removed the handicap of distance from Europe and thereby allowed the colonial powers of Southeast Asia to take full advantage of the new situation.

[359]

Within this framework it was Dutch policy that gave shape and direction to the developments in the Indies. The Culture System, based on compulsory native cultivation of export crops and Government trade monopolies, was abolished about 1870 in favor of private enterprise, free trade and the "Open Door." This new course and the ever-increasing demand for tropical commodities explain the rapid development of the Indies from an isolated somnolent group of South Sea islands to a land of bustling activity, where the capital of many nations, together with cheap labor and a variety of resources, has created one of the world's foremost production centers of tropical raw materials. It should be noted that many of the now prominent crops are not native to this region but were introduced from other parts of the world because of the favorable conditions of capital, land, and labor, for example: rubber, cinchona (the source of quinine), agave fibers (especially sisal), maize, cassava (tapioca), and tobacco came from the Americas, coffee from Arabia, the oil palm from West Africa.

Regional shifts in export agriculture.—Until the end of the nineteenth century, Java was the only intensively developed area. Dutch government over the other parts of the Archipelago was largely nominal, but the new aims of colonial policy and, to some degree, fear of foreign intervention led to an extension of effective military and political control over all islands, to the construction of ports, highways, railroads and to the exploitation of the resources. In the 1930's the so-called "Outer Provinces"—all islands except Java and adjacent Madura—had actually surpassed Java in the total value of exports; in fact, it was they that provided the large positive international trade balance of the Indies. Although Java's agricultural production is, of course, still its major asset, the island, before the invasion of the Japanese, was assuming in increasing degree the role of local metropolis and manufacturing center for the Archipelago. The economic growth of the Outer Provinces has, however, been very uneven. Sumatra, particularly the so-called "East Coast Province," is far ahead of the others, although Borneo and Celebes also have considerable export agriculture. The small eastern islands—off the main trade routes, and with a less favorable natural environment—have shared little in the material progress, whereas in Dutch New Guinea active economic exploration had only begun in the past decade.

Plantation and peasant economy.—After the abolition of compulsory native cultivation, it looked for a time as though the estates of Western entrepreneurs would take over completely the production of the more valuable export crops; in about 1890 only 10 per cent of

TABLE I

VALUE OF AGRICULTURAL EXPORTS FROM THE NETHERLANDS INDIES 1894–1939

Year	Total, in millions of guilders	Percentage of total		Percentage of total	
		Java and Madura	Outer provinces	Plantation	Native
1894..............	154	82	18	89	11
1913.............	419	65	35	76	24
1928.............	1,237	58	42	65	35
1933.............	306	50	50	59	41
1939.............	495	46	54	63	37

the agricultural exports of the Indies came from peasant holdings. Although it is still true that the Indonesian is primarily a subsistence farmer, in the last forty years he has shown a growing interest in money crops. (See table 1.) On Java, this development has been hampered by the crowded conditions—at present there are, on the average, 900 inhabitants per square mile—which has left little room for other than food production, but even here the peasant's share in the agricultural exports from this island rose from 6 per cent in 1894 to about 23 per cent in the late 'thirties. This was, no doubt, a welcome development and one would wish that Indonesian enterprise might gradually replace the Western plantation. There are, however, various difficulties which block, or at least retard, this process. The peasant has been successful primarily with products where cultivation and initial processing are of a simple nature, such as rubber, copra, kapok, pepper and other spices, low-quality tobacco, and tapioca. The future of at least some of these commodities is uncertain. On the contrary, several of the typical plantation products (sugar, palm oil, cigar-wrapper to-bacco, quinine) require either a large outlay of capital, a high degree of organization, or expert handling. All these responsibilities may eventually be undertaken by Indonesians, but the process of creating favorable conditions will take considerable time.

Shifts in commodities.—The increasing participation of the Indo-nesian population in commercial agriculture has been partly offset,

TABLE 2

PERCENTUAL SHARES IN EXPORT VALUE

Source of export	1910	1939
Estates...........................	56.6	41.6
Indonesian agriculture.............	21.2	24.8
Mineral production................	16.2	29.9
Other goods......................	6.0	3.7
Total.......................	100.0	100.0

however, by the rise of the mineral production which is almost en-tirely in the hands of Western concerns. In 1910 mineral products formed 16 per cent of the total export (671,000,000 guilders), but in 1939 their share was 30 per cent (774,000,000 guilders). The above table summarizes these observations.

The change in types of commodities deserves further comment. Formerly the chief output was foodstuffs and condiments such as sugar, tobacco, coffee, and spices. Indigo was an important exception, but has been eclipsed by the rise of synthetic dyes. The modern period in the commercial agriculture of the Indies has been charac-terized by the ascendance of industrial raw materials such as rubber, fibers, starches, fats, and oils. To these crops should be added the minerals, as petroleum, tin, bauxite and, of less importance as yet, coal, nickel, and manganese. In the 1920's rubber and sugar vied for first place among the Indies exports, followed by petroleum products, and then by tobacco, tea, and copra. After the decline of the sugar industry in the depression of the early 1930's, petroleum and rubber became the foremost commodities.

TABLE 3

Exports of Major Commodities

(In millions of guilders and percentages of total export)

Product	1900 Value	1900 Per cent	1913 Value	1913 Per cent	1928 Value	1928 Per cent	1933 Value	1933 Per cent	1938 Value	1938 Per cent
Total export..............	257	100	671	100	1,577	100	468	100	658	100
Petroleum products........	5	1.8	113	16.9	144	9.1	104	22.2	162	24.6
Rubber..................	16	6.2	31	4.6	281	17.8	38	8.1	135	20.6
Tea.....................	4	1.6	22	3.2	98	6.2	26	5.6	56	8.6
Sugar...................	74	28.7	153	22.8	373	23.6	62	13.2	45	6.8
Tobacco.................	32	12.5	92	13.7	96	6.1	32	6.8	39	5.9
Copra..................	10	4.0	55	8.2	107	6.8	39	8.2	38	5.8
Coffee..................	24	9.2	21	3.2	81	5.1	26	5.5	14	2.1
Share of these in total export......	165	64.0	487	72.6	1,180	74.7	327	69.6	489	74.4

Table 3 demonstrates how the relative and absolute values of the major export commodities have changed in the last forty years. Like other countries producing raw materials, the Netherlands Indies export is dominated by a few products; in comparison with other countries in this class, the Indies have, however, a relatively varied export trade. This diversification gives some protection against business cycles and it is, therefore, unfortunate that the trend since 1900 has been toward increasing the share of a few commodities in the export trade.

The items that now rank high in the export list are mostly produced in the western part of the Archipelago (West Java, Borneo, and Sumatra), whereas such products as coffee, copra, sugar, and the cheaper types of tobacco come chiefly from the eastern part. If one adds such goods as sisal fiber, palm oil, tin, and bauxite, all produced on Sumatra or on the islands off its east coast, one sees more clearly that the problems of prosperity are of a regional nature and will have to be viewed as such after the war.

Foreign investments.—The glib assumption that the Dutch have merely "drained off the wealth of the Indies" has no basis in fact, in so far as the modern period is concerned. The capital investment in primary production, in communication, transportation and manufacturing, in laboratories and hospitals has added enormously to the material equipment of the Indies. But one may criticize the share of the profits flowing to Western capitalists, outside the Indies, and may doubt if enough effort has been made to educate the Indonesian toward active partnership in the development of his country. These questions, which have received much attention in recent years are ready for radically different solutions after the war. On the whole, however, there is no doubt that the Netherlands Indies has become richer, not poorer, by its fertilization with Western capital, science, and technology.

Information on capital investments is likely to be misleading if given without detailed comment. It must suffice to mention here the results of a number of special studies. They indicate that in 1939 state and local government loans in the Netherlands Indies amounted to some 1,300,000,000 guilders, of which at least four-fifths were held by Dutch citizens. The investments in private industry were estimated at 3,500,000,000 guilders, of which amount about two-thirds was Dutch and one-tenth was Netherlands Indies Chinese. The remainder (some 850,000,000) was in the hands of foreign groups. About 320,000,000 was British, 290,000,000 American, 120,000,-000 Franco-Belgian, and the remainder Japanese, German, and other interests. On Java, the capital investments were almost entirely Dutch and Chinese, but in the more recently developed East Coast Province of Sumatra about half of the capital belonged to other investors. Here American interests were prominent in rubber, British in tea, and French and Belgian in oil-palm culture. In the petroleum production of the Indies, British and American capital had a predominant part.

Economic policy.—Like any colonial region, the Indies have had to make large payments abroad for interest, profits, dividends, and for the pensioning of officials. In order to fulfill its obligations as a debtor country, it needed a big surplus of exports over imports. Obviously this was derived from the sales of commodities abroad. Moreover, the Netherlands could absorb only a small part and so the Indies were largely dependent on foreign markets. The economic structure of the country was, therefore, highly sensitive to changes in world trade. Not only did a decline in the value of exports affect the capital structure, it also decreased the purchasing power of the population and this, in turn, reacted quickly on the volume of imports. Thus the World Depression of the early 1930's hit the Indies particularly hard. It soon became very clear that no salvation could be expected from the free play of economic forces as represented by the multifarious producer and consumer groups in the Archipelago, whereas in other countries increasing state control directed all exchanges of goods and currencies. Only the Government could create the machinery necessary to cope with the situation. And so, the Netherlands Indies, albeit reluctantly, changed from a "free" to a "directed" economy. The Government had to assist in reorganizing production of the export industries on a restricted basis. It had to protect the financial structure not only from collapsing under the strain of changes in trade but also

of reduced state income. And, finally, it had to promote the development of new means of livelihood for the population.

These measures for relief were begun as an emergency policy, but
the results were so satisfactory that the system was retained even after
the worst years were past. One of the important results was the attainment of virtual self-sufficiency in major foodstuffs. Another was the

TABLE 4

DIRECTION OF NETHERLANDS INDIES FOREIGN TRADE

(In percentages of total trade)

Foreign trade areas	Percentage of					
	Exports to			Imports from		
	1909-1913	1925-1929	1938	1909-1913	1925-1929	1938
Europe.....................	49	36	37	64	49	50
North and South America....	4	14	15	2	10	13
Asia (excluding Singapore)....	29	24	13	16	26	25
Singapore..................	17	22	17	18	13	7
Other countries*............	1	4	18	...	2	5
Total.................	100	100	100	100	100	100

* Includes trade via free ports within the Netherlands Indies, but outside the Netherlands Indies
customs territory. This influences chiefly the export figure for 1938, when seven per cent of the total
exports (practically all petroleum) left the customs area for some of these special ports.

initiation of manufacturing industries. Both developments proved
their worth in the years before the Japanese invasion.

Trade relations.—The foreign trade of the Indies in the last thirty
years has shown significant shifts in direction. (See table 4.) So long
as western Europe remained the hub of world commercial and industrial activity, the commerce of the Netherlands Indies was mostly
with that area. Before the First World War two-thirds of the imports
came directly from Europe, and most of the goods from Singapore
originated in Europe. Of the exports, half went directly to Europe,
and much went to Europe via Singapore. The reason for Europe's
smaller share in the exports was the market in Asia for Indian products, particularly sugar. Thus (in the period 1909–1913) British India

took an average of 13 per cent of exports, China (including Hong-kong) 8 per cent, and Japan 4 per cent.

The First World War disorganized the relations of the Indies with Europe and established new channels of trade with Japan and the United States. The industrialization of these countries naturally would have led to their greater participation in the commerce of the Indies, but the war hastened the process. As a result, Europe's share in the direct imports during the 'twenties was less than half, whereas the United States and Japan each supplied about ten per cent. Europe's part in the exports of the Indies also dropped, and the share of the United States increased, particularly because of the expansion of the automobile industry. Exports to Asia, however, fell off. This was caused principally by the policy of self-sufficiency followed in the Far Eastern countries, especially regarding cane sugar. The World Depression reinforced this trend toward autarchy. Petroleum, of which the Indies has a pseudomonopoly in an oil-poor Far East, became the only commodity for which East Asia formed the major market. The trade relations with Japan presented a grave problem in the early 'thirties. Indeed, Japan flooded the market of the Indies with cheap goods, but refused to increase its purchases in the Indies. Moreover, there was no doubt that the Japanese coupled political-military objectives with their commercial penetration. The Japanese menace was the primary cause of the regulations which the Nether-lands Indies Government had imposed on the import trade since 1934. These measures were aimed at benefiting the good customers of the Netherlands Indies and were reasonably successful. It should be noted, however, that even under the new restrictions Japan's share in the import trade remained at a higher level than it had been before the World Depression. (Table 5.)

Because of the claims of the Japanese concerning the new "Co-Prosperity Sphere" to be established in "Greater East Asia" under their leadership, the trade relations of the Indies with Asia are of particular interest. Even in 1934, during the great Japanese economic offensive, when the Indies still adhered to free trade, the imports from Asia—excluding Singapore—were well under half (43 per cent, including 32 per cent from Japan). It is, however, quite likely that this proportion would have increased if the Indies had not abandoned its free-trade policy. Instead it decreased, although remaining well above the 1930 level. But more significant was the export trend, which revealed a steady decline in the relative importance of the Asiatic markets. The Netherlands Indies, it may be repeated, because of its

TABLE 5

TRADE WITH JAPAN

(In million guilders and percentages of total trade.)

Period	Imports from Japan		Exports to Japan	
	Value	Per cent	Value	Per cent
1909–1913, average.........	4	1.2	21	4.3
1924–1927, average.........	82	10.3	96	5.9
1934......................	93	31.9	19	3.9
1938......................	72	15.0	21	3.2
1939......................	85	18.1	25	3.3
1940......................	101	22.7	48	5.5

colonial economy, must sell abroad in order to service foreign invested capital. Neither under conditions of bilateral trade relations, nor under a Japanese "Co-Prosperity Sphere," would Asia fulfill this primary need of the Indies.

Thus it was actually the Western world that gained importance, in the 1930's, as a market for the exports of the Indies, but this "Western world" had a different meaning from what it had had in 1913.

Table 4 shows the increasing relations with the Americas and "other countries," among which Australia is particularly noteworthy. The latter country bought in recent years about 5 per cent of the exports. The figure of 15 per cent, in 1938, for North and South America was exceptionally low because of a business depression in the United States. On the basis of both the preceding and the subsequent years, 19 per cent is more accurately representative of the direct export trade to the United States in recent years.

Singapore, because of its function as an entrepôt for world-wide commerce, forms an obstacle to a correct evaluation of destination and origin of the trade of the Indies. In recent years, the Netherlands Indies Central Bureau of Statistics has attempted to determine the ultimate destination of exports shipped to Singapore. Without explaining the method, the results are quoted in table 6, in a summarized form.

TABLE 6

EXPORTS BY CONTINENTS (CORRECTED FIGURES)

(In million guilders and percentage of total trade)

Destination	1937		1938		1939	
	Value	Per cent	Value	Per cent	Value	Per cent
Europe	410	41.4	282	41.0	234	30.3
North and South America	259	26.1	127	18.5	217	28.0
Asia	198	19.9	157	22.8	199	25.8
Other continents	124	12.6	122	17.7	123	15.9
Total	991	100.0	688	100.0	773	100.0

In reading the figures for Asia it should be noted that the percentage for 1938 was raised by the decline of exports to the United States, whereas the high figure for 1939 resulted largely from the exceptional sugar exports to British India because of a poor harvest in that country. In general, it appears that Europe bought about two-fifths, the Americas and Australia one-third, and Asia one-fifth of the exports. The conclusion is unescapable. The place of the Netherlands Indies is in the world, not in an artificial bloc.

Postwar problems.—The war in the Indies led to considerable destruction, partly because of actual fighting, and partly because of the demolition of port installations, railroads and bridges, petroleum refineries, and other factories before they fell into the hands of the enemy. Many ships were lost through one cause or another. The Netherlands Indies Government, however, in order to prevent famine, expressly forbade the destruction of any food warehouses or processing plants. It is, of course, difficult to envisage the situation which will confront the United Nations after the Japanese have been expelled from the Indies. The Netherlands Indies, as a whole, had become practically self-sufficient in basic food production but local deficit areas had to be supplied by interinsular trade. The growing Japanese shipping shortage may well mean famine for certain districts. It may be that the present loss of markets for export crops will result in a shift to food crops, but even where this is possible it will lead to a lower standard of living. It has been reported that, because of the severe shortage in east Asia, Japan has attempted to introduce cotton production in the Indies, but the execution of such a program will take time, and the benefit, if any, to the Indonesian peasant will be very slight. There is also a great lack of consumers' goods, other than food, especially cotton textiles. Industrial machinery, if not already destroyed, is wearing out and replacement, except for Japanese military needs, is out of the question. Moreover, in the event that war again sweeps over the Indies, it might lead to frightful destruction by the retreating enemy. The first problem after reoccupation will be that of relief and reconstruction. But what of the wider postwar economic questions that will confront the Indies?

Difficulties of the export industries.—It has been seen that the wealth of this region was primarily derived from the export of a number of raw materials. As may be seen in table 7 the world was also dependent on the East Indies for many finished products. The war has compelled the Western nations either to increase production elsewhere, or to find substitutes.

The central question is, therefore, how far will the Indies be able to regain its former position. Much depends on general international organization after the war, but even under relatively secure conditions and with multilateral trade the problem remains grave. Rubber may be taken as the best-known example. Europe and the United States are now producing synthetic rubber on a large scale; besides, cultivation of latex-yielding plants—not only the Hevea in tropical America and Africa, but also various plants in the temperate zone—is rapidly expanding. Whether the rubber from Southeast Asia will be able to compete in quality or price with that from new Western production remains to be seen, but even assuming that it could, there still might be other obstructions. For instance, the Good-Neighbor Policy toward Latin America might induce the United States to give preference to the newly created rubber industry of that region. Or, the lesson of uncertain reliance on other countries for this strategic

TABLE 7

SHARE OF THE NETHERLANDS INDIES IN THE WORLD EXPORT, OR WORLD PRODUCTION OF CERTAIN COMMODITIES

Commodities	Percentage of world production	
	1928	1939
Cinchona bark (production).................	93	91
Pepper (export)............................	70	86
Kapok (export)............................	79	72
Rubber (export)...........................	35	37
Sisal (export).............................	18	33
Coconut (export)..........................	30	27
Palm oil (export).........................	5	24
Tea (export)..............................	17	19
Tin (production)..........................	21	17
Sugar (export)............................	21	11
Coffee (export)...........................	8	4
Petroleum (production)....................	2.3	2.8

raw material may result in popular demand in Europe, as well as in America, for the maintaining of home production, whatever the cost may be; concern for the large capital invested in the synthetic-rubber industry would certainly add support to such a policy. If one realizes that some five or six million Indonesians, in prewar times, were dependent on rubber plantings for their cash income, one may readily see what the loss of markets for this product would mean for the population, not to speak of the rubber estates, owned by Westerners.

Many other products offer similar problems. Quinine will have to compete with atabrine, kapok with synthetic bulbfill or milkweed, tapioca with newly developed waxy corn and sorghum starches, and natural resins with their synthetic counterparts. The tin export will find that other materials have been substituted and less of the metal is used in the new tin-plating process. The sugar industry of the

Indies, always dependent on the free markets, may be up against increased home production in various countries and all-round lower consumption because of changed habits or impoverishment. Sisal fiber will certainly face a stiff competition from the expansion of cordage production in Latin America.

Possible solutions.—A résumé of these postwar hazards is likely to create too gloomy a picture. The Netherlands Indies has gone through many crises and repeatedly has had to adjust its export industries to changed conditions. The high degree of rationalization in the export agriculture guarantees that, if more efficient production methods are necessary in order to maintain sales, they will be forthcoming. As to external factors, much will depend on the attitude of the people of the United States regarding their position in international affairs. Those who believe in the precepts of the Atlantic Charter realize that the raising of the standard of living in Southeast Asia depends substantially on the ability of these peoples to sell their commodities abroad. This is not mere philanthropy, but recognition of the fact that the wealthy industrial countries cannot hope to maintain their present high standards unless the economically backward peoples of the world are enabled to produce more and, therefore, to buy more. After this war, more than ever before, the United States will need outlets for its industrial production, and the Indies, as well as its surrounding areas, will require equipment to re-create and increase its productivity. Again, if it cannot sell, it will not be able to buy, and whether this buying is done directly from the United States, or indirectly, will benefit the United States via the chain of multilateral trade. Besides, there are political considerations which urge in favor of reëstablishing commerce as much as possible. The American people certainly do not wish to acquire any territory or assume direct governmental responsibility in Southeast Asia, but the region has such strategic significance that its security and stability must be an American concern. It is possible that some international regional agency will be organized to supervise the political emancipation process, the economic development, and the defense of Southeast Asia. No doubt the United States would have an important role in such an organization; but participation in such a scheme demands in return the acceptance of responsibilities regarding this region. It is not enough to speak eloquently about the right of all peoples to various kinds of freedom; these good intentions must be translated into action, and giving the Indies an opportunity to sell its goods is one of the most urgent and sound policies.

New outlets needed.—Nevertheless, it is fairly certain that the almost complete dependence of America and Europe on certain products of Southeast Asia will not return. The Indies then will have to find markets elsewhere for at least a part of its exports, or will have to change to other forms of production. There are several possibilities. If China is helped to her feet after the war, one may expect a considerable expansion of manufacturing and means of communication. Besides, the Chinese people will need food, or better food, and medicine. It seems unlikely that China would attempt to produce synthetic materials, when to do so would require such highly advanced technological environment. The Indies might, therefore, find in China some compensation for lost markets, for instance, rubber, quinine, sugar, tin, industrial oils, and fats. The exports to China—including Hongkong—until about 1925 were some 8 per cent of the total exports of the Indies, but since then, no doubt as a result of civil strife, depression, and war, the figure has been less than 4 per cent. Inasmuch as the Indonesians need goods adjusted to Oriental levels of living, the elimination of Japan's "high-pressure" sales methods should give China a good chance to supply many of the articles the Indies cannot produce themselves. The same reasoning, although to a lesser degree, applies to India. In recent years there has developed a closer relationship between the Indies and Australia; not only has it been stimulated by considerations of common security, but also by increasing trade relations. In the future the exports of raw materials from the Indies may increase because of the rapid expansion of Australia's manufacturing industry during the war. In turn, Australia, because of this development, may be better able to compete with other Western countries in providing the Indies with machinery and other metal goods.

Other possibilities.—If the Atlantic Charter is to be more than an empty gesture, a determined attempt should be made to raise the standards of living all over the world. One of the basic needs is for more and better-balanced food. The production of the Indies in the past fifty years has shifted from food crops to industrial raw materials. It might revert partly to the production of foodstuffs in order to provide its own population, as well as that of other countries, with a better diet. Then too, the wealth of the Indies forests should be considered. In the past, the lumber industry, apart from the carefully managed teak forests of east Java, consisted principally of selective logging of special tropical woods. The rapid development of the cellulose and wood-plastics technology may open entirely new possibilities for utilizing the tropical forest resources. The quick tree growth, under prevailing climatic conditions, ensures a harvest of pulpwood in far shorter time than in the temperate zone. Under good management, mass production on the principle of sustained yield should be combined with protection from soil erosion.

Raising the standard of living.—All these suggestions are based on the conviction that the Netherlands Indies will need to maintain an export surplus in order to pay for foreign capital investments and for other services rendered in the process of building up the country. Local capital had notably increased in the past decades, but after the war help from abroad nevertheless will be greatly needed. It is certain, however, that the function of Western capital will be viewed more than ever in the light of Indonesian welfare. This will be an inevitable result of the far-reaching autonomy the Indies will obtain after the war. A small group in Western countries thus may reap smaller profits, but ultimately the internal development of the Indies will benefit the world as a whole. For the same reason it is to be hoped that the disparity between prices paid for agrarian products and those paid for manufacturing products will disappear. In industrial countries there is much criticism of price agreements, or restriction schemes, regarding tropical products, but it is usually forgotten that the agrarian countries, as consumers of industrial goods, were in a far worse situation, and one which deteriorated as time went on.

In 1913 an Indonesian rubber planter could buy, for instance, a sewing machine for one-sixth the amount of rubber he had to give for it in 1939. An Indonesian gum collector, in 1913, could obtain a bolt of imported cotton goods for one-third the amount of gum he had to pay in 1939. The objective of raising the purchasing power motivated the regulation of the rice trade in the Netherlands Indies in 1933; abundant crops in Burma, Thailand, and French Indo-China had pulled down the rice price to such a low level that it threatened to ruin the Indonesian producer. By restricting imports and stabilizing prices, the purchasing power of the peasant was lifted, thus resulting in great benefit for the whole economy. Here again is the central problem of the Indies and, as a matter of fact, of the whole Orient: how to raise the standard of living of the masses. Whatever the political reforms after the war, this question will confront any kind of government. But it cannot be solved by domestic policy alone; it is a world problem which concerns all nations, not only in a humanitarian sense, but also in terms of broad self-interest. Neither can export agriculture be the complete answer—after the war, even less than before. The development of manufacturing industries, so successfully begun in the 1930's, must be energetically resumed in order to raise the productivity which, in turn, makes possible the expansion of purchasing power.

The rapid rate of population growth is another great problem that has harassed the progressive groups in the Indies for years. Unless this can be checked, all social-economic improvements will be swallowed up by increased survival, as has occurred in Java. Here, the Westerners and the Chinese "have grown in wealth, the natives in numbers." In final analysis it is through education, in a wide sense, that this conflict between fecundity and a higher level of living will have to be solved.

CHAPTER XXIV

Industrialization of the Netherlands Indies

BY PETER H. W. SITSEN

THE PROBLEM which had confronted the Netherlands Government for many years regarding industrial expansion in the Indies had been whether or not the most efficacious solution would be found in directly transplanting modern mechanized industry to Java, or in establishing a definite beginning by a promotion of small-scale industry.

From 1914 to the invasion of the Japanese in 1941, the balance of trade of the Netherlands Indies had become decidedly unfavorable. Attempts had been made to compensate for this by encouraging more varied and new exports, but these attempts had been only partially successful. In order to prevent a decline in the already low standard of living and a further fall in exchange value, the Indies had resorted to borrowing abroad. For a time this policy narrowed the hitherto widening gap between imports and exports. Gold had to be exported each year, thus resulting in a constant drain on the gold supply. In order to strengthen the national wealth, production had to be increased. This could be done by endeavoring to maintain, as much as possible, the export value and by increasing at the same time agricultural and industrial production for home consumption.

A well-organized migration of Javanese farmers to lands in the Outer Islands had enabled fifty thousand yearly to find a new and more prosperous livelihood, and had brought about a small rise in individual and total agricultural production. With the tremendous

increase in population in Java, as well as in the Outer Islands, industrialization had to be promoted as much as possible.

Industrial development.—In the years from 1928 to 1939, the population of the Netherlands Indies increased from 60,000,000 to
70,000,000, and on the island of Java the population reached a
density of 1,360 persons per arable square mile. The grave problem
of feeding these masses was partially overcome by better irrigation,
by the introduction of fertilizers and higher-yielding plant varieties,
as well as by migration to uncultivated areas in the Outer Islands.
Thus, for the time being, complete self-sufficiency in foodstuffs had
been attained in 1938, but, however strenuous these efforts and encouraging the results, it was very doubtful whether this equilibrium
could be maintained in the future.

In the same period, some time between 1935 and 1939, a sharp increase in the demand for certain types of consumers' goods was wit-
nessed; this caused a rapid growth of the small-scale and factory
industries. What caused this change?

It is known that in the economic development of a country, primary
production tends to set the pace, forming the basis for an increase in
the purchasing power of the population. However, as income increases, the demand for foodstuffs becomes relatively higher. When
primary demands for food and clothing are satisfied, the increased
income is spent on various kinds of articles. This occurred also in the
Netherlands Indies and, as a result, the home industry was stimulated
inasmuch as the imports did not materially increase during this
period. The figures shown in table 1 demonstrate clearly what happened. Thus, because the growth of industrialization meant a further
addition to the national wealth, the foundation for a modest increase
in prosperity was laid. Behind this fortunate development, however,
there was a long period of planning by the Government.

The establishment of agricultural centers in formerly undeveloped
areas, such as the Outer Islands, had been stimulated and made
possible by the Government. In addition, the natives had been encouraged to produce a larger share of export crops. Not only had these
newly developed areas aided overpopulated Java by providing arable

lands for many Javanese emigrants, but the need for industrial articles in these areas had created new possibilities for Javanese industry and had given employment to thousands. At the same time the migration of farmers from Java to the Outer Islands, and from primary to secondary production in Java proper, had promoted a greater individ-

TABLE I

NUMBER OF WORKERS IN THE NETHERLANDS INDIES IN PRIMARY AND SECONDARY
INDUSTRIES, AND IN OTHER OCCUPATIONS, 1940

Nature of occupation	Number employed
Agricultural production, cattle raising, fishing, forestry, etc..	14,000,000
Small-scale industry ⎫	⎰ 2,500,000
Machine industry ⎬ secondary industry...............	300,000
Mining industry.......................................	600,000
Total, primary and secondary industries..............	17,400,000*
Commerce, transportation, clerical work and professions....	4,600,000
Grand total.......................................	22,000,000

* Contrary to usage in many other statistics, women are included here among the agricultural workers, in so far as their main source of income is derived from agriculture or cattle breeding. From investigations made in 1940 and 1941 it appears that there was an average of 1.7 workers per family. The number of workers in agriculture, if only men are counted, can be accepted as approximately 10,500,000.

ual farm production, and through this process a higher purchasing power. In this way the domestic market for consumers' goods encouraged the industrial entrepreneurs.

The place held by this industry in Indonesian economy was certainly important. The 17,400,000 workers mentioned in table 1 produced an income valued at about 2,500,000,000 guilders; of this amount industrial workers produced 450,000,000. Simultaneously, while raising the national income, increased industrialization had made possible a reduction in the prices of many goods which, until 1935, had been chiefly imported—woven sarongs, shoes, cutlery, flashlights, etc.—and in this way had promoted a higher standard of living.

The question many persons will ask is: would this decrease in certain imports have directly harmed the total volume of imports and indirectly the volume of exports of raw materials? This fear is not justified in the light of the established fact that there was, and had been, before the Japanese invasion, a marked increase in the importation of consumers' goods by all countries in times of industrial development. Undoubtedly there was then a trend in imports, away from certain articles, which, because of growing industrialization, could have been manufactured more cheaply at home, but the total volume of imports had grown. Some objections against such industrialization could be expected by the manufacturers who formerly had produced these imported articles, but there is no doubt that world economy as a whole would have profited materially from the new and increased demands for imports.

In the Netherlands Indies increased industry would undoubtedly have meant increased purchasing power available for imports. Of course, prices of the consumers' goods produced must range on a level suitable for the Indonesian market, protective tariffs not being a lasting necessity. For this reason it seems most desirable that the Indies should specialize in the production of those articles for which the principal raw materials could be found in the country.

Table 2 shows very clearly that in the years between 1928 and 1940 a situation was developing which corresponded more exactly to the logical place of the Netherlands Indies in world economy. Internally this fortunate economic development was linked with an enlightened social program which had found expression in a political decentralization, an increased educational program, and especially in the solution of hygienic and social problems. In the last years prior to the Japanese attack, forces had developed which seemed destined to carry the country rapidly to greater social and economic prosperity.

Indonesian industries.—Indonesian industry may be divided into three branches: (1) Cottage industry which was in the hands of agricultural workers who wanted to earn some money during their spare time; (2) Small-scale industry which comprised small shops with less than 50 employees who worked primarily with hand tools; and (3) Factory industry which included all other production. The cottage industry was almost entirely in the hands of the Indonesian farmers, and had the following characteristics: (*a*) the major part of the production was traded in the village; (*b*) a small part was bought up by middlemen and transported to other regions, sometimes even exported. In this event the middleman often provided the raw materials.

TABLE 2

ECONOMIC DEVELOPMENT IN THE NETHERLANDS INDIES, 1928 TO 1940
(Index Figures: 1928=100)

Economic factors	1928	1932	1935	1939	1940
1. Population increase..............	100	106	110	118	119
2. Cost of living for worker's family with stable standard of living.....	100	65	56.5	57	60
3. Price level of food..............	100	51.5	43.5	44.5	46
4. Income from native agriculture exports in units of purchasing power*.	100	52	64	88	116
5. Total exports in units of purchasing power......................	100	59	53	87	97
6. Income from industry in units of purchasing power...............	100	165	210	335	370
7. Total imports in units of purchasing power......................	100	61.5	48	90	85
8. Consumption of primary foodstuffs in kilograms per person...........	100	102	105	112	115
9. Calorie value of this food.........	...	...	100	110	112
10. Consumption of textiles in yards per person......................	100	...	92	136	?
11. Number of mechanically operated factories........................	100	132	134	162	184
12. Area technically irrigated.........	100	125	139	164	?

* The purchasing power of the income subsistence of a family with an income of about 360 guilders per year was taken as unit of purchasing power.

This industry added roughly 110,000,000 guilders to the national income each year, and used imports representing a value of approximately 20,000,000 guilders.

The small-scale industry, as it existed before the invasion of the Japanese, can be seen as a development of the cottage industry. Everywhere among the small-scale workers coöperative unions grew up with centers which finished off and sold the products, parts of which had been manufactured in the small-scale workshops. These centers also provided the small-scale industry with raw materials and implements. The rapid growth of this kind of industry, so well adapted to the Indonesian way of life, had been most encouraging. The advantages were to harmonize with the native's feeling of obligation toward his fellow villagers, and toward his village.

The interesting fact was discovered that the good quality of the products which the villagers felt obliged to give to their fellow villagers disappeared as soon as the small-scale workers had to produce for outsiders, toward whom no obligation of mutual assistance existed. The shrewd middleman, who, by taking advantage of the Javanese desire for credit, tried to make the latter dependent on him, failed either in obtaining products of good quality or in getting delivery of the goods at the time agreed upon. This result, naturally, was very undesirable. However, when the finishing plant of an industrial center, even though at times situated in another village, was managed by workmen who had family ties with the small-scale workers in the surrounding villages, again the workers felt they could not fail the plant, and the high quality which they had heretofore given to their fellow villagers, reappeared.

By means of this industrial development, centers with finishing plants, often financed by middlemen, were capable of competing with the older forms of small-scale industry. At the same time they brought about an appreciable change in the social position of the workers.

In the small-scale industry the obligation to give mutual assistance, or *"sambatan,"* gave birth to a flexible wage-and-gift system, which rose and fell with the variable Indonesian business cycles. Because this system was the perfect expression of the Indonesian conception of just treatment, difficulties with the workers seldom arose in an Indonesian enterprise.

Of the 2,800,000 workers employed in the manufacturing industry, the greatest number—2,500,000—worked in the small-scale industries; 2,400,000 of these were Indonesians, of whom 600,000 were women; the remaining 100,000 were mostly Chinese. Roughly estimated, in the years from 1935 to 1939 some 60,000 workers turned yearly from agricultural production to small-scale industry.

In the small-scale industry there was generally a high percentage of absenteeism. The average working day in a small-scale center of the weaving industry, with some 9,000 active workers, was about 6.4 hours, while, generally speaking, an average worker put in about 800 to 900 hours a year. Wages varied greatly; the people working in the small-scale industry for a middleman, called *"bakoel,"* received incredibly low wages, or from two to five Dutch cents (approximately 1 to 2½ U. S. cents) per hour. Here the money received was more in the nature of supplementary earnings than of real wages. In new industries the wages generally ran from three to eight Dutch cents per hour, while in the centers with finishing plants five to fifteen Dutch cents an hour was paid. This short survey shows clearly that the number of working hours and the low wages had remained the weak point of the small-scale industry, but that at the same time the newer forms of industry were gradually improving them.

The factory industry, sometimes working in close coöperation with small-scale enterprise, sometimes even with cottage industry, was capitalistic in character. The number of workers in these factories ranged from 20 to 5,000, and the development of these industries, as well as of small-scale industry, showed that a turning point had been reached some time in the period of economic expansion from 1935 to 1939. The larger of these factories were generally overseas factories, or were financed by managing agents.

Overseas factories are always subsidiaries of a foreign concern. Typical examples are the Goodyear Tire factory, the Heinekens brewery, the British-American tobacco industry, the Unilever soap industry, the General Motors plant, etc. The fact that these factories enjoy the benefits of intensive research conducted in the country of origin makes them a valuable addition to the economy of the more backward countries, which are enabled, in this manner, to rely upon the experiences and the new developments carried on so intensively in the highly industrialized countries.

The managing agency presents a much less attractive picture. Some importers who had become more or less superfluous because of the increased domestic production of previously imported articles, discovered that the newly established factories were eager to make use of their connections and experience as sellers. Consequently, a former importer often became the managing agent of such a factory and obtained exclusive rights for the sale of its products, thus forcing the manufacturer into a subordinate position.

In the factory industry in the Netherlands Indies, as in other countries, manual labor had been replaced in part by machines. However, the development of the machine had not been very rapid here, when compared with other countries, because the rate at which a factory can be profitably mechanized depends to a large extent on the price paid for the available labor. A comparison between the price and the productive power of manual labor, and the price and the productive power of the machine is, therefore, necessary, and up to now the use of manual labor for certain phases of a manufacturing process have often appeared to be the most profitable.

This situation certainly influenced the development of a modern factory industry, but there was, nevertheless, a decided increase in the mechanization of even small-scale factories. This was shown by a survey held in 1939 covering 52 branches of industry with 5,469 factories employing 324,210 workers; all these factories worked independently of the argicultural or mining estates. Sugar, tea, and rubber factories were not covered by this survey.

The year 1940 saw the establishment of about 500 new factories which engaged 23,000 new employees. On the basis of the available figures, it may be estimated that during the period 1939 to 1940 about 50,000 new factory workers were assimilated by the entire factory industry in the Indies. Tables 3 and 4 give data regarding the expansion of the factory industry.

Neither the factory industry nor the small-scale industry is centralized. The former was made up, for the greater part, of relatively small factories spread over the country and generally situated near their chief source of supply, or in the center of their market area. This was an efficient setup because of the geographical shape of Java and because of high transportation costs—two to four cents per long ton against an approximate rate of one cent in the United States.

TABLE 3

Number of Factories and Workers, and Amount of Production in the Leading Industries of the Netherlands Indies, 1939 and 1940

Type of industry	Number of factories		Number of workers		Production in 1939	Production in 1940
	Dec. 31, 1939	Dec. 31, 1940	Dec. 31, 1939	Dec. 31, 1940		
Canning	5	6	226	315	988,000 kgs.	1,418,000 kg.
Starch	220	220	13,872	7,566	187,138 tons	223,742 tons
Rice mills	1,040	1,137	26,618	28,560	1,114,825 tons	1,202,826 tons
Vegetable oil and margarine	105	113	6,788	7,107	202,530 tons	220,538 tons
Palm oil	31	31	5,102	3,950	298,290 tons	236,651 tons
Soap	13	14	1,743	1,864	15,307 tons	16,588 tons
Fireworks	20	21	3,699	1,936	1,256 billion pcs.	739 billion pcs.
Rubber articles	11	14	1,403	3,371	858 tons	2,200 tons
Sawmills	105	103	5,183	3,957	130,932 tons	118,917 tons
Furniture	10	12	397	813	436 tons	943 tons
Wooden barrels and cases	19	27	1,963	2,147	2,229,000 pcs.	2,605,000 pcs.
Other wood products	10	9	206	166	773 tons	231 tons
Printing	268	284	14,309	15,162	16,227 tons	18,000 tons approx.
Tanning	20	25	1,302	1,293	594,000 hides	1,185,000 hides
Weaving	131	200	37,342	50,168	36,618,000 meters	81,823,000 meters
Shoes	12	10	1,329	2,519	610,000 prs.	3,196,000 prs.
Public electricity	115	126	8,407	9,274	325,200,000 k.w.h.	969,600,000 k.w.h.
Tiles	14	21	1,702	2,497	18,700,000 pcs.	28,420,000 pcs.
Glass containers	5	6	829	1,617	3,455,000 pcs.	17,674,000 pcs.
Iron castings	5	5	439	392	3,118 tons	3,000 tons (approx.)
Tin-plate works	28	28	1,497	1,705	21,300,000 tins	31,500,000 tins
Steel barrels	5	6	251	463	479,000 pcs.	589,000 pcs.
Agriculture machinery	61	68	9,005	10,559	14,691 tons	30,062 tons
Repair shops, machinery	213	282	13,726	17,812	1,279 tons steel	
Repair shops, electrical	10	163	606	1,569	385.7 ton metal	
Shipbuilding and repair	12	16	4,303	7,268	4,037 ton metal	
Wagon building	23	23	6,993	5,895	5,537 ton metal	
Automobiles, repair and assembly	27	40	1,228	3,346	38 ton metal	
Totals	2,538	3,010	170,468	193,291		

In encouraging industry, the Netherlands Government attempted to create types that would fit in well with the national pattern, while, of course, some exceptions were made with respect to defense industry. Because the Netherlands Indies do not possess good iron ores or hard coal suitable for blast furnaces, a heavy industry does not fit so

TABLE 4

NUMBER OF FACTORIES AND WORKERS ON THE ISLAND OF JAVA AND ON OTHER ISLANDS OF THE NETHERLANDS INDIES, 1940

Industry	Factories on Java	Factories on other islands	Number of workers	Average per factory
Foodstuffs......................	1,002	605	43,068*	27
Beverages......................	177	163	5,005	21
Tobacco.......................	115	2	53,547	464
Vegetable oil, margarine, etc......	824	254	21,850*	20
Chemicals.....................	61	11	6,038	82
Rubber articles.................	10	4	3,371	240
Wood products.................	81	70	7,083	52
Printing, binding, etc............	251	59	15,842	51
Tanning.......................	23	2	1,583	63
Textiles.......................	231	8	50,168*	210
Clothing, shoes.................	24	1	7,624	30
Gas and electric................	518	212	11,232	154
Earthenware, glass..............	100	23	12,371	102
Metal.	34	12	3,710	81
Repair shops and shipbuilding....	476	116	46,449	78
Total......................	3,927	1,542	228,941	42

* Incomplete. Not available from certain branches. The total is, therefore, greater than these figures would indicate.

well into the pattern. Most of the newer factories produced consumers' goods for the domestic market. Table 5 gives information regarding the types of industry, the number of factories, the production and the percentage of production used for home consumption.

There has been much discussion of the usefulness of the Javanese worker in modern industry. This question has been answered by many years of experience, and it is encouraging. The Javanese worker is conscientious, and when engaged in light, routine work his ability is certainly not less than that of the Western laborer. However, heavy work is not the Javanese worker's best asset. He did an excellent job in the manufacture of bicycle tires, but was less skillful in producing truck tires. It was also feared that absenteeism would be very prevalent among the Javanese workers. This fortunately proved to have been less than had been expected, although it was certainly higher

TABLE 5

NUMBER OF FACTORIES, THE AMOUNT OF THEIR PRODUCTION, AND THE APPROXIMATE PERCENTAGE USED FOR HOME CONSUMPTION IN THE CHIEF INDUSTRIES OF THE NETHERLANDS INDIES, 1939

Industry	Number of factories	Production 1939, metric tons	Approximate percentage, home consumption
Sugar factories...............	138	1,500,000	25
Rice mills....................	1,137	1,200,000	90
Tea factories.................	273	120,881	30
Rubber remilling factories......	193	421,000	3
Tapioca factories.............	220	223,000	137
Fiber factories...............	31	108,000	0
Coffee hulling factories........	89	120,000	50
Palm oil factories.............	31	250,000	10
Vegetable oil factories.........	113	263,178	70
Etheric oil factories...........	100	5,193	5
Kapok cleaning...............	213	18,000	0
Saw mills....................	103	118,000*	90
Quinine factories.............	1	200	10
Tin refineries.................	....	14,000	1
Petroleum refineries...........	....	7,036,348	18
Saltponds and refineries........	....	160,000	100

* In cubic meters.

than in Western factories. As may be seen from table 6 the wages were low, but their exact value should not be judged according to foreign exchange quotations; rough calculations show that the purchasing power of one guilder in the Indies is about equal to that of $2.00 in New York for wages of this kind.

Industrial policy of the Netherlands Government.—It has often been claimed that the industrialization of the Indies was the practical result of the necessity of the times, and it certainly cannot be denied that the tremendous increase in population influenced industrial advancement. However, the primary factors were the substantial increase in agricultural income, and the demand by native farmers for certain goods, and the means by which to acquire such goods. But even when the total income is raised, the purchasing power of the individual farmer must also be strengthened. In order to achieve this, a definite program of irrigation, migration, crop improvement, and

TABLE 6

TOTAL NUMBER OF WORKERS AND WAGES, AND AVERAGE YEARLY INCOME OF
INDUSTRIAL WORKERS IN THE NETHERLANDS INDIES BY
INDUSTRY GROUPS, 1940

Groups	Number of workers Jan. 1, 1941	Estimated average in 1940	Total wages in 1,000 guilders	Wages per year per worker in guilders
1. Preserves, starch ricemills, foodstuffs, soft drinks, vegetable oil, and margarine......	40,918	38,000	7,665	202
2. Alcohol, ice, gas, soap, shoes.	7,665	7,120	2,149	302
3. Rubber, woodwork.........	19,797	18,420	4,461	242
4. Dyes, chemical, zincographic, limestone.................	20,108	18,690	6,524	349
5. Iron, steel, press work, repair and other metal constructions	58,283	54,600	22,734	416
Total.....................	146,771	136,830	43,533	314

the maintenance of a fairly high parity for farm products was carried out. The plantation owners, of course, did not always welcome this increasing share in the parity policy by the native farmer, but the policy adopted by the Netherlands Government was firmly carried through. The whole picture of the growth of industrial production shows that this attitude brought really good results. Meanwhile, it must be remembered that the achievement of these results demanded that various governmental actions be performed.

In order to stimulate the native's desire for certain commodities, successful expositions were organized; these expositions were held in the native schools. The school teachers, with their enthusiastic pupils, were excellent propagandists, and in this manner native industry was stimulated; meanwhile many regulations guided its development, encouraging healthy expansion, and restricting speculative ventures.

The guidance of this ambitious program was the function of a special industrial division created in the Department of Economic Affairs. It was composed of three sections, dealing with industrial policy, industrial research, and industrial field work. This essential socio-economic organization was well adapted to the needs of Indonesian society. It did not hesitate to intervene in instances where a managing agent seemed to restrict the healthy development of the industry he represented, or where capitalistic industry, by price-cutting, tried to wipe out the desirable small-scale industry, or government legislation established production quotas, and the factories were legally bound to licensing systems.

In conjunction with the section for industrial field work, regular reports on market prices of important raw materials and by-products were published, and the industrial division of the Department of Economic Affairs acted in an advisory capacity for the government on such questions as the granting of exemption from import duties, the establishment of quotas, and the setting of dates when part of the managing functions of newly established factories were to be allotted to Indonesians. Close contact was also maintained with the institutions for scientific industrial research, which had been established to study both the economic and technological problems of the various industries. This important section was subdivided into the following four branches:

1. Laboratory for chemical research
2. Laboratory for testing materials
3. Central bureau for technical research
4. Bureau for economic research.

Although large-scale industry may sometimes need some specific advice, it is clear that its research facilities and experience are generally sufficient, especially in the instance of overseas factories. However, the small- and medium-sized plants depend principally on the Government Information Service. At the same time the infant national industry was assisted by advice in its difficult struggle against foreign competition, and care has always been taken that only those industries should be advised and encouraged which were considered nationally beneficial.

Conclusion and prospects.—In Indonesian industry the village commodity production had evolved, in former days, into a small-scale industry. This native industry brought forth not only skilled laborers, but also men who proved themselves able managers capable of taking over many of the posts formerly held by Westerners. This development forced the latter to specialize in hitherto unknown or more complicated forms of manufacture, and gave a new impulse to the pace of industrial development.

In former years the existing industry had been chiefly connected with agriculture and exports, but since 1935 the evolution had been toward the production of more and more consumers' goods for home use. Some figures are shown in table 5 which represent the industries connected with the large estates, and there appears to be a possibility of having the exported materials, which up to the invasion had undergone partial processing, treated still further. In this way the bulk of the export goods would be reduced, whereas the value of the same quantity of goods would increase. The degree to which these processing industries can be developed after the war depends largely upon the requirements of the consuming countries, although a large field of industrial development is not probable. However, much more can be expected from the processing of industrial by-products. Up to 1941, the residue from molasses was for the greater part exported (200,000 tons annually) without any kind of processing locally, and no attempts were made to utilize bran, the by-product of the rice industry, and mountains of it were burned every year.

The development of heavy industries in the Indies has been hampered by a lack of iron ore and coal of good quality. Forestry and the manufacture of wood products offer somewhat better possibilities. Unfortunately, however, the extremely varied types of wood, and the high cost of transportation have handicapped the growth of this industry. The fishing, dairy, and fruit-canning industries have no great possibilities because of the absence of supplies. There are not many minerals—petroleum production is about 3 per cent of the world total; coal production is 2,000,000 tons a year, but coal is soft grade. This situation accounts for the unfortunate fact that while tin and bauxite deposits are important, and these ores can be mined on a competitive basis, the Netherlands Indies will continue to import finished and manufactured tin and aluminum articles inasmuch as there is little possibility of promoting local industries based on these raw materials.

This brief survey shows that the real wealth of the Indies lies principally in the soil and climate, which are especially suitable for agricultural activities. Agricultural production is the cornerstone of any economic development in the Indies. The great wealth of the fertile islands, the favorable climate, the excellent geographical situation on the sea lanes of the world and the 70,000,000 inhabitants, before the war, of which 62 per cent were agricultural workers, are the basic factors which a government must consider in formulating any long-range program for bringing prosperity to the Indies. Thus, in the first place, every effort was made to promote agricultural production for export, and this was one of the most effective means of attaining a certain degree of prosperity.

However, the rate of exchange for imported consumers' goods had become increasingly unfavorable since 1914—for instance, a tin of imported salmon could be obtained in 1913 for the equivalent of two pounds of copra; in 1939 this price had risen to six pounds. The only remedy for this problem seemed to be a greater self-sufficiency in the production of consumers' goods. The program of industrial development and the Netherlands Government industrial policy were based on these circumstances. However, today it is to be expected that not only will the pace of industrial development be adversely influenced by the unfortunate rate of exchange, but it is more than likely that the strides made in the synthetic-products field will mean a decrease in Indonesian exports. The development of industry—necessarily a consumers'-goods industry—will become more important.

In the future, however, new raw materials will be needed for the world markets, and the Netherlands Indies will then have the chance to produce new export products. The Indies have survived many such changes. The development of synthetic dyestuffs killed the indigo industry; synthetic resins drove 70 per cent of the Indonesian natural gums from the market, but, at the same time, entirely new products, for instance, palm oil and rubber, came into existence. Changes of this nature always cause depressions which, however, could be mitigated by a sound consumers'-goods industry. For this reason it is vital to expand such an industry as rapidly as possible, and this has been the goal of the Netherlands Indies Government since 1916.

The first attempts at transplanting large Western industries to the Indies were highly discouraging, chiefly because the transplanted industries were brought into a country not yet ready for them. The overseas factories generally thrived within a short time, but many disappointments were suffered by the entrepreneurs of other factories. Better results were derived from stimulating small-scale industries which, when well established, could be rebuilt along Western lines.

The program of industrialization to be followed by the Netherlands Government in later years, consequently, may be summarized as follows:

1. Rapid expansion of elementary education.
2. General and individual increase in agricultural production, with resulting increase in the purchasing power of the native farmer.
3. Gradual absorption of native farmers into small-scale industries, operated by and for the Indonesians.
4. Organization of small-scale industrial workers into production centers with finishing and sales divisions.
5. Development of factories organized by Westerners, as well as by Indonesian entrepreneurs.

The encouragement and development of Indonesian leadership to attain the fifth stage of industrialization have been, and will again become, after the war, an integral part of the Indies Government policy, and it is the general hope that more and more Indonesians will be able to take over the larger factories and to derive the benefits of a well-balanced relationship with local consumption, as well as with local customs. Such an industry could then become a real and vital part of this new development in the Indonesian way of life.

CHAPTER XXV

Dutch West Indies: Curaçao and Surinam

BY PHILIP HANSON HISS

THE NETHERLANDS WEST INDIES is the name given to all present-day Netherlands territories in the Western Hemisphere. For purposes of administration, however, the Netherlands West Indies is divided into the territories of Curaçao and Surinam, each with a separate governor, advisory council (*raad*), and legislative assembly (*staten*). The seat of government for the territory of Curaçao is Willemstad, on the island of Curaçao, and for Surinam, Paramaribo.

The territory of Curaçao, with an area of 384.1 square miles and a population, on July 1, 1943, of 119,585, is composed of six main islands: Curaçao, Aruba, Bonaire, St. Martin (St. Maarten), Saba, and St. Eustatius, and the two small, barren, and almost uninhabited islets of Klein Curaçao and Klein Bonaire. The six islands are further divided both geographically and administratively into two groups; the Leeward Islands (Benedenwindsche Eilanden) and the Windward Islands (Bovenwindsche Eilanden). The Leeward group, or the ABC Islands, as they are more popularly called, are Curaçao, (area 172.5 sq. m. and population 68,217), Aruba (a. 69.9 sq. m. and p. 31,522), and Bonaire (a. 111.9 sq. m. and p. 5,556). The Windward group are St. Martin (a. 13.2 sq. m. and p. 1,938), Saba (a. 4.8 sq. m. and p. 1,146), and St. Eustatius (a. 11.8 sq. m. and p. 1,213). The Leeward Islands, lying twenty to sixty miles off the north coast of Venezuela, make up more than 90 per cent of the total area of the territory and approxi-

mately 96 per cent of the population. The comparative insignificance
of the Windward Islands is apparent. They lie within sight of one
another, approximately five hundred miles to the east and north of
the ABC group and midway between the Virgin Islands and Antigua, though their nearest neighbors are the British islands of An-
guilla and St. Kitts, and French St. Barts.

Surinam, geographically speaking, does not form a part of the
West Indies, but historically it does, for both areas were developed
simultaneously by the Dutch West India Company. It lies on the
northeast coast of South America between 2° and 6° north latitude
and 54° and 58° west longitude, and is bounded by British Guiana
on the west, by Brazil on the south, by French Guiana on the east,
and by the Atlantic Ocean on the north. It has an area officially estimated as 55,143 square miles, though the boundary between Surinam
and British Guiana has never been definitely settled, and on December 31, 1941, it had a population of 183,730.

The recent tendency, not only in the Netherlands, but in Great
Britain and France as well, has been to discount the importance of the
West Indies and to stress the wealth and glamor of the East Indies.
The education of government officials in the Netherlands is directed
almost exclusively toward the administration of the East Indies, and
many Dutchmen have little or no knowledge of the West Indies
territories. It is therefore interesting to recall that from the time of
their discovery by Columbus until barely 150 years ago—a period
when the East Indies were already well known—the West Indies were
considered to be the most important and the richest colonies in the
world. There were several reasons for this. The West Indies were far
more accessible to Europe; at a time when a trip to the West Indies
was a matter of months, a similar trip to the Far East could be measured in years. During this period, sugar was in great demand in
Europe and brought a high price, and the West Indies islands were
ideal for sugar plantations. The population of the West Indies—composed almost exclusively of Europeans and African slaves—provided
an outlet for European manufactured goods, which were in small demand in the East Indies; consequently, many goods that had to be

paid for with gold in the East could be purchased by trade with a double profit to both the merchants and the ship owners. Finally, the trade in slaves was one of the most profitable businesses and was the basis for many fortunes, but as the East Indies already had an abundant labor supply, it was naturally not a market for slaves.

Following the discovery of the West Indies by Columbus on October 12, 1492, the Greater Antilles were quickly colonized by the Spaniards, whose treatment of the indigenous Indian population—the Ciboney and the Arawaks—resulted within a few years in their virtual extinction from wars, epidemics, unaccustomed labor in the mines that the Spaniards soon opened, and mass suicide. As early as 1502 the Spaniards were forced to import slaves. In the same year the cultivation of sugar cane had been introduced. Cattle had already been brought by the earliest settlers. All of these factors were to be of immense future importance.

Spanish claims to the entire new world by right of prior discovery remained practically undisputed for the first fifty years for the reason that Spain was all-powerful on land and sea. The Spaniards swept on from the Greater Antilles into Mexico and Peru, and an apparently endless stream of treasure flowed back to Spain in the heavily ladened galleons. Such wealth was certain to arouse the envy of the other maritime nations, which quite naturally refused to recognize Spain's claims to undisputed sovereignty over such a vast territory; from the middle of the sixteenth century, Spain was forced to defend her empire from the encroachment of the British, French, and Dutch.

It has already been stated that the Greater Antilles were immediately colonized, but this was not true of the many islands of the Lesser Antilles, for the reasons that the smaller islands did not promise the same wealth of gold; that the fierce Caribs, unlike the Ciboney and the Arawaks, provided unexpected opposition; that many of the islands lacked water; and that there were not enough men and ships to go everywhere at once. Furthermore, when the exodus to the continent began in 1519, even the Greater Antilles were drained of manpower, leaving the proportion of whites to blacks precariously small.

The Lesser Antilles probably seemed of minor importance to the

Spaniards, and the fact that they were not defended would have had little significance had the power of Spain not been seriously weakened during the latter part of the sixteenth century and the opening years

NETHERLANDS WEST INDIES

of the seventeenth century by almost continual conflict in Europe. While the "Sea Beggars" of the United Provinces waged successful warfare against Spanish shipping in the English Channel, Sir Francis Drake harassed the Spaniards in the Caribbean, but it was not until 1625 that Richelieu came to power in France and definitely shifted the balance of power to the side of Great Britain and the United Provinces by his enmity to Philip II.

The year 1625 also marks the beginning of the colonization of the Lesser Antilles by the British, French, and Dutch—a mass migration from Europe that by 1642 had brought the white population of the Lesser Antilles to the astonishing total of 100,000. When it was discovered that white labor was unsuited to the cultivation of cane, the white population was quickly reduced from this peak, and the entire Caribbean area was flooded with disappointed men, many of whom were desperate from hunger. They joined with the flotsam left in the wake of the Spanish conquistadores and with castaways to form the nucleus of bands of buccaneers, which later became such a menace to the peaceful development of the West Indies islands and the adjacent continental areas.

Many of the British and French colonists were seeking new homes with better living conditions and greater freedom of religious expression—a land of broader opportunities. They brought their wives with them and settled down to a life of agriculture. The Dutch, however, came as traders and middlemen. They had no real desire to found new homes or even an empire—they had already fought for freedom and tolerance in Europe, and won—but they were seeking an outlet for their growing trade, and a use for their seapower which had increased enormously during their long struggle with Spain. There was also the consideration of salt, which the Dutch needed badly for their herring industry, for they had been cut off from the Portuguese salt pans at the end of the sixteenth century at the time that Portugal was conquered by Spain. Even before 1625, Dutch ships had visited the salt pans of St. Martin and Bonaire.

Curaçao was taken from the Spaniards without opposition in August, 1634, by a Dutch expedition under Johannes van Welbeck. The island had originally been discovered by Alonzo de Ojeda in 1499 and had been colonized in 1527. By this simple move, the Dutch found themselves in possession of one of the finest harbors in the West Indies, from which they could both build up their trade and harass the Spaniards. During the next two years they fortified the island and occupied the neighboring islands of Aruba and Bonaire.

St. Eustatius was colonized by Zeelanders in 1632, but it is difficult to understand why, as it has no natural harbor, and its water supply is so uncertain that it is doubtful whether it had any permanent Indian population. Saba, which was colonized from St. Eustatius in 1640, is also without a harbor, but it may have been chosen because its precipitous slopes made it easily defensible. St. Martin, on the contrary, was valuable because of its salt pans and its roadstead. It was colonized jointly by the Dutch and the French in 1648, under a treaty of division, and for this reason was less valuable to the Dutch than if it had been their sole possession. The superior harbor of St. Thomas in the Virgin Islands, less than a hundred miles away, and at that time uncolonized, was not selected because the proximity of the Spaniards on Puerto Rico made the island unsafe. It was, in fact, a no-man's-land, untenable by either side. The Dutch, therefore, were obliged to develop the meager natural advantages of St. Eustatius as best they might, and, as may be seen later, they were so successful that St. Eustatius earned the epithet, "The Golden Rock," and brought down upon itself the wrath of the British.

As more and more Dutch merchants found their way to the Western Hemisphere, there was increasing insistence in the United Provinces that a Dutch West India Company, patterned after the East India Company, be founded, for it was believed that a single large company in which all of the United Provinces shared would be more profitable than to have individual merchants competing one against the other. The States-General, on June 3, 1621, granted the Company a broad charter giving it the right to exploit all territories in the Western Hemisphere and on the west coast of Africa, to conscript armies and navies, and to enforce its rights by arms; in fact, it was to enjoy all of the rights of sovereignty. The States-General was to supply the Company with troops, and, in event of war, with ships; and it was to have freedom of imports. Furthermore, the Company was to receive a subsidy of a million guilders for which the United Provinces were to be shareholders for half of that amount.

The West India Company started out promisingly enough. In 1628 a Dutch fleet under Admiral Hein captured nine Spanish merchant ships and four treasure galleons with booty amounting to nearly fifteen million guilders, and in the next two decades the Company established colonies in the West Indies, Brazil, and North America, and so many slave factories were captured from the Portuguese on the west coast of Africa that for a while the Dutch enjoyed a virtual monopoly of the slave trade. This was the period of greatest prosperity for the West India Company, but it was not to last long. By 1654 the Dutch had been driven entirely out of Brazil, and the Portuguese had recaptured many of the slave factories in Africa. The expense of maintaining huge fleets was not compensated for by occasional rich prizes, and colonies had to be defended by garrisons that had to be maintained. Furthermore, Dutch successes resulted in the inevitable jealousy of the British and the French and brought about the Anglo-Dutch wars of 1652 to 1654, 1665 to 1667, and 1672 to 1674, and, in spite of the fact that the West India Company was supposed to enjoy a monopoly, individual Dutch merchants continued to trade in both slaves and goods.

Finally, New Amsterdam (now New York) and the colony of New Netherlands were forced to surrender to the British on September 8, 1664, without a fight, and though Surinam was captured by a Dutch fleet during the second Anglo-Dutch War and was retained under the terms of the Treaty of Breda, it reverted to the province of Zeeland, which had sent out the expedition, and not to the West India Company. In 1675 the first Dutch West India Company was dissolved, and in the same year a second company was founded.

After struggling for fifteen years, the province of Zeeland decided that the problems of garrisoning Surinam were too great and sold it to the second Dutch West India Company, which, in turn, sold a one-third interest in the colony to the City of Amsterdam and a second one-third interest to the Van Aerssen family. The Chartered Society of Surinam (*Geoctroyeerde Societeit van Suriname*), was formed to administer the colony, and in 1683 Cornelis van Aerssen van Sommelsdijk was sent to Surinam as governor.

When Sommelsdijk arrived in Paramaribo, the city consisted of Fort Zeelandia and "only twenty-seven dwellings, more than half of which were grog shops." Colonization was confined to a small area within the protection of the fort. Sommelsdijk immediately sent out several expeditions and decisively defeated the Indians, who were then glad to make a treaty of peace in return for a guarantee of their liberty. He cleared more land and extended the area of protection, he set the soldiers to work digging canals, and he established courts and encouraged immigration. His strong methods, however, were distasteful to many, the soldiers in particular, many of whom had led an easy life in the carefree days before his governorship. On June 17, 1688, Sommelsdijk was killed by mutineers, but the reforms that he had made remained, and he had succeeded in putting the colony on a firm foundation.

The experienced Portuguese-Jewish agriculturists, who had come to Surinam from Brazil in 1666, formed a nucleus around which a sound agricultural economy now was built up, for Surinam, unlike the other Dutch colonies, sought profit in the commodities of trade as well as in trade itself. The earliest traders had planted tobacco, and the planting of sugar—the crop which had replaced the imagined gold of the Spaniards as the true source of wealth in the West Indies—had been started under Willoughby.

Unfortunately, the vagaries of European politics continued to control the destinies of the New World. The Dutch were able to repulse an attack by the French under Admiral Du Casse in 1689, but a second attack by Cassard in 1712 was more successful and almost brought about the ruin of the colony. Cassard's first demands of surrender were met by refusal, but when a part of his fleet slipped by the Fortress Zeelandia during the night and sacked many of the plantations further up the river, the importunities of the plantation owners, who had fled for their lives, were added to those of the inhabitants of Paramaribo, who had good reason to believe that Cassard would keep his word to bombard the city if they did not accede to his demands. With so much pressure brought to bear on him, and with no adequate means of defense, the Governor was forced to capitulate, and the colony was ransomed for 747,350 florins, of which the largest part had to be paid in goods and slaves.

The financial loss, in itself, was a severe blow to the colony, but far more serious was the fact that many of the Negro slaves who had been left behind when their masters fled at the appearance of the French fleet, joined the French in burning the plantation houses, then escaped to the jungle.

Slave insurrections were probably inevitable in a country where slaves far outnumbered freemen, and it is more correct to describe Cassard's attack as the occasion for revolt rather than as its cause. The first general uprising actually did not occur until 1730, eighteen years later, but from this time until 1786, the outlying plantations were never free from fear of attack.

Far too much has been said about the ill treatment of slaves in Surinam, and it is popular to recite the tortures that were inflicted by cruel and lascivious masters. There were undoubtedly instances of cruelty, but these have been seized on and used to point conclusions that are far from being true. It is a question that has been bitterly debated on both sides, but it is necessary to point out that, as there were never enough slaves in Surinam to meet the demand, and as slaves brought a high price (the Government paid an indemnity of 300 florins for each slave emancipated in 1863) any planter who resorted to such methods indulged his passions at the expense of his purse, a thing abhorrent to the shrewd traders and planters. Instances of cruelty were largely traceable to absentee ownership.

Disease contributed to the high death rate among plantation slaves, and infant mortality was obviously the fault of carelessness on the part of Negro mothers and occurred in spite of the precautions taken by the planters. Antislavery proponents in British Guiana, in spite of all their efforts, were unable to reduce slave death rates, when they were put in charge of estates.

As the insurrections gathered momentum, many of the outlying plantations were abandoned, and there was a gradual withdrawal toward the protection of Paramaribo or the forts. The colonists, now mortally afraid, resorted to excesses in the hope that they would act as a deterrent to the rebels, but the result might have been antici-pated—excesses on one side led to excesses on the other. In the end, the Government was forced to sue for peace on humiliating terms:

the granting of complete freedom to the former slaves and the payment of an annual tribute to the Negro chiefs. Peace was made in this way with the Saramacca and Auca Negroes, and although tribal success set the example for further insurrections, these were put down by a regiment of manumitted slaves, called Rangers, who were given their freedom in exchange for fighting, and by the Scots Brigade, which was sent from Holland by the Stadholder at the request of the colonists. The Scots Brigade was able to return to Europe in 1777, and during the next decade the last shreds of resistance were gradually overcome, but already the stage was being set in Europe and the West Indies for difficulties of quite a different nature. But first it is necessary to turn back to Curaçao.

Because of the strength of its defenses, the development of Curaçao proceeded in an orderly fashion. It became a vast entrepôt for goods and slaves destined for Santo Domingo and the northern coast of South America and, in turn, for quantities of dye-wood, hides, and sugar that were shipped to Europe. The island itself was too dry to be very productive, but its plantations raised a moderate amount of sugar, cotton, tobacco, millet, and indigo, and a comparatively small amount of orange peel was exported for the manufacture of the famed Curaçao liqueur. The wealth of Curaçao, however, lay in its commerce in goods and slaves.

Portuguese Jews were allowed to come to Curaçao from Brazil on the condition that they engage in agriculture, but the indications are that they almost immediately turned to trade in which they attained a preëminent position that was not seriously challenged until the development of the oil industry by foreign capital. Great liberalism was shown in the charter granted to the Jews and they, in turn, proved to be among Curaçao's most valuable citizens.

Bonaire remained a single large government plantation until 1863, and the population of Aruba continued to raise cattle until the discovery of gold on the island in the nineteenth century.

In 1775 the American Revolution cast its shadow across the Caribbean Sea. It brought with it a period of unequaled prosperity for St. Eustatius and Curaçao, but this prosperity also contained the seeds of disaster. The Dutch merchants were alive to the opportunities for profit in the struggle between Great Britain and her revolting colonies, but their sympathies were also aroused by the parallel between the American Revolution and their own long struggle for freedom against Spain, and they were not without a desire for revenge against the British who often were arrogant in their demands.

St. Eustatius played a leading role as a transshipment port for supplies destined for the rebels. American agents, British and French merchants, and sailors of all nations crowded the island, and hundreds of ships lay in the roadstead waiting their turn to discharge or load their cargoes. The warehouses were full to overflowing, and less perishable goods were piled high on the beach.

The British were not blind to what was happening, for British St. Kitts is within sight of St. Eustatius, and British merchants came to the island as freely as men of other nationalities; in fact, many were not averse to selling goods to the Americans. British anger, however, was tempered by an unwillingness to goad the Dutch into a declaration of war at a time when British arms were already confronted by a revolution on the one hand and the French on the other, but they eagerly seized an opportunity to protest a salute fired, on the order of Governor de Graaff of St. Eustatius, by Fort Oranje to the brig "Andrew Doria," which entered the roadstead flying the flag of the American rebels. The British received scant satisfaction from Governor de Graaff and little more from the States-General, who turned a polite but deaf ear to all demands that trade with North America cease. The States-General claimed to be unable to stop this trade, and the merchants made such an enormous profit that it was possible to lose two out of three ships in running the British blockade and still make money. There was something gallant in the Dutch attitude of defiance.

By 1780 the British realized that it was useless to continue diplomatic negotiations, and on December 20th they declared war on the United Provinces. An order was sent by a fast ship to Admiral Rodney, who was already in the West Indies, and on February 3, 1781, he appeared in the St. Eustatius roadstead and demanded the surrender of the island. When he saw the goods that overflowed from the warehouses onto the beach, Rodney was amazed and declared that had it not been for St. Eustatius the American Revolution could not have lived. All goods were confiscated and thirty-four fully laden ships were dispatched to England and others were sent to the neighboring British islands, after which the remaining goods were sold at a huge auction that netted a sum equivalent to $15,000,000 at the present time. The Lower Town and the harbor installations were then destroyed. The British had had their revenge; St. Eustatius was ruined. But they were to profit little from their booty; all the ships dispatched to England were captured by the French fleet or by American privateers, and, on November 26th, the French surprised the British on St. Eustatius and captured the island from them. Saba, St. Martin, and the Netherlands colonies of Berbice, Demerara, and Essequibo fell to the British during the war, but, together with St. Eustatius, they were all returned in 1783 under the terms of the treaties of Paris and Versailles, which ended the American Revolution.

With the beginning of the Napoleonic Wars in 1803, the pattern of conquest was repeated. Surinam surrendered to the British in 1804, Curaçao was captured in 1807, and St. Eustatius surrendered in 1810. In 1806 Louis Bonaparte became King of Holland, but in 1810 he abdicated, and Napoleon annexed Holland to the French Empire. In 1813 Holland revolted, and William of Orange was proclaimed King as William I. Finally, in 1814, Napoleon abdicated, and the *opéra bouffe* of European politics had temporarily run out of new situations except for a brief flurry during "the Hundred Days." The Treaty of Paris, May 30, 1814, restored Curaçao, St. Eustatius, and Surinam to the Netherlands—though they were not actually transferred to the Dutch until 1816—but later in the year Demerara, Berbice, and Essequibo were ceded to Great Britain at the London Convention, and in 1831 they were joined to form the colony of British Guiana. Since these two treaties, there has been very little change in the political geography of the West Indies, a fact partly attributable to the promulgation of the Monroe Doctrine by the United States in 1823, and partly to other unpredictable forces which would tend to push the Dutch West Indies from the forefront of history into a quiet backwater: beet sugar was to compete with cane, the steamship was to supersede the sailing ship and to reduce the sailing time between Europe and the East, the opening of the Suez Canal in 1869 was to make the East even more accessible, and the huge reservoir of cheap labor in the East Indies, Malaya, and India promised to aid in the development of the natural resources of these countries. Cessation of the slave trade with Africa in 1819 and the emancipation of slaves in the British, French, and Dutch colonies in 1834, 1848, and 1863 not only destroyed a profitable trade but resulted in the abandonment of many plantations which had been heavily mortgaged and the neglect of others because of the scarcity of labor.

The year 1816 found the inhabitants of Curaçao virtually in a state of starvation, the trade of all the colonies had been ruined, and the Government was in a state of utter confusion. Curaçao recovered only slowly from this debacle. Willemstad was made a free port in 1828 in an effort to regain its trade. Very gradually it again became a transshipment port for the Maracaibo Basin of Venezuela, but for years Curaçao was unable to balance its budget and depended on an annual subsidy from the Netherlands. The discovery of phosphate on Curaçao in 1875 and gold on Aruba at an earlier date led to no appreciable improvement. The phosphate was not fully exploited until after the First World War, and the gold proved so unprofitable that it was finally left to be mined by individual Indians and Negroes.

Aruba and Bonaire produced a large part of the world's supply of aloes, but the cash value of the crop was small. Divi-divi pods, used in tanning leather, goatskins, and orange peel were all exported in small quantities, but most of the orange trees were killed by a protracted drought, and the problem of plantation labor was serious, for the Negroes preferred to live a hand-to-mouth existence on small farms rather than to perform any labor reminiscent of slavery. Straw hat weaving was a home industry that engaged a large number of people, but it had never been very profitable.

By the opening years of the First World War, the pendulum of history, which for a century had been swinging away from the West

Indies, hesitated and began to swing back. For years there had been a growing traffic between North and South America in which the Caribbean lands had shared, Spain had been dispossessed of her remaining Caribbean colonies, the growing interest of the United States had brought fresh capital, and the opening of the Panama Canal in 1915 brought the hope that the West Indies would once more become a crossroads of world trade.

The entrance to the harbor at Willemstad was widened and deepened during the years 1915–1918 and coal-bunkering facilities were installed. The advantage of the latter, however, was offset by the fact that similar facilities were also established at Colon. Nevertheless, Curaçao recouped its shipping losses so that by 1929 it had surpassed the harbors of Amsterdam and Southampton in both tonnage and value of merchandise.

The discovery of oil on the shores of Lake Maracaibo in 1914 by the Royal Dutch Shell Company marks the beginning of Curaçao's real prosperity. Lake Maracaibo was handicapped by a shallow bar at its mouth, which made it necessary to locate a deepwater port. There was only a small market for petroleum products in Venezuela, for there were few roads, the country was politically unstable, and the coast was hot and malarial. Curaçao, only a short distance away, suffered none of these defects. It had for years been a transshipment port for Venezuelan goods, it had a magnificent deepwater harbor, it was cooled by the trade winds and was free from malaria, it had a good supply of labor that would have no prejudices against work in a refinery, and the Government was not only stable but was also Dutch. The choice of Curaçao was inevitable, and in 1915 the *Bataafsche Petroleum Maatschappij,* an operating subsidiary of the Royal Dutch Shell Company, began the construction of a refinery at Emmastad on the northern side of the Schottegat, Willemstad's inner harbor. The refinery was completed in 1918 and operation was begun in May of that year, but the refinery did not reach its full capacity until 1922. In 1925 a new operating subsidiary, *Curaçaosche Petroleum Industrie Maatschappij*—the C.P.I.M.—was created and the refinery has been considerably expanded and partly rebuilt since that time.

The Lago Oil and Transport Company, Limited, a subsidiary of the Standard Oil Company of New Jersey, entered the field in 1923, though at that time it was known as the Lago Oil Corporation and was controlled by the British-Mexican Petroleum Company, Limited. The Lago management was eager to find a site for a refinery that was even closer to the oil fields than Curaçao, and St. Nicolaas on the southeast end of the island of Aruba was finally selected. From 1924 to 1929 shipments in transit were made, but in 1928 the company started construction of a large refinery, and in July, 1929, the first refined products were exported, though the refinery was not completed until 1930. Like the C.P.I.M., Lago started to expand almost as soon at it was finished, and by 1935 it had supplanted the C.P.I.M. as the largest refinery in the world.

A third refinery, the *Arend Petroleum Maatschappij*, also a Royal Dutch Shell subsidiary, was started at Druif, Aruba, in 1927 and has been in operation since 1928. Though it is much smaller than either the C.P.I.M. or the Lago refineries, it has large storage facilities, and a part of its business is the transshipment of crude petroleum.

All three refineries are supplied with crude petroleum by shallow-draft tankers of subsidiary companies which take about thirty-six hours for the round-trip, and average ten trips a month from Curaçao and eleven trips a month from Aruba.

Most crude petroleum still comes from Venezuela, but recently a small proportion has been imported from Colombia. In 1938, the last year that petroleum figures were given out, the proportion was about fifteen to one.

Petroleum has greatly changed the Curaçao scene. Within three decades the population of Curaçao has doubled, and in the same period Aruba's population has more than trebled, the standard of living has risen to a higher level than on any other West Indies island, the per capita imports have rocketed, and small agriculture has been almost abandoned.

The history of Surinam in its broad aspects has paralleled that of Curaçao since the Treaty of Paris: recovery was slow for years and then was greatly accelerated. Two disastrous fires in 1821 and 1832 destroyed a large part of the city of Paramaribo, adding greatly to the problems of reconstruction. The emancipation of the slaves was much more severely felt in Surinam than in other West Indies islands. The problem of immigration had been considered ever since the cessation of the slave trade in 1819, and successive experiments were made with Dutch farmers, Madeirans, Chinese, British Indians, and Indonesians.

Large-scale immigration has been attempted only with British Indians and Indonesians. Altogether, 34,024 British Indians came to Surinam between the years 1873 and 1916, when the practice was discontinued, and of these, 22,374 remained. They are hard working and adaptable, but at the expiration of their contracts almost all prefer to leave the plantations for small holdings. Indonesians—for the most part, Javanese—have been, on the whole, the most successful immigrants. A total of 32,020 went to Surinam as contract laborers between 1894 and 1931, of which 24,792 remained, and since that time several shiploads of free immigrants have come to the country. They are the most skilled agriculturists, the hardest workers, though not the quickest, the most patient, and the least obtrusive. Their village communities, run on a communal system of mutual help (*desas*), are as successful in Surinam as in Java.

The Bush Negroes and the Aboriginal Indians, numbering 21,648, live in the jungle. Their only contribution to the economy of the country is a small trade in timber and in other forest products.

When the problems of immigration and a sufficient labor supply have been solved, many of the difficulties that have beset agriculture will vanish. Yet they are by no means the only reasons for Surinam's agricultural failures. The other reasons may be classed under three general headings: natural limitations inherent in the soil, climate, and location; historical reasons; and plant diseases. To these, a fourth reason might be added, which is particularly applicable today—lack of capital.

In spite of the fact that Surinam is essentially an agricultural country, the bauxite industry has been its financial salvation. Bauxite was first discovered in Surinam in 1915, but it was not until 1922 that the first shipments of crude bauxite were made from Moengo by the Surinam Bauxite Company (*Surinaamsche Bauxiet Maatschappij*), a subsidiary of the Aluminum Company of America. In 1925 the construction of a washing and drying plant was begun at Moengo, and it was completed in 1927, despite the combined handicaps of the climate, disease, and the lack of skilled labor. Another plant was built at Paranam, on the Surinam River above Paramaribo, by the Surinam Bauxite Company in 1939, and shipments were begun in 1941. In 1941 the Billiton Tin Company of the Netherlands Indies entered the field and built a plant at Onoribo, close to Paranam, which started production in the summer of 1942. Bauxite exports for 1941 totaled 1,093,764 metric tons, which was nearly double that of 1940, but the combined capacities of the three plants is probably at least twice the 1941 figure. However, bauxite production is at present controlled by available shipping space rather than by plant capacity.

Revenues from bauxite permitted the Surinam Government to balance its budget in 1941 for the first time in many years, whereas the annual subsidy from the Netherlands Government had previously amounted to from two to three million guilders.

The Second World War has already had several noticeable effects on both Curaçao and Surinam: the cost of living has risen enormously, and labor problems have been further complicated by the employment of native labor in the construction of camps, airfields, and roads by the United States Army and the civil services; imports and exports have diminished because of the shipping shortage; with the resulting decrease of essential commodities and loss of markets, many large Netherlands corporations have moved their offices to the West Indies; and although sea communication has been disrupted, the airlines have increased their services.

The Netherlands overseas territories have already been promised greater autonomy and a voice in empire affairs after the war, and it is to be hoped that one of the provisions of the peace will be the abolition of preferential empire tariffs, for, with a greater voice in their own destiny and with freedom of trade, a prosperous future for the Netherlands West Indies seems assured.

Part Seven

The Second World War and After

CHAPTER XXVI

Holland in the War

BY JAMES H. HUIZINGA

IN THE SERIES OF MILITARY AND POLITICAL miscalculations which have characterized Hitler's campaign for the conquest of the world, the Netherlands may claim to occupy an honorable place. There can be little doubt that to Hitler the reaction of this country, first to the military attack on its territory and subsequently to the psychological attacks on the spirit of its people, has been as unexpected as the unyielding attitude of the British after the fall of France. For to Hitler, Holland was not only one of the richest but also one of the ripest plums which, in theory, should have fallen into his lap at the first and slightest touch. Nor was the theory altogether ill-founded. For on the military side, Holland was as ill-prepared as any other democracy. And there were other and far more powerful arguments for the confident belief that the military and political conquest of the Netherlands would prove to be an uncontested victory. Few peoples were less war-minded or had a greater aversion to war than these stolid Dutchmen who had experienced a century of peaceful progress. Surely it was not an unreasonable hope, therefore, that these burghers and merchants, artisans and farmers, intellectuals and laborers would have no stomach for modern war. For even such military forces as the Dutch maintained could hardly be said to be imbued with a warlike spirit.

To put the matter bluntly—as German agents doubtless often put it in their reports to headquarters—the Dutch of all classes were skeptical not only of armed force as an instrument of national policy, but also of its use to good advantage in their own country.

[411]

In addition to what—for want of a better word—one might call the weakness of Holland's innate pacifism, there were other weaknesses which to the planners of the Nazi campaign must have been delightful to behold. Holland, like the other democracies, was no social, political, or economic paradise. For a number of years the structure and the fiber of the nation had been weakened by the same ills which had so direly afflicted the majority of Hitler's other democratic victims. Cut off from a large part of its former markets by the ever-rising trade barriers of the period, unemployment had climbed to dangerously high levels, bringing the usual social and political evils in its wake. Party strife, fed on Holland's intense individualism and aggravated by the system of proportional representation, more often than not appeared to divide the state in a number of sharply opposed factions. In short, the country suffered from a spiritual and physical malaise which could not but encourage the planners across the Rhine in their belief that a state seemingly so divided in body and in spirit, so inclined toward extremes of individualism and self-criticism was bound to collapse at the first imposition of strong dictatorial rule.

No wonder, therefore, that when at last the time to strike had come the directors of the military and political campaigns against the Netherlands were fully confident that the fruit they were about to pick was more than ripe. Even before the final attack, they had softened up their victim still further by an intensive and, in many ways, successful application of the war of nerves and the cultivation of a thoroughly organized German Fifth Column. Twice before the attack was launched, the calm of the Dutch people was subjected to the grueling test of a false alarm, purposely manufactured by the planners of the real invasion that was not to materialize until several months later. Rumor followed rumor, alarm followed alarm until at last the people of the Netherlands, weary of these successive shocks to their calm, took refuge in a spirit of indifferent and jocular skepticism.

If, therefore, the Nazi schemers ever had good reason to believe that their time schedule would be strictly adhered to, it was on the fateful tenth of May, 1940, when with inhuman, clockwork precision the vast machine of German military and political aggression began to roll into the green fields of Holland. One can almost imagine those in the German hierarchy who had been charged with the military subjugation and the political conquest of the Dutch, sitting back in their Berlin offices confidently watching the clock tick off the hours, every one of which was to bring the achievement of a carefully prepared military and political objective. But what consternation there must have been on these very same faces when in the course of this first Friday afternoon reports began to come in indicating that something had gone wrong. Already the clock pointed to 3 P.M. and yet, contrary to all orders, The Hague, seat of the Dutch Government, was still in Dutch hands. Did not the general in charge of the German parachutists have orders to capture the city within twelve hours of the first attack? Did not his instructions provide that a Guard of Honor was to be placed at the palace of Queen Wilhelmina who, of course, could be counted upon to abandon the unequal struggle the moment Holland had vindicated its honor by putting up a token resistance to the advance of the enemy.

These were indeed Berlin's instructions. But instructions are of no avail when those who are charged to carry them out are killed, or rounded up by Dutch infantry forces which, after four days of unceasing struggle, were able to report that the carefully planned parachute attack on The Hague had been finally and completely frustrated. With this failure of the central part of the German military campaign against the Netherlands, all the carefully planned program of the invaders was thrown out of gear. For, as documents found on German officers have proved, these plans were based on the confident assumption that with the conquest of The Hague and the capture of the royal family and the Government, all of which should have taken place on the first day of the invasion, resistance throughout the country would automatically come to an end.

It is true that the Germans had not altogether ruled out the possibility that, in spite of the hoped-for capture of the royal family, resistance might still continue. But even that unlikely eventuality had been carefully provided for. The Queen and her family, so the instructions ran, were to be accorded a Guard of Honor and to be treated with every courtesy. Should they, however, refuse to order an immediate capitulation of the armed forces, then they were to be taken by plane to Berlin, there to be dealt with in accordance with the measure of resistance offered by the Dutch people. How full that measure of resistance proved to be, none know better than the Germans themselves.

And yet, if it is true that the end of the fighting in Holland came considerably later than the enemy had so confidently calculated, it is also true that this end came very much sooner than the world at large had expected.

In fact, nowhere did the early collapse of military resistance come with more shocking unexpectedness than to the people of Holland themselves. What then is the explanation? It is not that Holland's water defenses had been overrated or that insufficient vigor was displayed in holding these natural positions, as proved by the fact that the Germans never succeeded in breaking through the famous water line. If they were nonetheless able to penetrate to the core of the country surrounded by this water line—known as the "Fortress of Holland"—it is only because of their employment of two unexpected weapons: mass parachute attacks and infamous trickery.

As already stated, the first of these unexpected methods did not prove successful in obtaining its immediate objective, the capture of The Hague. It did, however, succeed in upsetting the Dutch General Staff's carefully worked out plans for the distribution of its limited military forces. Suddenly confronted with thousands upon thousands of heavily armed and often disguised parachutists floating down from the skies into the very heart of the country and even into the center of its crowded cities, the General Staff, fully aware of the disorganizing effects of this large-scale enemy infiltration, was forced to throw vitally needed reserves into the task of annihilating the air-borne troops that were striking at the nerve center of the country. In this way, Dutch troops destined to support the defenders of the water line were withdrawn from their original allocations, thus leaving a fateful gap in the distribution of Holland's military forces.

At the same time, the Germans achieved an even more dangerous disorganization of the Dutch defense plans by the trick through which they obtained control of the vital bridge connecting the so-called "Fortress of Holland" with the south, whence French and British troops were expected to come to the aid of the Dutch. The story of this trickery has been told too often to need elaborate restatement. Suffice it to say that German soldiers, disguised in Dutch uniforms, succeeded in overpowering the Dutch soldiers standing guard over the bridge before there was time to throw the switch which would have destroyed the last remaining approach leading from the southern province to the water-encircled "Fortress of Holland."

From that moment, the fate of Holland was sealed as a heavily armed enemy column of some five hundred tanks and other mechanized equipment approaching from the southeast, now only needed time to make good its triumphant entry into the heart of the country. Even so, another four days of furious fighting had to pass before the end. Nor did these three days bring a series of sole German victories. In the north, where another German column tried to cross into the "Fortress of Holland" over the twenty-six mile barrier built to enclose the Zuiderzee, Dutch land and naval forces completely stopped the invaders. In the center of the country where the German forces made a frontal attack on the Dutch lines, the battle swayed to and fro with Dutch forces repeatedly counterattacking and inflicting heavy casualties on the enemy. In Rotterdam, the first and most intensive point of attack by the German air force and the German air troops, the airport continually changed hands as Dutch marines and army detachments time and again drove out the attacking forces only to be met with another and still larger wave of men and planes descending upon them from the skies.

But even though reports that reached headquarters in The Hague were not always tidings of disaster, those members of government who were able to form an overall picture of the situation, soon realized that even three days after the initial attack the military situation had already become hopeless.

It was with the knowledge of this inevitable and rapidly approaching end that on Monday, the thirteenth of May, the Queen and her

Government after many heart searchings finally made the historic decision to leave the country and set up a free Netherlands Government. It was a decision which required even more courage than far-sightedness; there can have been little doubt in the minds of those who had to make this decision that to depart in the hour of their country's gravest ordeal would inevitably expose their motives to painful misunderstanding. That the Queen who for more than forty years had stood by her people would now suddenly, at the moment when they most needed her, leave them to the mercy of their enemies, was something to fill every Dutch heart with bitterness and despair. Besides, would not such action give the enemy every opportunity to use the propaganda that the people of the Netherlands had been deceived and deserted by their rulers? Would it not also irreparably damage the position of the Queen as ruler and leader in the eyes of the outside world?

True statesmanship could not but recognize the weight of these considerations. But true statesmanship in itself is not sufficient to explain the decision of May 13th. True courage played its part, too, not only the courage of facing certain unpopularity, but also the far greater spiritual courage of refusing to accept what to so many in the desperate summer of 1940 seemed the inevitability of an ultimate Axis victory.

Thus, only a few hours before the home country was dealt its final shattering blow by the bombardment of Rotterdam, a handful of Dutch ministers and officials, led by their Queen, arrived in London to settle down to a long and what must then have seemed almost hopeless war for the reconquest of their country. Perhaps the only factor that made it physically possible for them to carry on at this desperate time in their nation's history, was the realization of the vast amount of work to be done.

For waiting on their guidance and their orders were not only Holland's sprawling and teeming territories in the West and the East Indies, but also thousands of hapless Dutch citizens who had escaped from burning Holland in the last forty-eight hours, contingents of soldiers and airmen who had fought their way out, a sizable naval force which had followed the Queen to England to reënter the fight and, finally, hundreds of ships of the merchant marine anchored in countless ports all over the world. To weld this considerable reservoir of energy into a properly functioning war machine was indeed a task which left no time for indulgence in sorrow. Somehow, the immense job had to be done. And somehow, with the wholehearted and generous coöperation of hospitable England, the job was done.

Meanwhile, and as so often happens in history, the ordeal with which the Netherlands Government found itself faced during the first few weeks after its arrival in London proved the wisdom of certain policies of earlier years. In this prewar period, the overseas territories had gradually been encouraged to develop an increasing degree of self-rule and independence from the central government in The Hague. Had a less enlightened policy been followed and had the East and the West Indies not acquired experience in the techniques of government and administration, the task of keeping the badly damaged ship of state on an even keel might well have proved too much for the handful of men who when they had first arrived in London had started to build their administrative machine from the very beginning. As it was, the overseas territories were able to manage their affairs successfully, even though for the moment the central government had been all but disrupted. More than that, it was to a certain degree these overseas territories themselves which, by the power of their energetic example and by throwing themselves wholeheartedly into a continuance of the struggle, inspired the Government in London to still greater exertion.

Immediately on the outbreak of war with Germany on May 10, 1940, both the East and the West Indies had taken forceful steps to guarantee the homeland the fullest measure of support. If it is true that to these outlying regions the German attack had come as an even greater surprise than to Holland itself, it is also true that for once the enemy was completely frustrated in his hopes of exploiting the advantage of surprise. Within a few hours, all German ships in Dutch East Indies ports and the several thousand German nationals residing in the Indies, had been rendered thoroughly harmless by action of the Dutch forces. The German Fifth Column, carefully built up and prepared as it had been in practically every country in the world, was stamped out before it had had even the slightest opportunity to fulfill its task. And thus, once again, Hitler who on attacking the Netherlands had adjured the people that he had only come as their "protector" and that he specifically "guaranteed" the integrity of Holland's overseas domain, found both his military and political calculations thoroughly upset.

But if the energetic attitude of the overseas territories provided at least one source of hope and encouragement to the reorganized Government in London, there was another side to the picture in those early months of struggle which at first caused grave misgivings. How would the backbone of the Kingdom, the common people of Holland itself, react to the direct and deceptive contact with the cunning enemy who now held their lands? If they should fail, if stunned by the soul-shaking experience of the five days of fighting, disillusioned by the departure of their Queen and Government, cajoled by the wiles and the promises of the occupier, they should succumb to defeatism and Petainism, not even the greatest exertions of the Government and the free parts of the Kingdom would be able to save the homeland from ignominy and disaster.

Even after making full allowance for the propaganda wrappings in which news reached the outside world, one dreadful and inescapable fact soon stood out. A considerable part of the population, as yet unable to understand the weighty reasons of state which had induced the Queen to leave her country, seemed to have lost faith in their sovereign. To a Dutchman it was all too clear why estrangement of the people of Holland from their Queen would almost certainly mean utter disaster. He knew that again and again in the history of his country, the intensely individualistic and democratic people of the Netherlands have been able to merge their strong differences only through an upsurge of loyalty to and belief in the House of Orange which through four centuries has helped them to surmount the greatest perils to their national and individual liberties.

Unfortunately, it was not only the Dutch who knew this. The

Germans knew it, too, and hence launched their desperate and temporarily successful efforts to estrange the people of Holland from the Queen who, as the German propaganda put it, "had left them in the lurch." Nor was this the only cunning game played by the Nazis in their early attempts to destroy the moral backbone of the Dutch nation. Knowing that the overwhelming majority of the Dutch had a violent aversion to Naziism and that the Dutch, too, during the long years of Hitler's rule, had read and heard of the atrocities committed by the Nazis upon their own people, they went out of their way to confuse and bewilder the population by instructing their occupying forces to behave in the most exemplary manner. Thus, the Dutch, some of whom had even killed themselves rather than face the known horrors of Nazi persecution and of concentration camps, suddenly found themselves confronted with the spectacle of orderly, disciplined, and extremely well-behaved German troops who molested no one, not even Jews, burned no books, erected no concentration camps and, in fact, avoided unnecessary interference with the ideology, the administration, and the normal day-to-day life of the people.

No wonder the cunning trick worked. No wonder thousands of Dutchmen were forced to confess to themselves that, after all, these Nazis were not half so bad as they had been painted. No wonder the Government monitors in London for a period of some five or six weeks had to record a growing number of indications that the people were settling down to a relatively peaceful and amiable life with their uninvited, but extremely well-behaved guests. And, then, the picture quickly changed.

It is difficult to say exactly what happened or what caused the rapid transition from easy acquiescence to violent resentment. The reason is to be found, no doubt, partly in the innate good sense of the Dutch who, after they had recovered from the first shock and confusion, began to realize that these well-behaved Germans might be trying to lull them to sleep and partly in the rapidly increasing realization that in leaving the country the Queen and her Government had not betrayed the nation but had, in fact, pursued the only policy consistent with honor and wisdom.

But, in addition to all this, some credit for this resurrection of the Dutch spirit must also go to the Nazis themselves. For just as the leopard cannot change his spots, the Nazi cannot conceal his instincts nor the German his psychological stupidity. Thus, while the tragi-comedy of apology, of noninterference, and of exemplary behavior were still being enthusiastically enacted by the German High Command and its troops, the policy-making authority in Berlin committed its first great blunder when it appointed the Austrian arch-traitor, Dr. Arthur Seyss-Inquart, as Reich Commissioner for the occupied Netherlands. If it were the intention—as it clearly was—to flatter and cajole the Dutch into submission, no more unsuitable official could have been appointed than this lawyer who already had become rightly execrated by the people of Holland when, two years earlier, he had betrayed his own country.

Even more fatal to the Germans' hope of success, however, was the manner in which the newly appointed Reich Commissioner made his first public appearance. With the grossest tactlessness imaginable, he chose the ancient Hall of the Knights in The Hague—revered by every child in Holland as the temple of Dutch liberty, where every year in a modest ceremony the Queen opened the session of the States-General—in which to stage a typical Munich circus complete with braying speeches, Wagnerian music, and all the trappings of a Nazi junket.

No doubt, therefore, that the Nazis had to thank only themselves for the rapid revival of Dutch resistance so aptly described by Holland's ace Quisling, Mr. Anton Mussert, when on March 7, 1941, he expressed the following bitter complaint in his weekly *Volk en Vaderland*:

" . . . After the first few weeks of occupation, romancing, in the worst sense of the word, made its appearance. It began with Prince Bernhard carnations, orange-coloured leg bands for chickens and similar exhibits. Soon it took on more serious manifestations such as the destruction of signposts and the cutting of wires and cables. Not to mention the most immoral utterances of mental degeneration in revolutionary times, such as the threat of assassination held out against National-Socialist compatriots."

Since then, Dutch hostility, whipped up by the ever-increasing brutality of the occupier who has long since thrown off the mask of gentleness and noninterference, has steadily increased until finally it reached the point where the paramount anxiety of the Dutch Government in London was no longer concentrated on the possibility that the people at home might compromise with the enemy, but rather on the danger of premature, widespread and bloody revolt. No attempt can be made here to describe either the ever-mounting horrors perpetrated on the people of Holland or the many different forms in which this people's defiance of the all-powerful enemy has expressed itself. Suffice to say that if in their persecution, their massacres, their tricks, and their looting, the Germans have not shown themselves unworthy of their Spanish predecessors of four centuries ago, neither have the people of the Netherlands failed to live up to the example of those sixteenth- and seventeenth-century Dutchmen who held out for eighty years and gained freedom as their reward.

Meanwhile, and at approximately the same time that the home-front in Holland itself was reconsolidated, the Government in London had obtained the means to give guidance, inspiration, and direction to the steadily growing resistance across the Channel. In the summer of 1940, facilities had been secured from the British Broadcasting Corporation to conduct regular daily broadcasts to the people of occupied Holland which not only enabled the Government to counteract the unceasing barrage of German propaganda to which all Holland had been subjected ever since May 15th, but also to encourage its listeners by keeping them informed of the active part which the Netherlands Kingdom was continuing to play in the war. There is no doubt that these broadcasts of "Radio Orange," as the Dutch Government's program came to be called, have exercised a powerful influence. Through them the people of Holland learned of the many steps their Queen and Government were taking to reassemble the scattered forces of the Kingdom for the second round. They learned of the financial measures taken almost immediately after the Government's arrival in England for the mobilization of Holland's extensive foreign exchange and security holdings throughout the world. They learned of the work being done in the battle of supply by Holland's two and one-half million tons of merchant ships, a large part of which was chartered to the British Ministry of War Transport. They learned of the establishment in England of Dutch training camps for soldiers, airmen, and naval personnel; of the exploits of Dutch warships, the great majority of which had managed to make safe port in England from which they were rapidly put to sea again under the operational command of the British Admiralty. They learned of the active preparations being made by the Government for the immediate relief of the starving multitudes after the enemy had been driven out; of the marshaling of Dutch manpower and economic resources throughout the world; of the provisions being made for the thousands of hapless refugees who had succeeded in escaping from the Netherlands in the five days of fighting.

Equally encouraging to the people of Holland as was the broadcast information about the many measures taken by the Dutch Government for their ultimate liberation, was the news they received through the same channels of the part played in the world conflict by their fellow countrymen and their comrades of many races in the East and the West Indies. Especially did the East Indies, situated on one of the most important nodal points of the world's strategetic and commercial highways and regarded with a covetous eye by the aggressor states both for their economic and military value, display a realistic awareness of the dangers threatening them and the measures required to guard against these dangers. Nowhere was there less inclination, even in the year 1940 when the war was still only a conflict between European powers, to underestimate the likelihood that before long all the world and certainly the neighbors of Japan, would be engulfed in the terrifying and sweeping struggle.

It was this clear realization of the impending spread of the conflict which induced the Indies, with the full approval of the Government in London, to make the maximum preparations for war in the Pacific when other nations were still content to flatter themselves with the hope of appeasing the Far Eastern member of the Axis. The small standing army of the Indies was greatly enlarged by the institution of compulsory military service not only for all Dutch nationals of military age but subsequently also Indonesians. Those over military age were enrolled in the rapidly organized home guard, while the women of the Indies, both European and Indonesian, answered the call to war by organizing themselves into various auxiliary services. Demolition charges were put into place at all important military and industrial establishments which might one day fall into the hands of the enemy. Everything that could be done was done but, unfortunately, much that was vital to the all-round preparation of the defense of the Indies and that could not be produced within that tropical region itself, proved unavailable. For it appeared all too soon that even the arsenal of democracy, aware at last of the dire perils threatening even the American continent, besieged by the demands for tanks, planes, guns, and ammunition from many other quarters and itself behind in its own defense preparations, was unable to meet the world-wide clamor for arms.

Thus, many months before war in the Pacific was declared, those in the Indies who knew the true state of affairs regarding military supplies, were forced to realize that, in spite of all their exertions, in spite of their willingness and ability to pay cash for every tank and every plane they could lay their hands on, the defense of their territories might well prove a repetition of the often-played tragedy "Too little, and too late."

But insufficiently equipped, therefore, as the Indies may have been in the military sense of the word, spiritually and morally they were indeed ready to face the worst. And face it they did without a moment's hesitation when, a few hours after the first bombs fell on Pearl Harbor and before even the United States themselves had formally declared war on Japan, the Governor-General called the nation to arms with these ringing words: "The Netherlands Government accepts the challenge and takes up arms against the Japanese Empire." Nor was this defiance of the powerful aggressor a defiance in words only. From the very first hour and for many weeks thereafter when the Japanese concentrated all their forces on the Philippines and on American and British positions in the Far East, the Dutch Indies navy and air force, far from conserving their scant strength for the inevitable attack on their own territories, immediately went forth to seek out the foe and to support the Allied forces fighting hundreds of miles away from Java. Over Malay and off the coast of British Borneo, wherever the enemy cast his superior forces against the Allies, Dutch bombers and naval units threw themselves into the fray. Many were the victories they scored during these desperate weeks following the outbreak of war in the Pacific; the pace was set by a Dutch submarine which, as early as the third day of the fighting, sank four heavily laden Japanese troop transports off the coast of Thailand. While the Tokyo radio was still broadcasting to Batavia to "keep out of the war," Dutch air and naval forces were already well on the way toward setting up their week's record of sinking one Japanese ship a day. Alas, neither the steadily rising toll of Japanese warships and transport vessels sunk by Dutch and Allied air and sea attacks, nor the embittered resistance put up by outnumbered Dutch land forces to the invading hordes, were able to stop the ruthless progress of the yellow flood. One after the other, the tremendous oil installations, whose destruction had been so carefully planned many months before, went up in flames. For a moment, a few days after the sky over Balikpapan in Borneo had been lit up by one of the greatest fires of all, hope flared again when a Japanese invasion fleet, clearly heading for Java, was routed in the Straits of Macassar with loss of eleven warships and seventeen heavily laden transports. Hope also fed on the arrival in Java of some small American and British reinforcements. But neither hope nor the handful of men and planes who had come to help the Dutch and Indonesian defenders of Java to hold this last defense bastion, availed against the seemingly inexhaustible power, the daring, and the cunning of an enemy who had made his preparations many years ago and who had struck when the forces of democracy were still scattered and dispersed across the surface of the globe.

Another month the fighting lasted, as with the fall of Singapore in the west and Amboina in the east, the net was drawn ever closer around beleaguered Java. Three weeks before the end, the islands of Sumatra and Bali, guarding the western and eastern flank of Java, fell.

A few days later, Americans, British, and Australians were still land-ing in the last remaining stronghold of the Archipelago. But their numbers were woefully small, their equipment was insufficient, and time was getting desperately short. At the same time, and just as the Japanese troops were making their first landings on Java, the Dutch Navy which by this time had once more earned its place in naval his-tory by its unbroken record of crippling blows against the enemy fleets, fought itself to death in the battle of the Java Sea. But again, for one brief moment, hope was reborn when, after the furious battling in the dark of night, the Japanese transports were reported retreating northward. Alas, the next day, the enemy pressed forward again. With the destruction of the proudest ships of the Dutch Navy and the loss of equal numbers of United States and other Allied cruisers, the fate of Java at last was sealed. Japanese troops, supported by overwhelming naval and air power, poured ashore at many different places. They still had to fight every inch of the way and repeatedly were driven back by the defenders. But, meanwhile, not a day passed without another important stronghold having been added to the long list of fallen cities. On March 5, 1942, Batavia, already abandoned as the headquarters of the Government, was lost to the advancing foe. On the other side of the island, the great naval base of Sourabaya burned fiercely as the retreating Dutch and Indonesian troops destroyed the last remaining military installations. In the south, Tjilatjap, the only remaining port through which reinforcements could be landed or the defenders evacuated, was utterly destroyed by Japanese bombers. Already the few squadrons of American fliers, who fought so bravely side by side with their allies, left the doomed island to fight again another time. Even Bandoeng, the last remaining center of organized resistance and the headquarters of the high command, was surrounded.

The game was up and on March 7th, exactly three months after Governor-General Tjarda van Starkenborgh Stachouwer threw his challenge in the face of Nippon, the voice of the Indies was heard for the last time when Radio Bandoeng signed off with this tragic mes-sage, "We are now closing down. Goodbye until better times. Long live the Queen!"

This, then, was the end of the second round. The third round of Holland's fight for freedom has begun. Much has happened in the intervening period to make stronger than ever before Holland's will to final victory. Out of common suffering and sacrifice has come a unity and a strength of purpose binding together in word and in deed all hearts and races of the Kingdom.

In the East, where for three months the Indonesians fought side by side with their Dutch comrades without one single instance of disloyalty having been reported and where from the beginning of the ordeal even the most extreme nationalist leaders declared and proved their transcendent solidarity with the cause of democracy, 70,000,000 Dutch subjects have been welded still more firmly within the framework of the Commonwealth by the assurance of a further development of East Indies self-government after their liberation from Japan. In the West Indies territories, the people of Curaçao and Surinam, equally assured of a new importance in the future commonwealth, have been further made to feel their association with the common effort by their immensely valuable contribution of the fuel oil and bauxite supplies that have kept the planes of freedom flying. In Holland proper, the inconceivable sufferings of a people which, with unflagging fortitude, strives to remain itself under the inhuman duress of a brutal and deceitful tyrant, have produced a desperate will to victory unsurpassed by the endurance and the faith of that earlier generation of Dutchmen who first gained the right to live, and think, and worship as free human beings.

Yet, it is not only moral preparedness which has made the Dutch ready and eager for the third and final round. In the material field, too, preparations have reached a far-advanced stage. In England and in Australia, in Canada and in the United States, Dutch soldiers and airmen—many of them veterans of the fatal battles for Holland and the Indies—are putting the final touches to their training for what they confidently trust to be the third and successful battle. What three years ago was a hapless band of unequipped, untrained patriots recruited from all over the world, has now been welded together into a small but highly efficient fighting force. While they train and wait, others, in the guerrilla bands still operating in the Indies, in the navy, the merchant marine, and in the Dutch squadrons of the R.A.F., remain actively at grips with the enemy. In Holland itself, a well-organized underground, in close contact with the Government in London, is not only regularly damaging the German war machine but is also making the most minute preparations for immediate coöperation with the longed-for liberators when they reach Holland's shores.

Finally, in the nerve center of Holland's war effort, in hospitable London, the Queen and her Government, now grown to a formidable machine, are not only preparing countless measures for the last round of the fight but also for the peace that is to follow. They know that this peace will not be won without further bloodshed on a vast scale. They know, as does each one of Holland's fighting men—whether he be a member of the underground, a guerrilla fighter in the Indies, or an eagerly waiting soldier, sailor, or airman—that much blood will still have to flow. Yet all of them, guided by the example of their Queen, are of serene mind, remembering ever the stout words of that seventeenth-century Dutch admiral who, falling in the course of battle, consoled his anxious comrades with these words: " 'Tis but a slight mishap to die for the fatherland in the midst of victory."

CHAPTER XXVII

Holland Among the Nations

BY ADRIAAN JACOB BARNOUW

HOLLAND OCCUPIES a very favorable position on the continent of Europe. Situated at the mouths of the Rhine, Maas, and Scheldt, the country is the natural meeting place of many trade currents and the natural base for large-scale commercial enterprise. Consequently Holland has always been a market at the crossroads of the Western world, and the Dutch have always been traders and seafarers. Since the early Middle Ages, they have rubbed elbows with foreigners of many lands. This continuous intercourse with strangers, and the knowledge it gave to them of different customs, laws, and beliefs has imbued them with an open-mindedness that is the mainspring of their tolerance. They are willing to believe that foreign customs and ideas are just as sound as their own and, when convinced that such ideas are better, are even willing to adopt them. The Dutch are singularly free from arrogance and from the vulgarity of chauvinism and, consequently, are immune to the sting of the master-race bug that has infected their German neighbors. Peace is the climate in which they thrive, and a land that is open to untrammeled trade with the world is their natural habitat.

But wars have a perverse way of playing havoc with habitats. The conditions that the Dutchman considers essential to his happiness are not apparent in the gloomy prospect that is vaguely seen, or believed to be vaguely seen, behind the flames and smoke of war. Peace? Will the return to disarmament usher it in? If peace is merely a negation, a nonexistence of war, there shall indeed be peace. The word is actually so defined by the New English Dictionary: a "freedom from, cessation of war." But Holland has learned enough in these last few years to know better. Men speak of the war of nerves, of economic warfare, of the war of classes, realizing too well that such warfare, even though conducted without physical force, can be equally destructive. Will the peace that must conclude this war preserve the world from these other, more insidious wars?

There will be hatred of all that is German in every Dutch heart when Holland has been cleared of German soldiers. Hatred, contempt, and distrust! And who can blame them for such emotion toward neighbors who have come among them to burn and sack and loot and murder, like savages weaned of all human feelings? No Dutchman will ever feel safe again, unless Germany be permanently restrained from rearming. But who shall restrain Germany? How long will international coöperation for the maintenance of the Four Freedoms over the whole world survive the restoration of the peace? Will not inertia soon relax the vigilance and allow the military caste to build up a new army while pretending to train merely a necessary police force and *heimwehr?* Only utter annihilation of that caste will quiet the fears which the Hollanders share with Germany's other neighbors. That caste, and the tribe of great industrialists are the ogres that must be emasculated before Europe can breathe freely again.

Americans, who have the good fortune to live far from the witches' cauldron that is Europe, talk hopefully of a future in which that unhappy European continent will have become a political duplicate of the United States. But few are the Europeans who either desire, or believe in, such an outcome. Those many nations, so different from one another in language, customs, traditions, and memories, will find it infinitely more difficult to federate than it was for the British colonists in America. The best one can hope for is a sectional grouping of states that have a common bond in old historical ties, in similarity of economic interests and democratic institutions. The Hollanders, as a seafaring nation, feel a much closer affinity to the British than to the Germans. The ocean does not separate nations; rather does it unite them. Political frontiers divide. For the sea, although giving a sense of safety, actually encourages peoples to seek one another. The political boundary, just because it is an imaginary barrier, induces the nation on either side to accentuate and to safeguard its separateness by estranging the frontier dwellers from one another. That happened along the boundary that now separates the Netherlands from Germany. In the Middle Ages, the ancestors of the people of present-day Westphalia were not conscious of being different from the inhabitants of the eastern Netherlands. They spoke the same language, they honored similar customs, and lived very much the same kind of lives. But after the Dutch Republic had come into being and had obtained its complete severance from the German Empire, the dwellers along the west side of the frontier became more and more Hollandish and those on the east side more completely Germanized.

But the Dutch see in the British, across the North Sea, like-minded people with whom they can get along. They remember, indeed, the naval wars with England, Britain's seizure of the Cape Colony and Ceylon, the Jameson raid against the Boer republics and the South African War that ensued; but all these memories cannot blind the Dutch to the truth that the British, both spiritually and politically, are much closer to them than are the Germans.

This is not a new discovery. The Dutch have always felt that way, if not through sentiment, then by necessity. The geographical situation of the two countries has made them natural allies. England has never felt safe when the harbors of the Netherlands were in the hands of a mighty continental power. That is why Queen Elizabeth, not for love of the Dutch but for the sake of England, had to assist the Dutch rebels against the world power of Spain. That is why Great Britain and Holland, under the King-Stadholder William of Orange, fought side by side against Louis XIV, England for her safety, Holland for her freedom. And now that it is Germany who is playing the villain's role of world conqueror, Holland finds herself again in close alliance with England. The North Sea, far from being a barrier, unites them more closely than ever. For if Hitler were all-powerful on the Continent, it would be exclusively a German Sea, whereas Holland and England, for the sake of their commerce, must maintain it as everybody's thoroughfare.

Denmark, Norway, and Sweden undoubtedly feel as do the Dutch. They, too, as seafaring nations, have developed that open-mindedness and tolerance that make for liberalism and for love of democratic institutions. Before the war, when the craze for autarchy started by Germany began to choke all the channels of international trade, these countries, together with Holland and Belgium, formed a kind of economic union for the purpose of their common defense against the selfish policies of mightier neighbors. But the whole body of Europe was then so seriously diseased that no one part of it could cure itself. The Oslo Convention had slight effect upon the ailments of its members. But the fact that each sought and felt the need of collaboration augurs well for the postwar period. A close association of the Oslo countries with Great Britain and the United States, an Atlantic Union of democracies brought together by the ocean that would seem to separate them, would constitute a safeguard against a recrudescence of the war psychosis on the Continent.

Among these Atlantic democracies Holland, historically speaking, would be *primus inter pares*. As far back as the days of the Dutch Republic, the Netherlands presented an early model of a democratically ruled nation. It was not, it is true, a modern democracy; but the men in power were enlightened autocrats who wisely granted freedom of speech and freedom of religion, and encouraged the founding of private institutions that gave destitute and underprivileged citizens freedom from want and freedom from fear. Suppression of liberating thought was never a part of their policy. The Leyden magistracy declared in a remonstrance addressed in 1581 to the not-so-liberal Dutch Reformed Synod, "Liberty has always consisted in uttering our sentiments freely; and the contrary has always been considered the characteristic of tyranny. Reason, which is the adversary of all tyrants, teaches us that truth can be as little restrained as light."

The ruling class in the Dutch Republic was not a caste of tyrants. The people, intent on their individual pursuits, were satisfied to let the upper ten run the State, but they insisted on the right to express their grievances. And the men in power knew the national temper too well not to respect their insistence on that freedom. Said the historian Hooft, writing in the 'thirties of the seventeenth century: "In this country, the greatest changes were brought about through the instigation or, at any rate, through the active compulsion of the common man; and in these days not the least art of the municipal government consists in managing and placating the multitude."

Freedom of religion was just as liberally conceded and maintained. The Prince of Orange declared, in an address delivered in the Council of State in 1564, "Although attached to the Roman Catholic faith, I cannot possibly approve that princes should wish to rule the consciences of their subjects and deprive them of their liberty of faith and worship of God." That noble sentiment became the guiding principle of the merchant rulers of the Republic. The Jews from Spain and Portugal, the Separatists from the Church of England, the Huguenots from France, the German Protestants who were unwilling to live under a Catholic Prince, all found a refuge in seventeenth-century Holland. Even the Church of Rome, though officially banned, was tolerated, and Roman services connived at.

In the care of the disabled and the aged they were equally progressive. Sir William Temple, who was British ambassador at The Hague in the 'sixties, said in his quaint English, "the many and various hospitals are in every man's curiosity and talk that travels their country."

The Four Freedoms, then, have been the prized possession of many generations of Hollanders. They are an integral part of the Dutchman's social inheritance, so much so that, in the early twentieth century every Dutchman's right to his enjoyment was universally recognized, and proposals for various legislative enactments that would embody in the written laws of the land the citizen's right to freedom from want met with slight opposition from any party. The objections raised against these proposals were not prompted by any desire to deny that right, but by a theoretical aversion to all state interference in the private lives of its citizens. Such meddling, tending to dull the sense of personal responsibility and initiative, was called un-Dutch and anti-national.

It is true that most, if not all, the charitable institutions that were so much admired by Sir William Temple were founded by private donors. But conditions in the early twentieth century were different from those in Sir William's age. The Industrial Revolution had greatly increased the number of workers employed in factories and work-shops, and had increased, also, the number of accidents and the preva-lence of occupational diseases. It was felt that private initiative was no longer adequate to cope with modern conditions; and thus, after long debates and repeated revisions of the original draft, legislation was enacted in the period between the two world wars which provided for compulsory insurance of the worker against disability, and for state pensions for the aged, for widows, and for orphans.

There were many, at the time, who feared that these laws would prove an intolerable financial burden which would drag the nation into bankruptcy. Those prophecies have not come true. By relieving the destitute from worry, by caring for the sick, by preventing the disabled from becoming clogs on the workers, this welfare legislation has improved the nation's happiness and health—the two watchmen best fitted to keep the wolf from the nation's door.

Yet, the wolf did enter, in the track of a mightier and more terrible beast: the German army. And the Four Freedoms, nurtured with care by successive generations as a precious heritage of the past were trampled upon and crushed under the hobnailed boots of barbarians. These men never knew freedom at home. They were accustomed to being barked at, to drilling and regimentation, to scraping and bow-ing—a race of bullies and moral cowards. And they turned the Dutch garden of freedom into a wilderness. Free speech was stricken dumb, the free press was gagged, freedom from fear was suffocated by the Gestapo, freedom from want was carried off with all the loot the rob-bers carted away. And what became of freedom of religion can be told by Holland's Jews who were denied all freedom, even the free-dom of choosing a place in which to live.

But the garden of Dutch freedom is a very old garden. The Nazis can trample across its soil and cut down the trees of free speech and free conscience, in whose shade the Dutch have lived happily for centuries. But the roots are too deep in the earth to be destroyed by German brutality; the roots live on underground, accumulating and preserving the sap that, in better days, will feed the new shoots which inevitably will begin to grow.

The Nazis know this. They feel it in the Dutch air they breathe, they see it in the defiant and hopeful faces of young and old, they can tell from their own depressing sense of disillusionment and frustration. They realize that their cause is doomed, that the will to freedom of these stubborn people has a tougher life than the brutal might of Hitler's bleeding army. When that army, bled white, is forced to withdraw, the love of freedom, pent up and strengthened by long suppression, will burst forth with the vigor of a new and prolific spring.

A Selected Bibliography

A Selected Bibliography

THE FOLLOWING WORKS have been selected and arranged by topics for readers who desire to continue their study of the Netherlands.

For further reading about the land and the people of the Netherlands (chap. i), see: (1) Hendrik Blink, *Nederland en zijne Bewoners* (*Handboek der Aardrijkskunde en Volkenkunde van Nederland*), Amsterdam, 1889–1892, 3 vols.; (2) H. Schuiling, *Nederland, Handboek der Aardrijkskunde*, Zwolle, 1934, 6th ed., 2 vols.; (3) Anton Albert Beekman, *Nederland als Polderland*, Zutphen, 1932; (4) J. P. de Vries, ed., *Volk van Nederland*, Amsterdam, 1938, 2d ed.; (5) R. W. P. de Vries, *Beautiful Holland: Dutch National Costumes* (historical notes), Amsterdam, 1925; (6) Samuel van Valkenburg, in Ellsworth Huntington, *Europe,* New York, 1935; (7) H. Riemens, *Les Pays-Bas dans le monde,* Paris, 1939; and *The Netherlands: The Story of a Free People,* New York, 1944; (8) A. J. Barnouw and B. Landheer, eds., *Holland's Contribution to the Sciences* (a symposium), New York, 1943; (9) Gratiana de Gardilanne and Elizabeth W. Moffatt, *The National Costumes of Holland,* London, 1932; (10) P. M. Hough, *Dutch Life in Town and Country,* London, 1901; (11) Adèle de Leeuw, *The Flavor of Holland,* New York, 1928; (12) Henry Asselin, *La Hollande dans le monde. L'Âme et la vie d' un peuple,* Paris, 1921; (13) Karel Čapek, *Letters from Holland,* London, 1933.

For the history of the Netherlands (chaps. ii and iii), see: (14) Hajo Brugmans, *Geschiedenis van Nederland,* Amsterdam, 1935–1938, 8 vols.; (15) Henri Pirenne, *Histoire de Belgique,* Brussels, 1902–1913, Vols. 1–4; (16) P. J. Blok, *History of the People of the Netherlands,* New York, 1898–1912, 5 vols., a standard work; (17) I. H. Gosses and N. Japikse, *Handboek tot de Staatkundige Geschiedenis van Nederland,* The Hague, 1927, 2d ed.; (18) P. Geyl, *Geschiedenis van den Nederlandschen Stam* (of which "The Revolt of the Netherlands, 1555–1609," London, 1932, and "The Netherlands Divided," London, 1936, have been translated into English), Amsterdam, 1930, 1934, 2 vols.

For the earliest history (archaeology and anthropology) of the Dutch people, see: (19) A. W. Bijvanck, "De Oorsprong van het Nederlandsche Volk en de Archeologie van Nederland," in *Jaarboek van de Maatschappij van Nederlandsche Letterkunde,* 1935–1936; (20) D. J. H. Nyessen, *The Passing of the Frisians,* The Hague, 1927, and J. Holwerda, *Nederland's Vroegste Geschiedenis,* Amsterdam, 1925, 2d ed.

For the medieval history of the Netherlands, see: (21) J. W. Moll, *Kerkgeschiedenis van Nederland voor de Hervorming,* Arnhem, 1864–1869, 4 vols.; (22) Léon Vanderkindere, *La formation territoriale des principautés Belges au Moyen Âge,* Brussels, 1902, 2 vols.; (23) O. Oppermann *et al., Bijdragen van het Instituut voor Middeleeuwsche Geschiedenis te Utrecht,* 1922.

For the Low Countries and Europe, see: No. 23, above, and (24) W. Kienast, *Die deutschen Fürsten im Dienste der Westmächte,* Utrecht, 1924; (25) Johan Huizinga, "L'Etat Bourguignon, ses rapports avec la France et les origines d'une nationalité néerlandaise," *Moyen Âge,* Vol. 40 (1930), and "Burgund, eine Krise des romanisch-germanischen Verhältnisse," *Historische Zeitschrift,* Vol. 148 (1933); (26) S. Lucas, *The Low Countries and the Hundred Years' War,* Ann Arbor, Mich., 1929.

The origin of the estates and the States-General may be found in: (27) E. Lousse, "Les Origines des Etats des Pays-Bas," *Revue d'histoire ecclésiastique,* 1933; the development of Dutch nationality may be traced in: (28) Johan Huizinga, "Uit de Voorgeschiedenis van Ons Nationaal Besef," *De Gids,* Vol. 1 (1912); and (29) L. van der Essen, "De Historische Gebondenheid der Nederlanden," in *Nederlandsche Historiebladen,* 1938, Pt. 1. The beginnings of Protestantism are traced in: (30) L. Knappert, *Het Ontstaan en de Vestiging van het Protestantisme in Nederland,* Utrecht, 1924; the Inquisition in: (31) P. Fredericq, *Corpus Documentorum Inquisitionis,* Gand, 1900; and the Brethren of the Common Life in: (32) A. Hyma, *Christian Renaissance,* Grand Rapids, Mich., 1924.

For the Eighty Years' War, besides the general histories (Nos. 14 to 18, above) there is the complete account by: (33) J. Romein, ed., *De Tachtigjarige Oorlog,* Amsterdam, 1941. Although now out of date, the well-known works of John R. Motley are: (34) *Rise of the Dutch Republic,* New York, 1913, latest ed., 3 vols., and (35) *History of the United Netherlands,* New York, 1909, latest ed., 4 vols. The following biographies are recommended for this period and later: (36) P. J. Blok, *Prins Willem I,* Amsterdam, 1909, 2 vols.; (37) F. Rachfahl, *Wilhelm von Oranien,* Halle, 1906, 3 vols.; (38) N. Japikse, *De Geschiedenis van het Huis van Oranje-Nassau,* The Hague, 1937–1938, 2 vols. For the political theories of the war, see: (39) A. de Frankrijker, *De Motiveering van den Opstand,* Nijmegen, 1933.

On toleration, see: (40) A. A. van Schelven, "De Ontwikkeling van de Idee der Politieke Tolerantie in de Nederlanden," in *Tijdschrift voor Geschiedenis,* 1931, and (41) the articles by H. Enno van Gelder in the same journal.

The standard bibliographies are: (42) Henri Pirenne, *Bibliographie de l'histoire de Belgique,* Brussels, 1932, and (43) L. Petit (continued by H. Ruys),

Repertorium van Tijdschriftartikels Betrekking Hebbend op de Vaderland-sche Geschiedenis, Leyden, 1907–1933, 4 vols.
For the Golden Age of the Netherlands (chap. iii), see, besides Nos. 16, 33, 34, 35, above, the following: (44) Anon., *Dutch Drawn to the Life,* London, 1664; (45) George Edmundson, *Anglo-Dutch Rivalry in the First Half of the 17th Century,* Oxford, 1911; and "The Dutch Power in Brazil," *English Historical Review,* 1896, 1899, 1901, 1903, and 1904; (46) R. J. Fruin, *Tien Jaren uit den Tachtigjarigen Oorlog, 1588–1598,* Amsterdam, 1861, and several later editions, and *Verspreide Geschriften,* The Hague, 1901; (47) J. Geddes, *History of the Administration of John de Witt,* The Hague, 1879; (48) Jan and Annie Romein, *Erflaters van onze Beschaving,* Amsterdam, 1938, Vol. 2; (49) Sir William Temple, *Observations upon the United Provinces of the Netherlands,* Cambridge, 1932, 1st ed., 1672.

For the period of the decline and reawakening (chap. iv), see: Nos. 16 and 46, above, and (50) Robert Fruin, *Geschiedenis der Staatsinstellingen in Nederland,* The Hague, 1922, 2d ed.; (51) H. T. Colenbrander, *Gedenkstukken tot de Algemeene Geschiedenis van Nederland, 1795 tot 1840,* The Hague, 1905; *Inlijving en Opstand,* Amsterdam, 1913; *De Bataafsche Republiek,* Amsterdam, 1908; *Schimmelpenninck en Koning Lodewijk,* Amsterdam, 1915; *Vestiging van het Koninkrijk,* Amsterdam, 1927; *Willem I,* Amsterdam, 1937; (52) Hendrik Willem van Loon, *The Rise of the Dutch Kingdom,* New York, 1915; (53) Joh. W. A. Naber, *Overheersching en Vrijwording,* Haarlem, 1909; (54) J. Huizinga, *Tien Studiën,* Haarlem, 1926; (55) G. K. van Hogendorp, *Bijdragen tot de Huishouding van den Staat,* Amsterdam, 1825, 10 vols.; *Brieven en Gedenkschriften,* The Hague, 1901–1904, 3 vols.; (56) De Bosch Kemper, *Staatkundige Geschiedenis van Nederland tot 1830,* Amsterdam, 1868; (57) B. D. H. Tellegen, *De Wedergeboorte van Nederland,* Groningen, 1913; (58) J. R. Thorbecke, *Historische Schetsen,* The Hague, 1860.

For the modern development of the Netherlands (chap. v), see: Nos. 16 and 17, above, and (59) A. J. Barnouw, *Holland under Queen Wilhelmina,* London, 1923, and *The Dutch,* New York, 1940; (60) H. Brugmans, *Schets eener Beschavingsgeschiedenis van Nederland,* Haarlem, 1928, and *Geschiedenis van Nederland onder de Regeering van Koningin Wilhelmina,* Amsterdam, 1938; (61) I. J. Brugmans, *Thorbecke,* Haarlem 1932, and *De Arbeidende Klasse in Nederland in de 19e Eeuw,* The Hague, 1925; (62) J. A. de Bruyne and N. Japikse, *Staatkundige Geschiedenis van Nederland in onzen Tijd, 1848–1917,* Leyden, 1921, 6 vols.; (63) H. T. Colenbrander, *De Belgische Omwenteling,* The Hague, 1905; (64) Hendrik Colijn, *Voor het Gemeenebest,* Utrecht, 1938, and *Saevis Tranquillus in Undis,* Amsterdam, 1940, 2d ed.; (65) P. A. Diepenhorst, *Dr. A. Kuyper,* Haarlem, 1931; (66) F. J. W.

Drion, *Vaderlandsche Jaarboeken, 1937,* Zeist, 1938; (67) George Edmundson, *History of Holland,* Cambridge, 1922; (68) F. H. Fischer (De Roever-
Dozy), *Het Leven van Onze Voorouders,* Amsterdam, 1929, Vol. 4; J. H.
Gosses and N. Japikse, *Handboek tot de Staatkundige Geschiedenis van
Nederland,* The Hague, 1920; (69) K. E. van der Mandele, *Het Liberalisme
in Netherland,* Arnhem, 1933; (70) P. H. Ritter *et al., Eene Halve Eeuw,
1848–1898,* Amsterdam, 1898, 2 vols.; (71) Henriëtte Roland-Holst, *Kapitaal
en Arbeid in Nederland,* Rotterdam, 1932, 4th ed.; (72) Jan Romein, *De
Lage Landen bij de Zee,* Utrecht, 1935; (73) W. J. van Welderen Rengers,
Schets eener Parlementaire Geschiedenis van Nederland, 1848–1891, The
Hague, 1918.

Constitutional and political aspects of Dutch life (chap. vi) are to be studied
further in Nos. 16 and 17, above, and (74) J. A. de Bruyne and H. Japikse,
Staatkundige Geschiedenis van Nederland in onzen Tijd, Leyden, 1921, 6
vols.; (75) J. T. Buys, *De Grondwet,* Arnhem, 1882–1886, 3 vols.; I. H. Gosses
and N. Japikse, *Handboek tot de Staatkundige Geschiedenis van Nederland,*
The Hague, 1920; (76) F. J. A. Stuart, *De Grondwetsherzieningen van 1917
en 1922,* Arnhem, 1925; (77) N. Japikse, *Staatkundige Geschiedenis van
Nederland* (1887–1917), Leyden, 1919; (78) H. Krabbe, *De Moderne Staatsidee,*
The Hague, 1922; (79) R. Kranenburg, *Het Nederlandsch Staatsrecht,* Haarlem, 1938; (80) A. F. de Savornin Lohman, *Onze Constitutie,* The Hague,
1921; (81) A. A. H. Struycken, *Ons Koningschap,* Amsterdam, 1909, and *Het
Staatsrecht van het Koninkrijk der Nederlanden,* Arnhem, 1928.

For Dutch political parties (chap. vii), see: Nos. 16, 64, 67, above, and (82)
A. J. M. Cornelissen, *Beginselen der Nederlandsche Politieke Partijen,* Nijmegen, 1935; (83) Hendrik Colijn, *Saevis Tranquillus in Undis (Toelichting
op het Anti-Revolutionnaire Beginselprogram*), Amsterdam, 1934; (84) P. W.
A. Cort van der Linden, *Richting en Beleid der Liberale Partij,* Groningen,
1886; (85) P. A. Diepenhorst, *Ons Isolement (Practische Toelichting op het
Program van Beginselen der Anti-Revolutionnaire Partij*), Kampen, 1935;
(86) C. K. Elout, *Onze Politieke Partijen,* Amsterdam, 1913; (87) *Gedenkboek
der Sociaal-Democratische Arbeiderspartij in Nederland, 1894–1919,* Amsterdam, 1919; (88) *Gedenkboek van den Vrijzinnig-Democratischen Bond, 1901–
1926,* The Hague, 1926; (89) G. Groen van Prinsterer, *Ongeloof en Revolutie,*
Utrecht, 1924, 5th ed.; (90) N. Kolff, *Over den Invloed van Politieke Partijen
op den Nederlandschen Regeeringsvorm,* Leyden, 1931; (91) A. Kuyper, *Anti-
Revolutionnaire Staatkunde,* Kampen, 1916–1917, 2 vols.; Leo XIII, *Immortale
Dei* (1886), Studiën dl. 25; Leo XIII, *Rerum Novarum* (trans. by L. Zeinstra,
1931); (92) K. E. van der Mandele, *Het Liberalisme in Nederland (Schets van
de Ontwikkeling in de Negentiende Eeuw*), Arnhem, 1933; (93) *Nationaal-
Socialistische Beweging in Nederland* [Brochure 1 en 2: *Program met Toelich-*

ting; Brochure 3: *Nationaal-Socialistische (Fascistische) Staatsleer;* Brochure 4: *Actueele Vragen*]; Pius IX, *Quadragesimo Anno* (trans. by L. Zeinstra, 1931); (94) *Het Program der Communistische Internationale aangenomen door het zesde Wereldcongres te Moskou,* Amsterdam; (95) A. F. de Savornin Lohman, *Bijdragen tot de Geschiedenis der Christelijk-Historische Partij,* The Hague, 1921, 2 vols.; (96) Schrift en Historie, *Gedenkboek bij het vijftigjarig Bestaan der Georganiseerde Anti-Revolutionnaire Partij, 1928,* Kampen, 1929, 2d ed.

For Dutch foreign policy (chap. viii), see: No. 77, above, and (97) *Annuaire Grotius International,* The Hague, 1913; (98) H. L. Asser, *De Buitenlandsche Betrekkingen van Nederland, 1860–1889,* Haarlem, 1889; (99) A. H. de Beaufort, *Vijftig Jaren uit onze Geschiedenis, 1868–1918,* Amsterdam, 1928; (100) Adèle de Leeuw, *Nederland in de Wereld Politiek,* Zeist, 1936; (101) W. J. Oudendyke, *Ways and By-Ways in Diplomacy,* London, 1939; (102) R. J. Renier, *Great Britain and the Netherlands, 1813–1815,* London, 1930; (103) Royal Institute of International Affairs, *Political and Strategic Interests of the United Kingdom,* London, 1939; (104) A. A. H. Struycken, *De Hoofdtrekken van het Nederlandsche Beleid,* The Hague, 1923; (105) Amry Vandenbosch, *The Neutrality of the Netherlands during the World War,* Grand Rapids, Mich., 1929; (106) W. J. M. van Eyzinga, *De Nederlandsche Tractaten sinds 1813,* The Hague, 1916; (107) J. A. van Hamel, *Nederland tusschen de Mogendheden,* Amsterdam, 1918; (108) H. A. van Karnebeek, *De Internationale Positie van Nederland in de laatste veertig Jaren,* The Hague, 1938, pamphlet.

The development of Dutch economy (chap. ix) may be traced in: Nos. 7, 15, 16, 72, above, and (109) O. van Rees, *Geschiedenis der Staathuishoudkunde in Nederland,* Utrecht, 1865–1868, 2 vols.; (110) Ernst Baasch, *Holländische Wirtschaftsgeschichte,* Jena, 1927; (111) Hendrik Blink, *Opkomst van Nederland als Economisch-geograpisch Gebied,* Amsterdam, 1925; (112) C. te Lintum, *Nederland en de Indiën gedurende de Laatste Kwart-Eeuw,* Zutphen, 1923; (113) J. A. Nederbragt, *La Politique économique des Pays-Bas des dernier temps,* The Hague, 1932; (114) H. Differee, *Geschiedenis van den Nederlandschen Handel,* Amsterdam, 1905–1908; (115) J. G. van Dillen, *Het Economisch Karakter van de Middeleeuwsche Stad,* The Hague, 1914; (116) T. P. van der Kooy, *Hollands Stapelmarkt en haar Verval,* Amsterdam, 1931; (117) O. Pringsheim, *Wirtschaftliche Entwicklungsgeschichte der Vereinigten Niederlande,* Leipzig, 1890; (118) J. van Ouwerkerk de Vries, *Verval des Nederlandschen Handels,* Haarlem, 1827; (119) H. Riemens, *Het Amortisatie-Syndicaat, een Studie over de Staatsfinanciën onder Willem I,* Amsterdam, 1935; (120) J. de la Valette, *British Trade with Holland,* London, 1934.

For Holland's role in world trade (chap. x), see: (121) A. Heringa, *Free*

Trade and Protection in Holland, London, 1914; (122) Christian Guenther, *Holland im Weltverkehr,* Bern, 1926–1927, 7 vols.; (123) *Nederland, het Continentale Centrum van Handel, Scheepvaart en Financiën,* Rotterdam, 1928 ff.; (124) Willem L. Valk, *Die Entwickelung des Aussenhandels der Niederlande nach dem Kriege,* Jena, 1934–1936; (125) Emilie de Cock Buning, *Die Aussenhandelspolitik der Niederlande seit dem Weltkriege,* Bern, 1936; (126) Franz Haumer, *Die Handelspolitik der Niederlande, 1830–1930,* Emsdetten-Westfalen, 1936.

For further reading on Dutch social structure (chap. xi), see: (127) C. A. Verrijn Stuart, "De Economische Structuur van ons Volk," *De Economist,* 1935; (128) W. B. Kloos, *Het Nationaal Plan,* Alphen aan den Rijn, 1939; (129) Centraal Bureau voor de Statistiek, *Bevolking en Oppervlakte der Gemeenten van Nederland op 1 Januari 1940; Afdeeling Bevolkingsstatistiek, Medeleelingen, 1936–1940;* (130) H. W. Methorst, "Leeftijdspyramide, de Spil van het Bevolkingsvraagstuk," in *Tijdschrift voor Sociale Geneeskunde,* 1934; A. B. Velthuizen, "Omvang en Samenstelling van de Bevolking van Nederland," *Tijdschrift, Nederlandsche Werkverschaffing,* 1938; (132) J. Ch. W. Verstege, "Het Migratie-vraagstuk in de Demografie," in *Tijdschrift voor Economische Geographie,* 1938; (133) A. C. de Vooys, " 'Stad' en 'Platteland' in de Statistiek," in *Tijdschrift voor Economische Geographie,* 1938; (134) H. J. Keuning, "L'Habitat rural aux Pays-Bas," in *Tijdschrift Koninklijk Nederlandsch Aardrijkskundig Genootschap,* 1938; (135) A. C. de Vooys, *De Trek van de Plattelandsbevolking in Nederland, Bijdrage tot de Kennis van de Sociale Mobiliteit en de Horizontale Migratie van de Plattelandsbevolking,* Groningen, 1923; (136) C. Busken Huet, *Het Land van Rembrandt,* Haarlem, 1898; 5th ed., Haarlem, 1930; (137) F. H. Fischer, *Historie en Cultuur van het Nederlandsche Volk,* Amsterdam, 1927; (138) J. de Vries, ed., *Volk van Nederland,* Amsterdam, 1938.

For Dutch labor conditions (chap. xii), see: (139) T. J. Brugmans, *De Arbeidende Klasse in Nederland in de 19de Eeuw, 1813–1870,* The Hague, 1929, 2d ed.; (140) B. Bymholt, *Geschiedenis der Arbeidersbeweging in Nederland,* Amsterdam, 1894; (141) H. Smits, *De Nederlandsche Arbeidersbeweging in de 19de Eeuw,* Rotterdam, 1902; (142) J. van den Tempel, *De Nederlandsche Vakbeweging en haar Toekomst,* Rotterdam, 1920, 3d ed.; (143) P. J. Troelstra, *Gedenkschriften,* Amsterdam, 1927–1931, 4 vols.; (144) Henriëtte Roland-Holst, *Kapitaal en Arbeid,* Rotterdam, 1932, 4th ed.; (145) P. L. M. Aalberse, *Een Onbekende Enquete naar de Arbeidstoestanden in Nederland,* Leyden, 1919; (146) Jan Oudegeest, *De Geschiedenis der Zelfstadige Vakbeweging in Nederland,* Amsterdam, 1926–1932; (147) J. R. Slotemaker de Bruine, *Vijf-en-twintig Jaren Sociale Verzekering,* Haarlem, 1928; (148) A. C. Josephus, Jitta and E. H. Bisschop Boele, *Sociale Wetgeving,* Vol. 8 of

J. H. F. Kohlbrugge, *Practische Sociologie,* Groningen, 1931; (149) K. Du Bois de Vroijlande, *Volksverheffing in de Roomsch-Katholieke Standsorganisatie der Werklieden in Nederland,* Louvain, 1924.

Further reading in philosophy and religious trends in the Netherlands (chap. xiii) may be found in: Nos. 30, 32, above, and (150) G. van Antal, *Die Holländische Philosophie im Neunzehnten Jahrhundert,* Utrecht, 1888; (151) H. Bavinck, "Mental, Religious and Social Forces," in *A General View of the Netherlands,* No. 17, The Hague, 1915; (152) R. Casimir, *Beknopte Geschiedenis der Wijsbegeerte,* The Hague, 1910, 2 vols.; (153) J. Clay, "Bolland en zijn Invloed," in *Pallas Leidensis,* Leyden, 1925; (154) A. Eekhof, *Religious Thought and Life in Holland* (Lectures on Holland for American Students), Leyden, 1924; (155) W. J. Hull, *The Rise of Quakerism in Amsterdam,* Philadelphia, 1938; (156) Albert Hyma, *Erasmus and the Humanists,* New York, 1930; (157) Rufus M. Jones, *Studies in Mystical Religion,* London, 1936; (158) L. Knappert, *Geschiedenis der Nederlandsche Hervormde Kerk,* Amsterdam, 1911–1912, 2 vols.; (159) J. P. N. Land, "Philosophy in the Dutch Universities," *Mind,* Vol. 3 (1878); (160) J. P. N. Land, *De Wijsbegeerte in de Nederlanden,* The Hague, 1899; (161) B. J. H. Ovink, "Die Niederländische Philosophie," in Ueberweg, *Grundriss der Geschichte der Philosophie,* Berlin, 1928, 12th ed., Vol. 5; (162) A. Vloemans, *Spinoza,* The Hague, 1931; (163) W. van der Vlugt, *De Geestelijke Wetenschappen—Eene halve Eeuw, 1848–1898,* Amsterdam, 1898, 2d vol.

For material on Dutch education (chap. xiv), see: (164) J. Versluis, *Geschiedenis van het Onderwijs in Nederland,* 1916; (165) C. Hentzen, *De Politieke Geschiedenis van het Lager Onderwijs in Nederland,* Nijmegen, 1920–1932, 6 vols.; (166) J. H. Gunning, *De Studie der Paedagogiek in Nederland, 1898–1939,* Amsterdam, 1940; (167) John C. Medd, "Education in the Netherlands," in *Special Reports on Education* (Education Board, Great Britain, 1902), Supplement to Vol. 8; (168) National Catholic Welfare Conference, *Public Education and Catholic Education in Holland,* Department of Education, Washington, D. C., 1932; (169) Centraal Bureau van Statistiek, Jaarcijfers, The Hague, 1918–1940.

Further references on art may be found in: (170) Paul Fierens, *L'Art hollandais contemporain,* Paris, 1933; (171) H. E. van Gelder *et al., Kunstgeschiedenis der Nederlanden,* Utrecht, 1930; (172) E. G. Greenshields, *Landscape Painting and Modern Dutch Artists,* New York, 1906; (173) Haldane Macfall, "The Dutch Genius," in *A History of Painting,* Vol. 5, Boston, 19—); (174) W. Martin, *De Hollandsche Schilderkunst in de Zeventiende Eeuw,* Vol. 1: *Frans Hals en zijn Tijd,* Vol. 2: *Rembrandt en zijn Tijd,* Amsterdam, 1935 and 1936; (175) Max Rooses *et al., Dutch Painters of the Nineteenth Century,* New York and London, 1901; (176) Regina Schoolman and Charles

E. Slatkin, *The Enjoyment of Art in America:* chap. x, "Flemish School," chap. xi, "Dutch School," New York, 1942; (177) R. H. Wilenski, *An Introduction to Dutch Art,* New York, 1928.

For architecture in the Netherlands, see: (178) Paul Bromberg, *De Kleine Practische Woning,* Amsterdam, 1937; (179) M. D. Ozinga, *De Protestantsche Kerkenbouw in Nederland van Hervorming tot Franschen Tijd,* Amsterdam, 1929; (180) F. Vermeulen, *Handboek tot de Geschiedenis der Nederlandsche Bouwkunst,* The Hague, 1923–1932, 3 vols.; (181) J. J. Vriend, *De Bouwkunst van ons Land,* Amsterdam, 1938; (182) J. G. Wattjes, *Nieuw– Nederlandsche Bouwkunst,* Amsterdam, 1930; (183) F. R. Yerbury, *Old Domestic Architecture of Holland,* London, 1924; (184) F. R. Yerbury, *Modern Dutch Buildings,* New York, 1931.

For the chapter on literature, the following list of references is added: (185) Frans Bastiaanse, *Overzicht van de Ontwikkeling der Nederlandsche Letterkunde,* Amsterdam, 1922–1927, 4 vols.; (186) Jan Ten Brink, *Geschiedenis der Noord-Nederlandsche Letteren in de XIXe Eeuw,* Amsterdam, 1888 and 1889; (187) Jan Ten Brink, *Geschiedenis der Nederlandsche Letterkunde,* Amsterdam, 1897; (188) G. Kalff, *Geschiedenis der Nederlandsche Letterkunde,* Groningen, 1906–1910, 6 vols.; (189) Jacob Prinsen, *Handboek tot de Nederlandsche Letterkundige Geschiedenis,* 's Gravenhage, 1928.

The history of Dutch music (chap. xviii) may be studied in the following: (190) Henk Badings, *De Nederlandsche Componisten,* Amsterdam, 1937; (191) Dirk J. Balfoort, *Het Muziekleven in Nederland in de 17de en 18de Eeuw,* Amsterdam, 1938; (192) K. Ph. Bernet Kempers, *Muziekgeschiedenis,* The Hague, 1932; (193) *Concertgebouw-Gedenkboek, 1888–1938,* Amsterdam, 1938; (194) J. D. C. van Dokkum, *Honderd Jaar Muziekleven in Nederland, (Een Geschiedenis van de Maatschappij tot Bevordering der Toonkunst, 1829–1929),* Amsterdam, 1929; (195) Sem Dresden, *Het Muziekleven in Nederland sinds 1880,* Amsterdam, 1923; (196) *Willem Mengelberg-Gedenkboek,* Amsterdam, 1920; (197) S. van Milligen and Sem Dresden, *Ontwikkeling der Muziek,* Groningen, 1928; (198) Edmond van der Straeten, *La Musique aux Pays-Bas avant le XIX⁰ siècle,* Brussels, 1867–1888, 8 vols.; (199) Sem Dresden *et al., Geillustreerd Muzieklexicon,* ed. by S. Keller and Philip Kruseman, The Hague, 1932.

For the anthropology of the Netherlands Indies (chap. xix), see: (200) J. P. Kleiweg de Zwaan, *De Rassen van den Indischen Archipel,* Amsterdam, 1925; (201) W. A. Mijsberg, "Het anthropologisch Onderzoek in Nederlandsch Oost Indië in de Periode 1911–1935," in *Feestbundel van het Genootschap voor Nederlandsch Indië,* 1936; (202) D. J. H. Nysessen, *The Races of Java,* Batavia, 1929; (203) D. J. H. Nyessen, *Somatical Investigation of the Javanese,* Anthropological Laboratory, Bandoeng, 1930; (204) J. van Gelderen, "The

Numerical Evolution of Population, with Particular Reference to the Population of Java," in *International Congress for Studies Regarding Population Problems,* Rome, 1932; (205) Raymond Kennedy, *The Ageless Indies,* New York, 1942; (206) B. Alkema and T. J. Bezemer, *Volkenkunde van Nederlandsch-Indië,* Haarlem, 1927; (207) J. Ph. Duyvendak, *Inleiding tot de Ethnologie van de Indische Archipel,* Groningen, 1940; (208) J. C. van Eerde, *De Volken van Nederlandsch-Indië,* Amsterdam, 1920, 2 vols.; (209) Raymond Kennedy, "A Survey of Indonesian Civilization," in G. P. Murdock, ed., *Studies in the Science of Society,* New Haven, 1937; and *Islands and Peoples of the Indies.* Smithsonian Institution, Washington, D. C., 1943.

For the history and culture of the Netherlands Indies (chaps. xx and xxii), see: (210) C. Lekkerkerker, *Land en Volk van Java,* Groningen-Batavia, 1938, Vol. 1; (211) P. J. Veth, Borneo's *Wester-afdeeling,* Zalt-Bommel, 1854–1856, 2 vols.; (212) F. W. Stapel, ed., *Geschiedenis van Nederlandsch Indië,* Amsterdam, 1938–1940, 6 vols. in 1940; (213) B. H. M. Vlekke, *Nusantara: A History of the East Indian Archipelago,* Cambridge, Mass., 1943; (214) N. J. Krom, *Hindoe-Javaansche Geschiedenis,* The Hague, 1931, 2d ed.; and *Inleiding tot de Hindoe-Javaansche Kunst,* The Hague, 1923, 2d ed.; (215) W. F. Stutterheim, *Indian Influences in Old Balinese Art,* 1935; (216) C. Wessels, *Geschiedenis van de R. K. Missie op Amboina,* Nijmegen, 1926; (217) J. K. J. de Jonge, *De Opkomst van het Nederlandsch Gezag in Oost Indië,* The Hague, 1862–1865, 3 vols.; and *De Opkomst van het Nederlandsch Gezag over Java,* The Hague, 1869–1878, 7 vols. (continued later by M. L. van Deventer and L. G. W. de Roo), 5 vols.; (218) J. E. Heeres and F. W. Stapel, "Corpus Diplomaticum Neerlando Indicum," in the series *Bijdragen voor Taal, Land en Volkenkunde van het Koninklijk Instituut,* Vols. 57, 87, 91, 93, and 96; (219) G. Gonggrijp, *Schets eener Economische Geschiedenis van Nederlandsch Indië,* Haarlem, 1928; (220) J. S. Furnivall, *Netherlands India, a Study of Plural Economy,* Cambridge, 1939; (221) Clive Day, *The Dutch in Java,* New York, 1904.

The story of the Dutch in the Far East (chap. xxi) is to be followed in: Nos. 205, 212, 213, 221, above, and (222) C. R. Boxer, *Jan Compagnie in Japan, 1600–1818,* The Hague, 1936; (223) P. de Kat Angelino, *Colonial Policy,* Chicago, 1931, 2 vols.; (224) Rupert Emerson, *Malaysia: A Study in Direct and Indirect Rule,* New York, 1937; (225) Albert Hyma, *The Dutch in the Far East,* Ann Arbor, 1942; (226) Amry Vandenbosch, *The Dutch East Indies: Its Government, Problems, and Politics,* Berkeley, 1942, 3d ed.

Useful material for further study on the economic significance of the Netherlands Indies (chap. xxiii) may be found in the following: (227) J. H. Boeke, *The Structure of Netherlands Indian Economy,* Institute of Pacific

Relations, New York, 1942; (228) Jan O. M. Broek, *The Economic Development of the Netherlands Indies,* Institute of Pacific Relations, New York, 1942; (229) *Bulletin of the Colonial Institute of Amsterdam, 1938–1941;* (230) H. G. Callis, *Foreign Capital in Southeast Asia,* Institute of Pacific Relations, New York, 1942; (231) G. H. C. Hart, *Towards Economic Democracy in the Netherlands Indies,* Institute of Pacific Relations, National Council for the Netherlands and the Netherlands Indies, New York City, 1943; (232) Pieter Honig, "Future of Export Agriculture in the Netherlands East Indies," *Far Eastern Survey,* Vol. 12, No. 4 (February 22, 1943); (233) *The Netherlands Indies,* Department of Economic Affairs, Batavia, 1936–1940, monthly; (234) Peter H. W. Sitsen, *The Industrial Development of the Netherlands Indies,* Institute of Pacific Relations, National Council for the Netherlands and Netherlands Indies, New York, 1943; (235) *Statistical Abstract of the Netherlands Indies,* Batavia, 1940, pocket ed.; (236) *Atlas van Tropisch Nederland,* Batavia, 1938; (237) *The Export Crops of the Netherlands Indies,* Central Bureau for Statistics, Batavia, annual; (238) *Indian Report in Statistical Abstract for the Netherlands East Indies,* Batavia, annual; (239) *Jaaroverzicht van den In-en Uitvoer van Nederlandsch-Indië,* Batavia, annual, 3 vols.; (240) *Verslag van de Commissie tot Bestudeering van Staatsrechtelijke Hervormingen,* Batavia, 1941, 2 vols.; (241) *Economisch Weekblad,* Department of Economic Affairs, Batavia, 1930–1941, weekly.

For materials on the industrialization of the Netherlands Indies, see: Nos. 227, 228, 240, 241, above, and (242) Harry F. Bain, *Ores and Industry in the Far East,* New York, 1933; (243) H. B. Butler, *Problems of Industry in the East, with Special Reference to India, French India, Ceylon, Malaya, and the Netherlands Indies* (Studies Series B, No. 29), International Labor Office, Geneva, 1938; (244) Victor A. Clark, *Labor Conditions in Java,* Bulletin No. 58, U. S. Bureau of Labor, Washington, D. C., 1905; (245) J. van Gelderen, *The Recent Development of Economic Foreign Policy in the Netherlands East Indies,* New York, 1939; (246) P. de Kat Angelino, *Some Remarks on the Wages Paid in the Netherlands Indies,* Institute of Pacific Relations, National Council for the Netherlands and Netherlands Indies, Batavia, 1936; (247) Henri Hubert van Kol, *De Ontwikkeling der Groot-Industrie in Japan,* 's Gravenhage, 1916; (248) Kate L. Mitchell, *Industrialization of the Western Pacific,* Institute of Pacific Relations, National Council for the Netherlands and Netherlands Indies, New York, 1942; (249) Hendrik C. Prinsen Geerlings, *De Rietsuiker Industrie in de Verschillende Landen van Productie,* Amsterdam, 1942, 2d ed.; (250) C. van de Koppel, *Forestry in the Outer Provinces of the Netherlands Indies,* Vol. 2, No. 1; Cecile Rothe, *Metaal Industrie,* No. 119; *Textielindustrie,* No. 125; *Industrial Development and Home Consumption in the Netherlands Indies,* Vol. 2, No. 1; *Keramische,*

Glas en Cement Industrie, No. 127; *Leder en Lederwarenindustrie*, No. 129 (Bulletins of the Colonial Institute of Amsterdam, 1919, 1938, 1939); (251) Dienst van den Mijnbouw, *IJzerertsen in Nederlandsch Indië*, *Weltevreden* (*Verslagen en Mededeelingen betreffende Indische Delfstoffen en hare Toepassing*), No. 7 (1919); (252) *Industrie in Nederlandsch Indië*, special number, May, 1941.

For additional reading on the Dutch West Indies, see: (253) Cecil S. Baker and Wallace Thompson, "Climatic Influences in the Caribbean," *Current History*, Vol. 31, No. 5 (February, 1930), pp. 908–918; (254) H. A. Ballou, "The Dutch Leeward Islands," *Tropical Agriculture*, Vol. 11, No. 12 (December, 1934), pp. 317–320; (255) Dr. H. D. Benjamins and Joh. F. Snelleman, *Encyclopaedie van Nederlandsch West Indië*, The Hague, 1914–1917; (256) F. Edler, *The Dutch Republic and the American Revolution*, Baltimore, 1911; (257) Melville J. and Frances Herskovits, *Rebel Destiny*, New York, 1934; (258) C. A. S. Hynam, "Agriculture in the Dutch Windward Islands," *Tropical Agriculture*, Vol. 18, No. 7 (July, 1941); (259) S. J. Kruythoff, *The Netherlands Windward Islands*, Antigua, 1939; (260) Lawrence Litchfield, Jr., "Bauxite Mining in Dutch Guiana," *Engineering and Mining Journal*, September 21, 1929; (261) A. P. Newton, *The European Nations in the West Indies, 1493–1688*, London, 1933; (262) Philip Hanson Hiss, *Netherlands America*, New York, 1943; (263) A. H. Redfield, *The Petroleum Trade of the Netherlands West Indies*, supplement to *International Petroleum Trade*, United States Department of the Interior, Washington, D. C., November 25, 1938; (264) C. W. Wardlow, "Agriculture in Surinam," *Tropical Agriculture*, Vol. 7, No. 2 (February, 1930), pp. 31–37; (265) John K. Wright *et al.*, *The European Possessions in the Caribbean Area*, New York, 1941.

For the Netherlands in the Second World War, see: (266) H. S. Ashton, *The Netherlands at War*, London, 1941; (267) F. Beelaerts van Blokland, *The Five Days of Holland*, London, 1940; (268) G. N. Clark, *Holland and the War*, Oxford, 1941; (269) Hermann B. Deutsch, "The Flying Dutchmen of Dixie," *Saturday Evening Post*, January 23, 1943; (270) Louis de Jong, *Holland Fights the Nazis*, London, 1941; (271) Louis de Jong and Joseph W. F. Stoppelman, *The Lion Rampant: The Story of Holland's Resistance to the Nazis*, New York, 1943; (272) *Ten Years of Japanese Burrowing in the Netherlands East Indies* (official reports of the Netherlands Indies Government), Netherlands Information Bureau, New York, 1942; (273) E. N. van Kleffens, *Juggernaut over Holland*, New York, 1941, and "The Democratic Future of the Netherlands Indies," *Foreign Affairs*, October, 1942; (274) Relman Morin, *Circuit of Conquest*, New York, 1943; (275) Vanya Oakes, *White Man's Folly*, Boston, 1943; (276) *The Peoples' Peace* (prepared by representatives of the United Nations), New York, 1943; (277) John MacCutcheon Raleigh, *Pacific Blackout,* New York, 1943; (278) *The Sixth Column* (inside the Nazi-occupied territory), New York, 1942; (279) J. M. Kenworthy, Baron Strabolgi, *The Campaign in the Low Countries,* London, 1941; (280) W. L. White, *Queens Die Proudly,* New York, 1943.

Current information may be obtained in: (281) *Knickerbocker Weekly,* New York; (282) *Vrij Nederland,* London; (283) *Netherlands News,* The Netherlands Information Bureau, New York, biweekly.

Index

Index

Aalberse, P. J. M., 198–199
Academy of Sciences, 48. *See also* Huygens, Christiaen
Achinese War, 342
Adat, 324, 357
Aertszen, Pieter, 243
Agriculture: intensive in nineteenth century, 4, 172; in transition zone, 9, 10; proletariat class in, 114–115; coördinated with world trade, 161; type of, 161, 172; effect of low prices in, 162; school for tropical, 174; Holland not country of, 185; Talma Minister of, 197; Academy of, 233; in East Indies, 322–323, 336, 340–341, 360–362, 377–378, 390; Agrarian Law for, 338; in Surinam, 399
Albarda, Johan Willem: "Constitutional and Political Aspects," 91–106; S.D.A.P. leader, 128, 201; Minister of Waterways and Communications, 201
Albert, King, quoted, 143–144
Albuquerque, Alfonso de, 317–318
Amsterdam: the capital, 9, 10; history of, 10–11; trade of, 11, 45, 154; Stock Exchange in, 11, 162, 169; financial center, 11, 158, 161; granary of Europe, 45; only theater of Golden Age in, 55; abortive insurrection in, 62; central revolutionary committee in, 63; poverty under Louis Napoleon in, 66, 159; insurrection in, inspired by Van Hogendorp, 67; harbor of, improved, 78, 160, 171; population of, 81, 159; Free University of, 84, 228; Bank, 168; trade unions, 191; general strike in, 195; Labadist community in, 214; refused Rembrandts, 246; center of Dutch art in twentieth century, 251; Zuiderkerk, 256; school of architecture in, 259–260; Concertgebouw orchestra of, 289

Anabaptists, 34, 208
Anti-Revolutionaries: condemned Liberal principles, 77, 117–118; interest of, in common people, 80; rapid growth of, 82; united with Christian Historicals, 83; in power, 84–85; conflicting class interests of, 111; history of, 118; leaders of, 118; Calvinist principles inspired, 118; a political party, 120; Free, 121; political strength before war, 122; agreed to universal suffrage, 198
Antwerp: thriving metropolis, 154; Spanish took, 155; realistic painting prevalent in, 243
"Architecture," by Paul Bromberg, 253–266
Architecture: Romanesque, 27, 238, 253; transition to Gothic, 27, 253; of housing projects, 128, 161; in Flanders in fifteenth century, 153; painting of, 244–245; church style of, 250; of Amsterdam Zuiderkerk, 256; influence of Italian Renaissance, 257; new materials in, 258; Neo-Gothicism in, 258; became craft again, 258; Amsterdam school of, 259–260; functionalism in, 260–263; *8 en Opbouw* periodical for, 261; Church, 263–264; individualism in, 264; influence of, 265–266
Arminius, Jacobus, 210
Army: improvement of, 84; coastline fortifications built for, 84, 138–139; mobilized, 85; Liberal State party advocated increased, 117; S.D.A.P. opposed expenditure for, 129; Colijn's bill to strengthen, 139
"Art," by Joep Nicolas, 238–252
Art: Flemish school of, 27; new subjects in, 57, 180; specialization in, 57–58; chief glory of Golden Age, 58, 244,